Crime and Community in the Cape Fear

Crime and Community in the Cape Fear

A PROSECUTOR'S GUIDE TO A HEALTHIER HOMETOWN

Benjamin R. David

District Attorney

SAN DIEGO

Bassim Hamadeh, CEO and Publisher
Kaela Martin, Project Editor
Celeste Paed, Associate Production Editor
Emely Villavicencio, Senior Graphic Designer
Alexa Lucido, Licensing Manager
Natalie Piccotti, Director of Marketing
Kassie Graves, Senior Vice President of Editorial
Jamie Giganti, Director of Academic Publishing

Cover image copyright © 2017 iStockphoto LP/Darwin Brandis

Printed in the United States of America.

3970 Sorrento Valley Blvd., Ste. 500, San Diego, CA 92121

The DA is inevitably in daily collision with life at its most elemental level. His job is somewhat akin to that of a young intern on a Saturday night ambulance call: he is constantly witnessing the naked emotions of his people—raw, unbuttoned, and bleeding ... By virtue of his job the DA is the keeper of the public conscience.

—Robert Traver, *Small Town D.A.* (1954)

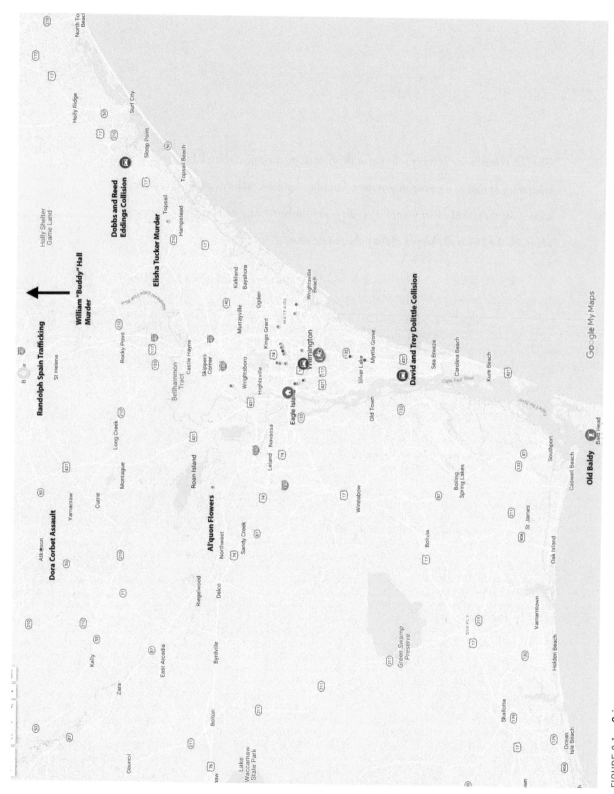

FIGURE 0.1 Crime map.

FIGURE 0.1 (*Continued*)

Brief Contents

Detailed Contents

Part II Community 183

Chapter 6

The First Two Arms of the Starfish 185

Author's Note

The case studies and experiences in this book are a snapshot of my journey of more than two decades as a prosecutor. The cases involve real victims and real defendants and were investigated, prosecuted, and presided over by people with whom I work every day. I have not tried to shield the identity of those involved since the events discussed in these pages have been the subject of intense publicity—jury trials, court hearings, and press conferences. Some details have been added for artistic license but none of this is fiction.

In order to make it clearer, persons charged with a crime are identified by their last name on second reference, the victims by their first, and all officials with their title and last name. This book is structured according to the case method, which is utilized in nearly every law school in America and is an excellent tool in supporting critical thinking and communication in discussion. Images are used with permission, are the personal photos of the author, are public record, or are part of a criminal case file.

These cases highlight large legal principles and magnify societal ills. Many have set precedent—laws that may help guide decisions when similar circumstances arise in the future. While the past can be a good teacher, every case is different. Subtle factual differences can greatly affect an outcome in a courtroom or whether a past case can speak to a present situation.

I have filmed eight lectures, each approximately 100 minutes in length, that are a companion to the eight chapters of this book. These lectures, filmed in the courthouses, police stations, detention facilities and other places of significance in my District, expand on the case studies and contain interviews with many of the leaders I have written about in these pages. To learn more, please visit BenjaminRDavid.com.

It is my hope that as you read about these individual cases, you will come to see the larger principles that run like currents in connecting legal concepts to each other. It is also my hope that you will see how we are all connected to each other and think of ways you can participate in making your hometown a better place to live. A portion of the sales from this book will go to the Unlock Hope Fund, to provide assistance to crime victims and to create opportunities for formerly incarcerated individuals at the Jo Ann Carter Harrelson Center in Wilmington, North Carolina.

I Crime

Chapter 1

Foundations of Prosecution

Dora told me later, after the attack, that she was lucky. At first I thought she meant that she was lucky to be alive because she should have been dead. But she surprised me when she said, "I have been on this earth for 78 years and in my whole life I have had only one bad hour. That must make me pretty lucky." This is the story about that one bad hour.[1]

Dora met the man of her dreams in high school and married him soon thereafter. They moved to a 500-acre farm in west Pender County outside the town of Atkinson, land that had been in his family for several generations. It was a place where neighbors knew each other and few people locked their doors at night. It was a place where you could scream and no one would hear you.

Dora and her husband raised a large family on the farm, and they spent their life together there. Dora's husband died when they were approaching 70, leaving her a widow for the last 10 years, but she was not lonely. With four children and 10 grandchildren in the area, Dora was the matriarch and her home was the family compound, especially during holidays, like it was on the recent Fourth of July celebration.

Dora could have retired many years earlier, but she still loved her job. She was a reporter for the *Pender Post*, a weekly newspaper concerned more with community affairs than hard-hitting journalism or world events. Most people in Pender County read the *Post*

FIGURE 1.1   Dora Corbett.

because at some point over the prior three decades Dora had knocked on their door and asked them to subscribe.

The night before the attack, Dora asked her daughter Emily to give her a wakeup call—a backup to her alarm clock. She had to be up early in the morning to interview a pastor for her weekly column, and, as everyone knew, Dora was a notoriously sound sleeper.

With curlers in her hair, dentures still in her mouth, and eyeglasses perched on her nose, Dora drifted off to sleep reading a book. She could not have known that as she kicked off the special orthopedic shoes her son-in-law (Emily's husband) had fashioned, it would be the last night she would ever sleep in the bed she had only shared with her husband, at a farm she had lived on for the better part of five decades.

The "monster," as she later would refer to him, tried the front door first. It was locked. The windows were also locked. Dora's compound was a secure fortress, out of place for the area. Then he saw it. About nine feet up was a window that led into the kitchen. It was slightly ajar. By stacking cement flowerpots to create a makeshift mound, he gained just enough height to climb up and, with gloved hands, propped open the window and squeezed in.

We think he rifled through the drawers in the house first. By appearances, Dora should have had plenty to steal. The home was straight out of a Norman Rockwell painting and the land it sat on was more than 10 times the holdings of most neighbors. (Eleanor Roosevelt had come to the area in the 1930s to extoll the virtues of having forty acres and a mule, and much of the surrounding plots were configured in this fashion).[2] But Dora's money was in the bank as was her best jewelry—the stuff she wore on a more regular basis was of the costume variety. At some point, we believe he became frustrated and took the burglary in a more sinister direction.

The first punch broke her glasses. The next series of punches broke eight bones in her face. Her dentures and curlers were scattered about the room during the attack. What would you do if you were sound asleep and someone started punching you in the face? Dora told me that she instinctively drew up both hands. But as she reflexively tried to fend off the attack, she realized in horror that her arms had been bound to both sides of the bed with her own bed sheets. Her legs were tied, too. Dora was indeed a sound sleeper. "Please, take whatever you want from me!" Dora begged. "Just let me live." The intruder laughed.

I will spare you the details of the assault. Suffice it to say we later proceeded on charges for first-degree rape, first-degree sexual offense, first-degree kidnapping, and assault inflicting serious bodily injury. Dora said, "God made me pass out so the monster would think I was dead." When she awoke, the intruder was gone.

No one is quite sure how she wriggled free from her bindings. The blood trail through the home shows Dora's next movements. First, she went to the bedside table to use the phone. There was no dial tone. Next, she tried the phone in the living room. She sat on the couch and blood began to pool beneath her as she tried to place a call for help. Again, nothing. The rotary phone hanging on the kitchen wall was also dead. All the phone lines were cut.

It was then that Dora made an important decision. She knew that if she remained at home she would bleed to death. Dora got into her car and set out to drive toward civilization, navigating the winding dirt roads mostly by memory. Her eyes were swollen shut. Dora had to use her thumb and forefinger on her left hand to spread the lids apart on one eye while she used her right hand for the steering wheel. After driving approximately four miles, she came to a beautiful home located on the banks of the Black River, a tributary of the Cape Fear River that separates Pender County from even more remote Bladen County.

Dora left her car on the main road and ran down the crooked driveway to a truck parked in front of the home. Opening the unlocked door, she found the horn and immediately started pounding on it. The noise woke the occupants, a mother and father and their two young children. The time was just past 5:00 a.m.

The family that ran outside was shocked at the sight. Standing in their driveway was an elderly woman, incoherent and drenched in blood. The attacker had choked her so badly that Dora could only squeeze out with difficulty the words "help me" over and over again. They assumed that she had been hit by a car and had wandered into their yard for help. The family immediately took Dora into their home, tended to her wounds, and called for help.

Approximately five and a half minutes into the 911 call, the Good Samaritan treating the injuries of a woman whom she thought was a stranger looked down at the victim's shoes. She recognized them. She realized in horror that, for the last several minutes, she had been looking at her own mother. Dora had gone to Emily's house. (We will return to Dora's case in chapter 2).

A Place Called Home

Dora escaped to a place she knew was safe. What do you run from and run toward? We flee from things that scare us and seek out things that give us comfort. Where do you call home? Where do you belong? Wherever that place is, when you are lost or experiencing real trauma, instinct will lead you there.

This is a book about my home. This is also a book about my job. For over 20 years, I have been prosecuting crime in the Cape Fear region of Southeastern North Carolina. I have had to run toward the things that scare us. Along the way, I have found a home.

Today, in my hometown, the crime rate is at the lowest level in decades.[3] It has never been safer to go to sleep at night or walk down the street for the average citizen than as I write these words. Violent crime, to be sure, still exists but it is overwhelmingly visited upon those who are in street gangs, doing drugs, or who are in abusive relationships. Random acts of violence have almost ceased to exist.

It is only when we stopped caring about who received the credit for the success of these efforts that we finally started making real progress. And it was when we began to focus more on the humanity of all victims, and the larger factors that were contributing to people perpetrating crimes, that we saw our crime rate drop. This book will explore how we have fought crime by building community.

Giving Victims a Voice

My phone rings every time someone is murdered inside the 1,000 square miles that make up the place where I live and serve as the elected district attorney (DA). I have never felt more alive than when speaking for the dead in a courtroom. It can be more gratifying, however, when I have the opportunity to be the voice for a victim who should be dead but survived to confront their accuser.

Meeting people like Dora, and the family members of those whose lives have been taken by crime and giving them a voice in the courtroom, has been the greatest privilege of my professional life. Mixed into their cases are not only horror and helplessness, but beauty and bravery. Sharing their stories in the courtroom is about getting justice. The purpose of sharing their stories in public and in this book is to create community and bring about positive change.

In these pages you will read about the long investigation and eventual trial of the man who attacked Dora and the journey of those who attempted to convict him. But you will also meet a grandmother who held a press conference after the verdict, inspiring many other victims of sexual violence to come forward and raise needed funds for a local rape crisis center.

Crime rips apart and destroys; community brings together and builds up. The role of the prosecutor is not simply to avenge individuals. The DA speaks for all people. What if we could stop or at least prevent much of the victimization we see? That would be a noble effort. What leads to crime and who should we enlist to fight it? These are some of the bigger questions that we will attempt to answer.

In rare cases like Dora's, evil and innocence are easily defined. Bad things happen to good people, but far more often, the water is murky. Many victims are engaged in illegal or immoral conduct at the time of their victimization. How can we prevent them from being blamed and keep the focus on the defendant's conduct?

There are other cases where defendants are not bad people—they are people with bad problems or people who have made bad choices. Sometimes, defendants commit crimes that cannot be labeled in a way that all observers would universally agree. How do you separate feelings from reason, justice from mercy, and forgiveness from punishment? We will explore what goes into a prosecutor's decisions when seeking justice in these tough-call cases.

And then there is the past. We live with our history. At the courthouse we call that history "precedent" or "case law," and we rely upon it time and again. When confronted with making a choice, we look to the law as a ship's captain looks to a lighthouse to guide the way forward. Broad protections in the Constitution, statutes, and case law inform our movements as we encounter new situations. When we are lost and alone, we look for the light.

The past shapes us in other ways too, both consciously and subconsciously. This is true for both individuals and society at large. If we only look to the past, we might stay in a dark place. Slavery, for instance, would still be legal if we failed to realize that we were on the wrong course and had not changed direction. These issues also arise in police shootings, the war on drugs, and the debate over mass incarceration. Thinking about how we think, including participating in bias training and conducting critical case reviews as a group of prosecutors and detectives, prevents wrongful convictions and ensures everyone is treated equally.

This book is my attempt to have you, the reader, stand on the shores of the place you call home and look deep into the water to see the crime that I see every day. The faces reflected in those waters may very well surprise you. When society looks at the water, the image reflected is a side of our collective selves we wish would remain hidden: poverty, broken families, inadequate mental health services, and failing public schools. I refer to this sad reality as the "Mirror Image Rule," which holds that defendants and victims tend to look a whole lot alike: overwhelmingly, they have in common the same race, religion, national origin, and socioeconomic status.[4]

While many only consider the plight of defendants, prosecutors in my office keep our focus on their victims and the immediate surrounding community where these defendants live. If victims have the same challenging circumstances as those who are being prosecuted in the criminal justice system, then giving them a voice and uplifting their community will make all of us safer.

For example, the high rate of incarceration has unquestionably impacted poor minority communities. Several years ago, I asked the Sheriff to look at the people who were incarcerated at the New Hanover County Jail. We found that of the 520 inmates, 49 percent were African-American.[5] That is nearly three times what should be expected from a county-wide demographic of 18 percent African-American. An analysis of serious violent crimes was even more disheartening: of the 34 pending murder cases, 30 involved African-American defendants. The numbers were equally staggering for assaults with a deadly weapon (25 total, 16 African-American); sex crimes (29 total, 13 African-American); armed robbery (40 total, 28 African-American); and drug trafficking offenses (37 total, 22 African-American).

What is lost in these numbers, however, is the impact it has on the victims. Not only are open-air drug transactions disproportionately taking place in neighborhoods where these defendants live but the victims of violent crime mirror the demographics of the perpetrators. For instance, of the 34 murder cases just mentioned, 28 of the victims were African-American and almost all lived below the poverty line. This, unfortunately, is not unique to Wilmington. Murder is the leading cause of death in North Carolina for African-American males, and they are 4.5 times more likely to die of a homicide than their white counterparts.[6] These same numbers show up for violent assault, armed robberies, and the like. Simply put, the most frequent victims of crime look a lot like the offenders in jail.

Helping both defendant and victim, wherein statistically we know they will be coming back to court for a return trip, is not only good policy, it is morally the right thing to do. Forcing us to look hard into the mirror will help us see the sometimes forgotten innocent children living in a place called poverty being caught in the crossfire of a war not of their own making.

FIGURE 1.2   Office of the District Attorney, March 2018.

These things are not unique to my town. The root causes of crime are predictable and often preventable. We will look at how my office is redefining the role of what it means to be a prosecutor by labeling high crime areas as high victim areas. Fighting crime means helping everyone. Justice means not only punishing the wicked but uplifting the poor and the oppressed. Who fights for this group in your community? If it is not the chief prosecutor, it should be.

My prosecutors handle serious felonies in Superior Court and misdemeanor and traffic offenses in District Court. We advise police officers in station houses and listen to cooperating criminals in holding cells. My victim-witness legal assistants provide comfort to people who have been aggrieved and walk them through the bizarre and unfamiliar world that is the criminal justice system. We have been given a vast amount of responsibility and much is expected of us in return.

When I graduated from Wake Forest School of Law in 1995, I went to work for the largest law firm in North Carolina. I was soon convinced that there was a different path ahead for me. Like many people in public service, I believe that you can make money or you can make a difference.

I started my career as a prosecutor in Wilmington the day after the Columbine Shooting in the spring of 1999. My identical twin brother, Jon, who was a prosecutor in Miami at the time, later joined me in the office where we would prosecute violent criminals together over the next decade.

Five years into that job as a violent crime prosecutor, my predecessor, John Carriker, announced that he would retire and the role of DA would be up for election. I was 34 years old at the time, and Mr. Carriker asked if I would run to become the next DA. It was a close five-horse race and I won it. Overnight, I was running the largest law firm in Wilmington and was responsible for handling 5,000 felonies, 20,000 misdemeanors, and 50,000 traffic tickets every year. Jon stayed on for six years as my first assistant in the violent crimes section.

FIGURE 1.3   District Attorney Ben David (D-New Hanover and Pender) and District Attorney Jon David (R-Bladen, Brunswick, and Columbus). *Source: Wilmington Magazine.*

Today, Jon and I both serve as elected DAs in Southeastern North Carolina in neighboring districts. The Cape Fear River separates the places where we live and work, but we talk almost every day. I represent the Sixth District, covering a territory roughly the size of Rhode Island.[7] Jon represents the Fifteenth District, which is about the size of Delaware. His district is bigger than mine, but I represent more people (did I mention that we are competitive?).

The Sixth District

Out of my office window is downtown Wilmington, also known as the Port City, which abuts the Cape Fear River to the west. Eight miles to the east is the Atlantic Ocean. The land is shaped by the hammer and anvil of the ocean and the river. Visually it makes my district look like a big ice cream cone: the 900 geographic square miles of Pender County balance precariously on the cone-shaped peninsula of the 180 square miles of New Hanover. The district ends where the river and ocean meet.

There is a dichotomy about the place where I prosecute crime; it is both metropolitan and rural. New Hanover County has over 230,000 people jammed into the second smallest county in the state.[8] It has beautiful beaches, a historic riverfront in downtown Wilmington, vibrant art centers, and institutions of higher learning, like the University of North Carolina Wilmington (UNCW) and Cape Fear Community College (CFCC). A large movie studio, Screen Gems, makes Wilmington immediately recognizable in movies like *Iron Man 3* and television shows like *Dawson's Creek* and *One Tree Hill*. We also have the unfortunate distinction of leading the nation in opioid abuse rates.[9]

Pender County, home to over 60,000 people, is spread out over vast forests and farms.[10] Life-long residents live here, and tourists are confined to I-40 as they pass through on their way to the beaches. The line of demarcation in Pender is US Highway 17, separating the rural west of the county from the exploding seaside communities. If Atticus Finch were practicing law, you would expect to see him walking outside of the courthouse, which is guarded by a Confederate soldier training his eyes toward the North.[11]

The Sixth District of North Carolina is a bellwether in a battleground state.[12] In a sense, it is a microcosm of the country—a collision of cultures, classes, religions, and races. With every presidential election come the candidates: Since being in office, I have seen Obama, Clinton, Trump, and McCain. They come knowing that if they can carry this region, they can win the state and maybe the country.

There have been only five DAs in the Sixth District in the last half century. Through the years, the successes of the DAs have been celebrated. The freeway running across northern New Hanover County, I-140, is named for DA John J. Burney, who came home from WWII a hero and served as the top prosecutor before becoming a renowned defense attorney and state senator. The courthouse where I work today is named for his successor, Allen "Papa" Cobb, the four-term DA who hired John Carriker, who later became DA and hired me.

The failures are equally acknowledged. I, along with the other DAs in North Carolina, watched the implosion of Mike Nifong, Durham County's DA (who grew up in Wilmington), as the Duke Lacrosse case unraveled in front of an international audience.[13] Then there was Jerry Spivey, the DA in Wilmington for a decade between Cobb and Carriker, who was thrown out of office for uttering a racial slur during a Wrightsville Beach bar fight with an NFL football player in 1995.[14]

DAs are the only elected officials who can be removed from office when a petition is filed by a member of the general public.[15] Much like any elected official, DAs are held accountable by the communities they serve.

Statewide Justice System

The North Carolina Constitution, like the United States Constitution, created three branches of government. Each branch has certain responsibilities and checks and balances that ensure all three branches work together in service of the people. The Legislative Branch writes the laws, the Executive Branch enforces the laws, and the Judicial Branch interprets the laws. The DA straddles all three branches. We are executive officers who work with and advise law enforcement. We go to the legislature to suggest law changes and resources that are needed to uphold the law. We work daily in courtrooms with judges to uphold the Constitution.

North Carolina is divided into 100 counties, each with a county seat where local government is headquartered.[16] Every county seat has a courthouse. There are 43 prosecutorial districts in the state.[17] Some districts contain multiple counties (like District 1 in the Outer Banks and District 43 in the mountains, each of which has seven counties in their district), while others, primarily the metro areas of Wake (Raleigh) and Mecklenburg (Charlotte), contain only a single county in their districts.[18]

Administering justice is inherently local. In 99 percent of cases, police powers are carried out through state and local representatives of the Executive Branch in individual communities. The North Carolina Constitution gives crime victims a Bill of Rights—including the right to meet with the DA at an early stage of a criminal case, speak at the time of sentencing, and be notified when a defendant is released from custody.[19] The Constitution also makes the DA the legal advisor to law enforcement agencies in the region.[20]

Every county has a jail, where people who are presumed innocent remain awaiting trial if they cannot make bond. Those who make bond are frequently put on electronic monitoring. Jails also house defendants who are convicted of minor offenses where the sentence is less than six months. In the New Hanover County Detention Center, there are approximately 550 prisoners at any given time.[21] The Pender County Jail holds nearly 100 inmates (92-bed facility).[22]

There are 55 prisons around the state.[23] Prisons house inmates who are convicted of their crimes and are serving out their sentences. Inmates are housed according to the offense for which they were convicted and other security considerations. There is a minimum-security prison in Wilmington housing approximately 400 prisoners, and a medium-security prison in Burgaw holding approximately 800 prisoners.[24, 25] Statewide, there are more than 37,000 inmates.[26] The North Carolina Department of Adult Correction and Juvenile Justice supervises and runs the prisons.

When the community is your client, you need to stay in touch with tens of thousands of people at once. While press conferences and public speaking engagements are a daily part of my job, my office has embraced technology to keep that line of communication open with a website. Weekly press releases give a running account of how cases are resolved. Much of what I am writing about in these pages is expanded upon in press releases and articles that we provide to the public. There are also sections for victim services, more about our law enforcement partners, and next steps if you receive a traffic ticket.[27]

Community-Based Prosecution

There are, of course, many other people standing on the banks of the shore horrified by the same things that I see every day in my job. Much of this book is devoted to the work that they have done or are doing, both within and outside of the justice system. The collaboration has led not only to success in individual cases but fundamental change in the Cape Fear region. In these pages you will be introduced not only to great officers and scientists who solved cases like Dora's, but also to leaders from diverse backgrounds who have joined together in the model of "community-based prosecution."

Being the DA requires balance: building alliances while remaining independent; being humble while not playing small; doing what is right rather than what is popular right now. It means taking a tough love approach by remaining tough on crime while simultaneously showing people you care.

I have had many great mentors, career prosecutors who learned through trial and error that the job is not all about them but about the people they serve. They include former DAs Peter Gilchrist in Charlotte, Tom Keith in Winston-Salem, Ed Grannis in Fayetteville, and Clarke Everett in Greenville. If there were a Mount Rushmore of great DAs, they would be on it. I had the privilege of being in their company as a very young elected DA toward the end of their careers.

They showed me the importance of remaining calm and saving my strength for the big fights, the importance of working with others, and celebrating successes jointly.

Another mentor, Colon Willoughby, was the DA for Wake County for nearly 30 years. He was asked a question by a student while we were co-teaching the inaugural prosecution clinic at Campbell Law School, his alma mater: "What has it been like to be the most powerful man in the Triangle [Raleigh-Durham-Chapel Hill] for the last three decades?"

Without hesitating, Colon replied that he had very little power. "The only power I have is the power to dismiss a case," he said. Colon went on to explain that the DA cannot make an arrest—only an officer can make an arrest. He cannot set a bond—only a magistrate and later a judge can do that. He cannot convict. That is the job of a jury (or a judge in a bench trial). And he cannot sentence. That is mapped out by the legislature in structured sentencing and handed down by the court.

Of course, that is only part of the story. The DA advises officers and can call for investigations. The DA is present at first appearances and advises the Court about the defendant's degree of danger to the community and the risk of flight for the purpose of setting bond. While a jury or judge convicts, the DA presents the evidence, then uses persuasion to convince the fact-finder of a verdict. Through argument and presentation of the defendant's prior record, the DA greatly affects the sentence. Since nearly all cases in the criminal justice system are resolved through plea negotiations or dismissals, DAs must work with and gain respect from the defense attorneys to reasonably resolve cases that come through the system.

In short, Colon conveyed that DAs are not people of great power. Rather, DAs are people of great influence. Community-based prosecution means working with everyone to achieve justice.

In the summer of 2020 protestors around the country held up signs to "defund the police," following the murder of George Floyd at hands of police in Minneapolis, Minnesota.[28] It would be a tragic mistake to abolish the police function, especially in areas where crime runs most rampant. Instead, we need to "re-fund the police," deploying them to the areas of greatest need to engage in community policing that reinvents their roles as "guardians" to serve and protect, rather than as an occupying force of "warriors" who are in conflict with everyday citizens.

There is no question that in modern times we have asked too much of law enforcement officers. In addition to carrying guns, officers now carry life-saving drugs to reverse drug overdoses. They must also be proficient in mental health counseling for encounters in schools and on the street. Greater investment to treat addiction and mental illness is long overdue and would be welcome by the officers I advise. Like prosecutors, they want to work collaboratively with professionals from other fields in a common pursuit of doing justice.

The power that comes from working in a group is celebrated in many venues. In business it is called synergy. In the nonprofit world it is called collaboration. In a church it is called unity. On a field it is known as teamwork. In an investigation, officers who are the first responders to a crime scene have a different role than the Crime Scene Investigation (CSI) Unit that collects evidence or the detectives who conduct follow-up investigations. Seen this way, professionals throughout the system are like chess pieces with different abilities, rather than like checkers where all pieces move in the same fashion.

Critical Thinking

In all criminal cases, the prosecution must prove two things beyond a reasonable doubt: the *mens rea* (guilty mind) and the *actus reus* (guilty act) of the defendant. Both must come together for there to be a crime. Stated another way, people cannot be arrested for merely having bad thoughts (we would need a much bigger prison system), and people who do a bad thing but lack criminal intent are not always criminally punished. The public mistakenly focuses solely on the criminal *act* while the guilty mind is just as crucial to the crime equation—often the harder of the two for prosecutors to prove. In other words, the guilty mind refers to intent and that's what must be coupled with the act in order to convict someone of a crime.

There are only two ways to prove a case beyond a reasonable doubt. The first is through witnesses who are called to the stand to testify about what they saw, heard, or knew. Defendants can cross-examine witnesses and juries can assess their credibility. The second is through the presentation of physical evidence, called "silent witnesses," which include fingerprints, DNA, ballistics, and videos. Many crimes are committed in private with few or no witnesses. In murder cases, the only witness may be dead. Crime scenes talk; you just need to know how to listen.

We need to label conduct in order to identify the crime. The same conduct, like taking someone's life, is treated much differently by the court when it is labeled as murder rather than manslaughter. To conceptualize the different types of crimes that can be charged, think of the elements of various crimes like the ingredients of a recipe. These elements must be proven beyond a reasonable doubt. The more ingredients, the more complex the flavor and the harsher the punishment. If all of the ingredients are not present, a defendant's conduct may only be involuntary manslaughter, instead of first- or second-degree murder.

When telling a story, journalists start with identifying the five Ws: who, what, where, when, and why. Then they set out to find answers for them. In proving a crime beyond a reasonable doubt, prosecutors must prove who (identity), what (*actus reus* and *mens rea*), where (jurisdiction), and when (date of offense). Yet the question of why (the motive) is not part of the recipe in nearly every criminal case.

As a prosecutor, I have an additional checklist. It is called the FIRAC method: Facts, Issues, Rules, Application, Conclusion.

Good lawyers start with the Facts. Our job is to pursue the truth. We don't have the luxury of creating "alternative facts" or rewriting endings to the story. The saying "you are entitled to your own opinion but not your own facts" applies to anyone conducting investigations and trials.

Issues are the questions that arise in a case. Good lawyers do not always know the right answers, which can be learned through legal research, but they know the right questions to ask. Spotting the issues can clearly define the case and possible controversy, as well as highlight the way forward.

Rules are the law, and we are a nation of them. Laws are usually created by the legislative branch, although sometimes they are created by the courts and become case law. In this book, you will see some cases where the law is clear and some cases where we have created precedent in the context of a new case.

Application is where the law and the facts come together. This is the great work of analysis and advocacy. It is the skill that separates the good from the great. It involves marshalling all of the evidence and testing it against the various defenses. This is the part of the case where trials are won or lost and pleas are either accepted or rejected.

Conclusion is the result, the end product of the analysis. It can be a charging decision by a police officer or a prosecutor, a judge's ruling, or a jury's verdict, to name just a few. It is the destination of the journey.

Using FIRAC frames the way I analyze cases, and I encourage you to use this method and see if you agree with the outcomes and my use of discretion for the cases in this book. I don't pick the easy ones. Some are controversial. You are, of course, welcome to disagree.

Thinking critically, and constantly testing facts against assumptions, will be a recurrent theme over the next seven chapters. The book is divided into two parts. In part 1: Crime (chapters 2–5), we will look at the legal principles and types of evidence that prosecutors use to prove cases and the five defenses that are raised by defendants. In this part of the book, you will meet the five pigs. In part 2: Community (chapters 6–8), we rely on the case method but go outside the courtroom to explore how crime can be reduced through outreach efforts. In this part of the book, you will be introduced to the Starfish model. In both part 1 and part 2, we will see how legal concepts (shifting the blame, the power of the past, the cost of silence, the duty to act, and group responsibility) arise not only in crime but in community.

Pigs in the Creek: The Five Defenses

Only Iowa has more pigs than North Carolina.[29] Most of these pigs live their short lives in Eastern North Carolina. Many hog farms, in need of water and lagoons, populate the shores of the Cape Fear River. The five defenses are more easily conceptualized as pigs that we can name. Imagine as you read these cases that you are a juror and that you are standing on the bank of a creek, a tributary to the river. Your job in analyzing the evidence is to get to the bottom of the case, to see the creek bed. This is where the truth lies. Sifting through the evidence is tedious. Making the task more difficult are pigs. When the pigs get into the creek, they muddy the waters.

The term "verdict" means "to speak the truth." Defendants and defense attorneys muddy the water by throwing pigs into the creek, creating reasonable doubt. Your job as a juror, like mine as a prosecutor, is to search for the truth. As we analyze these cases, we will get to a point where we must consider the nature of the defense. Let's call the pigs by name: 1. "SODDI: Some Other Dude Did It"; 2. "I Did Not Do It"; 3. "Of Course I Did It"; 4. "The Devil Made Me Do It"; and 5. "Maybe You Did It." Our job will be to pull these pigs out of the creek to get to the bottom of what happened and to see the truth.

It does not matter what type of offense is charged. Property crimes, violent assaults, drug sales, driving offenses, and incidents between close family members or total strangers all have the same burden of proof. Prosecutors must prove the guilty act and the guilty mind, notwithstanding the nature of the charged offense. Anyone seeking to avoid responsibility for a crime, in whole or in part, has several avenues to defend themselves.

It must be said at the outset that defendants are presumed innocent and are not required to put on any defense when they are charged with a crime. Oftentimes, charges are not filed or are dismissed prior to trial because the totality of the evidence (both testimonial and physical evidence) falls short of fully satisfying or entirely convincing a finder of fact (e.g., the judge or jury) of the defendant's guilt. Prosecution of an indefensible crime is over before it begins without anyone getting justice because investigators and prosecutors cannot meet the burden of proof beyond a reasonable doubt.

There are only five ways to defend a crime. These defenses are not mutually exclusive: one or more may be raised by the same defendant during an investigation or a defense attorney during a trial.

1. **Some Other Dude Did It (SODDI).** The defense contends the wrong person has been charged. A terrible crime has been committed, but the defendant denies any involvement. The real perpetrator is still out there and thus "Some Other Dude Did It." The crime is terrible, but prosecutors are further compounding the tragedy by wrongfully accusing an innocent person. These are the classic "whodunit" cases, the real-life murder mysteries. We will explore these cases in depth (chapters 4 and 5).

   This defense pushes all the poker chips into the middle of the table. It is an "all or nothing" play. Either the defendant will get convicted as charged or walk away as a free man. When a suspect waives the right to remain silent and denies any involvement in the crime, I like to get the detectives to ask him this question: "Can we agree that whoever did this should be punished to the fullest extent of the law?" If he says no, we get him to explain his answer, which frequently leads to a change in defense or an outright confession. If he shares everyone's horror about the crime but denies involvement, and he is later shown to be the perpetrator beyond a reasonable doubt, I like to remind the judge and jury of his answer at the time of sentencing.

   This defense may also be raised among co-defendants. A person may claim to know the identity of the party who committed the crime but contend that they bear little or no responsibility because of their diminished role. As we will see, however, the person serving as the look-out to the crime or as the getaway driver can be charged with the same crimes as the trigger man, though their punishment is frequently reduced at the time of sentencing (chapter 7).

2. **I Did Not Do It.** Here the emphasis is placed on the word "it." The defendant may have done something illegal but contends that he is overcharged. The defendant claims that the injustice is at the hands of overreaching and overzealous police and prosecutors. With this defense the emphasis is on labeling the crime correctly since the label vastly changes the potential punishment.

   For example, a homicide is punished very differently when it is deemed an involuntary manslaughter instead of a murder. A daytime breaking and entering of a home is a relatively minor offense. The same crime committed at night when people are home is burglary, which is punished far more harshly. A defendant may admit to taking property by force (a common law robbery) but deny that he had a deadly weapon at the time of the theft (robbery with a dangerous weapon). These distinctions can be the difference between probation and long-term imprisonment. With this defense, the defendant claims that the crime lacks all of the necessary ingredients or elements that make up the offense (chapter 3).

3. **Of Course I Did It.** This defense does not deny the act but rather says that it was legally justified. "Of course I shot the other guy," the defendant may claim. "He tried to shoot me first." Everyone has a right to use deadly force to defend themselves or others if they face the threat of imminent deadly force. The defendant is essentially contending that he would rather be judged by twelve (a jury) than be carried by six (pallbearers at his funeral).

   In a sexual assault case, the defendant may claim that the sex was consensual. A thief may claim that he had permission to be in the house where he was caught. "You will find my fingerprints and DNA—I had consent." With this defense, the defendant is proclaiming that he or she committed the act but for some reason it is justified.

4. **The Devil Made Me Do It.** This defense does not deny the actual crime or *actus reus* (guilty act) but denies that it was done with the necessary *mens rea* (criminal intent). The classic defense in this category is that of insanity. Here, the defendant cannot appreciate the difference between right and wrong because of mental illness. If this is established, and it is quite rare, the defendant escapes any responsibility for the actual crime. However, the defendant may be confined to a treatment facility for the protection of himself and others until he is well enough, if possible, to return to society.

Far more common in this category is the claim that the defendant lacked the ability to form the alleged guilty intent because of chemical impairment through drugs or alcohol. Even a claim of "voluntary intoxication" can partially excuse some crimes (but not all) if it is established that the defendant's mental or physical faculties are so overcome that the defendant essentially acted without thinking.

In the case of "diminished capacity," the defendant claims that drugs or alcohol prevented him from acting intentionally (for instance, in a first-degree murder case involving premeditation and deliberation). Without denying the crime, the defendant is contending that he acted recklessly and therefore should only be convicted of something less (for instance, involuntary manslaughter). With this defense, the defendant claims that the crime is lacking an essential component of the criminal equation—guilty intent.

5. **Maybe You Did It.** This involves the murky waters of conspiracy. The frame job. Bad cops and bad prosecutors have put an innocent person on trial or have acted so incompetently that we cannot know the truth. This is putting the criminal justice system on trial. With this defense, the defendant is claiming that either investigators added evidence or that the cops and prosecutors are so incompetent or corrupt that the truth can never be known. You cannot connect the dots if you did not correctly collect the dots.

These last three defenses attempt to shift the blame to someone or something else. The defendant is attempting to blame the victim ("Of Course I Did It"), blame drugs or a mental defect ("The Devil Made Me Do It") or blame the system ("Maybe You Did It") for why they find themselves charged with any given offense. We will explore how to keep the focus on the defendant and cut out the blame game (chapter 2).

All five defenses overlap and intersect. For example, it is not uncommon for a defendant to say that his actions were not a crime ("Of Course I Did It") but in the event the jury says otherwise, he will claim to be overcharged ("I Did Not Do It"). Alternatively, a defendant may claim that the sexual encounter was consensual (and therefore not rape) and further claim that they did not technically have "sexual relations." Sexual battery and assault on a female are only misdemeanors and carry sentences that are far less serious than the decade or more in prison for rape or a sex offense where there was penetration.

Frequently, the claim of "The Devil Made Me Do It" (gross impairment) is coupled with the defense of "I Did Not Do It." Now sober, the defendant is horrified by his conduct and claims not to have been thinking clearly. This is a plea for a reduced charge (second-degree murder because he used a gun) but not first-degree murder (because there was no premeditation and deliberation) or reduced punishment for the ultimate charge.

It is harder for a defendant to claim, though I have seen it many times, that the police arrested the wrong suspect ("SODDI") but whoever did it should not be guilty because the victim bears the responsibility ("Of Course I Did It") or that the crime is not as bad as everyone thinks ("I Did Not Do It"). When I see multiple defenses being advanced simultaneously, I remind the jury that there is a reason for the loud protests. In these instances, the defendant is trying to get away without being held fully responsible. Defendants and their attorneys who try to use more than one defense at a time can lose credibility.

Before a case gets to the courthouse and we are forced to confront the five defenses, we can proactively try to stop crimes from ever occurring. There is a reason I allow every one of my employees to take two hours off each week to volunteer in the community: We can prevent much of the crime that we see through outreach efforts. To understand the structure that we give to this approach, let's travel downstream to where the Cape Fear River empties into the Atlantic Ocean and meet the starfish.

FIGURE 1.4   My son Fitz throwing a starfish back into the ocean.

The Starfish Model

The parable of the starfish is one you have likely heard. A wise old man is walking along the beach when he comes across a young child looking for starfish that have washed ashore with the tide and are now slowly cooking to death under the glowing sun. "What are you doing?" the old man asks the busy boy. "I am saving starfish," answers the boy. "But look down the beach," says the elder. "The tide has receded, there are dozens of them, and time is running out. You cannot possibly make a difference." Without looking up, the young boy picks up another starfish and, throwing it into the water, says to the old man, "It made a difference to that one."

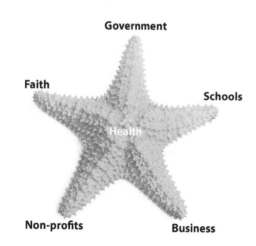

FIGURE 1.5   The Starfish model.

My children and I frequently go to Wrightsville Beach to unwind after a big week of school and court. When considering the outreach efforts that prevent crime and the way to structure the work we do here in this community, I came up with the starfish as an analogy to organize my thoughts.

The Starfish model represents our outreach efforts and a way to give people a sense of belonging in the community. These five arms are: government, schools, business, nonprofits, and faith organizations. We will look at how leaders from government and the faith-based community have come together to focus on reconciliation and keep the calm, especially around the thorny issue of race and justice (chapter 6). We will look at how schools, businesses, and nonprofits have teamed together to reduce crime and promote the pursuit of happiness (chapter 7).

Holding it all together at the center of the starfish is health. This includes physical health and mental health to be sure, but also healthy relationships and a healthy lifestyle. I rarely see healthy people in the criminal justice system. Many defendants are weighed down by drug dependencies, behavior disorders, and severely dysfunctional relationships. The same root causes that contribute to poor health and overrun the hospital also wash up on the courthouse steps.

New Hanover Regional Medical Center (NHRMC), with over 7,000 employees, is the largest employer in southeastern North Carolina.[30] The former CEO, Jack Barto, and I started in our respective posts in 2004 and worked together in many ways on trauma, prevention, and community outreach for over a decade. At the end of 2016 Jack retired, causing the leadership team at the hospital to draft a new mission statement. They noted that while less than 10 percent of the population goes to the hospital in any given year, NHRMC is concerned about 100 percent of the citizens.[31]

These medical professionals could no longer see themselves merely as a repair shop for injuries and disease. They had to think about health. That meant going out into the community, focusing on healthy lifestyles, diet, and exercise. An ounce of prevention is worth a pound of cure.

In shifting the paradigm, the hospital articulated what I have long contended about the things I see at the courthouse. Peace and safety must be the entire community's concern. Police and prosecutors cannot just be reactive—we must be proactive. The Starfish model is our effort to get to the root causes of what we see at the hospital and the courthouse. We may have only a limited number of cases in front of us at any given moment, but we want justice for all. We will look at how we focus on the center of the starfish (chapter 8).

One characteristic of a starfish is worth mentioning. When an arm breaks off, a starfish will regenerate the lost appendage. Communities that are broken can still fix themselves. People who have been traumatized can be resilient and not let the crime define their lives. This concept is so profound that I have devoted chapter 8 to exploring its implications in the form of Adverse Childhood Experiences (ACE) scores. As we think about prevention efforts, the parable of the starfish reminds us that while murder, rape, and armed robbery existed 100 years ago and will exist 100 years from now, it is also true that current efforts can make a significant difference right now. We might not save everyone, but we can save one.

The Ripple Effect

Evil dropped into the water creates a tidal wave of grief. Crack rocks, pills, and bindles of heroin have collateral consequences that range from traffic fatalities, to property crimes, to gang violence, and overdose deaths. The same is true of a bullet fired from a gun: it has an impact on an individual, a family, and people far outside of its immediate harm.

There is also a tremendous impact through genuine acts of kindness and compassion. Throwing the starfish back into the water creates waves that lap onto distant shores that we cannot yet see. When one person gets a job, a family of five might be lifted out of poverty. When a girl learns to read, her future children have a much better chance for success. When victims receive needed care at an early stage and defendants receive treatment, we break the cycle of abuse, stop the revolving door at the courthouse, and change the arc of their lives.

These outreach efforts leave not only a legacy but make an immediate difference to one person. When we travel upstream to find the source, we can catch the evil before it hits the water and deal with it when it is still manageable. Police officers, prosecutors, probation officers, and prisons deal with tidal waves. The ripples are easier to contain.

Crime and Punishment

How defendants are punished, and whether they are even punished at all, comes down to the labels the law affixes to their conduct. Labels have meaning. Most people have heard: "The punishment should fit the crime." The critical questions to ask when a tragedy occurs are 1) is this a crime at all, and 2) if it is a crime, what do we call it?

- FIRST-DEGREE MURDER
- SECOND-DEGREE MURDER
- VOLUNTARY MANSLAUGHTER
- INVOLUNTARY MANSLAUGHTER
- ACCIDENT

FIGURE 1.6   The ladder of guilt.

Many of the crimes you will read about in this book involve the loss of life. Every loss is a tragedy. Whether that conduct is punished, and the degree of punishment involved, depends upon how the conduct is labeled. Imagine walking up a ladder of guilt, from the bottom rung to the top.

Accident: There may still be civil liability for negligence, exposing the defendant to massive monetary damages, but there are no criminal penalties.

Involuntary Manslaughter: Unlawful killing of a human being, unintentionally and without malice, proximately resulting from the commission of an unlawful act not amounting to a felony. Involuntary manslaughter is also defined as an act done in an unlawful or culpably negligent manner, when fatal consequences were not improbable under all the facts existent at the time, or resulting from the culpably negligent omission to perform a legal duty. Punishment for a first-time offender is 10 months to three years.

<u>Voluntary Manslaughter</u>: Killing in the heat of passion OR killing in imperfect self-defense (the defendant is either the first aggressor or uses excessive force). Punishment for a first-time offender is 3.2 to nine years.

<u>Second-Degree Murder</u>: Killing with malice. Malice can be either expressed (hatred, ill will, or spite) or can be implied from the circumstances (the intentional use of a deadly weapon or conscious disregard of rights and safety of others). Punishment for a first-time offender ranges from 12 to 31 years when there is express malice (B1 offense on the Felony Punishment Chart, figure 1.7). Second-degree murder sentences range from 7.8 to 20.6 years for implied malice offenses (B2 offense on the sentencing chart).

<u>First-Degree Murder</u>: Killing with premeditation and deliberation OR felony murder (killing during the course of another violent felony like armed robbery or rape). Punishment for first-degree murder is either life in prison without the possibility of parole or death, no matter the criminal record of the offender.

Structured Sentencing

In North Carolina, like many places, crimes at the felony level are divided into categories under structured sentencing. A defendant is sentenced to a range of months based upon the offense (in the vertical column, felony offenses are separated into ten classes of seriousness from A to I) and prior record level (in the horizontal row, records are defined from level I for first time offenders, to level VI for people with very serious criminal histories).

Going up the ladder of seriousness, starting at the lowest rung are class I felonies (possession of drugs, for example), class H (breaking into a home), class G (felon in possession of a firearm), class D (robbery with a dangerous weapon), class B1 (sex offenses with children and second-degree murder), and class A (first-degree murder). The higher up the chart, the bigger the punishment. The legislature effectively handcuffed trial judges under structured sentencing by prescribing the punishment based in months upon a chart.

Across the nation, 94 percent of all felony cases are resolved through pleas.[32] This does not necessarily mean a "plea bargain," where the defendant is given some lesser sentence in exchange for taking full responsibility or cooperating in testifying against co-defendants. Plea offers are sometimes extended because a case is weak and the chance of the state prevailing at trial are slight. It is the prosecutor's use of discretion, through plea offers, that puts the vast majority of people in the box that prescribes the sentence.

Sentences can be consolidated, meaning that they are all placed into one box with the highest sentence controlling for all, or they can be run consecutively, meaning they can run back-to-back ("boxcar") with each other so that the sentences are added together. Additionally, within every box, a defendant can be sentenced in the "aggravated range" (the top range of months), the "presumptive range" (middle range of months), or "mitigated range" (bottom range of months). For a judge to deviate from the presumptive range, they must find that the scales of justice tip toward aggravating or mitigating based upon statutorily created factors.[33]

It is impossible to take all emotion out of the criminal justice system, especially when it comes to punishment. Great decisions are made not only with the head but the heart. Of all the professions that may one day be replaced by artificial intelligence, lawyering will not likely be on the list. Computers cannot advocate. We do our best to remove feelings and focus on facts—to assign numbers to conduct on punishment charts. The truth is more complicated because humans are complicated. Justice can be a messy business.

In the heartbreaking case that follows, let's look at how we decide which label to affix to conduct. Critically important to this process is to ask an even more profound question: Why do we punish people in the first place?

In re Wilkins[34]

The screams coming from the parking lot outside the daycare center were piercing. Nancy Wilkins pleaded for help. Moments earlier, around 5:30 p.m. on May 25, 2016, she had been inside the daycare center to pick up her four-year-old and nine-month-old sons, only to be told by staff at the center that the toddler was present but that the baby, Jefferson, had not been dropped off that day.

In a panic, Nancy ran outside, only to realize that Jefferson was in the back seat of her car and had been there for over nine hours. CPR efforts to revive him proved futile. He had been dead for hours. Nancy was so overcome with grief that she was unable to stand or walk. She had to be assisted into a rolling chair before she was able to communicate with emergency personnel.

FELONY PUNISHMENT CHART
PRIOR RECORD LEVEL

OFFENSE CLASS		I 0-1 Pt	II 2-5 Pts	III 6-9 Pts	IV 10-13 Pts	V 14-17 Pts	VI 18+ Pts	
	A	Death or Life Without Parole — Defendant Under 18 at Time of Offense: Life With or Without Parole						DISPOSITION
	B1	A 240 - 300 **192 - 240** 144 - 192	A 276 - 345 **221 - 276** 166 - 221	A 317 -397 **254 - 317** 190 - 254	A 365 - 456 **292 - 365** 219 - 292	A *Life Without Parole* **336 - 420** 252 - 336	A *Life Without Parole* **386 - 483** 290 - 386	*Aggravated Range* **PRESUMPTIVE RANGE** *Mitigated Range*
	B2	A 157 - 196 **125 - 157** 94 - 125	A 180 - 225 **144 - 180** 108 - 144	A 207 - 258 **165 - 207** 124 - 165	A 238 - 297 **190 - 238** 143 - 190	A 273 - 342 **219 - 273** 164 - 219	A 314 - 393 **251 - 314** 189 - 251	
	C	A 73 – 92 **58 - 73** 44 - 58	A 83 - 104 **67 - 83** 50 - 67	A 96 - 120 **77 - 96** 58 - 77	A 110 - 138 **88 - 110** 66 - 88	A 127 - 159 **101 - 127** 76 - 101	A 146 - 182 **117 - 146** 87 - 117	
	D	A 64 - 80 **51 - 64** 38 - 51	A 73 - 92 **59 - 73** 44 - 59	A 84 - 105 **67 - 84** 51 - 67	A 97 - 121 **78 - 97** 58 - 78	A 111 - 139 **89 - 111** 67 - 89	A 128 - 160 **103 - 128** 77 - 103	
	E	I/A 25 - 31 **20 - 25** 15 - 20	I/A 29 - 36 **23 - 29** 17 - 23	A 33 - 41 **26 - 33** 20 - 26	A 38 - 48 **30 - 38** 23 - 30	A 44 - 55 **35 - 44** 26 - 35	A 50 - 63 **40 - 50** 30 - 40	
	F	I/A 16 - 20 **13 - 16** 10 - 13	I/A 19 - 23 **15 - 19** 11 - 15	I/A 21 - 27 **17 - 21** 13 - 17	A 25 - 31 **20 - 25** 15 - 20	A 28 - 36 **23 - 28** 17 - 23	A 33 - 41 **26 - 33** 20 - 26	
	G	I/A 13 - 16 **10 - 13** 8 - 10	I/A 14 - 18 **12 - 14** 9 - 12	I/A 17 - 21 **13 - 17** 10 - 13	I/A 19 - 24 **15 - 19** 11 - 15	A 22 - 27 **17 - 22** 13 - 17	A 25 - 31 **20 - 25** 15 - 20	
	H	C/I/A 6 - 8 **5 - 6** 4 - 5	I/A 8 - 10 **6 - 8** 4 - 6	I/A 10 - 12 **8 - 10** 6 - 8	I/A 11 - 14 **9 - 11** 7 - 9	I/A 15 - 19 **12 - 15** 9 - 12	A 20 - 25 **16 - 20** 12 - 16	
	I	C 6 - 8 **4 - 6** 3 - 4	C/I 6 - 8 **4 - 6** 3 - 4	I 6 - 8 **5 - 6** 4 - 5	I/A 8 - 10 **6 - 8** 4 - 6	I/A 9 - 11 **7 - 9** 5 - 7	I/A 10 - 12 **8 - 10** 6 - 8	

A – Active Punishment   I – Intermediate Punishment   C – Community Punishment
Numbers shown are in months and represent the range of <u>minimum</u> sentences

Revised: 09-09-13

FIGURE 1.7   Felony Punishment Chart.

The Child Fatality Protocol

I am immediately notified anytime a child dies in the Sixth District and the same goes for the directors of the Departments of Social Services (DSS) in New Hanover and Pender Counties. When I became DA, I enacted a Child Fatality Protocol that established a course for investigating these very sensitive cases to ensure that our actions never vary.

DA's Office representatives respond to the scene of child fatalities to advise local law enforcement to make sure that a criminal investigation occurs. The job of law enforcement is clear—presume innocence but prove guilt. They should trust that a caretaker's remorse is sincere, but it must be verified. That means interviewing witnesses and collecting all physical evidence. It also means taking a blood draw of the caretaker to see if there are any impairing substances present, as well as seizing their cell phone.

It is the responsibility of DSS to ensure the immediate safety of any other minor children (in this case, the four-year-old brother) and to see if there are other instances of abuse or neglect in the family. Jeffrey and Nancy Wilkins did not have any previous contact with law enforcement or the Department of Social Services regarding the care or welfare of their children. Interviews with close and extended family, as well as with friends, underscored Nancy's care and concern for both of her children. Her vigilance regarding their safety and her abhorrence of harming them was paramount.

The Investigation

Interviews with the couple revealed they alternated taking care of the baby when he woke overnight, and the night before the incident was Nancy's turn. She was up with the baby at 3:30 a.m. It was her morning routine to drop off both children at daycare, get coffee, and then drive to work. Documents at the daycare center confirmed this.

On this day, there had been a change in the family's routine. Jeffrey drove the four-year-old son to school and Nancy took the infant to the pediatrician for a regular checkup, which he passed with flying colors. Mother and baby left the doctor's office, stopped for coffee at the same donut shop she visited every morning (the one she would normally go to directly after drop-off at daycare), and headed to work. She simply forgot that Jefferson was still in the backseat. There, the baby remained in his rear-facing car seat, behind heavily tinted windows, hidden from view by anyone else who might have parked in the lot.

Nancy's cell phone records showed that during the time she was driving her car to and from work she neither placed nor received any calls or texts. Business records provided by her employer show that she clocked in at 9:36 a.m. and that she did not leave her place of business that day until she clocked out at 5:17 p.m. A co-worker picked up take-out for several of the employees, including Nancy, who did not go out to lunch on this day.

Nancy's co-workers would later say that Nancy behaved as usual, that she seemed in good spirits. Video from the business corroborates these statements. The investigation of Nancy's phone, which included looking at her online activities, texts, and calls, indicated nothing out of the ordinary.

Throughout the investigation both parents were fully cooperative with law enforcement's efforts to determine the facts of what had happened. Nancy consented to a request for a blood draw, which was collected at the scene. The sample was analyzed at the state's request by a private lab routinely used in criminal investigations. The lab results confirmed the presence of medically prescribed substances within therapeutic levels and corroborated the medical history provided by her physicians. There was no presence of alcohol or illegal drugs and no evidence of impairment.

The death certificate indicated that Jefferson died as a result of "death by hyperthermia due to environmental exposure/accident." The temperature on this date reached a high of 86°F. That means that temperatures inside the car would have reached 135°F.[35]

In making my decision not to prosecute Nancy Wilkins for any crime, I consulted with the Wilmington Police Department (WPD) chief of police, the head of DSS, and Chief District Court Judge J. Corpening (who serves as head of the Community Child Protection Team).[36] We decided that it was best to hold a joint press conference to announce the decision to decline prosecution and also to use this as a forum for educating the community to employ safeguards to prevent another tragedy like this from occurring. For good measure, I also invited Chief Dan House of Wrightsville Beach and Chief Chris Spivey of Carolina Beach. Hot car deaths involving children and pets are more likely in their jurisdictions during the warm summer months. This was my statement:

There is no victim more innocent than a baby and none of us could think of a more torturous death than an infant being left to spend its last moments alone and afraid in a blistering hot car. The men and women of law enforcement and my office see the very best and worst of our community every day. By any objective measure, this is one of the most tragic cases to ever visit our region, and it reduced hardened career professionals to tears. If we punished merely on emotion, many of us in the law enforcement family and this community would want the sanctions to be swift and severe.

Sadly, we are not the first community to confront this issue. Across the country, approximately 37 children die each year under similar circumstances.[37] The decision of whether to charge and what charges are appropriate must always be guided by the particular facts of each case. Broadly speaking, these cases fall into the following four categories:

Intentional behavior: Where a parent intentionally leaves a child in the car while they run an errand and an unintended death or injury is caused by a car that quickly overheats. The conscious choice to leave a vulnerable infant in an unattended car is child abuse.[38] Where serious injury or death result, serious felony charges can and should be filed.[39]

Impairment: It should surprise no one that a parent is held responsible for the intentional choice of using alcohol, drugs, or other impairing substances when a child who is entirely dependent upon them for safety is seriously injured or dies as a result of the omission of a duty to act or the commission of an act causing death.[40]

Reckless behavior: When a parent engages in conduct or a pattern of behavior that shows a "conscious disregard" of a substantial risk, recklessness to support involuntary manslaughter is appropriate.[41]

Accident: Death that results from an otherwise loving parent who simply forgot that their child was in the car. According to a national survey of heatstroke deaths of children in vehicles, approximately 54 percent of all hot car deaths fall into this category.[42]

Where death is the result in this fourth category, many authorities in jurisdictions across the country do not file charges. As one legal scholar noted, "where the death of a human being is the result of accident or misadventure, in the true meaning of the term, no criminal responsibility attaches to the act of the slayer. Where it appears that the killing was unintentional ... with no wrongful purpose ... while engaged in a lawful enterprise ... the homicide will be excused on the score of accident."[43] More than mere civil negligence is required. To be actionable as a crime, the conduct must carry with it "*wantonness, recklessness or other conduct, amounting to culpable negligence.*"[44]

The statutes and case law from North Carolina specifically remove accidental death from any criminal penalty.[45] Without some intentional act in the chain of causation leading to the death, there can be no criminal responsibility. Death under such circumstances is rather the result of accident or misfortune.[46] Nineteen states have laws making it illegal to leave unattended children in cars.[47] North Carolina is not one of them.[48]

The case before us was the result of an accident: the "perfect storm" of circumstances arising from a change of routine, sleep deprivation, and outright forgetfulness. No criminal charges will be filed against Wilkins for this unthinkable tragedy. As is my practice for critical incidents such as officer use-of-force cases, where I have determined that no charges are warranted, I detail the findings of fact and conclusions of law in support of that decision.

Prosecutors cannot abdicate their responsibility to make tough calls where the evidence does not support the filing of criminal charges. Our oath is to do justice, not to convict at all costs. Stated differently, the question is not *can* we charge, but *should* we? To answer, look at the four reasons we punish, none of which apply to this incident:

> *General deterrence:* Punishing conduct to show society that this type of behavior will not be tolerated and will deter others from engaging in similar behavior. Accidents have never been criminally punished because accidents happen and are not the product of intentional choices. Stated another way, no parent is more or less likely to accidently leave their child in a car if we punished Wilkins.

> *Specific deterrence:* Punishing a specific individual to protect society from them through either incarceration where they cannot hurt others, or putting the world on notice of their identity so that they may be avoided. Wilkins poses no public threat and the streets would not be made safer by punishing her.

> *Rehabilitation:* Some offenders, through treatment, are less likely to reoffend in the future through court-imposed counseling, addiction therapy, and the like. The state is aware that Wilkins has sought professional help since the very moment this occurred and there is no

indication that any additional treatment a court could impose would reduce the risk of a similar tragedy from occurring again.

Retribution: Punishment for punishment's sake, under the proverbial "eye for an eye" adage. It should be asked rhetorically, "Is there anything the justice system can do to Wilkins to punish her beyond what she is already doing to herself?"

In my district we have always put our children first and have taken a very aggressive approach in prosecuting anyone who would do them harm. Over the last decade we have established precedent and procedures to make the following objectives clear: (1) prosecuting violent crime is our first priority; (2) impairment is no accident; (3) a pattern of reckless behavior is tantamount to intentional conduct; and (4) parents and caregivers owe a special obligation to the children in their care.

The Child Fatality Protocol we have in place for the Sixth District requires a team of dedicated professionals, comprised of law enforcement, court officials, and the Department of Social Services, to contact members of the DA's office anytime a child fatality occurs to make sure that a complete investigation is conducted and the immediate safety of other siblings is assured. In the Wilkins case, this protocol was invoked within minutes of the 911 call being made, and many of us worked together throughout the night of this incident and over the next several weeks to conduct a thorough investigation.

Those of us on the Child Protection Team (CPT), who are entrusted with serving, protecting, and doing justice, take that obligation very seriously. If there is any good to come from this tragedy it is increased public awareness. To help prevent an event like this from ever occurring again, the CPT is buying billboards and printing placards to launch a "Look Before You Lock" campaign. Additionally, I have instructed law enforcement officers not to charge anyone who breaks through the window of a locked vehicle to help a child, pet, or other vulnerable person left inside. The public is urged to immediately call 911 to report these situations.

An innocent baby is dead and all of us grieve. Filing criminal charges will not make us safer, balm our hurt, or bring him back. For those of us who serve and protect and uphold the Constitution, we will stop at nothing to conduct thorough investigations and use every law at our disposal to hold people accountable when appropriate.

We should not elevate a tragedy to a crime merely to say that grave accidents cannot happen and must be the result of something more sinister. Accidents can happen and they break our hearts. We *call upon the entire community to put measures in place to reduce the risk of accidents like this from occurring again.*[49]

A Higher Duty

Statistics in Washington have names in Wilmington. I know the names behind the statistics. Makeshift memorials, road signs, and parks all bear the names of the victims I have represented in a courtroom. Their stories are shared here not to glorify death but to celebrate their lives and to extract lessons learned from their cases.

Some of the defendants from the cases discussed in this book are out among us, walking on the street. Others are in prison, death row, or the cemetery. Many of these cases have set precedent and have established broad legal principles.

Being a prosecutor also means being a strong advocate for victims of all shapes and sizes. That has been my life's work—whether speaking for the dead in a murder trial or putting victims on the stand to find the courage to confront a defendant. The best part about my job is that eventually I meet everyone. The worst part are the circumstances that bring us together.

Decades ago, the United States Supreme Court left no question that prosecutors have a higher duty than anyone else in the criminal justice system:

> The [DA] is the representative not of an ordinary party to a controversy, but of a sovereignty whose obligation to govern impartially is as compelling as its obligation to govern at all, and whose interest, therefore, in a criminal prosecution is not that it shall win a case, but that justice shall be done. As such, he is in a peculiar and very definite sense the servant of the law, the two-fold aim of which is that guilt shall not escape or innocence suffer.[50]

While putting criminals away is the primary objective, it's just as important to see what we can do to prevent crime from happening in the first place. While I still visit crime scenes and try cases, much of my time is spent working with people inside and outside my office to help victims, and even some defendants, out of the stale waters of despair. Shaping how our justice system works and identifying what we can do to make it better drives me every day. Part of this is being actively involved in my community.

After a tragedy, we try to make individuals and communities as whole as possible. But DAs should do more than just look back to help victims; we should look forward to prevent victimization. If there are issues that keep leading defendants or victims to the courthouse (poverty, drug addiction, and intergenerational abuse to name a few), the DA can bring other people in the community together to work on solutions that stop the abuse, stop the trauma, stop the cycle.

Making sure that the focus is not on convicting at all costs means considering mercy and second chances. Prosecutors keep young adults' records clean when they make mistakes by deferring prosecution and, when appropriate, we send people struggling with addiction and mental illness to treatment rather than a prison cell. While we take a very hard line on the violence and drug trafficking that comes out of young people joining forces to commit crimes, we also join together as adults to provide long-range solutions that break up gang violence. We even hold back on the visceral reaction to punish in the worst case imaginable, like when a baby dies, when proceeding with charges would serve no useful purpose.

Being a servant of the law means dismissing a case when we are not sure of a defendant's guilt. It also means putting policies and practices in place that help to guard against unfair treatment and prevent wrongful convictions. While everyone has seen the horror stories of wrongfully convicted people languishing in prison for decades until being exonerated by DNA or other new evidence, these stories have not been part of the narrative coming out of the Sixth District.[51]

Staying loyal to your oath as a prosecutor, however, also means making sure that the guilty do not escape. This includes fighting to create precedent that sends an impaired driver away for the rest of his life or holding someone responsible for the death of an officer that occurs two miles away from the killer. It also means convicting a serial killer or a serial rapist who has escaped justice, in part, by moving around the country and learning how to conceal evidence. Prosecutors also give a voice to the voiceless. When we build trust in the communities most affected by crime, we enable individuals to seek justice at the courthouse, not on the street.

Speaking for innocent people and bringing awareness and change for communities most affected by crime are a driving force behind my work. Who is the victim in a drug transaction between a willing buyer and seller on the street corner in a public housing project? In some respects, the buyer, who is an addict, may be the victim. But increasingly, I have come to see the residents of the neighborhood where the transaction takes place as the biggest victims. People in poverty who are living behind bars in their own homes, terrified by the violence that surrounds drug deals, are frequently unwilling to report the crimes they see for fear of reprisal. Innocent people are literally caught in the crossfire or pulled into crime themselves.

Growing demand for criminal justice reform to confront structural inequality, racism, and police use of force, to name a few topics, are not theoretical headlines for the local DA, but are very much a daily reality. These issues are not unique to my district, and the solutions to them can be replicated elsewhere. Some of the ideas in this book have come from other prosecutors and professionals, and I am in their debt. Many others are my original ideas and have been developed, sometimes after painful trial and error. If they can work in your community, be a thief.

In the end, prosecution is about connecting details to solve crimes and connecting people to each other to help prevent them. It is about the things that pull us apart and the things that bring us together. It is about the things we run from and run toward. This is a book about crime and community in the Cape Fear.

Notes

1   As a research guide, I list the cases that will be discussed in each chapter in the introductory paragraph and include an endnote that will give the case file or, where applicable, the published opinion. A case at the Superior Court trial level will have a file number such as *State v. Deans*, 15CRS00114, which means Deans was charged in 2015. Where the cases have been appealed to the Court of Appeals or Supreme Court, they can be found in published volumes. A case cited as *State v. Carter*, 156 N.C. App. 446 (2003), is a Court of Appeals opinion that can be found on page 446 of volume 156 that was decided in 2003. A case cited *State v. Cummings*, 361 N.C. 438 (2007), is a Supreme Court opinion that can be found on page 438 of volume 361 that was decided in 2007. Dora's case is *State v. McAllister*, 190 N.C. App. 289 (2008). Co-counsel was Barrett Temple.

2   *First Lady Eleanor Roosevelt Visits Homesteaders at Penderlea, 1937*, N.C. Natural and Cultural Resources, (Aug. 2, 2017), https://www.ncdcr.gov/blog/2015/06/11/first-lady-eleanor-roosevelt-visits-homesteaders-at-penderlea-1937.

3   http://crimereporting.ncsbi.gov; see also, Jonathan Haynes, "Violent Crime Is Down, Though There Has Been a Sudden Increase in Motor Vehicle Theft, *Wilmington Star News*, February 19, 2020. Violent crime is down by half since 2002 despite an increase in the population by 30,000 people.

4 Some scholars refer to this phenomenon as the Equivalent Group Hypothesis. James F. Anderson, *Criminological Theories.* (Jones & Bartlett Learning, 2015), 50.

5 Memorandum from the New Hanover Sheriff's Office to author (Jan. 31, 2008) (author file).

6 Tom Keith and S. Stanley Young, "Racial Justice Act Repeal Should Stand," *Winston-Salem Jounrnal*, Jan. 4, 2012, *available at* http://www.journalnow.com/news/2012/jan/04/wsopin02-tom-keith-and-s-stanley-young-guest-colum-ar-1775245/.

7 My district was known as the Fifth Prosecutorial District until December 31, 2018, when statewide redistricting changed the district numbers for several jurisdictions.

8 *Quick Facts New Hanover County, North Carolina*, United States Census Bureau, U.S. Department of Commerce (July 1, 2016), https://www.census.gov/quickfacts/fact/table/newhanovercountynorthcarolina/PST045216.

9 Paul Stephen, "Study—Wilmington No. 1 in Opioid Abuse," *Wilmington Star News*, GateHouse Media, LLC (Copyright 2006–2017), (Updated June 24, 2016), http://www.starnewsonline.com/news/20160421/study---wilmington-no-1-in-opioid-abuse.

10 *Quick Facts Pender County, North Carolina*, United States Census Bureau, U.S. Department of Commerce, (July 1, 2016), https://www.census.gov/quickfacts/fact/table/pendercountynorthcarolina/PST045216.

11 See Harper Lee, *To Kill a Mockingbird*. Pender County is named for 29-year-old William D. Pender, who was killed in action during the Civil War. His monument is at the entrance to the courthouse. In Wilmington, a monument to George Davis, senator and attorney general for the Confederate States of America, stood next to the courthouse since 1911. The statue was removed by the City of Wilmington on June 25, 2020, and the pedestal was draped in a black cloth by the city five days later.

12 Ann McAdams, Investigative Reporter, "AP: New Hanover County Bellwether for Presidential Election," WECT6, Fox Wilmington, (Updated November 9, 2016), http://www.wect.com/story/33661926/ap-new-hanover-county-bellwether-for-presidential-election.

13 Associated Press, "Mike Nifong Disbarred over Ethics Violations in Duke Lacrosse Case," Fox News Network LLC (2017), (June 17, 2007), http://www.foxnews.com/story/2007/06/17/mike-nifong-disbarred-over-ethics-violations-in-duke-lacrosse-case.html

14 Jeff Turrentine, "The N-Word," *Indy Week* (March 6, 2002), https://www.indyweek.com/indyweek/the-n-word/Content?oid=1185947.

15   N.C. Gen. Stat. § 7A-66 (2015).

16   *North Carolina Counties*, North Carolina Association of County Commissioners, Government Websites by Civic Plus (August 2, 2017), http://www.ncacc.org/171/Links-to-Counties.

17   *North Carolina Prosecutorial Districts*, NC General Assembly (June 15, 2018), http://www.nccourts.org/Courts/Trial/District/Documents/prosecutorialdistrictsmap15.pdf.

18   *Id.*

19   N.C. Const. Art. 46, Chapter 15A. (2019).

20   N.C. Const. Art. IV § 18 ("The District Attorney shall advise the officers of justice in his district").

21   *Detention Division*, New Hanover County Sheriff's Office, New Hanover County, North Carolina (August 2, 2017), http://www.newhanoversheriff.com/about-us/divisions/detention-division/.

22   *Jail*, Pender County Sheriff's Office, Pender County, North Carolina, (August 2, 2017), http://www.pendersheriff.com/jail-division/.

23   *Prisons*, N.C. Public Safety, North Carolina Department of Public Safety, (August 2, 2017), https://www.ncdps.gov/Adult-Corrections/Prisons (North Carolina currently houses more than 37,000 inmates in 55 state facilities).

24   *New Hanover Correctional Center*, N.C. Public Safety, North Carolina Department of Public Safety, (August 2, 2017), https://www.ncdps.gov/Adult-Corrections/Prisons/Prison-Facilities/New-Hanover-Correctional-Center (Inmate Capacity: 384).

25   *Pender County Correctional Institution*, N.C. Public Safety, North Carolina Department of Public Safety, (August 2, 2017), https://www.ncdps.gov/Adult-Corrections/Prisons/Prison-Facilities/Pender-Correctional-Center (Inmate Capacity: 740).

26   *Prisons*, N.C. Public Safety, North Carolina Department of Public Safety, (August 2, 2017), https://www.ncdps.gov/Adult-Corrections/Prisons (North Carolina currently houses more than 37,000 inmates in 55 state facilities).

27   See newhanoverda.com and penderda.com.

28   Amanda Arnold, "What Exactly Does It Mean to Defund the Police?" *The Cut*, June 12, 2020. https://www.thecut.com/2020/06/what-does-defund-the-police-mean-the-phrase-explained.html

29   Anne Blythe, Jury Awards More Than $25 Million to Duplin County Couple in Hog-Farm Case. *The News and Observer* (June 29, 2018), https://www.newsobserver.com/news/local/article214096384.html

30 Cammie Bellamy, Top Employers in the Cape Fear Region, *Star News Online*, (April 21, 2019), https://www.starnewsonline.com/news/20190421/top-employers-in-cape-fear-region.

31 Philip Brown, M.D., *NHRMC on a Mission—New Mission Statement: Leading Our Community to Outstanding Health*, New Hanover Regional Medical Center (Copyright 2017), (January 25, 2017), https://www.nhrmc.org/blog/2017/01/nhrmc-on-a-mission ("Statistics show that 80% of health has nothing directly to do with medicine and that only 8% of a given population annually will admit to a hospital.").

32 Clark Neily, Prisons Are Packed because Prosecutors Are Coercing Plea Deals. And Yes, It's Totally Legal, *NBC News*, August 8, 2019, https://www.nbcnews.com/think/opinion/prisons-are-packed-because-prosecutors-are-coercing-plea-deals-yes-ncna1034201

33 N.C. Gen. Stat. § 15A-1340.16 Aggravated and mitigated sentences.

34 There are many press accounts. Co-Counsel was Christa Lawler.

35 Jan Null, CCM (Certified Consulting Meteorologist) at San Jose State University states that "with an outside air temperature of approximately 86 degrees, the inside air temperature of the car could have been in excess of 135 degrees. Objects or a person inside the car in direct sunlight would have been significantly hotter." Jason Samenow, "Children left in hot cars a deadly combination that must stop," *Washington Post*, July 8, 2013, https://www.washingtonpost.com/news/capital-weather-gang/wp/2013/07/08/children-left-in-hot-cars-a-deadly-combination-that-must-stop/.

36 As Amber Rollins, the director of KidsandCars.org, remarked in a *New York Times* article, her organization had identified 494 deaths involving caregivers said they were not aware they had left their babies in hot cars. In 43 percent of those cases, no charges were filed. In 32 percent of the cases, the caregiver was charged and convicted. And in 11 percent of the cases, the person was charged with a crime, but the judge or jury did not convict. The other 14 percent accounts for cases that are still open, or the status is unknown. See, Otterman, S. "He Left His Twins in a Hot Car and They Died. Accident or Crime?" *New York Times*, August 1, 2019, section A, page 1.

37 *Heatstroke*, KidsAndCars.Org (Copyright 2017) (August 2, 2017), http://www.kidsandcars.org/how-kids-get-hurt/heat-stroke/ ("On average, 37 children die from heat-related deaths after being trapped inside vehicles.").

38 N.C. Gen. Stat. § 14-318.2.

39 N.C. Gen. Stat. § 14-318.4; *State v. Wilkerson*, 295 N.C. 559 (1978).

40 *Arteaga v. Texas*, No. 01-00-00482-CR, 2002 WL 1935268, at *1-4, 2002 Tex. App. LEXIS 6096, at *3, *8-10 (Ct. App. Aug, 2002) (Eight-month-old died of exposure after being left in car overnight by his impaired mother who took her other young child from car, leaving baby in it, to get a ride home after first attempting to drive); *Louisiana v. Small*, 2012 La. Lexis 2705 (Mother left children at home to go drinking; house caught on fire and one child died. Mom found criminally negligent).

41 *Illinois v. Kolsowski*, 301 Ill. App.3d 1, 3-5, 703 N.E.2d 424, 226-27 (Ct. App. 1998) (Mother who had habit of leaving baby in car for up to 20 minutes while visiting friends and running errands, also in an effort to get uninterrupted sleep was convicted where child died of exposure after being left in hot car for four hours); Small, *supra* (Fact that mother had previously pled guilty to child abandonment relevant on issue of knowledge that leaving unsupervised child was illegal and reckless).

42 Samenow, "Children left in hot cars."

43 26 Am. Jur. Homicide, s.220, p.305. More than mere civil negligence is required.

44 *State v. Faust*, 254 N.C. 101, 112-13, 118 S.E.2d 769, 776 (1961). See also, *State v. Phillips*, 264 N.C. 508, 142 S.E.2d 337 (1965).

45 N.C. Gen. Stat. § 14-318.2(a) (Child abuse must be established "by other than accidental means").

46 *State v. Everhart*, 291 N.C. 700, 231 S.E.2d 604 (1977); *State v. Church*, 265 N.C. 534, 144 S.E.2d 624 (1965).

47 *State Laws*, KidsAndCars.Org. (Copyright 2017), (August 2, 2017), http://www.kidsandcars.org/resources/state-laws/ ("Currently only 19 states in the U.S. have laws that specifically make it illegal to leave a child unattended in a vehicle.").

48 *Id.*

49 These remarks were made at a press conference held at the Carolina Beach Town Hall on January 1, 2016.

50 *Berger v. United States*, 295 U.S. 78, 88 (1935).

51 There has not been a substantiated claim of actual innocence in the Sixth District in the 20 years I have been in the office. Our people believe: "It is better to let a hundred guilty people escape than to let one innocent suffer," which has been attributed to both English jurist William Blackstone (the Blackstone ratio) and Benjamin Franklin.

Figure Credits

Chapter 2

The Blame Game

In this section, we look at three defenses: "Of Course I Did It," "The Devil Made Me Do It," and "Maybe You Did It," as defendants seek to shift the blame to the victim, or to impairing substances, or to the police and prosecutors handling the case. Keeping the responsibility squarely on defendants means not only focusing on the facts but also shifting our focus. This may involve a cultural shift, or the courage for leaders to take on some of the blame and commit to do better.

The Search for Dora's Attacker

There were few leads in Dora's case. Between losing her glasses and her vision during the onslaught, the most that Dora could say was that she thought the intruder was black. The search for physical evidence proved more fruitful and corroborated Dora's limited description of the attacker. Wrapped up in Dora's bed sheets was a hair fragment, which investigators believed may have come from the intruder.

There are two types of DNA. The first type of DNA is nuclear and is unique to every individual, except identical twins, to the exclusion of every other person on the planet. Blood, semen, skin cells, and, importantly, hairs with roots, have nuclear DNA. When nuclear DNA is present, it can be put into a database, known as the Combined DNA Index System (CODIS), to compare the unknown sample to all other convicted felons (and, in North Carolina, people who have been charged with a felony) to see if there is a match. Many cold cases are solved using this method.

The second type of DNA is mitochondrial. While not unique to every individual, it is common to every maternally related relative in a family line. For example, each of three brothers from the same mother will have the same mitochondrial DNA as one another. Mitochondrial DNA is found where samples are limited (for example, bone fragments and hair fragments with no roots). A huge limitation with mitochondrial DNA found at crime scenes (like with the hair fragment found on Dora's bed) is that the DNA cannot be put into the CODIS database to compare it to all other felons. Instead, to conduct a comparative test, investigators and scientists must have a sample from the actual suspect or his mother.

The challenge was identifying a suspect capable of such a heinous attack. The good news was that few people resided in western Pender County, limiting the pool of possible perpetrators. Fewer still were African-American males. And far fewer had a criminal history that would suggest being capable of such a brutal crime. To conduct a test to obtain DNA for comparison, all that was needed was a buccal swab (obtained by rolling a cotton swab along the inside of a subject's cheek) from the suspect or his mother.

Obtaining DNA samples was, of course, tricky. The Fourth Amendment prohibits unreasonable search and seizure.[1] This means that without probable cause and a search warrant, investigators cannot approach an individual and demand that they submit to a DNA test.

This limitation, however, is overcome with the consent of the governed. Investigators are allowed to ask individuals to voluntarily submit to such a test: there is no Fourth Amendment violation if someone waives his or her right to privacy. The Pender County Sheriff's Office took this approach and started by confronting men in the area who were convicted felons.

Many in the community knew about the crime and all were horrified that a woman as nice and revered as Dora was violently assaulted. People in the possible pool of suspects (African-American men, many with criminal records) lined up to help. If this was to be a process of elimination, they wanted to remove any cloud of suspicion, and quickly. The common refrain was, "I did not touch that lady and I want to help you find the man who did it." Some convicted felons fled the area, among them a homeless man who had been chased out of a nearby mobile home around the same time as the attack. The property in which he had been squatting was within walking distance of Dora's farm. His name was Antonio McAllister.

A thief by trade, McAllister had done time for minor breaking and entering charges. Years earlier, McAllister was charged with a sex offense in neighboring Bladen County, but it was dismissed when the woman who had accused him of rape refused to cooperate. Once word of the dragnet in Dora's case started to spread, McAllister fled.

McAllister's mother, a registered nurse who worked at a local hospital, was all too happy to provide a DNA sample when asked by authorities, since her son could not be found to provide one himself. She maintained that her son was incapable of such a crime. After several weeks, DNA results from her buccal swab came back from the State Bureau of Investigation (SBI) Crime Lab. She was a match. It was established that McAllister's two biological brothers were in prison on the date of the attack (making it impossible for them to be the mitochondrial DNA contributors). We knew we had our man. Working with the U.S. Marshals, a SWAT team found McAllister hiding in an attic in Florida months later. He was quickly extradited back to North Carolina.

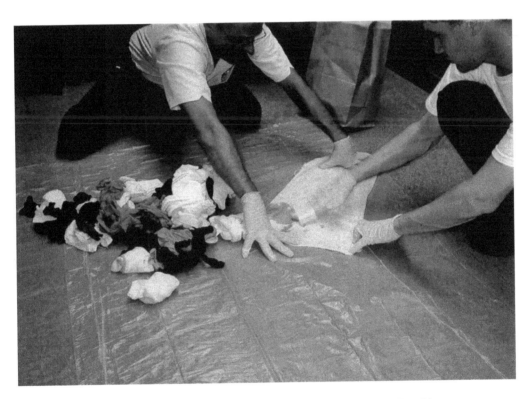

FIGURE 2.1   Detective Scott Lawson examines evidence collected from Dora Corbett's residence.

Detective Scott Lawson with the Pender County Sheriff's Office obtained a search warrant to retrieve DNA from McAllister for confirmatory testing. Meanwhile, Detective Lawson continued to comb through the evidence to determine if the initial review of items seized from Dora's house would yield any new clues. We were fortunate; Detective Lawson found an additional hair hidden in one of Dora's socks. Unlike the first hair, this one had a root, making it possible to conduct nuclear DNA testing. The subsequent DNA test confirmed, statistically into the millions and billions, that Antonio McAllister was the perpetrator of the crime. This new piece of evidence allowed us to proceed to trial without the crime lab testing the rape kit collected from Dora. At the time, the crime lab had a severe backlog for this type of testing. It took more than two years to get results—longer than Dora might live.

The Trial

The trial, which was moved to Wilmington because we could not find a fair jury in Pender County, started without much controversy. Dora bravely took the stand and held the jury captive as she provided the horrific details of her experience. Dora's testimony eliminated nearly every possible defense. Provided that we could establish the identity of the perpetrator, McAllister would be convicted as charged of all offenses.

Next, Pender County Detective Cordelia Johnson described the discovery of the hair fragment and the subsequent dragnet investigation that eliminated many

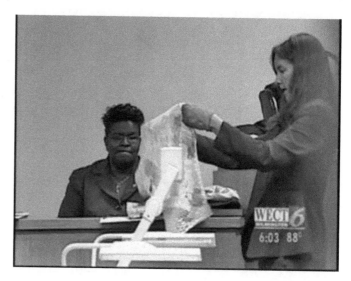

FIGURE 2.2　Detective Cordelia Johnson testifies as ADA Barrett Temple shows the jury evidence. *Source*: WECT.

other suspects. A scientist from the SBI Crime Lab also testified about eliminating the other suspects through the buccal swab.

Then Detective Lawson took the stand. He testified that he took the original hair fragment to LabCorp, an independent laboratory, because the SBI Crime Lab did not have the capability to perform mitochondrial DNA testing. Detective Lawson explained that he immediately took out warrants for McAllister when the hair fragment proved to be a mitochondrial match.

Then came the bombshell. DNA experts hired by the defense took the stand and testified that they had reviewed the DNA profile from the hair fragment from the data provided by LabCorp. In the view of these scientists, the hair fragment did not match the DNA of Antonio McAllister! The defense attorneys went further, alleging that Detective Lawson planted the second, more complete hair. When the second hair was found, McAllister was already in custody and forced to give a hair sample for testing, which they alleged gave Detective Lawson the evidence he needed to frame McAllister. The defense wanted the Internal Affairs file on Detective Lawson to see if he was a bad cop. Suddenly, he was the one on trial. My team and I were shocked. The "Maybe You Did It" pig had walked into the creek to muddy the water.

With absolutely no notice of the defense's DNA results, Assistant District Attorney Barrett Temple and I requested that the judge grant a two-week recess in the middle of the trial. Over this break, two things were confirmed. First, Detective Lawson did not have any Internal Affairs complaints that even remotely suggested that he might have planted evidence against an innocent man. Second, and even more damning for the defense, further DNA testing on the original hair fragment (found the morning after the attack and months before McAllister was a suspect in our custody) confirmed that the hair was a mitochondrial match with McAllister and his mother. The reason for the defense expert's opinion that the DNA profile was different than McAllister's profile was that the hair fragment also contained a mixture of a second person's DNA. Further analysis of that profile established that the second DNA was that of a woman. A female had not attacked Dora. The most likely reason that the hair also had a mixture of female DNA on it was that it came from a female lab agent who handled the hair in the chain of testing and had inadvertently contaminated the sample.

With the confusion cleared up, the trial resumed. After several more days of testimony, the State rested. McAllister did not testify, and his defense experts were easily cross-examined with the new testing we had obtained during the recess. After brief deliberations, the jury returned guilty verdicts on every charge. The judge ensured that McAllister, age 37, would be older than Dora before he ever got out of prison.

Dora's Legacy: Advocacy and Actual Innocence

Most survivors of sexual assault do not want publicity, for obvious reasons. While the press is legally permitted to print the names of rape victims and incest survivors, there has always been an unwritten rule that this information will not be made public—to do otherwise would discourage reporting and hurt the healing process. Dora rejected anonymity and used her status as a survivor of sexual assault for good in the community.

Dora held her own press conference immediately following the verdict. A reporter herself, Dora understood the power of the pen. "If it could happen to me and I can come to court to tell it, I encourage other women to do the same," she said. The most under-reported crime in the criminal justice system had a new spokeswoman.[2] In the weeks that followed, many of us took pride in New Hanover County having the highest number of reported rapes in the state.[3]

Years later, Dora was able to continue this advocacy work in Wilmington. She, along with Detective Lawson, joined me at a fundraising breakfast benefitting Coastal Horizons Center, an organization that provides support services for sexual assault survivors in Southeastern North Carolina and runs the area's only rape crisis hotline.[4] I shared Dora's story with the hundreds of people in attendance and tens of thousands of dollars were raised.

While Dora never returned to her home, she lived out her remaining days in Pender County, surrounded by her family and friends and admired by all. When she passed away in 2011, I joined other friends and family at Dora's funeral and was honored to be asked to give her eulogy.

Then, within a month of the funeral, the letter came. Despite paying lip service to the fact that it would reopen an old wound and cause concern to Dora's family, there was some unfinished business. The North Carolina Center on Actual Innocence (or "the Center"), a private group in Durham, seized on McAllister's defense strategy. They wanted the untested rape kit to be processed to establish that someone other than McAllister had committed this heinous crime.[5]

Verdicts are supposed to speak for all time. A wrongful conviction is a twin tragedy: an innocent person is punished for a crime they did not commit, and the real perpetrator escapes justice. More collateral damage comes to victims and their families who cannot get legal closure and may have to relive the case again in the court system. The victim, the prosecutors, the police, the jury, and the Court of Appeals were all convinced that McAllister was guilty. Now we would be placed on trial again, and this time without Dora.

Truth, trust, and transparency must be the standard for everyone in the criminal justice system. We welcomed the scrutiny of an outside review to resolve the conspiracy theory that Detective

Lawson planted evidence, and we agreed to send the untested rape kit to the Center's lab for testing. The Center incurred the cost for having the rape kit examined.

The timing of the Center's request, however, presented a problem for Detective Lawson. The year after the verdict, he traveled to Afghanistan to serve as a consultant to military forces conducting sexual assault investigations in the war-torn region. Now, having returned to America and between jobs, Detective Lawson was an "untouchable," as a cloud of suspicion hung over him. The Center's investigation dragged on for months.

Finally, almost a year after the case had been reopened, and after repeated phone calls to the Center, I received word that they were abruptly closing the case and that they would not be contesting the jury's verdict. Only after pressing them for documentation to support their reasoning did I learn why they had come to agree with the verdict.

The testing conducted by the independent lab that the Center had hired put the nail in McAllister's coffin. The sample that the defense had collected from Dora's rape kit and had paid thousands of dollars to put through tests that had not been run at the State lab, contained nuclear DNA that *matched* Antonio McAllister. In other words, his semen was inside a 78-year-old woman. He was actually guilty, without any doubt.

The conspiracy theory that Detective Lawson had planted the hair on the mattress was difficult to believe, and the jury did not. Now there was evidence, collected within hours of the attack by medical professionals at a hospital, which contained more of the defendant's DNA. Either there was a massive conspiracy involving nurses, doctors, and detectives to convict an innocent man they never met, or McAllister really was the rapist. The "Maybe You Did It" pig was slaughtered. Case closed.

There is a larger point to this story, one that is overlooked because it is rarely discussed and almost never on the front page of a paper. There are no press conferences to show when police and prosecutors get it right—only quiet letters months or even years after the fact confirming guilt. Moreover, just as defendants can be wrongfully accused, so can police and prosecutors. Should a similar duty exist for the defense to immediately clear up this cloud of suspicion when the truth comes to light that their client was actually guilty?

It was only after my persistent phone calls to the Center (calls that I made each time Detective Lawson called to tell me that he was still unemployed) that documents closing the innocence inquiry, and showing additional damning test results, were even provided to me. More troubling is the fact that the lawyers at the Center knew these results for more than six months before telling me and Detective Lawson.

There is an old adage that defense attorneys often use when describing this last-ditch "Maybe You Did It" defense: "If you do not have the facts, pound the law. If you do not have the law, pound the facts. And if you do not have either, pound the police and prosecutors." The Fifth Defense, "Maybe You Did It," puts the process itself on trial. This was McAllister's ultimate end game. In the end, he lost.

Duke Lacrosse Case

While I was trying McAllister for his heinous crimes, another case was taking shape two hours away in Durham. The Duke Lacrosse case arose when an African-American female alleged sexual violence by a group of white lacrosse players from an elite school. DA Mike Nifong was embroiled in a hotly contested election, and many have speculated that his rush to judgment in seeking an indictment against the Duke players had more to do with pandering to his base than with getting justice.[6]

What would become clear over time is that Nifong had not properly vetted the case, nor had he done the necessary background investigation prior to publicly staking himself to a position. Instead, he began a community quest to slay the larger giant of race and justice using the well-established teaching tool of the case method. Nifong looked into the muddy waters, past obvious pigs, and claimed to see clearly where others had doubt. His certainty reassured many in the short term, but caused everyone to doubt the veracity of prosecutors across the nation in the long run.

The world watched as the case began to unravel, with the realization that Nifong withheld DNA evidence that exonerated the lacrosse players, all the while making incendiary public statements accusing them of being "hooligans."[7] I was in the room when several of the most senior and most respected DAs in the state sought to intervene and tell Nifong that he needed to let someone else handle the case. Ultimately, under pressure from the other elected DAs, Nifong recognized that he had a conflict of interest and agreed to send the case to the Special Prosecutions Unit of the Attorney General's Office.

Attorney General Roy Cooper concluded that the players were "actually innocent," a claim that went well beyond the expected conclusion that there might be insufficient evidence to convict them. Nifong was ultimately disbarred, sent to jail for a day for contempt of court for the way the case was handled, and filed for bankruptcy after the players sued him civilly. Another sad postscript to the story was that the woman who made the report of sexual assault, Crystal Mangum, was subsequently involved in a violent killing of her boyfriend and went to prison for second-degree murder.

State v. Mintz[8]

In the summer of 2004, the homeless population wandering the streets of downtown Wilmington seemed to jump dramatically, almost overnight. It did not take long to learn the cause. When arrested for minor offenses, like aggressive panhandling and public urination, many were found in possession of one-way bus tickets from Myrtle Beach, SC. Upon further investigation, authorities learned that a group called Helping Hand of Myrtle Beach had provided full fare for the tickets, for the stated reason that the Port City had better resources for those in need than those resources that could be provided by leaders in their city. This reasoning sounded hollow to people in my hometown and created a dangerous situation—at our jail and on the street.

Tension grew as several young women living in the downtown historic district reported that they had been sexually assaulted by an unknown intruder. The suspect's description suggested that one man was responsible for all of the attacks and that he was likely homeless. This narrative did little to make the local population more welcoming of the nameless new arrivals.

Around 2:30 a.m. on November 29, 2004, David Allen and Barry Mintz, two white men ages 28 and 31, respectively, stumbled out of the Liquid Room where they had been drinking for most of the night. Both men were bouncers who worked at various clubs in the area and owed their considerable size to a combination of genetics and, as Mintz would later admit, steroids. This evening, they were off the clock and drinking heavily.

Whether Mintz and Allen knew that a suspect in the downtown rape cases had recently been arrested is an open question. What they would later claim is that they were, "standing on Market Street and Front, herd [sic] a girl yell and did not actually see a girl but chased a black male down an alley."[9] The man they cornered in the alley was Joe Bradshaw, a homeless, 42-year-old

African-American man who, at times, was known to be aggressive and use abusive language. He fit the general description of the downtown rapist that had been widely circulated.

No one saw the beginning of the attack, but one resident, Ira Blaustein, who lived three floors over the alley, heard it. "Break his leg" one yelled. "I'll crush his f*ing skull," said the other. Ira called 911.

Kathy Francis, a bartender who was returning to her vehicle after a long night of work, walked by the alley at about the same time. She knew Mintz and Allen, had waited on them earlier in the night, and recognized them in the dim light. She believed, at first, that they were stomping liquor boxes, breaking them down for trash pickup the next day. She then realized that the men were kicking and stomping another human being. She was about to call 911 when police arrived.

Upon hearing the approaching sirens, both men fled. Allen ran out onto Front Street and was quickly apprehended. Mintz ran further down into the alley believing that it would wind through the many buildings before spilling out onto Water Street, next to the Cape Fear River. The alley was a dead end, sealed off by the Federal Courthouse. He was soon captured. Both men were literally caught red-handed and taken into custody.

At the station, Mintz and Allen were administered breath tests and their gross impairment was confirmed. They were separately interviewed. Allen lawyered up and did not talk. Mintz admitted to the attack, changing up the story slightly to say that they were standing in the same location when someone yelled "there goes the guy who attempted to rape a girl a few days ago."[10] Mintz and Allen were booked on charges of a Assault with a deadly weapon inflicting serious injury. While neither was armed, hands and feet can be considered deadly weapons in some circumstances, and we believed those circumstances applied in this assault.[11]

Joe was rushed to the hospital with severe head trauma. After emergency surgery to reduce swelling to his brain, he was moved to the ICU. He remained there for several days before being transferred to a long-term treatment facility. On February 2, 2005, he succumbed to his injuries and was pronounced dead. Charges against Mintz and Allen were elevated to first-degree murder that same day.

The Trial

Just before jury selection, David Allen agreed to plead guilty to second-degree murder and testify against Mintz. Both men were equally culpable for the heinous assault but only one was accepting any responsibility for his role. It would be up to a jury to decide Mintz's fate.

We began by calling a member of the Bradshaw family. Joe was from a rural community and a member of a large loving family. He came to the big city of Wilmington, seasonally, making the streets his home before returning to his hometown, where a bed in a nice home waited for him. Essentially, he took a vacation without a hotel room. He had his demons, but he was also someone's baby.

Kathy and Ira both took the stand and gave chilling first-person accounts of the callous nature of the assault. Crime scene investigators with the WPD documented blood spatter on the alley walls to highlight that Joe was on the ground for the duration of the attack. Inflicting lethal wounds while a victim is down is the essence of premeditated murder. Even if there was no intent to kill at the start, it could be inferred that Mintz and Allen formed this intent during the course of the assault given the number and nature of the wounds to Joe's head and body and considering the vicious circumstances of the beating.

Mintz took the stand in his own defense and threw several pigs into the creek. He admitted to his role in the killing but said the "Devil Made Me Do It," contending that his gross impairment negated his ability to form the specific intent to kill. In addition to drinking 13 beers, Mintz claimed to use cocaine that night. He also hired an expert witness to testify about the documented side effects of steroid use. According to his expert, Mintz was overcome with such emotion that he could not premeditate and deliberate, because he was in the grips of a "roid rage" during the attack.

In cross examination, we played Mintz's videotaped interview from the night of the arrest. While two hours had passed, allowing for some of the effects of alcohol to leave his system, Mintz was clear on the details of the attack and why it began. He claimed to be justified because Joe was a dangerous man who had either attempted to attack a young woman that night or had tried to rape a young woman days earlier. Essentially, he said "Of Course I Did It," claiming that the attack was akin to defense of others.

There were two deep flaws with this defense. First, while deadly force can be used in self-defense as well as defense of others who are experiencing a sexual assault, it must occur while a threat is imminent and must be reasonable for the circumstances. Obviously, this attack did not meet that criteria and was not legally justified.

Second, the implication that Joe was beneath the law's protection because he was the fabled serial rapist was exploded when the jury learned that another individual, Jerome Bostic, had been arrested for the multiple downtown rapes, had confessed, and by the time of Mintz' trial, had pled guilty and received a sentence of over 44 years.[12] Moreover, the suggestion that Joe may have attempted to sexually assault a young woman was undermined by testimony that he was homosexual. Essentially, Joe had been tried and convicted by two strangers who played judge, jury, and executioner. He had been killed for crimes he was blameless of committing.

It did not take the jury long to deliberate. Barry Mintz was convicted of first-degree murder under the theory of premeditation and deliberation. For his part, David Allen received a sentence of 15.75 to 19.66 years in prison. Mintz was sentenced to life without the possibility of parole.

After the trial, the Chief of WPD and I called Helping Hand of Myrtle Beach and held a press conference to explain that they were helping no one with their actions.[13] The one-way bus ticket practice ended. Moreover, the city teamed with several area nonprofit leaders to begin a strategic plan to end chronic homelessness in the Port City over the next decade.[14]

Blaming the Victim

For years sexual assault survivors have been blamed for their victimization. "She asked for it" is the insidious suggestion in these "he said, she said" cases. Similarly, in self-defense cases, the defense will frequently try to assassinate the character of the deceased who is unable to speak about their murder. Removing labels from victims and keeping the blame squarely upon the defendant is the challenge when the "Of Course I Did It" defense is raised. Removing labels does not apply only in individual cases; it is a cultural shift.

State v. Spain[15]

I once heard a prominent children's advocate share with a large crowd how she "saved a 14-year-old prostitute" by coaxing her into a car, taking her to a shelter, and getting her out of the lifestyle.

This was admirable work and the crowd applauded the leader's efforts. But as I listened to the story, I had a different reaction. Both the speaker's narrative and the crowd's enthusiasm failed to appreciate the nuance that I also missed when I first became a prosecutor. There is no such thing as child prostitutes; there are only children who are being prostituted.

Changing our thinking about prostitution from a noun to a verb transfers the blame from the victim onto the slave-trading pimps where it belongs. The 14-year-old girl was not a prostitute; she was being prostituted. By focusing on the child and her rehabilitation, we were losing sight of the perpetrators that had exploited somebody's child or grandchild. I finally came to realize this well into my career as DA.

In 2012, I met a young lawyer named Lindsey Roberson. She reached out to me after we attended a human trafficking summit regarding the exploitation of women and children in South Sudan. "Slavery is going on in your district too," she said to me. "I want to come to Wilmington and fight it." I was inspired by her willingness to earn less than a third of her salary (giving up a job at a private law firm in New York City) to return to public service. I hired her immediately.

Lindsey and I understood that plenty of women (and some men) didn't have pimps or slave-keepers, but listed themselves on websites and social media, thus serving as their own agents. They were not being prostituted; they were prostitutes. Many prostitutes have serious drug addictions and almost all are victims of child sexual or other abuse. Though not necessarily held in bondage by pimps, threats of violence and captivity are entrenched in their hearts and minds. Fear and trauma create invisible prison walls and chains.

However, there were many other cases hiding in plain sight. They became visible as Lindsey got to work. She changed my perspective and that of many officers whom she trained across the district, proving to us that the problem was bigger than we had imagined. Two cases stand out. In one case, Randolph Spain was charged in Pender County with misdemeanor assault on a female. We typically handle hundreds of domestic violence cases each year in our district courts.

"Spain is a human trafficker," Lindsey said.

"Convince me," I replied.

"He grew up in Rocky Point, in Pender County, but he moves around a lot. He has a felony conviction for pimping in Virginia, and he's wanted by Maryland's child abduction task force. He's on the run from those charges and is facing a half-million-dollar bond," Lindsey explained.

I was impressed.

"There's more. The victim does not want to prosecute him. She is pregnant with his baby and claims to love him," Lindsey added. She explained that this dynamic was common throughout his assault cases. "It's his MO. He gets his 'girls' pregnant when they try to leave or report him to authorities. He claims that if he 'puts a baby in their belly' it becomes his 'insurance policy.'"

"How many women are pregnant or have had a baby by this 25-year-old?" I asked as I thumbed through his record.

"Six," said Lindsey.

There were federal charges that could be filed against Spain to hold him fully accountable, but North Carolina law still regarded his egregious conduct as a misdemeanor. I asked Lindsey to join me at dinner with State Senator Thom Goolsby and Representative Susi Hamilton. For good measure, Lindsey and I brought a survivor to dinner with us to share her journey. Far apart on the political spectrum, Goolsby and Hamilton saw eye to eye on toughening up the laws regarding human trafficking. Using the Safe Harbor laws from New York as model legislation, Lindsey helped to draft the comprehensive law that Goolsby and Hamilton co-sponsored before the North Carolina General Assembly. Their bill passed with overwhelming bipartisan support.[16]

Pimping became a felony and prison sentences were made substantially harsher. Victims were given immunity for coming forward, and those charged were eligible to have their prior convictions removed, or expunged, from their records. After the law changed, it shifted the perspective of lawmakers and law enforcement officials across our state. Lindsey made Spain the first North Carolina defendant to be indicted under the new law. Where he once faced just 150 days in jail for misdemeanor assault on a female, he now faced years in prison for multiple felonies. Lindsey worked with federal prosecutors to concurrently charge Spain in the federal system where the laws on human trafficking have long been severe. She won. The case went to a jury trial in federal court, Spain was convicted, and was sentenced to over a decade in prison.

In another case, Wendy, a 17-year-old who dropped out of high school and was reported missing by her mother, was arrested one year later in a small rural town in Tennessee. She was in a car with several other young women. The vehicle had been purchased in Wilmington by a well-known local pimp. Some of the young women under his control were branded like cattle, either with a tattoo of his lips on their body or the letters HUSH, an acronym for "Hustle Until Something Happens."

Wendy faced human trafficking charges in Tennessee, but prosecutors there were missing the larger picture. Lindsey and I explained to our counterparts that the young woman was a "bottom," a former prostitute who, after months of abuse, now assisted the pimp in finding new girls. As such, she was a victim of human trafficking and not a defendant. The Tennessee prosecutors shifted their focus from the young woman to go after the real pimp.

Closing Down Dens of Iniquity

We also focused our full attention on seemingly legitimate business people who lived far above the fray of drug and human trafficking but were indirectly profiting from these vice crimes. The attention to prostitution expanded beyond just the people involved to the facilities where this criminal activity was taking place. On November 29, 2015, the WPD was called out to the Carolinian Inn on Market Street to investigate a serious crime. Inside was the body of a career criminal who was dealing black tar heroin. He had enlisted the services of a prostitute and was shot by the woman's pimp, in her presence, as the two men fought over the price of the transaction.

The young woman rejected all efforts by law enforcement to get out of the lifestyle and she did little to help with the prosecution of the case. Ultimately, because of a self-defense issue, no homicide charges were filed. The "Of Course I Did It" pig muddied the waters too much to prosecute the pimp for murder. Instead, we were left to prosecute him for a firearm charge because, as a convicted felon, he was prohibited from possessing one.

The individual case was outrageous, but even more so was the activity that had been festering at the motel for years. Motels along the Market Street corridor, which is a main street of Wilmington, were becoming cesspools for all sorts of vice. Frequent arrests involving drug and human trafficking were the norm; serious violent assaults and overdose deaths were commonplace. Locals would rent a room for the sole purpose of engaging in drug-fueled parties that might last for days. Unknowing tourists who checked in had comments like this:

To Whom It May Concern:

I want to report a very scary situation. We arrived to at the Ramada Inn - 5001 Market Street. We arrived in late (2AM) with no room. We tried several locations with no luck. My husband went in to the Ramada Inn get the room and in the meantime. I watched a scene play out like in a horror movie. I looked over to see a very young girl, the one in the attached photo, maybe 12–14, with a man who looked at least 28.

He proceeded to train her as a prostitute. No joke. He made her stand up and begin to walk, which was the sign she was young and unexperienced. She walked awkward, did a turn and slung her hips. He made her "try again" and put her chest out. They then walked around to the side of the building that was dark. Once I found the security I begged him to call 911 since my phone was dead. He just watched them for a second and walked away. I was so upset.

We regretfully went to the room which was out of control. Room 235 was covered in drug baggies (like the attached picture), blood splatters on the walls, stains every-where, heavy smoke, and lack of sanitary sheets, etc. I fell asleep in fear and only kept the room for about 5 hours so my kids could sleep. I woke to being covered in bed bugs and bites. I will be reporting the bed bugs, but I want awareness for this poor girl and that yucky man.

I hope my photo saves lives. Please have this motel shut down asap for safety of others. If you need to contact me you may at (mobile number withheld), or this email. I am from Arizona and will be here and able to assist in any way for a week.

In response, I held a press conference with WPD Chief Ralph Evangelous in order to put the motels on notice that we would use the nuisance abatement laws at our disposal. The owners of the six motels with the most crime, based on reports over the preceding years, would be getting letters. The message was clear: clean up your act or we will clean it up for you. In other words, we were not putting the blame merely on the drug users and those being trafficked, who were tenants in the motel, but on the landlords who were secondarily profiting from the drug and human traf-fickers who were renting their rooms. Legitimate business owners needed to separate themselves from that activity or face closure of their motels.

Nuisance abatement laws were passed in 1913 in North Carolina during an era when our country was debating Prohibition. More than 100 years later, the laws remain in effect. The law empowers the district attorney, sheriff or local chief, or attorney general to request the North Carolina Alcohol Law Enforcement (ALE) to investigate alleged public nuisances.[17] Nuisances can range from illegally selling alcohol or drugs to promoting prostitution.

Star News

BRANDED: NUISANCE

HIGH SCHOOL FOOTBALL | WEEK 10

Hoggard	34	Topsail	51
West Brunswick	26	South Brunswick	7
New Hanover	43	North Brunswick	21
Ashley	0	Dixon	6

)ED HOUSE

creates logjam
tern Conference

er 22, 2016   StarNewsOnline.com $1 f StarNewsMedia   @starnewsonline

PUBLIC SAFTEY

2 targeted hotels risk losing national ties

By F.T. Norton
StarNews Staff

WILMINGTON –

Two of the six Wilmington motels marked by law enforcement as public nuisances are now at risk of losing their national name recognition, according to statements from their parent companies.

The Ramada Inn, America's Best Value Inn, Red Roof Inn and Budgetel – four of a half dozen hotels along Market Street which New Hanover County District Attorney Ben David and Wilmington Police Chief Ralph Evangelous have said are havens for drugs, prostitution and violence – are franchised locations for large national chains.

Those four, along with The Carolinian Inn and the Red Carpet Inn (formerly Travelodge), are under increased

SEE HOTELS, A5

THE RAMADA INN   RED CARPET INN

AMERICA'S BEST VALUE INN   BUDGETEL INN

THE CAROLINIAN INN   THE RED ROOF INN

Six hotels on Market Street in Wilmington are being targeted as nuisances by the New Hanover County District Attorney's Office and the Wilmington Police Department as a result of links to criminal activity. The parent companies for Ramada Inn and Travelodge, now Red Carpet Inn, said they were dismayed by the seedy reputations of their Wilmington franchises.
MATT BORN PHOTOS/STARNEWS

FIGURE 2.3 *Star News*, "Branded Nuisance."

This civil remedy focuses on the property, not the people, who are creating harm to the surrounding community. The primary goal is not to seize property but to eliminate the nuisance. The complaint comes from the community, not law enforcement. Everyone expects law enforcement to deal with problems, but ordinary citizens should not be continually exposed to criminal activity emanating from a particular location.

The burden of proof for a civil nuisance action rests on a preponderance of the evidence, not proof beyond a reasonable doubt, as it does in the criminal arena. But the threshold for the government to take property and deprive a business of the right to lawfully conduct business should be quite high. It should be sought only after traditional law enforcement efforts have failed.

Multiple instances need to be documented to show that an establishment has taken on the status of a public nuisance, including 911 calls, requests to check welfare, probation violations, and numerous criminal violations attached to a specific property.[18]

We documented the information for each of the six motels that were identified as the greatest offenders and sent certified letters to the motel owners, and more importantly, to the banks that owned the motels through deeds of trust. For example, the out-of-town owners of the Ramada Inn received our letter, but the first call we received was from representatives of the Yadkin Valley Bank that stood to lose the over $2 million collateral on the property's loan. When the City Attorney and I met with the various motels and banks, we laid out the case that the properties had taken on the status of being a nuisance, and that merely selling the property and changing owners would not cure that designation since the nuisance label runs with the property, not with the individual people.

To keep the property and avoid a lawsuit, the motel owners had to agree that all guests must present a valid, nonlocal driver's license at check-in; pay with a valid credit card (not cash); complete a registration card that includes vehicle information and personal identification (available for inspection by law enforcement); and display a parking permit. In addition, the motel must also agree to employ at least one privately licensed overnight security guard; have a 24-hour on-site manager; install multiple video cameras in the parking lot and hallway and make the recordings available for inspection by law enforcement; and conduct training for front desk and housekeeping staff in recognizing and reporting the signs of human trafficking. Within months of initiating this nuisance action, several of the motels came into compliance. Crime in these areas dropped precipitously.

Calls for Service for Nuisance Abatement Market Street Motels

Hotel Name	2010–2014	2015–2019	% Change
America's Best Value	599	258	–57%
Budgetel	809	787	–3%
Carolinian Inn	491	525	7%
Ramada	573	512	–11%
Red Roof Inn	647	490	–24%
Travelodge	789	399	–49%

FIGURE 2.4   Calls for service for nuisance abatement at Market Street motels.

Crimes committed by invited guests are not confined to motel rooms in crowded cities. Sometimes they occur in private residences down remote roads. And just as human traffickers are quick to blame victims for their "chosen profession," defendants are apt to blame the "lifestyle" of those they kill in the sanctity of the victim's own home. Such were the circumstances that brought me to a crime scene over 20 years ago, where I saw a dead body for the very first time.

State v. Campbell[19]

The year was 2000, and I was young, hungry, and eager to learn. Less than a year into being a prosecutor, I asked a group of detectives who covered the rural reaches of the district to call me when they got their next homicide. It didn't take long.

Three days later my phone rang after midnight. It was time for me to make good on my word. Crime doesn't conform to a nine-to-five schedule. So, there I was, bombing down I-40 at 100 miles per hour, heading to a small town 35 miles and a world away from Wilmington.

I arrived at an old man's home in Willard, North Carolina, before anyone else outside the investigation even knew what had happened. I stepped into the dark house and encountered a gruesome murder scene. The only noise was the whirring of a TV as a VHS tape had long come to its end. The blue light from the screen flickered over a man who lay facedown. Blood was everywhere, even covering the walls and a velvet wall hanging of the Last Supper. Rigor mortis had just started to set in, an indication that the killing had happened several hours earlier.

What a surreal feeling it was. On the kitchen table stood a kid's lunchbox. It had a cartoon on it—The Shadow—the superhero who knows what evil lurks in the hearts of men. The victim was 71-year-old William "Buddy" Hall, and just hours earlier he had eaten Kentucky Fried Chicken, *his* last supper. Now, he lay in a puddle of his own blood, being picked over by strangers wearing gloves and carrying clipboards. Two houses away slept his extended family, not yet realizing that they would awake to the first day of the rest of their lives without him.

The Interview in Aiken

A 22-year-old rookie officer in Aiken, South Carolina, first broke the case open. She received a 911 call from a local Kmart employee reporting that there was a man in the parking lot who was staring at her from his car and watching her movements over several hours as she collected shopping carts. It appeared that he was staking out the store. The officer approached the vehicle and found Terrance Campbell at the wheel. On the front seat next to him was a bottle of urine; apparently, to avoid going into the store and being caught on video, Campbell had relieved himself in an empty container rather than leave the vehicle. When asked for his license and registration, the officer discovered that the car was registered to Buddy Hall and that Campbell had Buddy's wallet as well. Concerned, she asked her department to call Pender County and request a safety check at Buddy's home. Had the officer not gone the extra mile, Campbell likely would have gotten away.

While Campbell was detained in Aiken, a Pender County Sheriff's deputy arrived at Buddy's home and found a brutal murder scene. Campbell was advised of his right to remain silent but quickly told the Aiken authorities that he wanted to talk. He willingly produced a nine-page handwritten statement and indicated that he welcomed the arrival of the Pender County Sheriff's detectives so he could "clear this whole thing up." A confession is where a defendant unburdens his soul and comes clean about his crimes. This was no confession.

Campbell's story included some details that could be verified. He was a convicted felon and had very little money. He had fallen in love with a woman who had kicked him out of the house only hours earlier. Destitute and with nowhere to go, Campbell ended up at the Walmart parking lot in Warsaw, nearby the even smaller community of Willard.

Sitting outside the store while contemplating his next move, Campbell was approached by an elderly man who showed him instant kindness. After hearing of Campbell's predicament, William Hall, or "Buddy," as this nice stranger called himself, offered to buy Campbell a bus ticket to South Carolina to be with his family. Since the Greyhound bus would not leave until early the next morning, Buddy also offered him a place to stay, and Campbell accepted. A trip to the local liquor store (confirmed on video) ensured that the new friends would have plenty to drink while they shared a meal. Buddy appeared to be an angel.

Back at Buddy's house, the two drank and ate a lot. They watched TV, drank and talked, and drank some more. When it was over, Buddy had a suggestion. Would Campbell be interested in watching a pornographic video? Campbell's answer was yes. Buddy quickly popped in a VHS tape and pressed play.

According to Campbell, it was at this point that the man he thought was an angel turned into the devil. As they were watching a particularly charged scene in the movie, one in which a woman was apparently wearing a dildo and having anal sex with a man, Buddy put his hand on Campbell's leg and said, "She has it in the good hole, don't you think?"

Campbell claimed not to remember much after that point. Rage burned in his heart and, fueled by the vodka in his system, anger took over. He had been duped by a stranger and was now being groped. Buddy was not a Good Samaritan: he was a predator. Campbell felt trapped, and in fear of getting sexually assaulted, he picked up whatever lay closest to him and started swinging. He ran out of the house in a hazy state, got into Buddy's car and started driving. He did not stop for several hours, eventually ending up in the Kmart parking lot in Aiken.

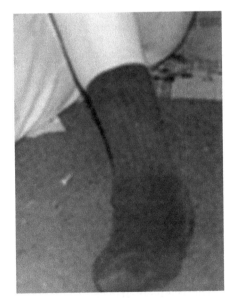

FIGURE 2.5   Cigarette found near Buddy Hall's body.

The Devil Is in the Details

There were several holes in Campbell's story. First, there was the testimony of a store clerk at the Kmart in Aiken. It was lost on no one that Campbell had met Buddy at a Walmart hours earlier. An MO was emerging.

Back in Pender County, the crime scene yielded additional clues. First, detectives noticed that all the lights in Buddy's home had been turned off. Would someone running out of the house fearing for their life—or a sexual assault—take the time to turn them off? Second, the murder weapon was never found since Campbell had taken it with him. Third, he never reached out for help or called the authorities after he left—completely inconsistent with self-defense. Fourth, several cigarette butts were found next to the body, and saliva on the cigarettes matched Campbell's DNA. It was reasonable to infer that he had not smoked and left cigarette butts on the floor of the home in Buddy's presence, but instead that he had taken time to smoke after the killing. There was cool deliberation, not panic.

Then there was the pornographic tape. The blue screen on the TV indicated that the movie had come to an end. When investigators played back the VHS tape, the scene that Campbell had described was nowhere on it. There were, however, several other tapes of a similar nature in a closet in Buddy's room. After watching 28 hours of footage, detectives finally found the scene that Campbell had described. This could only mean one thing: Buddy and Campbell watched the movie with the controversial scene much earlier in the night. If Buddy had made a pass a Campbell, it had not suddenly aroused violent passion in Campbell as he had suggested.

Evidence in Buddy's car offered the next clues. According to Buddy's niece, it was not her uncle's habit to leave his wallet in his car. Additionally, Buddy kept a coin collection in his closet; several rolls of quarters and dimes were found in the trunk of his car, matching the empty coin wrappings left in his closet. Campbell had not run from the house in a fugue state, as he had claimed. He had killed a man and then robbed his corpse. This made Campbell guilty of first-degree murder under the felony murder rule.

This was more than just a botched robbery; it was a cold and calculated killing. The wounds all over Buddy's body gave investigators the most insight into the nature of the attack. He had been whacked several times with a meat cleaver. According to the medical examiner, all of the blows to the back of the head were immediately incapacitating, if not fatal. The injuries were consistent with a sneak attack on an unsuspecting victim, not with defensive wounds to ward off a sexual assault. The repeated blows were also indicative of overkill.

Several Pigs in the Creek

Campbell first raised the "Of Course I Did It" defense, claiming the killing was in self-defense. A person may validly use self-defense when death or great bodily harm is imminent. This same right allows someone to use deadly force to repel a sexual assault. Unfortunately for Campbell, the wrong VHS tape, the robbery of items after the fact, and his past robberies and assaults revealed his true motive and undercut this defense. Most significantly, the number and nature of the wounds on Buddy's body screamed the loudest: this was an ambush, not an act of self-defense. Buddy was not the predator; he was the prey.

Blaming the victim has been raised time and time again, because it often works. Jurors, and those who sit in judgment of these cases, want to distance themselves from the horror of the victim's experience by rationalizing that it could never happen to them or someone they love. At its core, this defense is about dehumanization, blame, and taking responsibility away from defendants. It is a prosecutor's job to remind the jury who is on trial.

Campbell next raised "The Devil Made Me Do It" defense and coupled it with the "I Did Not Do It" defense, claiming that alcohol negated his ability to formulate the specific intent to kill, meaning he could not be convicted of premeditated first-degree murder. But the physical evidence suggested something far different. Not only was he able to drive away from the scene and travel six hours down the road without being stopped for impaired driving, all the actions that occurred after the killing, especially the robbery (as well as turning out the lights and taking the murder weapon), showed that he appreciated the gravity of his crime and was trying to get away with murder.

The jury did not buy any of it. The physical evidence contradicted everything that Campbell was saying to justify the killing. He could not blame alcohol or Buddy for this attack. It was a cold-blooded murder and nothing less. The jury rejected every defense and convicted Campbell of premeditated first-degree murder and felony first-degree murder.

The Sentencing Phase

Buddy's murder was especially heinous, atrocious, and cruel. It was also a premeditated act done in the course of an armed robbery, which was motivated by Campbell's desire for monetary gain. Campbell also had a lengthy, violent criminal record. Because these "aggravating circumstances" were present, the state tried him for his life (we will discuss the death penalty in much greater detail in chapter 5).

Since Campbell was convicted of first-degree murder, the jury next had to consider whether he should receive life without parole or the death penalty. Prior to the trial, I offered Campbell a plea to first-degree murder in exchange for a sentence of life without parole. Campbell rejected the offer. He, like many others at the time, believed it was unlikely that a jury in rural and conservative Pender County would convict him of murder, let alone sentence him to die in a case involving "gay panic."

In nearly every case, motive is not part of the burden of proof. The reason is simple: most crime, especially murder, is aberrant behavior, and having to prove why a defendant broke the law is like trying to chase a ghost. Sometimes there is no good explanation—the defendant is just mean. The only cases where prosecutors must prove motive are hate crimes.

In hate crimes, the allegation is that the victim was specifically targeted for a particular reason. Equal protection not only protects against discrimination of race, religion, or national origin, but if someone is targeted because of an immutable, unchanging characteristic that makes up their identity, the crime is especially deserving of harsher punishment.

Three months before Buddy Hall was murdered, Aaron McKinney was convicted of the brutal 1998 murder of Matthew Shepard, a gay college student who was beaten, tortured, and left to die in Wyoming.[20] The case made international news and sparked debate on whether sexual orientation should be a protected category for designation as a hate crime. McKinney was sentenced to two life sentences during death penalty deliberations following his trial. (His co-defendant, Russell Henderson, pled earlier to murder and kidnapping and received two life sentences). The Shepard killing was an obvious hate crime, but no law existed that allowed the jury to consider the motive for the killing as an aggravating factor for sentencing.

At the time of Buddy's murder, the law in North Carolina was the same as in Wyoming and every other state. While the brutal nature of the assault made Campbell eligible for the death penalty, the fact that he may have been motivated to kill Buddy in part because of his sexual orientation could not be considered. Hate crime legislation was not passed until 10 years later when President Barack Obama, citing the Shepard case, signed it into law.[21]

While motive was not part of the burden of proof, the trial judge allowed the state to present evidence of Campbell's past to show what truly motivated his behavior. Two women, tellers from two different banks near Campbell's hometown of Fairmont, North Carolina, testified about the bank robberies he had committed years earlier. They recounted the incidents, both thinking they were going to die, when Campbell threatened to kill them if they did not fully cooperate. It was for these offenses that Campbell had served most of his adult life in prison prior to 1998.

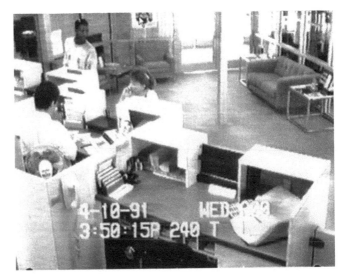

FIGURE 2.6   Surveillance footage of Campbell's bank robbery.

The true insight into Campbell's sadistic nature, however, came from someone closest to him. Campbell's ex-wife recounted a long history of domestic violence while the two were married and living in South Carolina. When she finally made her escape, Campbell tracked her down, laid in wait, and kidnapped her from the porch of her new mobile home. Over the next three days, he repeatedly raped and physically assaulted her.

When Campbell was finally arrested for his crimes, he was not charged with any sexual offenses. The marital rape exemption laws that existed in several states at the time (which basically provided that a man could not rape his own wife) limited authorities to charging Campbell only with kidnapping and physical assault—crimes that are punished far less severely. Because of an antiquated provision in the law, Campbell never received full justice.[22]

Now, with Campbell's past fully on display, the jury had no trouble seeing that Buddy's attack was just the latest act in a long line of violent crime committed by a predatory defendant. The defense of blaming the victim, of assassinating his character after he had been murdered, had backfired. The jury returned a death sentence. Campbell remains on North Carolina's Death Row to this day.

Campbell is not the only person on death row who has played the blame game and lost. And just as his actions before, during, and after Buddy's killing were crucial in establishing his motive, and proving that the murder was premeditated and deliberate, the case that follows is a study in confronting "The Devil Made Me Do It" defense. By highlighting the defendant's actions, weeks before and minutes after an innocent woman was tortured to death in her own home, the jury was able to see that, sometimes, the devil is in the details.

State v. Cummings[23]

As she drove to Wilmington, Joni Carson called her mom, Jane Head, to say that she was running late. When she arrived, her mom was lying in a pool of blood on the floor of her mobile home. CPR efforts were futile. Jane had been stabbed to death 18 times, mostly in the neck and head. At the exact moment Joni was trying to breathe life into her mom, the next-door neighbor, Paul Cummings, was three miles away attempting to drain Jane's bank account.

The bent knife used to kill Jane had the defendant's DNA all over it. The bank surveillance video also left little doubt about the defendant's motive. When Cummings was apprehended a few days later, he confessed to detectives but claimed he had not meant to harm Jane, a sweet elderly woman who treated him with kindness his whole life, but that he had been overcome by drugs and alcohol. Under this theory of "diminished capacity," Cummings would be guilty of second-degree murder.

Cummings put two pigs into the water: "The Devil Made Me Do It" and "I Did Not Do <u>It</u>." The guilty act was undeniable. The guilty intent, or *mens rea*, was the issue. To pull these two pigs out of the creek, we focused on his actions before, during, and after Jane's murder.

FIGURE 2.7   Bent knife found outside Jane Head's residence.

First, there was a job application for a Wendy's restaurant found in Jane's stolen van, which was found abandoned in a remote area of Brunswick County in the first few hours after the crime. It turned out that Cummings had gone to Wendy's after the murder to visit his girlfriend who worked there. He obtained a job application while at the restaurant and no one noticed any signs of impairment.

Second, soon after the murder, a cab driver came forward to say that she recognized the picture of Cummings from the paper and that he was the same man who had robbed her at knifepoint two weeks earlier. The cab driver had picked up the suspect from a Market Street motel and had driven him back to the same mobile home park where Jane and Cummings both lived. As she stopped the vehicle

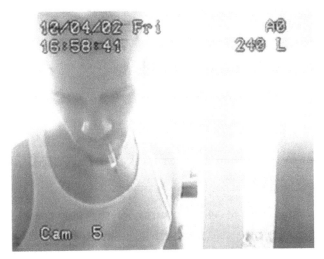

FIGURE 2.8   ATM video of Cummings using Jane's debit card.

at what turned out to be an abandoned trailer, Cummings slid in behind her, put a knife to her throat, and demanded money. In fear for her life, she complied, but not before he ripped out her earrings for good measure. He fled into the woods. WPD officers showed up but the trail went cold as the K9s were unable to track a scent in heavy rain.

Judge Jerry Cash Martin conducted a hearing and ruled that Cummings' prior bad act was relevant to the issue of motive and intent. The robbery and assault of the cab driver also showed a violent pattern of conduct with a knife and gave insight into his premeditation and deliberation in killing Jane. When I asked the cab driver if Cummings was impaired during the armed robbery and assault, she pointed to the bench and said, "He was as sober as that judge the whole time."

Third, and most damning, was the bank video. When a defendant raises the defense of "The Devil Made Me Do It," he must waive his right to remain silent and agree to be interviewed by state doctors. We had only one question for Cummings: how did he know the PIN number for Jane's account?

Jane's PIN number had not been written down anywhere, and only her daughter knew that it was S-E-A-N, the name of Jane's grandson. Without blinking, Cummings told doctors who were evaluating his mental state that he slowly tortured Jane, stabbing her multiple times in the face until she yelled it out. Being able to memorize the name, translate it to numbers on the keyboard, and withdraw the maximum amount is not consistent with gross impairment, but rather the work of a calculating killer.

The Silly Political Season

The Cummings trial occurred in the summer of 2004 during the same time that my longtime boss, John Carriker, announced that he was retiring from office. He shocked many by endorsing me to succeed him. During a break from jury selection, I walked into the courthouse courtyard and held a press conference to announce that I would run in a special election two months later.

Four seasoned defense attorneys, all with large constituencies behind them, quickly filed to run against me. Four of us had to face off in a special Democratic primary that was to take place on September 14, 2004, with the winner advancing to the general election to face the lone Republican candidate in November when the president, the governor, and several other races would be on the ballot.

For the next two months, I tried Cummings for Jane's murder. After hearing all the evidence, the jury convicted Cummings of premeditated first-degree murder and felony murder (burglary and armed robbery). The jury not only rejected the impairment defense, but they found the murder was especially heinous, atrocious, and cruel, and done soon after the armed robbery of the cab driver (a violent course of conduct is also an aggravating circumstance). The jury returned a verdict of guilty on all counts. In a separate sentencing hearing, they unanimously agreed to sentence Cummings to death. He was transported to North Carolina's death row later the same day on September 8, 2004.

It was a hectic time. With only one week between the verdict and the election, I was busy in the community seeking support from voters that I could not meet during the weeks I was in trial. Meanwhile my wife, Stephanie, was nine months, pregnant with our first child, and we were preparing to go from a couple to a family (Maddie was born on September 16). It was during that week that I received a call from the press.

On September 12, two days before the special election, the press was sent an email accusing me of being a racist and comparing me to former DA Jerry Spivey, who had lost his job after uttering a racial slur.[24] The basis for the allegation was a motion that had been filed earlier that day by the Center for Death Penalty Litigation, led by an adjunct faculty member at Duke University School of Law. Gretchen Engle, whom I had never met, sought to have Cummings' death verdict overturned on the grounds that I tried the case for political motives.[25] The motion was also distributed throughout several African-American precincts on the day of the special election.

The essential allegation was that I had sought the death penalty against Paul Cummings, who looked white (but was actually Lumbee Indian), in order to have political cover for seeking the death penalty against Curtis Dixon, a black suspect, who had recently sexually assaulted and killed Jessie Faulkner, a fellow classmate at UNCW, who was white. There was no legal reason for Engle to have filed the motion in such a hasty fashion. The timing was clear: she wanted to get the allegations into the public dialogue before the election. Fortunately, the community knew me better. I won the special Democratic primary and beat my Republican rival in the general election two months later.

When the dust settled and I took my new office, I met the allegations head-on during a hearing in January of 2005. Cummings was brought back from death row, and Judge Martin, who had presided over the trial, listened to many witnesses and considered many exhibits. In a scathing eight-page order following a four-day hearing, Judge Martin found that the motion was a naked attempt to "play the race card" and was tantamount to "blatant political sabotage."[26]

Judge Martin also found compelling the documentation relating to the death penalty review committee (discussed in chapter 5) that was convened for the Cummings case. The senior prosecutors who met with Mr. Carriker two years before the trial made the determination to seek the maximum punishment. This was long before any election, and I was not even on the committee. Judge Martin dismissed the defense motion to set aside the verdict and Cummings was returned to death row. The professor who lodged the allegation was fired, and Duke quickly severed its connections with the Center for Death Penalty Litigation.[27]

Returning to Duke Law School to Right a Wrong

Could there be any place more concerned about removing the collateral sting of wrongful accusations than Duke University? An online word search of Duke is scarred with the association of the elected DA making unfounded charges against its students. Meanwhile, a prestigious clinic at Duke's Law School was summarily closed after a Duke professor's unfounded accusations against me. Both cases magnified the ugly intersection of race, justice, and politics that led to false claims to advance agendas.

In 2012, when I began my one-year term as president of the Conference of District Attorneys, I reached out to the faculty at Duke with this simple message: DAs and Duke professors needed to come together to reduce errors in the criminal justice system. The leaders at Duke agreed that it was time to forge a new history and enlist DAs as partners, not adversaries. Prosecutors, defense attorneys, judges, and academics from around our state and country came to the summit, called Integrity and Accuracy in Prosecution. Gathering different viewpoints around the same table was an important step in recognizing that, even in an adversarial system, we all want the same thing.

My opening remarks at the conference began with recalling Dora's attack. Everyone agreed that she was innocent and that the justice system was designed to protect her and punish her attacker. Yet it was also true that defendants who look like McAllister have been wrongfully accused and convicted for crimes they did not commit, especially when considering the South's painful racial history. We must be committed to reducing human error leading to these wrongful convictions and confront the insidious role of race that seeps into many aspects of the criminal justice system.

The crowd then heard that after Cummings was sent to death row, I was wrongfully accused by a Duke faculty member (many in attendance were colleagues of disgraced professor Gretchen Engle). I shared that police and prosecutors are increasingly being falsely accused of misconduct: ethics complaints against prosecutors to the North Carolina Bar increased tenfold in North Carolina in the wake of the scandal involving DA Mike Nifong.[28] Moreover, during the McAllister trial and for months after, Detective Lawson was wrongfully accused of professional misconduct and suffered mightily for it. Self-governing professionals, even those in adversarial systems, should save charges of racism, bias, and misconduct for egregious cases and not resort to these insults as the first line of attack—to do otherwise harms innocent people and undermines real instances that need to be addressed. Those are important issues and we will discuss them in greater detail in chapter 6.

Thinking about How We Think

The summit that we held at Duke brought together not only police, prosecutors, and law professors, but also neuropsychologists to think about how we think. The criminal justice system has long been plagued by claims of racism: from profiling to police shootings to mass incarceration. Many criminal justice officials run the other way when they hear this blame. The police and prosecutors present at the Duke summit ran toward the problem. We wanted to better understand our roles and make the system fairer for everyone.

We started with use-of-force cases. Nearly all decisions made by officers that involve shooting a suspect happen in a rapidly evolving and tense environment. The part of the brain that keeps officers alive, the fight or flight frontal lobe, takes over. Split-second decisions that are formed out of fear and/or misunderstandings are contributing causes of these shootings. To reduce the risk of harm to officers and the public, training and dialogue offer the best chance to prevent future tragedies from occurring.

In an effort to help all the participants at the Duke summit better understand the environment of a use-of-force situation, we all went through a Fire Arm Training Simulator (FATS), a computer simulated shoot/don't shoot scenario.[29] The experience gave us all a much better understanding of these esoteric concepts and what officers confront in the moment of an encounter. I now require all my senior prosecutors to go through this training so that they can stand in these officers' shoes, at least virtually, when deciding whether their use of force was reasonable.

I encouraged other prosecutors to bring that awareness back to their hometowns. As the "top cop" in the district, the DA has an important opportunity to shape the policies and procedures of police agencies through the constitutional mandate to advise local law enforcement.[30] In my district alone, there are more than 1,000 sworn officers in 20 different police agencies. Getting to know them, and staying involved in their lives, is a priority for me.

We also looked at the role that "implicit bias" may play from the time of the stop of a

FIGURE 2.9   Patches of District Six law enforcement agencies. There are 20 police agencies in my district with over 1,000 officers.

suspect to handling a plea in court. As the National Center for State Courts says, "unlike explicit bias (which reflects the attitudes or beliefs that one endorses at a conscious level), implicit bias is the bias in judgment and/or behavior that results from subtle cognitive processes that often operate at a level below conscious awareness and without intentional control."[31] Everyone has some form of bias in their background and the key is to recognize it in decision-making.[32]

To reduce instances where race may play a role in a police encounter, officers must be trained on de-escalation techniques and the role of implicit bias in decision-making.[33] The ugly intersection of split-second thinking and racial bias leads to this startling statistic in America: a black man is 2.5 times as likely to be shot by the police as a white man.[34] Working together in teaching new officers good habits at the beginning of their careers engrains in them the culture of doing justice and not simply arresting at all costs. There are ways to reduce the impact of implicit bias that exists in every individual and human system and we all have a role in doing better.[35]

A Charge to Law Schools

It is easy to regard Dora as a victim since she was asleep in her own home when a stranger attacked her. Frequently, however, victims are engaged in illegal or immoral conduct when they are victimized, leading many to blame the victim. All victims need the protection of the laws, and changing laws and peoples' attitudes about who is to blame is a job for all leaders, inside and outside the justice system.

While there are innocent defendants, the vast majority are actually guilty. Most defendants are not bad people; they are good people with bad problems and habits. We should all be focused on exonerating the innocent. Errors will happen in any human endeavor. Reducing errors and improving accuracy should be a continuous process for all of us in the criminal system. We should also commit our resources to focus on the social determinants of health and attack the root causes of crime.

I have long advocated that law schools must create clinics to work with DA's offices to train the next generation of prosecutors.[36] This will be better in the long run for victims and defendants. As Professor George Fisher, faculty co-director, Criminal Prosecution Clinic at Stanford Law School noted: "The Criminal Prosecution Clinic helps students learn what it means to act morally with power. Prosecutors are the system's line of defense against wrongful convictions."[37] Many of our state law schools have listened. Now the young professionals who will be giving voice to victims, guarding the guardians, and ensuring against wrongful convictions will get the appropriate instruction while they are still in school, and not just learning on the job.

FIGURE 2.10   Duke Law School Professor Neil Vidmar and DA Ben David.

Defendants who seek to escape responsibility will frequently blame everything and everyone but themselves. We must address the underlying conditions that give rise to much of the crimes they commit while simultaneously holding them accountable for their actions. Moreover, by humanizing victims and removing labels from them, we go a long way toward getting them justice. We do not excuse individual malfeasance when we call for greater public accountability. For those of us to whom so much responsibility has been given, when we hear the larger criticisms about a "broken system" we can either defend it at every turn or be humble enough to realize that in a human system, we should constantly work to improve it.

Notes

1   US Const. amend IV.

2   https://www.rainn.org/statistics/criminal-justice-system

3   "More Rape Victims Come Forward for Help," WECT.com. Undated. The story reports that for every 100,000 residents in New Hanover County, 61.5 rapes were reported in 2005.

4   Coastal Horizons Center, (August 2, 2017), http://www.supportrcc.org/index.html.

5 The very lengthy and expensive testing by private labs would take time and money we could not afford, considering Dora's age and the urgency to bring the case to trial. We also regarded this evidence as duplicative since we had a nuclear DNA hit on the suspect's hair in her sock.

6 See generally, Howard M. Wasserman et al., *The Phases and Faces of the Duke Lacrosse Controversy: A Conversation*, 19 Seton Hall Journal of Sports and Entertainment Law 181 (2009).

7 David Barstow and Duff Wilson, Prosecutor in Duke Case Faces Ethics Complaint, *The New York Times*, December 29, 2006, https://www.nytimes.com/2006/12/29/us/29nifong.html

8 *State v. Mintz*, 654 S.E.2d 833 (NC Ct. App. 2008). Co-counsel was Dru Lewis.

9 Voluntary statement of Barry Dean Mintz, given to police at 5:09 a.m. on November 29, 2004.

10 *State v. Mintz*, DA Investigative Report of lead investigator WPD Det W.H. Hyman.

11 *State v. Jacobs*, 309 NC 463 (1983).

12 *State v. Bostic*, 04CRS 064977. Counsel was Jon David and Connie Jordan. (Defendant pled guilty February 23, 2005, to multiple sexual offenses and was sentenced to over 44 years in prison.)

13 Si Cantwell, "Efforts to Help Local Homeless People Should Begin at Home." *Star News*, December 18, 2005. Of 55 homeless surveyed, 15 had one-way bus tickets and 5 of those were from Helping Hand of Myrtle Beach.

14 Spiro Macris et al."The Street Is No Place to Live: Ten Year Plan to End Chronic Homelessness in the Cape Fear Region." CapeFearHomeless.org Fall 2006.

15 *State v. Spain*, 13CRS009034. Counsel was Lindsey Roberson.

16 NC GS 14-43.11 was signed into law in July 2013.

17 North Carolina Gen. Stat. 19-2.1

18 Civil remedies are contained in N.C. Gen. Stat. § 18B-901(c) (9) (2000). Three professionals need particular recognition for their work on nuisance abatement: Jim Gardner, Chairman of the ABC Commission and Agents Alan Fields and Josh Batten of NCALE.

19 *State v. Campbell*, 359 N.C. 644 (2005). Co-counsel was Barrett Temple.

20 See generally "Mathew Shepard" at Wikipedia.org for extensive background of case and legacy.

21 Hate Crime Prevention Act (Oct. 28, 2009).

22 While the "marital rape exemption" law was finally repealed in 1993 by the North Carolina Legislature, thereby subjecting a person who rapes their spouse to the same laws and penalties as a stranger, Campbell escaped full punishment for the rape and torture of his estranged wife. Campbell would

have served a much longer sentence and would never have been out to meet Buddy if the laws were stronger at the time.

23   *State v. Cummings*, 361 N.C. 438 (2007). Co-Counsel was Dru Lewis.

24   See, Ken Little, "D.A. Denies Race a Factor in Case," *Star News*, Jan. 27, 2005, at 1B. In 1998, DA Jerry Spivey became the first district attorney in North Carolina to be removed from office. See generally *In re* Spivey, 480 S.E.2d 693 (N.C. 1997).

25   See, Ken Little, "Judge Asked to Overturn Cummings Conviction," *Star News*, Sept. 15, 2004, at 4B.

26   Maggie Alexander, Race, Politics Not a Factor in Murder Trial, Judge Rules, WECT, Jan. 28, 2005, http://www.wect.com/story/2867127/race-politics-not-a-factor-in-murder-trial-judge-rules; *see also State v. Cummings*, No. 02-CRS-20548 (Sup. Ct. New Hanover County Jan. 27, 2005) (order denying Motion for Appropriate Relief).

27   Veronica Gonzalez, "Racial Disparity Remains Wide in Death Sentences," *Star News* Aug. 8, 2011, http://www.starnewsonline.com/article/20100808/ARTICLES/100809739?p=1&tc=pg.

28   According to the North Carolina Conference of District Attorneys, the year before Mike Nifong was prosecuted, there were only five opened files on grievances filed against prosecutors. In 2006, the year Nifong was prosecuted, there were 17 files. In 2007 there were over *80* grievances filed against prosecutors, with the number of grievances against prosecutors remaining between 80 and 90 per year thereafter. Email from Peg Dorer, Director, NC Conference of District Attorneys, to author (April 3, 2012, 10:51 EST)(on file with author).

29   A participant, gun in hand, is placed in front of large video screens that are programmed to record the participants' responses. The video begins. A routine traffic stop plays out with standard questioning for license and registration. Suddenly, the suspect picks up a weapon, or is it a phone? Or an armed co-defendant bursts out of the passenger door, or is it a lady with a baby in dire need of medical assistance? In an instance, the participant is faced with a life-altering choice: shoot or don't shoot? If the participant begins to fire, the machine records it all. If the suspect(s) is armed and begins firing, these shots are also recorded. When the simulation ends the participant can see the shots he or she landed and those that the suspect landed. Next, a deputy enters the room. He asks the participant for their service weapon and tells them that as a fellow law enforcement officer, the participant does not have the right to remain silent. This is not a criminal investigation; this is an internal investigation. They are asked to commit everything you did to writing and to be detailed about why you did or did not

shoot. It is enlightening to see how participants describe the facts after the shooting in their written incident reports. Frequently, the reported account is far different than the reality of what is on the video when it is replayed for the entire group. Tunnel vision is real. The participants are not lying or being evasive; they are mistaken because the part of their brain that was thinking fast during the incident is different than the brain that is now thinking slowly in the retelling of events on paper.

30 N.C. Const. art. IV, § 18(1).

31 National Center for State Courts (ncsc.org), "Helping Courts Address Implicit Bias, Frequently Asked Questions," 1.

32 Harvard University created the definitive test, the Implicit Association Test, or IAT, to give individuals insight into their bias.

33 The Attorney General's Training and Standards Division, Criminal Justice Education and Training Standards Commission is responsible for this certification. See "Instructor Certification," NC Department of Justice, http://www.ncdoj.gov/getdoc/b92dba07-e030-4022-8e95-e3b64202566e/2-6-3-1-2-4-Instructor-Certification.aspx. I obtained my certification in order to teach at area law enforcement agencies to give legal updates on case law and statutes that is required each year for officer certification.

34 Willem Roper, "Black Americans 2.5X More Likely Than Whites to Be Killed by Police." *Statista*. June 2, 2020. https://www.statista.com/chart/21872/map-of-police-violence-against-black-americans/

35 ncsc.org, "Strategies to Reduce the Influence of Implicit Bias." Among the things that help reduce implicit bias leading to discrimination include: 1) raise awareness of implicit bias; 2) identify and acknowledge real group and individual differences; 3) routinely check thought processes and decisions for possible bias; 4) identify distractions and sources of stress in decision-making and remove them; 5) identify ambiguity in decision making and establish concrete standards; 6) institute a feedback mechanism; 7) increase exposure to stigmatized groups.

36 Benjamin R. David, "Community-Based Prosecution in North Carolina: An Inside-Out Approach to Public Service at the Courthouse, on the Street, and in the Classroom," *Wake Forest Law Review* 47, no. 2 (Spring 2012).

37 Criminal Prosecution Clinic, https://law.stanford.edu/criminal-prosecution-clinic/#slsnav-overview

Figure Credits

Fig. 2.1: Pender County Sheriff's Office CSI, "Scott Lawson Evidence Collection," Pender County Sheriff's Office, 2006.

Fig. 2.2: Copyright © 2007 by Gray Television, Inc.

Fig. 2.3: Copyright © 2016 by Gannett Company, Inc.

Fig. 2.4: Barry Coburn, "Calls for Service for Nuisance Abatement Market Street Motels." Copyright © 2020 by Wilmington Police Department. Reprinted with permission.

Fig. 2.5: Pender County Sheriff's Office, "Cigarette Found near Hall Body," Pender County Sheriff's Office, 2000.

Fig. 2.7: Wilmington Police Department, "Bent Knife Found outside Head Residence ," Wilmington Police Department, 2002.

Chapter 3

The Power of the Past

In this section we look at the "I Did Not Do <u>It</u>" defense and see how the labels that we affix to a defendant's conduct can change dramatically when their past is admitted into evidence. We will go on a journey from an accident to a murder by looking at the prior bad acts of an impaired driver who had never been in trouble with the law. We will also see how a fleeing felon can be held responsible for a police officer's death from two miles away. And when it comes to domestic violence, an abuser's past may show that his crimes were not merely done in the heat of passion but were cold blooded.

State v. Hewson[1]

"My husband keeps shooting me," Gail Tice gasped. "Please come quick, I am bleeding to death." Gunshots continued to ring out in the background as the 911 operator attempted to get more information. The call for help was placed after the victim had been shot multiple times. There was a pause in the shooting, then one final loud bang. There was no more talking, only audible grunting and labored breathing—the "death moan."

When the 911 operator realized that the frantic call was coming from inside the gates of Wilmington's affluent Landfall community, it could have easily been mistaken for a prank call. Violent crime is almost unheard of in the exclusive enclave, which is surrounded by an eight-foot wall. Patrol officers sometimes joke that the biggest danger in Landfall is getting hit by a golf ball from one of the 45 holes of the Nicklaus or Dye courses. The call, unfortunately, was very real.

When officers arrived, they encountered Gail's estranged husband, Robert Hewson, in the front yard. He was clearly distraught. "If we had arrived any later, he would have used the gun on himself," reported the first arriving officer. The police yelled for Hewson to put down the gun that was still in his hands. Hewson complied and threw it into the corner of the home's front porch. The large oak door to the home was locked and Hewson did not have a key.

Officers and firemen hacked down the door and found Gail in the study near the front entrance, face down on the floor with the phone still in her hand. She had been shot multiple times, including in the back of the head. Gail was pronounced dead at the scene.

Hewson claimed to love his wife and said that the shooting was nothing more than a lovers' quarrel that went terribly wrong. But was this a heat of passion killing (making this a case of voluntary manslaughter) or a straight up execution carried out with premeditation and deliberation? Detectives soon learned the rest of the story.

Gail Tice was one of the rare women who recognized the signs of intimate partner violence and tried to get away from her abuser. She seemed to have it all: a successful real estate career, a wide circle of friends, and a beautiful home in the city's best zip code. She also had a bad relationship with a husband whom she had met late in life and now wanted to divorce.

The couple met at a restaurant a few years earlier. Gail, a widow, was intrigued by the possibility of a new romance in her life. Her friends and adult children did not approve of Hewson but were happy for her happiness and therefore supported their hasty marriage. Hewson moved into Gail's home in Landfall.

Despite initial appearances, Hewson was not wealthy, and certainly was not in the same socioeconomic league as Gail. He had been recently let go from his position as a Burger King manager. Worse, he had previously set court precedent with the court of appeals for resisting arrest when officers confronted him for nonsupport of his ex-wife. It didn't take long for Hewson's true character to surface and for Gail to become afraid of him.

In the summer of 2004, Gail wanted out of the relationship and took active steps to protect herself. The couple had been building a dream home on a beach in the northern part of the state. Gail, concerned that he might one day use them against her, took Hewson's firearms to the local sheriff's office in that county and asked them to take possession of the weapons.

After sharing her suffering with family and friends, Gail sought a domestic violence protective order in New Hanover County District Court. The order directed Hewson to move out of Gail's Landfall house immediately and forbid him to possess any weapons. Authorities removed the parking decal on his vehicle that allowed access to the gated neighborhood. Hewson had effectively been kicked off the island, and the privileged life he knew for a brief time was now a distant memory.

Despite the court order, Hewson attempted to purchase a gun from a local gun dealer near his former home. A background check at the time of purchase showed the existence of the protective order, which prohibited Hewson from possessing a firearm. The gun shop would not sell him the pistol. Undeterred, Hewson sought other means to obtain a weapon and ultimately found an old revolver at an area yard sale. He purchased the gun mere days before the killing.

Investigators could not determine how Hewson gained access to Landfall on the day of the murder, but they speculated that he either scaled the eight-foot wall or slipped past an unmanned gate. His vehicle was found parked behind a strip mall just outside the neighborhood. He was familiar with Gail's daily routines and knew that she usually came downstairs to feed the cat around 6:30 each morning. Investigators believed that he laid in wait until she descended the back staircase into the kitchen. It was at the base of those stairs that he first fired at Gail from outside the house.

Drops of blood marked her movements as Gail frantically ran from the breakfast nook into the kitchen and down the hall before finding a phone in the study. Picture windows that had provided a scenic view of a nearby lake gave Hewson a clear view of Gail as she ran through the gilded cage. As she moved throughout the house, Hewson would find another window and fire into it as Gail tried to take cover. When he ran out of bullets, Hewson had enough time to manually extract the six spent shell casings from the revolver and reload the weapon. While this provided time for Gail to get on the phone, it did not provide enough time for her to get away.

The Trial of Robert Hewson

When the trial began, Hewson's attorney claimed that Gail's 911 call, in which she identified her husband as the shooter, was inadmissible hearsay evidence. Because Gail's statement was made out of court and not under oath, and since she could not be cross-examined, the defense claimed that what she said was unreliable and inadmissible: the definition of hearsay. My brother Jon and I tried the case together and made two arguments in response. First, dying declarations and statements made for medical purposes are exceptions to the hearsay rule, which allow for the admission of these statements because of the statement's inherent reliability. People are unlikely to lie about their medical condition when they are seeking aid for life-threatening injuries.

Our second argument rested on the principle of fairness. The only reason Gail was not able to testify was because Hewson killed her. Because he was the reason that Gail was not available at trial, his attorney could not claim that he was being denied the benefit of cross-examination. The judge agreed and admitted the recording of the 911 call.

Hewson's True Intent

Most intimate partner crimes are not whodunits but rather what-do-you-call-its. As we saw in chapter 1 when looking at the sentencing chart, the labels we affix to tragic events can vary widely. Because the same act (the *actus reus*) can be treated very differently depending upon the defendant's mind-set (the *mens rea*), holding a defendant fully responsible frequently comes down to proving intent. Killing in hot blood (where someone claims that reason was overcome by provocation of the victim) is voluntary manslaughter. Killing in cold blood is first-degree premeditated murder.

Hewson raised the "I Did Not Do <u>It</u>" defense. This defense does not deny the crime, but rather denies that the crime is as serious as the one charged. He claimed that he killed Gail in a jealous rage. If the jury agreed, he would face a potential sentence of only three to nine years rather than a mandatory life without parole sentence for first-degree murder. Proving Hewson's intent to kill, and that he acted with premeditation and deliberation, was the issue confronting the jury in his trial.

The state argued that Hewson's deadly intent was clear by looking at his actions before, during, and after the killing. Before the killing, he had a history of domestic violence against Gail and other women, he attempted to purchase a gun while under a protective order, and he breached an eight-foot wall to reach the home of his estranged wife. Gail's expressed fear to girlfriends and her efforts to take Hewson's weapons to the sheriff's office were also very telling.

Prior Bad Acts

Many defendants who commit terrible crimes have done other bad things before. Some have lengthy criminal records. Others may have committed a series of acts leading up to the crime that provide greater insight and context into their mind-set at the time of the actual crime. Giving the jury the fuller picture is often vital in telling the whole story to prove the crimes beyond a reasonable doubt. Are these prior convictions and prior bad acts admissible?

Rule of Evidence 404(b) deals with the admissibility of a defendant's "prior bad acts." The rule states that evidence of crimes, wrongs, or other acts may be admissible to show a defendant's mental processes like motive, intent, knowledge, absence of accident, and premeditation and deliberation.[2] Prior bad acts may also be admitted in order to prove the identity of the killer, or to establish their plan and preparation, as well as *modus operandi* (MO), that is, their "method of operation."[3]

For evidence to be admissible under Rule 404(b), a trial judge must make several findings to ensure a fair trial.[4] First, the court must conclude that there is substantial evidence that the defendant actually committed the prior bad act. This is obvious with prior convictions, such as Hewson's prior conviction of domestic violence, but uncharged conduct, such as Hewson's attempt to purchase a firearm in violation of the domestic violence protective order, must be proven in a hearing outside the jury's presence before the court will rule on the admissibility of the evidence.

For prior bad acts to be admitted, the trial judge must next rule that the probative value of the other crimes evidence outweighs the prejudicial effect of them. If the scales tip too much toward distracting the jury or creating the likelihood that the defendant will be viewed unfairly, the court will keep the prior bad acts evidence out.[5] Finally, the judge must find that the prior bad act occurred close in time to the crime on trial and that the facts of the prior bad act are substantially similar to the crime on trial.[6] When all of these tests have been satisfied, the trial judge has the discretion to allow the jury to hear this other crimes evidence with instructions that the evidence may only be considered for the limited purposes described in 404(b) and for no other purpose.[7]

Think back to the Campbell and Cummings trials discussed in chapter 2. The jury in both cases ultimately voted to sentence the defendants to death. Their behavior before, during, and after the crimes (the rule refers to prior bad acts but includes acts that occur subsequent to the crime as well) contradicted their claims that they were grossly impaired. Their violent criminal histories were admitted in the sentencing phases to establish their true intent for committing the murders: money. As you will see throughout this book, the evidence from other crimes is frequently vital in establishing the identity of the perpetrator and proving him guilty of the highest crimes charged.

Overwhelming Evidence of Guilt

The judge admitted all of Hewson's prior bad acts leading up to the murder, from his history of prior violence to his attempted purchase of a pistol from the gun store. Gail's expressed fears to her girlfriends and to law enforcement, including taking his guns to a sheriff's office, were also admitted under Rule 404(b).

Gail's 911 call took listeners to the horror of the moment of the attack. During the assault, Hewson lay in wait outside the window at the base of the stairs and then fired multiple shots, a clear indication that his specific intent was to end Gail's life. As she bled to death, the recorded phone call to 911 revealed that Hewson had time to reload the weapon and fire additional shots. Infliction of lethal wounds after a victim is down is the essence of premeditation and deliberation. This was not hot-blooded manslaughter; it was cold-blooded murder.

Additionally, even though Hewson claimed to be in the house when the shooting occurred, ballistics evidence left no doubt that he fired into the home through several windows. Because the killing occurred in the course of firing into an occupied home, the state argued that he should be convicted of first-degree murder under the felony murder rule, irrespective of his premeditation and deliberation.

The jury did not take long to deliberate. The physical evidence left at the scene, from the shattered windows to the shell casings outside, left no doubt that Hewson was guilty of first-degree felony murder. The prior bad acts also made it clear that he did so in a cool state of mind, making him guilty of first-degree murder with premeditation and deliberation. The jury convicted him of first-degree murder under both theories. At age 72, Hewson was sent to prison for life without parole. He died there, ten years later, in 2014.

Domestic Violence Does Not Discriminate

At its core, domestic violence is about power and control and frequently involves shifting the blame to the victim. Combating this violence means taking hidden secrets out of the closet and keeping the blame squarely on the perpetrators.

Anyone can fall victim to predators despite socioeconomic status, age, sexual orientation, race, or religion. Gail's case is a reminder that sometimes not even the strongest survive. She was a financially independent woman who lived in a very safe neighborhood and took all measures provided by law to protect herself. If it could happen to her, it could happen to anyone. There is no wall high enough to stop domestic violence when the problem comes from within the home.

Many victims lead lives of quiet desperation, and few reach out for help. When they do summon the courage to report their abuse, it is very common for them to ask for the charges to be dropped at the first court appearance. The abuser is still their husband, the father of their children, the breadwinner. As if that weren't enough, these victims must also face their abusers in court, since the Sixth Amendment of the US Constitution gives the accused the right to confront his or her accuser. Witnesses frequently recant testimony or refuse to come to court after charges are filed. This phenomenon is known as "battered woman's syndrome" and makes it extremely difficult for investigators and prosecutors to help the abused.

Vulnerable victims are easy targets; predators go after the weakest in the herd. It should not be surprising that many of these cases involve the very young or the very old. Victims of domestic violence usually are or become economically dependent and socially isolated by the abuser. To take this violence out of the shadows and into the light, several public events are held each year to remind the entire community of a topic that was once taboo to discuss.

While the law compels people to report crime when they witness child abuse, there is no similar law that requires reporting when grown adults are similarly victimized.[8] Moreover, there was a time in our country when there were more shelters for battered pets than for battered women.[9] Abused women and children need our best, too.

Past conduct of defendants, like the type Hewson perpetrated against other women, should certainly heighten punishment. In depth analysis of a decade of killing of women in 47 major US cities revealed that almost half were murdered by an intimate partner. Moreover, 36 percent of the men were publicly known to be a potential threat prior to the attack because of a prior restrain-

ing order or a prior conviction for a violent crime.[10] In July 2017, a new law was passed in North Carolina called "Britny's Law."[11] When a defendant has engaged in past abuse, or when the victim has sought out the protection of a domestic violence protective order (like Gail did), this evidence is specifically recognized as heightening a killing done with malice (which by itself is second-degree murder) and, therefore, elevates the killing to first-degree murder.

Our laws in North Carolina reflect society's evolving views. At the turn of the 20th century, a man was still legally allowed to beat his wife with a stick as long as it was less than the width of his thumb.[12] "The rule of thumb" was based

FIGURE 3.1 Ben David addressing the crowd at 20th Annual Take Back the Night Rally in front of Battleship *North Carolina.*

on the idea that since a man could be held responsible in civil court for the actions of his wife, he could choose how to keep her in line.

In October, when the community focuses on domestic violence prevention, we hold a public march and rally at the Cape Fear River to "Take Back the Night." Silent memorials of women and children who have been killed stand sentry while their stories, written on life-sized silhouettes, are read by family members. The message is simple: intimate partner violence must stop. These prevention efforts have undoubtedly saved many lives and improved the circumstances of people living in fear.

Because domestic violence cases need extra attention, my office was spurred to start the Family Violence Unit in 2004, the year I was elected district attorney. Gail was one of six victims murdered that year through domestic violence. The unit consists of a full-time prosecutor and two assigned detectives who follow up with photographs of injuries and collect physical evidence for future use.

Victims are told about the unit when they go to the courthouse to obtain a civil domestic violence protective order and are counseled about the availability of a 24-hour domestic violence shelter. Our collective efforts have caused many more offenders to be held accountable and have undoubtedly prevented future violence, leading many to call the Family Violence Unit the "Homicide Prevention Team." We know that past abuse is a strong indicator of future abuse and that murders, like Gail's, are both foreseeable and preventable.

State v. Grooms[13]

It was Sunday morning, about 10:00 a.m., on April 3, 2011. David Doolittle and his son, Trey, were riding their bikes down River Road, an 11-mile-long stretch that winds at the start, then parallels the Cape Fear River before meeting Carolina Beach. They were training for an Ironman triathlon, a race they had successfully finished in Florida just a year earlier. The scenic views and even terrain made River Road a popular training area for cyclists who traveled this road often. By all accounts, Trey, whose senior prom was a week away and graduation was just after that, could keep up with his dad. They were both the ideal picture of health.

Thomas Grooms was a study in contrasts with David and Trey. A man of 62 years, he had the liver of a much older man, the result of many years of hard drinking. While he had never been charged with driving while impaired (DWI), there were many people who would ultimately come forward to talk about his uncharged exploits. He bragged at bars that he managed his double vision by driving with only one eye open. On a prior occasion, his girlfriend had a panic attack while he swerved to avoid mailboxes while driving on River Road at night. She demanded that he pull over and warned him that he was "going to kill somebody." That incident occurred on February 22, 2011.

Six weeks later, this unfortunate prophecy came true. First on the scene was a truck driver who was on his way home. He called 911. Grooms had been all over the road for miles, swerving into oncoming traffic then veering over the fog line into the grass, traveling long stretches in the dirt before correcting back up on the road. Three women, also cycling on River Road, had to bail into the ditch lining the road to avoid being run over by Grooms' car.

Grooms struck David Doolittle first. David shattered the windshield, rolled over the roof, denting it along the way, and then destroyed the back windshield. He died instantly. Trey, who was in front of his dad, was thrown, upon impact, 187 feet from his bike. His pulse was weak once help arrived, but he was still alive. Twenty-four hours later his mom watched as he was taken off life support. In a last selfless act, Trey Doolittle's organs were donated.

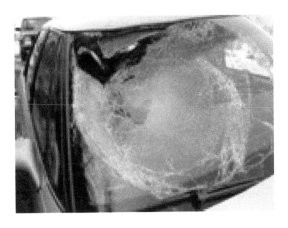

FIGURES 3.2 AND 3.3   Defendant's windshield and back window. David Doolittle rolled over the top, dented the top, and blew out the back window. Trey flew 187 feet on impact.

Grooms tried to flee, but his car was badly damaged, and the trucker's vehicle blocked his path. While others tended to David and Trey, Grooms never left the driver's seat to render aid.

Trooper Bryan Phillips of the State Highway Patrol was one of the first to arrive. The crash reconstruction team that followed Trooper Phillips' arrival noted that there were no skid marks on the road or the grass, and no signs of braking to avoid the collision. This was confirmed by

Grooms' vehicle's "black box," which showed that the car only slowed upon impact with David and Trey Doolittle's bodies. Grooms never hit the brakes. Nor did he even slow down before, during, or after hitting David and Trey.

Trooper Phillips was perplexed by his handheld Alco-Sensor reading. Despite smelling of alcohol, Grooms' breathalyzer registered .00. He denied drinking anything since the night before, and while having some indications of impairment, he was able to perform some components of the Standardized Field Sobriety Tests at the roadside. Doubting Grooms' claim that this was all a terrible accident, Trooper Phillips called a certified drug recognition expert in order to detect if substances other than alcohol might be responsible for Grooms' reckless driving. While there were bottles of wine and hard liquor in Grooms' car, the most interesting item for law enforcement was a half-chewed straw with a white substance still in it.

FIGURE 3.4   Grooms was asked to perform a Standardized Field Sobriety Test roadside by Trooper Bryan Phillips.

Grooms was transported to the station for further assessment. A sample was drawn for a better reading of his blood alcohol concentration and confirmed the suspicion that other impairing substances were present. Grooms' mustache glowed like a Christmas tree when evaluated under a black light. Swabs stuck up his nose indicated the same white substance. Analysts at the North Carolina State Crime Lab revealed that it was mephedrone, also known as "bath salts," which were just gaining popularity at this time as a synthetic cocaine and not yet illegal under North Carolina law.

More than 500 investigation hours eventually revealed Grooms' actions in the hours before he ran over David and Trey, elevating the event from a terrible accident to two counts of second-degree murder. Second-degree murder is the killing of another human being with malice. Malice means not only hatred, ill will, or spite, as it is commonly understood. It also may be implied where the defendant commits an intentional act in conscious disregard for the rights and safety of others. In other words, when a defendant acts in a wanton manner that reflects a callous disregard for human life and social duty, he may be convicted of second-degree murder under a theory of implied malice.

There were 29 cases in North Carolina that upheld the conviction of the defendant for second-degree murder where the defendant had been convicted of DWI in the past.[14] The theory was that the prior DWI should have put the defendant on notice of the potentially deadly choice of future impaired driving. To consciously disregard it constituted malice.

The reason we could elevate Grooms' charges to second-degree murder was the abundant evidence of prior bad acts—his prior behavior, while not captured in a criminal record, clearly showed a conscious disregard for everyone else and painted the picture of a man who was deliberately bent on mischief. This uncharged 404(b) evidence was the subject of a hearing out of the presence of the jury where we were able to establish many things about Grooms in the hours, days, and even weeks leading up to killing David and Trey.

FIGURES 3.5, 3.6, AND 3.7   From left: The straw found in Grooms' backseat, his nose, and his moustache were examined for evidence of impairing substances by analysts at the North Carolina State Crime Lab, who testified at trial.

Grooms drove impaired on numerous occasions, openly bragged about being a skilled impaired driver, and had been warned by his girlfriend not to drive impaired (on the very road where he would kill David and Trey less than two months later). This was sufficient to supply the malice for murder, the first of its kind under North Carolina Law.[15]

Additional relevant factors included Grooms' gross level of impairment (analysis of the blood draw showed a blood alcohol concentration of more than twice the legal limit—the breathalyzer Trooper Phillips used at the scene was faulty); the presence of bath salts in his system; his erratic driving earlier that day on River Road that included running three female bikers off the road; and his attempt to flee after the fact.

In the weeks that followed, investigators uncovered many other grossly aggravating factors. Grooms' story that he had only two glasses of wine the night before and then went to sleep in his office in Southport (about 30 minutes from Wilmington) was a lie. The schoolteacher with whom he had been on a blind date, and whom he was trying to call at the time of the wreck, confirmed that he drank two glasses of wine at dinner, but his night did not end after that date. A hidden video camera trained on his bed at the business (which in itself is disturbing) showed that he had not slept there as he claimed. When investigators checked his bank records, an ATM withdrawal of $400 at 4:00 a.m. in northern Wilmington jumped out. Grooms had only $100 in his pocket at the time of the crash. Bars closed at 2:00 a.m. Where did the rest of the money go in the six hours between the withdrawal and colliding with the Doolittles on River Road?

Look closely at the photograph in figure 3.8. There is another person in the vehicle (but it was not the schoolteacher). The silhouette belonged to a prostitute named Pat, who Grooms picked up next to the Cape Fear Memorial Bridge after leaving his date. It was Pat who took Grooms to a drug dealer's house to get the bath salts found in the straw. This was the same substance found in Grooms' nose at the time of the incident. Mephedrone is an amphetamine that is "synergistically impairing" with alcohol, according to Dr. William Meggs, East Carolina University Emergency

FIGURE 3.8   Landfall ATM at 4:00 a.m.

Room Toxicologist who testified at trial. Far from offsetting the depressive effects of alcohol, bath salts amplify the impairment.

Since the time of this case, mephedrone has been declared illegal in North Carolina and in many other states.[16] The world is now aware of the severity of this drug, and cases are treated seriously in many jurisdictions.

The most unsettling behavior was Grooms' choice to remain in his vehicle rather than render aid to the Doolittles. When questioned on the stand about this last point, Grooms indicated that he was in shock. They say a picture is worth a thousand words. Here, in figure 3.9, is Grooms minutes after the crash. Rather than displaying fear or confusion, he eerily seems to be grinning.

I reminded the jury that this was a case about the heart: the broken heart of a mother and wife, the heart of a boy that now beats in the chest of an organ recipient, and the depraved heart of a defendant who took the life of two innocent people. His lack of remorse was heartless.

FIGURE 3.9   Grooms at the crime scene after completing Standardized Field Sobriety Tests. Grooms would later testify that this image captured him while he was in shock.

The jury's verdict was as swift as the judge's sentence was severe. In a case that set precedent, Grooms was convicted of two counts of second-degree murder.[17] Judge Paul Jones ultimately said: "It's sad for everybody that we had to have this trial. I'm a veteran of a lot of trials, over 300 jury trials, and this is one of the saddest. I've presided over 200 murder trials. Some people pled guilty. You pled not guilty, which is your right. Vengeance only belongs to one person, and that's the Lord. But my job is to punish." Judge Jones then sentenced Grooms to consecutive sentences totaling nearly 25 years in prison. Given his age at the time of conviction, he will likely never get out.

State v. Pierce[18]

Police officers are sworn to protect and serve the public, and their jobs are both difficult and dangerous. Every time they clock in, their lives are at risk because they don't know what their next call will yield. When putting on that uniform, they have a duty to act.

When these officers lose their lives in the performance of their duties, there is no higher priority case in the criminal justice system. In the last three decades, only one officer has been killed by a suspect in the Sixth District. His killer never came closer than two miles to him. How the defendant was ultimately convicted of second-degree murder raises legal issues of foreseeability, contributory negligence, and proximate cause. We also relied on his prior bad acts to hold him responsible for the series of events that he set in motion.

In the early morning hours of February 18, 2009, Corporal Will Richards, an experienced vice and narcotics detective, drove a patrol car in a neighborhood near UNCW. Corporal Richards was widely respected on the force. When he spoke, other officers listened. On this night, he was acting supervisor in charge of B-Platoon and was in radio communication with Officer Rich Matthews.

At approximately 1:15 a.m., Corporal Richards observed a GMC Yukon traveling on Kerr Avenue. Richards believed that this vehicle matched the description of an SUV that had been involved in a kidnapping incident the night before. He followed the vehicle, searching for suspicious activity. The Yukon initially stopped in a business parking lot and appeared to be hiding. Soon after, it exited the parking lot and began speeding on South College Road. Corporal Richards turned on his blue lights and siren, which simultaneously started a video recording device in the car. The ensuing pursuit was caught on video.

When Corporal Richards activated the emergency equipment, the Yukon initially pulled over near the intersection of South College Road and Long Leaf Hills Drive. They remained parked for a few seconds. As Corporal Richards attempted to exit his vehicle, the car took off unexpectedly. Corporal Richards gave chase. During the pursuit, the Yukon reached speeds of 65 mph in a 25-mph-zone, sped through three stop signs without slowing down, crossed into the oncoming traffic lane several times, and swerved off and on the road. Five one-pound bags of marijuana were thrown from the vehicle at various points along the chase route. The video from Corporal Richards' car shows that three bags were thrown out of the driver's side and two bags were thrown from the passenger's side of the Yukon.

Given Corporal Richards' extensive experience with narcotics, he immediately recognized the substance being thrown from the car and understood by the volume of drugs what caliber of dealers he was chasing. In the course of the pursuit, Corporal Richards yelled, "I need somebody," over the radio, requesting assistance from other officers. He also identified the bags and their locations. Officers around the city were listening.

The Crash

Officer Matthews and Officer Allison Jahreis, both with the B-Platoon, were parked next to each other on Carolina Beach Road near the intersection of Shipyard Boulevard. Both turned on their blue lights and sirens and drove toward South College Road.

The in-car cameras from both assisting officers' vehicles show their route of travel and their manner of driving. Officer Matthews was in the lead with Officer Jahreis following. For the 2.2 miles of Shipyard Boulevard, from Carolina Beach Road to the point where Officer Matthews wrecked, there are three intersections with traffic lights. Between the lights, Officer Matthews traveled at high rates of speed, reaching up to 105 mph at one point. At all intersections with red lights, Officer Matthews slowed to a near stop, making sure that it was clear before proceeding through. Officer Jahreis followed Officer Matthews at a distance of nine seconds, closing in to four seconds since she did not encounter red lights.

Shipyard Boulevard is an almost entirely flat, straight road. It affords drivers the ability to see far ahead. There are few side streets, hardly any vegetation blocks the view of parallel roadways, and it is a commercial area with very light traffic during the night. There is also an extensive network of streetlights on either side of Shipyard Boulevard, and on the night of February 18 the roadway was dry. Officer Matthews experienced very light traffic during the 2.2-mile stretch of road before the crash.

As Officer Matthews reached a top speed of 105 mph, a cardboard box (which was later determined to be empty) suddenly came into view in the middle of the road. He instinctively jerked the steering wheel to the left, a move that proved fatal. The back end of the vehicle (which had recently been serviced and was working properly) slid out and the car bolted across the median. At this point, the feed for the in-car camera was lost.

FIGURE 3.10   Officer Matthews' patrol vehicle crashed on Shipyard Boulevard near Partridge Road in Wilmington.

Officer Matthews' vehicle continued to the other side of the road and struck a stand of trees. Officer Jahreis pulled off the road, called for backup and medical assistance, and began attempts to help Officer Matthews. It was no use. Officer Matthews was dead within seconds of impact.

Officer Matthews wrecked just 0.6 miles from the location from which the defendants first fled. Records from the WPD establish that Corporal Richards' chase was still active when Officer Matthews wrecked and did not end until 20 seconds afterward, when the driver of the Yukon finally pulled over. Corporal Richards was able to stop the vehicle without the assistance of the other pursuing officers.

The Three Defendants

Corporal Richards stopped the Yukon for a second time near Hugh MacRae Park at the intersection of Pine Grove Drive and Oleander Drive, just north of the Long Leaf Hills residential area. By then the driver had eluded him throughout the Long Leaf Hills neighborhood and the suspects had gotten rid of their contraband. In the Yukon were Anthony Pierce (the driver), Eric Smith (front seat passenger), and Matthew Hendy (in the back).

Along the chase route, officers located all five bags of marijuana. Together the drugs had a street value of approximately $30,000. A .40 caliber Glock handgun, loaded with multiple rounds of hollow-point bullets, was also found.

Later, investigators determined that Pierce, Smith, and Hendy had robbed other drug dealers of the five pounds of marijuana, mere minutes before being stopped by Corporal Richards. The other drug dealers, who were also armed, chased Pierce, Smith, and Hendy after they took off with their drugs. In essence, one chase turned into another. Pierce, Smith, and Hendy were outrunning other criminals from a lucrative and very dangerous robbery when Corporal Richards first attempted to stop them.

The Reasonable Officer Standard

All WPD officers on duty and involved in the chase that night reported that Corporal Richards' call for help was one that required an emergency response. Due to the large quantity of narcotics, many of these same officers perceived that there was a high likelihood that a dangerous encounter with three subjects would ensue.

Analysis of the response times of six other officers in Wilmington who heard the call and responded to assist reveals that many, if not all, were traveling at high rates of speed, even upward of 100 mph. Some officers diverted to help Officer Matthews while others continued straight to Corporal Richards, who had stopped the defendant's car seconds after Officer Matthews collided with a tree.

It is easy to second guess the split-second decisions of officers in the calm of an office, your living room, or even in a courtroom. In looking at the reasonableness of their decisions, whether talking about a use-of-force incident or engaging in a chase, prosecutors assess what a similarly situated officer would do if confronted with the same circumstances. We also look to see if they complied with their training and the standards set forth by their internal policies.

All officers with the WPD receive training and are bound by departmental policies regarding rendering assistance to other officers, as well as the times when a chase can be initiated and when a chase must be terminated. The WPD also has a policy regarding pursuits, which spells out the circumstances when officers can both exceed the speed limit and ignore traffic control devices in their pursuit of criminal suspects.

The policy does not put a limit on the speed at which an officer can travel while in pursuit of a fleeing suspect. Instead, it discusses the factors to be weighed by an officer both in decisions to engage in and continue a pursuit. An officer must consider the following: whether the need for apprehension outweighs the risks to the officer or the public; pursuit location and direction (i.e., school zones, playgrounds, neighborhoods); time of day; pedestrian and vehicular traffic conditions; the speeds involved in the pursuit; visibility and weather conditions; road conditions; and the capabilities and limitations of the police vehicle.

You Cannot Outrun the Past

None of the three defendants were strangers to law enforcement. In fact, all had extensive felony records that included charges and convictions for flight from arrest or failing to appear in court. As convicted felons, all were prohibited from possessing the loaded firearm that was later recovered. Additionally, all were either on probation or parole and faced a return to prison if apprehended.

Eric Grant Smith, who lived four hours away in Winston-Salem, was on federal probation, having been released from prison after serving a two-year sentence for transporting drugs and firearms across the Canadian border. Smith also had numerous marijuana and paraphernalia offenses throughout North Carolina. At the time of this incident, he was wanted in Yadkin County for failing to appear in court on February 21, 2006, for a possession of marijuana charge. He was also wanted for failure to appear in New Hanover County on February 12, 2009, for a speeding charge. Thus, there were active warrants for Smith's arrest at the time of this stop.

Matthew Gerard Hendy, who lived in Hampstead in Pender County, also had multiple prior contacts with the law. Just one week earlier, on February 12, 2009, Hendy pled guilty to felony fleeing to elude arrest in Johnston County. At the time of that arrest, $181,000 was seized from Hendy's vehicle and another $10,000 was found on his person. Hendy was also convicted of trafficking in cocaine on February 4, 2004, in Lenoir County, and was convicted of three separate marijuana offenses in Forsyth County.

Anthony Pierce, who lived in Wilmington, had a troubled past as well. At the time of this incident, he was on parole and faced the prospect of returning to Pennsylvania to continue serving a lengthy sentence for which he had already completed 10 years. The facts of the underlying conviction provided insight regarding the lengths to which Pierce would go in order to avoid apprehension.

On January 17, 1994, Pierce and a co-defendant, Thomas Anthony Lee, conspired to rob others engaged in criminal activity at a gambling house in Philadelphia, Pennsylvania An undercover officer alerted other officers to the crime taking place and back-up quickly arrived. Pierce and Lee took hostages and used their intended victims as human shields as they exited the residence. When commanded to drop their weapons by the Philadelphia Police Department, officers heard either Pierce or Lee yell, "I am not going back to jail," before both men opened fire on the police. Officer Deatrice Kennedy narrowly avoided being shot. Lieutenant Kevin Wong was struck in the chest; fortunately, he was wearing a bulletproof vest and his injuries were minor. Pierce's co-defendant, Lee, was shot and killed in the incident.

FIGURE 3.11   Lieutenant Kevin Wong of the Philadelphia Police Department testified in the Pierce trial about the shooting incident there 15 years earlier. *Source*: WECT.

Pierce fled from the scene and remained at large for almost three months until his arrest on April 9, 1994. Pierce was initially charged with 54 separate offenses from the incident. On August 11 of that year, he was convicted in Philadelphia of felony robbery, felony aggravated assault, criminal conspiracy, and carrying firearms. He was released from prison and put on parole on April 12, 2004, after serving 10 years. This meant that he was a free man but would return to prison to serve out his remaining sentence if he violated the law again.

Prosecutor Discretion and Charging

Prosecutors have great discretion in pursuing people who have committed bad acts. Frequently, the conduct for which a defendant is convicted and punished is different from the crimes he committed to first attract the attention of law enforcement.[19] In Officer Matthews' case, we all believed that had it not been for these three defendants, he would be alive today. While many contended that he was going too fast, all agreed that he was driving at a high rate of speed in order to apprehend violent and dangerous felons who were fleeing from his colleagues. The speed of the other six officers showed that Officer Matthews' response was hardly out of bounds.

My first exercise of discretion as a prosecutor came with Hendy and Smith. They were not driving but they were complicit in the risks that were created that fateful night. They were felons who had joined forces to rob other drug dealers at gunpoint, with the intention to resell the marijuana in our community. Given their lengthy records and the severity of the case, I asked one of my senior prosecutors, Tim Severo, who was cross-designated as a Special Assistant United States Attorney (SAUSA), to take the case into the federal system.

Soon after taking office, I formed a partnership with George Holding, who at the time was the US attorney for the Eastern District of North Carolina. I worked with him to have one of my senior ADAs cross-sworn to handle drug cases in the federal system. The success of this partnership

FIGURE 3.12   DA office staff with former US Attorney George Holding of the Eastern District of North Carolina. Holding and I know each other from attending law school together at Wake Forest, thereafter working as associates at Kilpatrick Stockton. He went on to serve as a US congressman, and we have maintained a friendship despite being on opposite ends of the political spectrum. *Source: Star News Online.*

has been dramatic from the standpoint of prison years for serious offenders and in the volume of weapons and drugs taken off the street. The program was replicated at the local level throughout the three federal districts of North Carolina.

There are several benefits to this partnership. First, the biggest traffickers, like Hendy and Smith, frequently move across large geographical areas and the territorial reach of the federal system is essential to getting these dealers brought back to Wilmington. Second, sentencing laws are usually much tougher at the federal level; my cross-sworn prosecutor can file a minor drug case in federal court in order to harshly punish defendants who may otherwise escape full justice in state courts. Federal sentencing laws for drugs, especially where firearms are involved, are much harsher than in state court.

Hendy ultimately went to prison for nearly 12 years for possession of a firearm in furtherance of a drug trafficking crime. Smith received a 20-year sentence for federal conspiracy to possess with the intent to distribute more than 50 kilograms of marijuana.

As for Pierce's charges, he was clearly guilty of fleeing to elude arrest causing a death, a class E felony. (For an overview of different types of felonies, see the sentencing chart in chapter 1.) We also believed that Pierce was guilty of murder. When the grand jury heard all of the evidence and watched the chase videos, they indicted Pierce not only for the gun and drug charges but also for fleeing to elude arrest causing death and for the charge of second-degree murder.

Implied Malice

As we saw in the Grooms case, a defendant who kills another human being while driving impaired may be charged with second-degree murder under an implied malice theory. Although never previously convicted, Grooms' prior conduct was admissible under 404(b); his prior bad acts established that he intentionally disregarded deadly consequences and was deliberately bent on mischief.

No one suggested that Pierce killed Officer Matthews with express malice or that he targeted anyone for death during the incident. Death was not his aim, but it was a reasonably foreseeable side effect. There were plenty of circumstances, both from the night of the incident and in Pierce's past, to show that he met the criteria for a murder charge under a depraved heart theory.

Pierce was deliberately bent on mischief the night he encountered Corporal Richards. Robbing other dealers of more than $30,000 in drugs just moments earlier, he intentionally fled from Richards to avoid apprehension. During the chase, Pierce drove in wanton disregard for the safety of everyone. He recklessly disregarded the imminent danger that his conduct might cause with the full realization that it would inevitably lead officers to respond at great risk to themselves and others.

His prior bad acts, both on the night of the incident and years earlier in Philadelphia, made it clear that he consciously disregarded the safety of others, and intentionally endangered the lives of officers, in order to escape the consequences of his criminal conduct. Moreover, no one could better appreciate that his flight from police might have deadly consequences than a man who spent over a decade in prison for doing it once before.

The incident in Philadelphia and the murder of Officer Matthews featured remarkable similarities. In both cases, Pierce joined forces with at least one other armed and convicted felon to achieve his criminal purpose, targeting individuals who were themselves engaged in illegal conduct. In both incidents, Pierce's criminal scheme was interrupted by police and he refused to submit to persistent commands to surrender. During the course of his attempted flight, Pierce's actions brought about deadly results—to a co-conspirator in Philadelphia and to a police officer in Wilmington. The violent encounter in Philadelphia showed a mind utterly without regard for social duty and one that will consciously disregard the rights and safety of officers who are performing their duties to effect his arrest.

Judge Phyllis Gorham conducted an extensive hearing at trial to determine the admissibility of this other crime's evidence. She ruled that Pierce's past, both 15 years earlier in Philadelphia and in the 15 minutes leading up to the fateful chase in Wilmington, were admissible to show his intent and malice.

There was, however, another mountain for the State to climb in order to convict Pierce of second-degree murder: prosecutors were required to show that Pierce was the actual, or proximate, cause of Officer Matthews' death. This brought up issues of foreseeability and contributory negligence.

Proximate Cause and Foreseeability

Proximate cause means "but for" an event having occurred a harm would not have resulted. In lawyer speak, proximate cause is defined as that which, in a natural and continuous sequence, unbroken by any independent cause, produces injury and without which the result would not have occurred. Simply put, Officer Matthews would not have been speeding to assist a fellow officer (resulting in a crash that caused his death) but for the fact that Pierce sped off and drove recklessly. As such, Pierce proximately caused the death of Officer Matthews.

In similar cases in other states, several defendants who were charged with causing the death of an officer while fleeing arrest have made the same argument that Pierce's attorney used: the officer's death was not foreseeable because he died more than two miles from where the defendant was at the time of the wreck. This "logic" has been consistently rejected across the country.

The issue for proximate cause is "foreseeability," not "seeability." A defendant who lights a fuse and is far away when a bomb explodes is obviously responsible for the death of victims he never encountered. The fact that Officer Matthews was not right behind Pierce when he crashed was irrelevant and not even surprising.

Wayne Gretzky once said, when asked what made him such a successful ice hockey player, that he did not skate toward the puck, but to where he thought it would be going next.[20] The same principle applies to officers involved in a chase, as they anticipate where a suspect is going to be while keeping in constant radio communication. A defendant can outrun an officer but not the officer's radio.

As one Ohio court said in a similar context, "[I]n the highly charged atmosphere of a high-speed chase, a police officer may disregard the safety of others and speed through an intersection in order to catch up with the vehicle being pursued. Certainly, in a perfect world such errors in judgment would not happen; but the fact is they do. It is difficult to believe, furthermore, that [the defendant] could not foresee that one or more of the officers chasing him would be so caught up in the chase that they would become reckless in their attempt to catch up to him."[21]

Even if other factors intervene, such as an empty box in the middle of the road, the defendant is not excused from his conduct. Nor does it matter if other factors combined with that initial cause to bring about the death. When Pierce stepped on the gas, the resulting chase was inevitable. Accordingly, he could be held responsible for the foreseeable consequences of his actions even though he never even saw the officer he killed.

Contributory Negligence

If an officer who is pursuing a reckless driver complies with all traffic laws (maintaining a safe speed, stopping at red lights, etc.), it would be impossible to apprehend the suspect. Yet when an officer dies in the performance of this very duty, the defendant who instigated the chase is frequently quick to point to the officer's conduct as the cause for his or her own demise. In this case, Pierce suggested that Officer Matthews was responsible for his own death by traveling twice the posted speed limit, when the defendant himself was traveling in excess of nearly three times the limit during the chase.

Sadly, dozens of officers die each year in the line of duty, many in high speed chases. So do innocent bystanders who are struck by these fleeing felons or by those officers in pursuit of them. Invariably, defendants attempt to shift the blame to the dead officers and bystanders, suggesting that their actions may have contributed to their own demise. Pierce was no exception. Precedent from North Carolina and all other states left no question that the law of contributory negligence has no place in the criminal laws.

Officer Matthews' actions were in direct proportion to Pierce's actions. He would have been derelict in his duty in failing to act. The fact that officers sometimes have to act in a manner counter to our "fight or flight" instincts to survive at all costs does not make them reckless. Indeed, it makes them heroes.

Conclusion

Pierce was convicted on May 6, 2010, of second-degree murder, felony fleeing to elude causing death, two counts of possession of a firearm by a convicted felon (one for the gun found on the side of the road and another for a gun found in his home during a search after the incident), and possession with intent to distribute marijuana. He was sentenced to prison for 19 years. Pierce's conviction was ultimately appealed to the court of appeals and the Supreme Court, where all the judges upheld Judge Gorham's evidentiary rulings and subsequent sentencing.[22]

State v. McCoy[23]

After spending years in prison for murder, Leon McCoy was released back into his hometown of Wilmington as a much older man. Now in his late fifties, his job prospects were dim. McDonald's gave him a chance and hired him. The night manager, "Kayla," was a young woman who worked hard and was a good employee by all accounts. She had the key to the restaurant's safe. She was also young and petite and not likely to put up a fight if an armed intruder came into the store demanding all the money under the roof.

McCoy had an idea. Instead of working for minimum wage, why not rob the place? The restaurant had more than $3,000 in the safe on any given night. Because Kayla knew him already, McCoy reasoned that it would be impossible for him to carry out the crime alone. He enlisted the help of a young man from his neighborhood, Keith Bellamy. As a built-in alibi, McCoy actually planned to be in the restaurant during the heist. This would serve two purposes: since only two employees worked at closing time, it would eliminate all witnesses other than Kayla, and it would give McCoy the alibi that he too was a victim. It was the perfect inside job.

The plan was set. Bellamy would be the thief, and McCoy would play the part of a hapless victim. The only other witness to the armed robbery would be a scared young woman who would take Bellamy straight to the safe. At closing time, Bellamy burst into the restaurant wearing a ski mask and wielding a revolver. He immediately ordered McCoy to the ground. In a theatrical display worthy of an Oscar nod, the old man reluctantly complied.

Bellamy then pointed a gun to Kayla's head and marched her to the back office. After getting her to empty the safe, Bellamy decided he was not finished. With a gun to her head, Bellamy told Kayla to remove her clothes and then sexually assaulted her.

Police arrived and watched the surveillance video in disgust. Cameras throughout the restaurant captured not only the encounter between Bellamy and McCoy, but Bellamy walking Kayla back to the office. To prevent embezzlement, McDonald's also had a hidden camera above the safe, which captured the entire sexual assault on film.

While the armed intruder may have been long gone, detectives knew they had another defendant in McCoy as they watched him rolling around on the restaurant floor in fake distress. McCoy knew about the camera at the front of the McDonald's and directed his acting toward it. Unfortunately for him, he was not aware of the second camera. Mounted in the hallway, it showed the footage of a completely different plot, showing McCoy repeatedly looking around and yelling to his partner in crime to hurry up. After initially lying to the police, McCoy eventually confessed and owned up to the plan, as well as the identity of his co-conspirator.

He was clearly guilty of the conspiracy to commit the armed robbery, but that was all. My brother and I, who tried the case together, disagreed. Bellamy and McCoy were arrested and charged with armed robbery and first-degree kidnapping (since Kayla was removed from one room to the next by the use of a gun). We also decided to charge both defendants with first-degree rape.

As we have seen, defendants must answer for foreseeable consequences. Pierce, who sets the wheels in motion by fleeing to elude arrest, was held responsible for the murder of an officer in hot pursuit. Similarly, co-defendants can be held responsible for each other's actions, so long as all the acts are in furtherance of a shared purpose and are foreseeable. (We will see this theory of acting in concert in greater detail in chapter 7.) We believed that the sexual assault was a foreseeable consequence of the conspiracy to commit an armed robbery of a young woman who was alone and isolated from any help.

Bellamy and McCoy were tried together; neither defendant took the stand. Kayla bravely testified. Both men were convicted as charged of all offenses. The trial judge, believing that this was an especially heinous event, went out of his way to run the sentences consecutively to each other for all of the various offenses. Bellamy received over 45 years in prison. For his role in the crime, McCoy received just over 31 years—effectively a life sentence for a man of his age.

The North Carolina Court of Appeals agreed that all of the charges against Bellamy were appropriate and affirmed the trial court's ruling and sentence. As for McCoy, the court upheld the armed robbery and kidnapping conviction but reversed the rape conviction. The Court held that while a murder is a foreseeable consequence of an armed robbery, a sexual assault is typically not. It vacated the rape conviction and drastically reduced the time McCoy now had to serve in prison. His sentence was reduced to 12.5 years.

The Right Context

Actions have consequences, and people are held responsible for the things they can reasonably foresee, even if those results were not originally intended. Context is important when looking at the reasonableness or recklessness of actions. As circumstances change, so does our view of appropriate actions.

It was, for instance, more reckless of Grooms to be driving impaired at 10:00 a.m. on a Sunday morning than in the middle of the night on a Saturday, because the number of potential victims greatly increases on crowded roads and bike lanes during the day. Pierce's speed, three times the legal limit, was more reckless because he was fleeing through a neighborhood and not on an open country road.

A hunter deep in the woods who accidentally shoots and kills a fellow hunter may be guilty of only involuntary manslaughter. That same hunter who shoots at an animal in a subdivision and kills a child instead is more likely to be guilty of second-degree murder. In neither case did the hunter intend to shoot or kill another human being. While the intent was the same, the degree of recklessness was much different.

Context is important not only in looking at the reasonableness or recklessness of what we do, but of what we say. And where and when something is said can transform a prank into a threat.

State v. Mortimer[24]

On May 4, 1999, two weeks after the Columbine school shooting in Littleton, Colorado, students and their parents were on edge around the country.[25] Schools had always been perceived as sanctuaries. Now, after a mass killing in a once safe haven, everyone was left to question if the same event could happen at a school in their community. Hoaxes, fake bomb threats, pulled fire alarms, and anonymous tips of more school violence were occurring in different areas as copycats were seeking to get attention and cause pandemonium.

At Hoggard High School during a computer class, a message suddenly flashed across several students' terminals that read "The end is near." Panic ensued. Students were quickly evacuated and sent home. Members of the New Hanover County Sheriff's Office (NHSO) bomb squad conducted routine K9 searches for explosives throughout the campus. They came up empty. Five hundred students didn't come to Hoggard the next day, and the trend continued for the next several days.

Gossip was hissing like a snake. Eventually, a 16-year-old junior named Gail Plordes was charged with filing a false police report in an apparent attempt to throw investigators off the trail of a friend who was the likely culprit. Investigators then learned that teachers caught 17-year-old Joshua Mortimer, a loner who had been bullied, writing graffiti on a desk the same day as the other incident. He had written, "Violent J will rule the day," an apparent reference to himself and his ability to make normal operations come to a screeching halt. The same day as Plordes' arrest, investigators arrested Mortimer for communicating threats.

Both teens were brought into the courtroom. Wearing orange jumpsuits, handcuffs, and shackles, the two stood before the court as first-time offenders, were informed of their right to an attorney, and were notified of the charges against them. In North Carolina, the law provided that a person reaches adulthood at age 16 for all criminal purposes. In all other states, the age of majority is 18. (We will revisit the age of majority law later in chapter 7.) Historically, in North Carolina, we reasoned that if a young person can drive a car, get a job, and consent to sexual activity beginning at the age of 16, they should be old enough to appreciate the permanent consequences of their choices.

The charge of filing a false police report is relatively straightforward. If someone gives misinformation to the police in order to impede the investigation, they can be charged with a misdemeanor. To establish that someone is guilty of communicating a threat, the elements are more difficult to establish. The state must prove four elements: (1) The defendant willfully threatened to physically injure the person or damage the property of another; (2) the threat was communicated to the other person, orally or in writing; (3) the threat was made in a manner and under circumstances which would cause a reasonable person to believe that the threat is likely to be carried out; and (4) the threatened person believed that the threat would be carried out.[26]

Looking at the elements, the second and fourth were not in dispute. The statement was conveyed in writing and there were dozens of students who could testify that when they read "the end is near," they believed that a bomb was about to go off or that a shooter might be coming through the school. The first and third elements, however, were more questionable. The defense contended that what Mortimer had written was not a threat. Moreover, the defense argued that it was not reasonable for the students and teachers who fled the school to believe that this threat would likely be carried out.

The crimes the teens were charged with were misdemeanors and were tried in district court in front of a judge, not a jury. This is known as a bench trial. Plordes and Mortimer were both convicted, Plordes for filing a false police report and Mortimer for communicating threats. Plordes received a relatively light sentence given her limited role, although the intense media attention brought with it a very public shaming. Mortimer, on the other hand, was given a long probation sentence filled with onerous conditions. Many believed that this punishment fit the crime given the terror that his conduct had caused.

Mortimer appealed the case. Any defendant convicted in a bench trial in district court has an automatic right to appeal the case to Superior Court, the place usually reserved for felonies, to have their case heard anew or "*de novo.*" The defendant also has the right to a jury trial.

The community now had a chance to weigh in with a verdict. I argued that to understand the gravity of the threat it was essential to look at the circumstances that existed at the time the statement was uttered and received. If a person is standing behind a deli counter and says "you're next" to the next customer in line, we are unlikely to perceive that as a threat. But if the person behind the counter has just opened fire in the deli and killed three people, "you're next" would have a far different meaning to the same listener.

Mortimer had written "the end is near" in the days after Columbine. This changed the whole context of the message, and he knew it. Just as pranks at the airport were treated far more seriously after the September 11th attacks, the timing of Mortimer's statement made the reaction of those around him completely understandable. Moreover, his intent to cause chaos was given context by what he had written on the desk just before he posted the message on the computers. The judge allowed this prior bad act under Rule 404(b) to show that Mortimer's intent was to spread fear of violence. The jury agreed and Mortimer was convicted of communicating threats.

Mortimer claimed that his statement was a prank and not a threat. Mortimer again appealed, this time to the North Carolina Court of Appeals in Raleigh, which is tasked only with looking at whether legal errors occurred, not in deciding facts that the jury already found beyond a reasonable doubt.

Mortimer's attorney contended that the statement was too vague to constitute a threat—Mortimer could have been referring to the end of the approaching school year or even the end of the millennium. (A magazine cover of Billy Graham saying "the end is near" was admitted into evidence at trial.)

Mortimer's attorney also contended that her client "Did Not Do It" because he had not intended to incite violence or instill fear. The court of appeals agreed with this argument and overturned his conviction. My office respectfully disagreed with the decision and thought that the court of appeals did not appreciate the environment and context of the statement. Nonetheless, the message had been sent that threats would be taken seriously. "If the people in Raleigh believe that we are trying too hard to protect our school children in Wilmington, that is a criticism we will have to live with," Mr. Carriker said.

A couple of larger points remained, however, and I have thought about them many times since the resolution of this case. First, young people do not appreciate the consequences of their actions the same way that adults do. Should we really be treating these 16-year-olds in the same fashion? Who is having an adult conversation about choices and consequence before they make a choice that changes their lives forever? We will return to these issues in chapter 7.

Second, as we have seen throughout this chapter, the past can give insight to a person's behavior and may change the label we affix to their conduct. If we can look to a child's past to help explain their present circumstances and even help predict their future, don't we have a duty to act now to make that future as healthy and safe as possible? We will take up this larger question in chapter 8.

Notes

1   *State v. Hewson*, 182 N.C. App. 196 (2007). Co-counsel was Jon David.

2   N.C. Gen. Stat. § 8C-404(B).

3   Ibid.

4   In order for Rule 404(b) evidence to be relevant, there must be sufficient evidence that the defendant committed the other act in question. *State v. Haskins*, 104 N.C. App. 675, 679 (1991). Only once that preliminary threshold is satisfied, does the standard Rule 404(b) analysis of similarity and temporal proximity apply. Id. at 679-80 ("the trial court is required to make an initial determination pursuant to Rule 104(b) of whether there is sufficient evidence that the defendant in fact committed the extrinsic act").

5   *State v. Coffey*, 326 N.C. 268, 278-279 (1990): Rule 404(b)"a clear general rule of inclusion of relevant evidence of other crimes, wrongs or acts by a defendant, subject to but one exception requiring its exclusion if its only probative value is to show that the defendant has the propensity or disposition to commit an offense of the nature of the crime charged."

6   *State v. Beckelheimer*, 366 N.C. 127 (2012). "Prior acts are sufficiently similar 'if there are some unusual facts present in both crimes' that would indicate that the same person committed them." Id. (quoting *State v. Stager*, 329 N.C. 278, 304 (1991)). The acts admitted under 404(b) must be similar in nature and proximate in time to the charged offense.

7 *State v. Peterson*, 361 N.C. 587, 601 (2007) (in a case in which the defendant was tried for murdering his wife, the trial court properly admitted 404(b) evidence regarding another woman's death where there was "sufficient circumstantial evidence that defendant was involved in [the other woman's] death—such as defendant being the last known person to see [her] alive; defendant being with [her] the night of her death; and there being no sign of forced entry and nothing missing from the residence, which indicated that [she] likely knew her assailant").

8 N.C. Gen. Stat. 7B-301 (2015).

9 Staff of Senate Committee on the Judiciary, 102d Cong, 2d Sess, Violence against Women: A Week in the Life of America 26 (GPO1992). http://library.niwap.org/wp-content/uploads/2015/VAWA-Lghist-SenateJudiciary-10.92.pdf. "We live in a county with three times as many animal shelters as battered women's shelters."

10 *Washington Post*, as reported by San Diego News 7, December 10, 2018.

11 Britny's Law Senate Bill 600, S.L. 2017-94, Amended N.C. Gen. Stat. 14-17.

12 *State v. Rhodes*, 61 N.C. 453, 459 (1868). "We will not inflict upon society the greater evil of raising the curtain upon domestic privacy, to punish the lesser evil of trifling violence."

13 *State v. Grooms*, 230 N.C. App. 56 (2013). Co-counsel was Doug Carriker.

14 More DWI Suspects Face Murder Charges, WRAL.Com, Capital Broadcasting Company, Inc. (Copyright 2017), http://www.wral.com/news/local/story/8635263/.

15 NC Court of Appeals Upholds Grooms' Sentence, WECT6, Raycom Media (Copyright 2017) (2013), http://www.wect.com/story/23578905/nc-court-of-appeals-upholds-grooms-sentence ("'This case sets important precedent that impaired driving, especially by someone who drives habitually impaired, is no accident; where a defendant causes death, it may very well be murder,' said DA Ben David, who tried the case along with ADA Doug Carriker. 'Mr. Grooms will almost certainly spend the rest of his life in prison and David and Trey's legacy will help future victims for years to come.'").

16 N.C.G.S. 90-85(5)(h). Brian Freskos, Bath Salts Abuse Down, New Drugs on the Horizon, *Star News* Wilmington, GateHouse Media LLC (Copyright 2006–2017), (November 13, 2011), http://www.starnewsonline.com/news/20111113/bath-salts-abuse-down-new-drugs-on-the-horizon ("Abuse of the potent stimulant widely known as "bath salts" seems to be tapering off months after North Carolina and several other states banned the drug.").

17 NC Court of Appeals Upholds Grooms' Sentence, WECT6, Raycom Media (Copyright 2017) (2013), http://www.wect.com/story/23578905/nc-court-of-appeals-upholds-grooms-sentence.

18 *State v. Pierce*, 216 N.C. App. 377 (2011). Co-counsel was Doug Carriker.

19 Al Capone, the notorious mobster who was reputed to have killed many people, never spent a day in prison for murder. Skilled investigators and prosecutors managed instead to convict him of multiple counts of tax evasion and incarcerate him on a lengthy sentence behind bars. *This Day in History: Capone Goes to Prison*, A&E Television Networks LLC (Copyright 2017), (Oct. 17, 2016) http://www.history.com/this-day-in-history/capone-goes-to-prison. ("On this day in 1931, gangster Al Capone is sentenced to eleven years for tax evasion and fined $80,000, signaling the downfall of one of the most notorious criminals of the 1920s and 1930s."). Similarly, many people believe O.J. Simpson killed his ex-wife and her boyfriend, but he was acquitted of killing both after a double murder trial. O. J. Simpson Trial: Where Are They Now? ABC News, (June 12, 2014), http://abcnews.go.com/US/oj-simpson-trial-now/story?id=17377772. While he escaped that crime, O.J. did serve time in prison for an armed robbery where no one was injured. ("[Simpson] was arrested in September 2007 during a botched robbery in Las Vegas when he led a group of men into a hotel and casino to steal his own sports memorabilia at gunpoint. He was charged with a number of felony counts, including kidnapping and armed robbery.")

20 Houston Mitchell, *Steve Jobs Used Wayne Gretzky as Inspiration*, Sports Now: Sports from Los Angeles and Beyond, *Los Angeles Times*, Oct. 6, 2011, http://latimesblogs.latimes.com/sports_blog/2011/10/steve-jobs-used-wayne-gretzky-as-inspiration.html ("[Steve Jobs] gave a glimpse into the concept he believed in at the end of the Macworld Conference and Expo in January 2007 by quoting hockey legend Wayne Gretzky: 'There's an old Wayne Gretzky quote that I love. "I skate to where the puck is going to be, not where it has been." And we've always tried to do that at Apple. Since the very beginning. And we always will.'")

21 *Ohio v. Lovelace*, 137 Ohio App. 3rd 206, 217 (1999).

22 *State v. Anthony Pierce*, 365 N.C. 560 (2012).

23 *State. v McCoy*, 360 N.C. 290, 628 S.E.2d 384 (2006).

24 *State v. Mortimer*, 142 N.C. App. 321 (2001).

25 Columbine High School Shootings Fast Facts, CNN Library, Cable News Network, Turner Broadcasting System Inc., (April 5, 2017), http://www.cnn.com/2013/09/18/us/

columbine-high-school-shootings-fast-facts/index.html ("Here is some background information about the deaths of 13 people at Columbine High School in Littleton, Colorado, on April 20, 1999.")

26 N.C.G.S. § 14–277.1 during the relevant time period as follows (it has since been amended).

Figure Credits

Fig. 3.2: New Hanover County Sheriff's Office CSI, "Grooms' Windshield," New Hanover County Sheriff's Office, 2011.

Fig. 3.3: New Hanover County Sheriff's Office CSI, "Grooms' Back Window," New Hanover County Sheriff's Office, 2011.

Fig. 3.4: North Carolina Highway Patrol, "Grooms Field Sobriety Test," North Carolina Department of Public Safety, 2011.

Fig. 3.5: New Hanover County Sheriff's Office CSI, "Straw from Grooms' Car," New Hanover County Sheriff's Office, 2011.

Fig. 3.6: New Hanover County Sheriff's Office CSI, "Grooms' Nose," New Hanover County Sheriff's Office, 2011.

Fig. 3.7: Copyright © 2012 by Gray Television, Inc. Reprinted with permission.

Fig. 3.9: North Carolina Highway Patrol, "Grooms at Arrest Roadside," North Carolina Department of Public Safety, 2011.

Fig. 3.10: Wilmington Police Department CSI, "Rich Matthews' Crashed Patrol Vehicle," Wilmington Police Department, 2009.

Fig. 3.11: Copyright © 2010 by Gray Television, Inc. Reprinted with permission.

Fig. 3.12: Copyright © 2011 by Gannett Company, Inc. Reprinted with permission.

Chapter 4

The Cost of Silence

I n this section, we look at the importance of putting the right person on trial as we study the "Some Other Dude Did It" defense. We also see how defendants get away with their crimes for weeks, months, and even years when others choose to remain silent. In a place where speaking up can get a witness killed, few come forward to help. And silence on the part of neighbors in fear of reprisal, as well as complicit government officials, proves to be even more deadly.

State v. Delgado[1]

"If I am dead, Roger did it." That is what Melissa Mooney said to her boss, Larry Bonney, special agent in charge of the Wilmington field office of the FBI, just two weeks before she was found murdered in the sanctity of her own home.

When Melissa made this statement, she had just reached the front door of the courthouse, the place she went for the purposes of seeking a divorce from Roger Mooney. She had been so afraid of how Roger might react that she had asked Larry to accompany her. While the proceeding went smoothly and the couple parted amicably, agreeing to equitably divide their property and share custody of their only child, four-year-old Samantha, Melissa was still fearful.

A year earlier, Larry noticed a bruise on Melissa's face. What happened and was she okay? Melissa confided in her boss that her husband, Roger, had become mad again. Did she want to leave him? Yes, she did. Melissa further confided in Larry that it had never been love. Roger and Melissa had met at a mutual friend's wedding a few years earlier. A quick affair and pregnancy followed. They decided to do the right thing, in their minds, and get married and raise the baby together.

Larry pulled some strings to get Melissa a nice apartment around the corner from the FBI office, a nondescript building in the suburbs where seven agents conducted bank robbery investigations and background checks that they routinely performed to support the local sheriff and police agencies. Melissa wanted a divorce and to start her life over with her daughter, whom she called Sammy. Moving out was the first step: North Carolina law requires that a couple live separate and apart for one year before they are lawfully allowed to file for divorce. Melissa was getting her house in order.

Roger was a Marine, a sergeant at Camp Lejeune, 75 minutes north of Wilmington in Jacksonville, North Carolina. He was physically imposing and a good shot. Despite keeping his composure in court, Roger was not happy with the prospect of divorce. Fellow Marines would later say that he used his wife's picture for target practice, telling his men, "I shoot better when she's in the bull's-eye."

Two weeks later, on August 5, 1999, Melissa was late for work. She was never late, and of all days, this should not have been one of them. Most of her co-workers had shown up on this Thursday morning in casual clothes, ready to help with the heavy lifting. Melissa was moving from her small apartment to a new home that she had just purchased in the Apple Valley subdivision in Castle Hayne, a community just north of Wilmington. Her work family would be there for her.

An hour passed. It was 10:00 a.m., and there was no sign of Melissa. The mood at the office was tense. This was out of character; at the very least, Melissa would have called in. The decision was made to send out four agents to do a safety check. Two went to her old apartment nearby, but there was no answer and no sign of anyone at home. Two other agents, Paul Cox and John Wolsky, traveled out to Castle Hayne to see if Melissa was perhaps at her new home.

When Paul and John arrived at Melissa's new home, both men became immediately concerned. Melissa's car was in the driveway. There was a big, muddy boot print on the front of the door near the handle. It appeared that the door had been kicked in then put back in place on its frame. Paul was calling Melissa on his mobile phone, but there was no answer. He called Larry. No time for a search warrant: these were exigent circumstances. Paul went in while John covered him.

"Sammy? Melissa? Sammy? Melissa?" Paul kept yelling their names as he walked through the hall. Paul didn't know it, but Sammy was not responding because she was up the road in Jacksonville. Melissa was there but could no longer speak. Paul saw her body as he entered the master bedroom. Wedged between a bare mattress that had been knocked off its bed frame and the freshly painted walls of her new home was Melissa's nude and lifeless corpse. She had been strangled to death, both through throttling (hands clasped around the neck) and with a ligature (most likely a telephone cord). She was 28 years old.

Paul knew that he was not only looking at the body of a good friend, he was standing in the middle of a crime scene. He backed out of the room and did a safety sweep of the house as he made his way back to the entrance. At the front door he told his partner what he had just observed. John immediately threw up.

Processing the Scene

The FBI does not usually conduct murder investigations. That duty falls to the local law enforcement agency with jurisdiction over the crime scene. In this case, it was the New Hanover County Sheriff's Office (NHSO). Paul called them directly to keep the call off the scanners and away from media attention. The first officer, Deputy Steven Blissett, arrived 20 minutes later. This new neighborhood was not yet on county maps, and few deputies knew it existed.

Melissa's FBI family descended upon the scene, along with numerous CSI detectives and others from the NHSO and agreed to divide up the responsibilities. The FBI fanned out to conduct knock-and-talk interviews of the approximately 70 homes that had recently been built in the sprawling neighborhood. None of the neighbors reported having heard or seen anything and were alarmed by the sudden police presence.

Meanwhile, the NHSO methodically collected the physical evidence in and around Melissa's home. Melissa was now literally a body of evidence. Her nudity suggested that she may have been sexually assaulted. While the medical examiner found no semen or other signs of injury, Dr. John Butts would later testify that no such evidence is found in approximately 50 percent of adult rape cases. It remained our theory, however, that her attacker had sexually assaulted her.

Strangulation is the most intimate form of murder. It requires close proximity to the victim and almost always occurs between a victim and defendant who are acquainted. A gun can be shot across the room. Even a knife can be wielded indiscriminately. Choking the life out of someone takes several minutes.

Whatever the reason for Melissa's killing, it was not robbery. Her purse containing $80 and her car keys were plainly visible to detectives, and her car was in the driveway. Melissa had apparently been watching a movie, ironically titled *Cruel Intentions,* and physical evidence suggested she watched it alone. Fingerprints on the Pepsi can and DNA on the popcorn bag in front of the TV came back only to her. This did not appear to be a date that had gone bad.

Investigators were drawn to the unplugged phone cord found in the kitchen. In addition to believing that it may have been used as a murder weapon, disabling the phone also had the benefit of cutting off Melissa's ability to call for help. Investigators also found burned baby blankets in the kitchen. The killer had apparently placed the blankets on the stove in an attempt to burn the house down as he left. Because the blankets contained a fire retardant, they failed to light. Whoever committed this crime was cool, calm, and deliberate enough to be conscious of evidence left behind.

Boot prints on the kitchen linoleum matched the boot print on the door. There was also a boot print found nearly 200 feet from the home in a sandy lot. It, too, matched the boot print on the door and was located near sandy tire tracks that were left on the hardtop surface running past Melissa's home. The working theory was that the killer had parked the vehicle, walked to Melissa's home, kicked in the door, killed her, and then drove away.

The Target of the Investigation: Roger Mooney

Melissa was a low-risk victim. She had a good job, lived in a nice neighborhood that few even knew existed, and was killed in her own home. It was originally thought that her death was the result of intimate partner violence. When a woman like Melissa is murdered, there is more than a 50 percent chance that she had breakfast with her killer at some point in her life.[2]

The FBI was sure they had their man. The history of domestic violence and the contentious divorce certainly provided Roger with a motive. He also had the physical strength needed to kick in a door and choke his wife to death with his bare hands. A call was quickly made to the Naval Criminal Intelligence Service (NCIS) at Camp Lejeune and Roger was pulled out of the morning lineup.

Roger expressed disbelief upon hearing the news. He wanted to be the first to tell his daughter. "Where is she?" the investigators demanded. To everyone's great relief, Sammy was safe at a

FIGURE 4.1   Grocery store surveillance footage captured Roger and Sammy in the early evening hours the night before Melissa's murder.

babysitter's house. "Where were you last night?" investigators asked. Roger explained that he and Sammy had shopped for hamburgers and ice cream at a local supermarket and had gone home to enjoy the meal. This fact was confirmed on store surveillance cameras. "Did anyone else see you after you left the store?" The answer was no.

Undigested popcorn in Melissa's stomach, phone records, and the condition of Melissa's body all pointed to the murder taking place sometime between midnight and 3:00 a.m. This would have given Roger more than enough time to travel to and from Jacksonville, either with or without his daughter, to get away with the perfect crime.

Would he be willing to take a polygraph and provide a DNA sample? Surprisingly, he complied. Roger failed the polygraph exam. He claimed to be nervous and distraught. Agents offered him a second opportunity, and he failed again.

Back at the scene, Roger's DNA was found on the mattress. Although this initially seemed like compelling evidence, investigators knew that this was Roger and Melissa's former marital bed. As DNA has no time stamp, they could not determine when the semen had been left. It could have been hours or years old. This evidence was not going to help them solve the crime.

Investigators pulled cameras from the Marine base and from any surveillance cameras that pointed toward the route between Melissa's and Roger's homes. Roger's car did not appear on it. They also came up empty trying to compare the tread and boot prints near the scene to Roger's tires and shoes. They simply were not a match.

For the next several months, investigators turned Roger's world upside down in an effort to unbury his past. They spoke to fellow Marines, ex-girlfriends, and others he came in contact with, but were unable to prove that Roger killed Melissa. In fact, it became clear that Roger had a motive for her to be alive. As a newly single dad, his career as a Marine would be greatly hampered since travel was now out of the question. Agent Bonney summed it up when he said, "It should be Roger, but it isn't."

Widening the Circle

Investigators follow a matrix in playing the process of elimination when considering suspects. Intimate partners are the obvious focus, the bull's-eye in the target, for the death of a woman killed in her own home. If Roger was not the killer, the next most likely suspects were men whom Melissa had dated in the first year of her newfound freedom. A man she had met online, the builder who reviewed the punch list in her new house, and a married FBI agent (whom she met while on assignment in the mountains of North Carolina, looking for Olympic bomber Eric Rudolph), all became suspects. She had sexual relations with each of them. They were cleared of any criminal wrongdoing, but suffered the consequences of having their adultery revealed to their spouses and coworkers.

Investigators also moved out to the next circle of acquaintances, to interview people whom Melissa had casually met at a coffee shop, Blockbuster video, or grocery store. When their phone numbers popped up in her phone records, agents appeared at their doors asking questions. The newspaper delivery driver and mailman were even interviewed. Nothing. The trail went cold.

When the crime scene had originally been processed for DNA evidence and fingerprints, the NHSO obtained numerous samples. As the model home in the neighborhood, dozens of real estate agents and potential buyers had come in to touch the Formica countertops, twist open the door handles, and test the sturdiness of a doorframe. In doing so they would have inadvertently shed their hair on the carpets. Through a process of elimination, nearly all the fingerprints and hairs were accounted for. The hairs that could not be matched to any of these interviewed subjects were run in the Combined DNA Index System (CODIS) database. No hits. Investigators had already run a list of registered sex offenders and newly released prisoners in the area, and no suspects had surfaced. Investigators were out of leads.

Two Years Later

At the two-year anniversary of Melissa's murder, the FBI and NHSO held a press conference to announce that they were reopening the investigation. An $80,000 reward was offered for new information, and the FBI flew in dozens of agents to help with the investigation. They fanned out around the much more developed neighborhood and reinterviewed some of the same people who initially provided information two years earlier. A spirit of cooperation had gripped the residents. A young mother was dead and everyone wanted to help.

An agent from Kansas City was tasked with knocking on the door of Ana and Tyrone Delgado. Their home was just down the street from Melissa's, and they had been home on the Thursday morning that her body was discovered. They had even watched the investigators process the crime scene. One crime scene photo taken in the direction that the boot print had been traveling showed the Delgado home in the distance.

Paul Cox and another agent, Craig Ackley, had knocked on the Delgados' door within an hour of discovering Melissa and had talked to the married couple. At the time, nothing seemed out of the ordinary. Notes from the interview reveal that Tyrone Delgado was cooperative during the 1999 interview. But now, in 2001, he was combative. The agent was concerned by his attitude and shared this information with Paul. In this agent's view, Delgado was acting "hinky." Paul obtained Delgado's Social Security number and conducted a background check. What he saw horrified him.

Outrunning a Past

Five years earlier, "Laura," a single mother of four, answered a knock on her door. She was alone and would be for the next two years, as the uninvited guest well knew, since he had been cellmates with her incarcerated boyfriend. Now this young, pregnant woman was left to fend for herself in a little town called Leesville, Louisiana.

As she slid off the chain, the door flew open and Tyrone Delgado grabbed her by the throat. She heard every bone in her neck crack. For the next several agonizing minutes, she was brought in and out of consciousness as this stranger controlled her breathing by squeezing her neck and pinching the airway around her nose while covering her mouth with his large hand. He kept

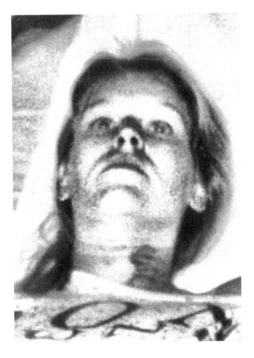 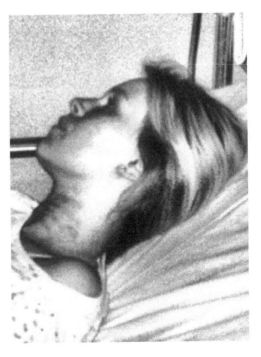

FIGURES 4.2 AND 4.3   Laura in hospital after attack.

saying, "look into my eyes." He removed her pants and penetrated her with his fingers after he failed to maintain an erection.

When he was finished, he was immediately concerned about what he had done. He quite literally threw money at her and told her not to talk. After he fled, Laura called the police. Delgado was apprehended two months later while on the run with his high school girlfriend, Ana, in Oklahoma. He was extradicted back to Louisiana to face sexual assault and burglary charges. The charges were dismissed when Laura signed a document indicating she did not wish to proceed against Delgado.

When Paul Cox listened to Laura's audiotaped interview following her assault, he felt like he was listening to Melissa's ghost. The attack of this vulnerable young woman, it turned out, fit a familiar pattern. Delgado had enlisted in the Navy and traveled around the country. Wherever he went, he left a wake of terror in his path. Women were sexually assaulted, only to have the cases dismissed or pled down to misdemeanors in exchange for payments and Delgado's agreement to leave town. Delgado was never convicted of a felony. Accordingly, his DNA was not in the CODIS database nor was he a registered sex offender.

More Crimes Lead to More Evidence

Agents with the FBI went to question Delgado, and he refused to cooperate or talk to them or to provide a DNA sample. North Carolina law today says that if a person is arrested for a felony, the state draws their DNA to keep on file. Back in 2001, however, a DNA sample could be drawn only after a person was convicted of a felony. Delgado had been charged many times but never convicted of more than misdemeanors. He was not going to voluntarily give his DNA to anyone.

The NHSO was ultimately able to draw Delgado's DNA, but not for a few more months, and only after another terrible crime occurred. Delgado shot and killed a teenager and seriously injured another as he sat in the backseat of their car on the way to purchase beer for them. The young man who lived testified that the shooting was because Delgado felt disrespected; Delgado claimed that it was self-defense. The jury ended up not knowing who to believe, and they acquitted Delgado of shooting and paralyzing the young man. The jury could not agree on a verdict for the murder of the driver, and Delgado ultimately pled to involuntary manslaughter. He received just over two years in prison.

This conviction, while clearly not justice for the the two young men, led to some big breaks in Melissa's death investigation. First, the state now had the ability to collect Delgado's DNA and compare it to DNA found at the crime scene. A hair fragment found on Melissa's bed was a mitochondrial match to Delgado. Unlike Roger and others, Delgado had no explanation for why his hair would be in her home. Delgado denied ever setting foot in the home and, in fact, the home had not yet been built when Delgado had completed construction of his own home—leaving him with no reason to tour the model home.

The second big break came when inmates who were serving time with Delgado came forward. He had bragged to them that he killed Melissa and stole the bedding to conceal his crime. The absence of sheets and pillows had never been publicly released and was a detail that only the killer would know.

Despite having this new evidence, most felt that authorities still did not have enough evidence to convict Delgado, and he was not arrested for Melissa's murder. After serving out his manslaughter sentence, Delgado was released from custody and returned to Leesville, where Ana had moved after his conviction. Delgado wasted little time in assaulting her, believing that she had been unfaithful during his incarceration. During the assault, he held a sword to her stomach and threatened to plunge it in, only refraining from killing her when she lied and told him she was pregnant with his unborn child.

But there was another aspect of the assault that proved to be even more interesting. As with Laura, Delgado had controlled Ana's breathing by pinching her nose and covering her mouth. Delgado had bragged to the other inmates in jail that this is what he had also done to Melissa. By

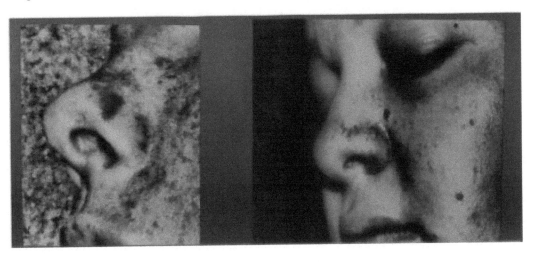

FIGURE 4.4   Dr. Bill Oliver's imaging of Melissa Mooney's nose (l) and Ana Cruz Delgado's nose (r).

using a special imaging technique to review the autopsy photos, the same distinctive bruising pattern around Melissa's nose was consistent with the bruising to Ana's nose. This was a true signature crime—a bizarre and unique style of attack. It was also a detail that corroborated the jailhouse informants: Melissa's internal bruising to the nose was unknown, even to investigators, and Ana's bruising had not yet happened when Delgado made the statements in jail.

After Delgado assaulted her, Ana went into hiding and was provided witness protection by the FBI. For the first time, she was ready to cooperate and disclosed new details about her husband. He had been abusive for years. She was raped on a weekly basis and was now increasingly concerned that Delgado was sexually assaulting the couple's daughters, who were approaching adolescence.

Ana also no longer covered for her husband as she had when first questioned by the FBI. Delgado had a tendency to wander at night, and she could not be certain that he was by her side when Melissa was killed. She also shared that Delgado was paranoid about the investigation and fired a gunshot into the roof over Ana's head when she questioned him about why he had been evasive with the FBI agent at the two-year anniversary. Delgado had cut out press clippings of the case to

FIGURE 4.5   Relation between Mooney and Delgado houses.

follow details of the investigation. He destroyed the boots he frequently wore at the time by burning them in his backyard after he saw investigators take cast impressions of footprints in the field near Melissa's home. It was later determined that the boot print was consistent in size with Delgado's.

It was at about this point in the investigation, at the end of 2004, that I became the elected district attorney. I had heard my boss and other senior prosecutors talk about the case over the years and now wanted to see if, taken in full, we had enough evidence. The clock was ticking, and a zebra does not change its stripes. Delgado was still assaulting women, mostly those who were alone and vulnerable, and who did not want to cooperate when it came time to testify in court.

After listening to all of the evidence, I made the decision to send the case to the grand jury. They returned a true bill of indictment, charging him with first-degree murder and burglary in Melissa's death. I utilized a very rare provision to seal the indictment, meaning that their decision to indict Delgado would not be made public until he was arrested. He was found in Leesville and taken without incident. He was extradited back to Wilmington to face trial.

The Trial

After firing his attorney, fighting with others, and filing motions against the FBI accusing the government of kidnapping him, the case against Delgado finally reached a courtroom in 2008, nearly three years after his arrest and more than nine years since Melissa's body had been discovered.

Expert witnesses of every stripe testified. DNA experts, footwear experts, bruise-patterning specialists, medical examiners, and crime scene investigators came from the FBI's "dream team," with cases on their resumés that included O.J. Simpson, Scott Peterson, Wayne Williams (the Atlanta child murderer), and Ted Kaczynski. The crime scene investigators who re-examined Melissa's home in August 2001 were the same professionals who were called to process the evidence at the World Trade Center the following month in response to the 9/11 terrorist attacks.

Home movies of Delgado kicking and practicing karate were admitted to illustrate how he knocked down Melissa's front door. (Note how Delgado's stamping kick is consistent with the size, height, and direction of the boot print found on the door.) His hulking physique and knowledge of pressure points also left no doubt that he was capable of rendering Melissa, and his other victims, physically helpless to the point where they would have no defensive wounds.

FIGURES 4.6 AND 4.7   Boot print on Melissa Mooney's front door (l) and Delgado practicing martial arts kicks at his residence on a home video (r).

The best witnesses, however, came from around the country. They were women who often lingered in the shadows of their respective hometowns, seemingly invisible. After a nationwide search, the FBI found a dozen women who were separated from each other by hundreds of miles and by many years. None had ever met each other, yet all told remarkably similar stories. The one thing they all shared in common was an encounter with Delgado they would never forget. In short, Delgado had a MOM (motive, opportunity, and means).

Melissa could no longer speak for herself, but these women were able to testify in a courtroom, all for the first time. Judge Charles Henry conducted a 404(b) hearing to compare details we knew about Melissa and evidence at the crime scene to the crimes these women endured. Ultimately, of the nine women who were brought to town, Judge Henry ruled that six would be allowed to testify. In comparing 20 points of similarity between their assaults and what we knew about Melissa's murder, there were as many as 17 common factors. The chart that follows illustrates why their cases were admitted to show Delgado's modus operandi, motive for attack, plan, preparation, premeditation, and deliberation.

Delgado raised the SODDI defense and made identity the key issue in trial. It is one thing for a defendant to claim that someone else committed a crime, but it is quite another for investigators and prosecutors to point the finger directly at a different suspect. All signs initially pointed to Roger Mooney, and we had plenty of documentation suggesting that he alone killed his ex-wife.

State v. Delgado	Tracy 1992 Bremerton, WA	Laura August 13, 1994 Leesville, LA	Melissa Mooney August 6, 1999 Wilmington, NC	Patricia February 6, 2002 Wilmington, NC	Ana November 10, 2003 Leesville, LA	Gabrielle July 20, 2004 Leesville, LA
Victim						
Vulnerable	X	X	X	X	X	X
Alone (w/children)	X	X	X	X	X	
Phone disabled	X	No Phone	X		X	Missing
D aware of victim	X	X	X	X	X	X
Before Attack						
Close proximity	X	X	X	X	X	X
Darkness		X	X	X	X	X
Impulsive, no plan	X	X	X	X	X	X
During Attack						
Forced/unlawful entry	X	X	X			X
Overpowered	X	X	X	X	X	X
Grab wrist	X	X	X	X	X	
Choking strangling	X	X	X		X	X
Threatens life	X	X	Murdered	Interrupted	X	Interrupted
After Attack						
D claims consent	Dating			X	Married	X
Evidence conscious		X	X	X		
D enlists help mom/wife		X	X	X	X	
Sexual component						
Forced sex motive	X	X	X	X	X	X
No semen noted	X	X	X	X	X	X
No vaginal trauma noted	X	X	X	X	X	X
No lubricant(s) noted	X	X	X	X	X	X

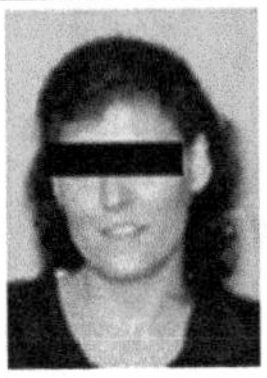

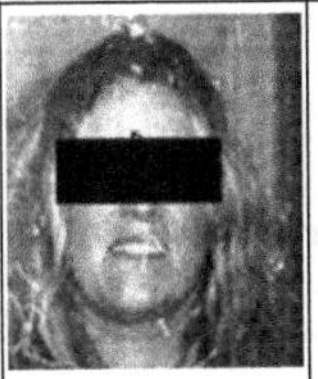

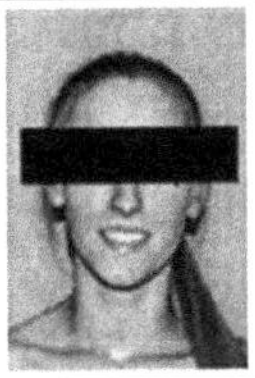

FIGURE 4.8   Delgado victim chart.

Even when we indicted Delgado, it would have been just as easy to walk into the grand jury room and make them believe that Roger, and not the stranger next door, was responsible for Melissa's murder. Roger may not have been a loveable person, but he did not kill his ex-wife.

The investigators and prosecutors who sought justice for Melissa over an excruciating 10-year struggle were only able to slay the SODDI pig because we moved slowly and deliberately, testing and retesting our initial assumptions against the evidence that we did and did not have. In chapter 3, we saw how 404(b) evidence could be used to show someone's intent, MO, and premeditation and deliberation. With Delgado, we did the same and also used the 404(b) evidence to reveal the identity of a ruthless and sadistic serial rapist who strangled his last victim to death.

After a nine-week trial that involved over 80 witnesses and 600 pieces of evidence, the jury convicted Delgado of first-degree murder and burglary. They found that he committed felony murder with premeditation and deliberation in choking the life out of a woman who was spending her very first night as his new neighbor. Delgado was sentenced to life without parole, and he will spend the rest of his days behind bars.

When to Talk and When to Remain Silent

Talking to the press while an investigation is ongoing is a bad practice. It is important to keep some details confidential in order to be able to corroborate or impeach witnesses (like the jailhouse informants) who may come forward days, or even years, later. Moreover, had prosecutors and agents publicly staked themselves to a position, they may have been less willing to keep an open mind when facts emerge that change that theory (think back to the Duke Lacrosse case from chapter 2).

It would have been easy to try Roger Mooney in the court of public opinion, but we would have missed out on prosecuting Delgado in the court of law. As proud as the team was to remove a dangerous predator from the streets, we took equal pride in knowing we did not convict an innocent person. When the trial was over, the investigation and trial received substantial national press.[3] The investigation and conviction of Delgado was personal to the FBI and was recognized by FBI Director Robert Muller when he presented the team with the Director's award in Washington, DC, for the top criminal prosecution in the country for 2009.

I am frequently asked whether Delgado's crimes would have been uncovered if Melissa had not been a member of the FBI. The short answer is no. The FBI expended extraordinary resources solving Melissa's murder and the significant lengths they went to are not afforded to every case. If we had these resources in every case, we would solve more of them and keep our communities safer.

Delgado, like James Bradley, a serial killer who you will meet in chapter 5, preyed upon women and those who had limited financial means, few social networks of support, and, in some instances, substance dependencies. Both men used physical isolation (remote areas where the victim can scream and no one will hear) or social isolation (prostitutes and drug addicts can scream and few

FIGURE 4.9   Ann Curry interviews Paul Cox and Ben David on the *Today Show* prior to the airing of a *Dateline NBC* episode about Melissa's murder.

FIGURE 4.10   The Delgado prosecution team. Pictured from left: Jon David, Paul Cox, FBI Director Robert Mueller, Ben David, Tim Flynn, and Craig Ackley.

will listen) to carry out their attacks. The end came for both men when they chose victims who broke the mold and had friends and colleagues that would make sure the case remained in front of everyone in the criminal justice system.[4]

There is a second larger point to this story and it is a cautionary tale for police and prosecutors. After he brutally raped Laura, Delgado fled the jurisdiction. He was arrested in Oklahoma and extradited back to Louisiana to face the charges. Delgado's mother, a prominent woman in the community who had befriended the chief prosecutor, agreed to pay $2,500 for Laura's pain and suffering in exchange for Delgado agreeing to leave town. The agreement dismissing the criminal case, which was also witnessed by an elected school board member, was signed not only by Laura but by the elected district attorney himself.

Had Delgado's past crimes been handled appropriately when he first began his reign of terror, he would not have outrun them all the way to Wilmington to kill Melissa on August 5, 1999. "Get out of town pleas," as they are sometimes called, may protect the local community but not the rest of the world. It is a complete violation of our oath as public officials to fail to protect the public, especially when the victims are voiceless and the defendants are politically connected.

As prosecutors and investigators, our client is not the individual victim, like Laura, standing in front of us. She may be so afraid of her attacker and the system itself, to say nothing of being financially desperate (Laura had four children at the time of her attack and was living in public housing), that she would be willing to take money in exchange for her abuser being allowed to walk away. DAs represent the people, and that includes not only the community that elects them, but society as a whole. Officials in Leesville, like those in so many other places Delgado perpetrated his violence across our country, decided to let a guilty man walk, and did not listen to the voiceless in their community.

Sadly, the inability to speak up for the voiceless is widespread. It includes not only public officials in cases involving sexual violence against forgotten members of the community but neighbors who are unwilling to report the street violence that happens in their front yards. In a place of high poverty where talking can get you killed, the cost of silence can be even more deadly. Consider these next two cases.

State v. Porter[5]

The shooter moved lazily through the morning light, past playing children, barking dogs, and a gathering of grandmothers. It was 9:30 a.m. on July 27, 2012, at the height of summer on a clear and hot Friday morning in Creekwood.

The end came quickly. When Brian Grant opened the front door to loud knocking, an assailant pressed a revolver against his nose and fired without warning. The slug traveled through Brian's head and transected his spine, killing him instantly. He was 30 years old. The assailant fled to a parked car and drove off as several residents looked on.

Brian grew up in Wilmington, the son of a longshoreman and a loving mother who had raised a close family of five children. Brian was staying in Creekwood only because his girlfriend, Ebony Hines, lived there. Brian's offense, if there was one at all, appeared to be that he loved a girl who others desired. At 28 years old, Ebony was a lifelong resident of Creekwood and already had three children by three different men, ages 14, 13, and 8, at the time of Brian's death. Two of the fathers were in prison, and the third had been murdered four years earlier in an unsolved homicide in the neighborhood. Now Brian was dating Ebony and helping to raise her children, together with his seven-year-old son, with the assistance of his parents.

We later learned that the night before the murder, Nashid Porter had words with Brian. Porter, who grew up with Ebony and now lived about 45 minutes away in rural Duplin County, was couch surfing at a friend's house, Obediah Hester, who lived across the street. The ensuing shouting match between Porter and Brian had been broken up, and the two men went their separate ways. This was apparently the sole motive for Porter to shoot Brian in the face the next morning.

Police immediately responded to the scene, but no one in the neighborhood wanted to help. In the "Ain't No Snitch" culture that was as much a part of Creekwood as oxygen itself, anyone caught talking to authorities might risk a fate similar to Brian's, who now lay lifeless at the threshold of his girlfriend's home. Nonetheless, the shooter's identity and the description of his vehicle emerged through hearsay accounts emanating from the crowd gathered behind the crime scene tape.

Porter spent the previous night in Obediah's home and fled in a distinctive vehicle, heading in the direction of Duplin County immediately after the shooting. The WPD was now looking for both Porter and Obediah. Meanwhile, crime scene investigators processed the scene, dusting for fingerprints on the door and collecting cigarette butts, a ball cap, and a chair for DNA testing. They also canvassed the area for any video cameras that might have caught the incident on film.

Obediah's uncle, Patrick Bragg, was home when detectives arrived but claimed not to have seen anything. Patrick called Obediah, who was out shopping at the time of the incident. Obediah returned to Creekwood and reported that Porter stayed with him the night before and had an argument with Brian. Porter was still at his house when he left to go shopping that morning. Surveillance video from a sportswear store confirmed that Obediah was far away when the shooting occurred. Law enforcement had little help and few leads.

Porter remained on the run for seven weeks before being apprehended by US Marshals in Fayetteville, North Carolina, with more than $2,500 in his pocket. He had changed his cell phone account several times to defeat tracking devices and had sold his car to a junk yard to be crushed within days of the incident. He immediately lawyered up and said nothing.

The Case's Journey through the System

When police file a warrant, they only need probable cause to believe that a defendant has committed the offense in order to make an arrest. The burden of proof for arrest is by a preponderance of the evidence (when the scales of justice tip slightly to the side of guilt) that it is more likely than not that the defendant committed the crime. Porter was charged with first-degree murder under theories of premeditated and felony murder (a murder committed during the commission of another felony). He was also charged with possession of a firearm by a convicted felon (he had been convicted of dealing drugs and violent felony assaults in the past) and firing into an occupied dwelling inflicting serious injury (because he fired through the threshold of the home that was also occupied by Ebony's 13-year-old daughter in order to kill Brian).

Bond must be set in every case except when the defendant faces the death penalty. Not every case of first-degree murder qualifies for this maximum punishment. There must be exceptional circumstances (called "aggravating factors") that qualify the defendant for the death penalty (this will be discussed in greater detail in chapter 5). Because there were no aggravating factors in Brian's killing, the state did not seek the death penalty and bond had to be set.

When setting a bond, judges must factor in two important considerations: 1) risk of flight: that is, the likelihood that the defendant will not show up for court proceedings, and 2) dangerousness to the community, which considers someone's criminal record and the nature of the offense. Bonds are secured or unsecured. If they are secured, a defendant needs to post the money or have a bail bondsman post the money for a percentage. If the bond is unsecured, the defendant is released on his word to reappear for court and will have to pay the bond only if he fails to appear in court.

Upon announcing to the court that my office would not seek the death penalty, a secured bond was set. Porter remained in the New Hanover County jail to await trial.

The evidence that we collected came back from the state crime lab after more than 15 months of testing, not an unusual wait for the busy crime lab. No physical evidence linked Porter to the crime scene. During the months that the evidence was at the lab, Porter sat in jail awaiting the test results. When the results came back, they were immediately turned over to the defense attorney, who now knew, like my prosecutors, that we had no physical evidence tying Porter to the murder.

Unlike most murders, the killing of Brian Grant was not perpetrated in secret. It was committed in broad daylight in front of several people. But Porter, who was originally from Creekwood, understood that people would not be coming forward. He was right. Prosecutors had only the sworn statement of Obediah who, acknowledging great risk to himself, provided some help by confirming that Porter was staying with him. But Obediah did not witness the incident itself.

There was still the damning circumstantial evidence. Porter fled from the scene (a jury is instructed that they may consider flight as consciousness of guilt, but standing alone it is not sufficient for conviction). It was also true that Porter changed his cell phone numerous times to avoid detection by the US Marshals tracking him and was found with a large amount of cash at the time of arrest. He also scrapped an entirely operational car just to destroy a vehicle that had been seen leaving the scene of the crime. Finally, in his first recorded jail calls to his girlfriend, Porter did not profess his innocence but was obsessed with learning the identity of any witness who might testify against him and with recovering the cash seized from him at the time of his arrest.

Still, the state had very little evidence. Following the discovery from the lab that showed no new evidence, the motion to reduce the bond came from the defense attorney almost as fast as the bullet from Porter's gun. With no cooperating eyewitnesses and no physical evidence to link him to the killing, a superior court judge released Porter from jail under an unsecured bond on February 14, 2014. However, as a precautionary measure, he was placed on house arrest and was required to wear an ankle monitor with a GPS tracker to show the pretrial release office his whereabouts in real time. He was allowed to leave his residence if he found a job, but he could not have contact with Brian's family or any potential witness and could not possess weapons. His trial was set for later in the year, and, at this point, my prosecutors had serious questions about whether we had sufficient evidence to proceed to trial.

Porter Strikes Again

The phone rang at the New Hanover pretrial release office in the late night hours of November 12, 2014. A signal had been sent from Porter's ankle monitor indicating it had just been cut off in a remote wooded area near his home in Duplin County. An hour later, the Pender County 911 Center received a frantic call from Obediah's grandmother. She was calling from a car headed up I-40 toward Duplin County from Wilmington. In the car with her were two young men who had come to her instead of calling the authorities. They told her that they had just witnessed Porter execute Obediah behind an abandoned trailer near the chicken plant where Obediah and the two men had been working.

Once again, Porter had committed a heinous murder and again he was on the run. However, unlike in Brian's killing, two brave witnesses were willing to tell detectives what they had seen. There was also physical evidence placing Porter at the murder scene: the GPS tracking device showed him, in real time, traveling without authorization from his home to the crime scene, then leaving the area immediately after the killing. It also showed him going deep into the woods to cut off the monitoring device. Detectives found the device in a hole a few hours after the incident. Obediah had been shot 11 times at close range. Porter then bludgeoned Obediah with a cinder block, just to make sure he was dead.

Porter was captured after a week of being on the run, during which he again changed his phone number multiple times in an attempt to evade detection by the same US Marshals who apprehended him two years earlier for Brian's murder. Porter was brought into court again, this time with no bond. He now faced the prospect of the death penalty in Duplin County. Obediah's murder case was aggravated because he was a state's witness and the murder was especially heinous, atrocious, and cruel. Additionally, if we were able to convict Porter in Brian's murder, he would then have the additional aggravating factor of being previously convicted of murder.

Porter Bucks Up

Evidence in the Duplin County case was much stronger than the one in New Hanover County. The plea offer Porter was now receiving was also much more severe. Duplin County DA Ernie Lee and I joined forces. In our joint plea offer, Porter would plead guilty to both first-degree murders and receive two consecutive life without parole sentences. He would die in prison. In exchange for avoiding the prospect of the death penalty in Obediah's murder, Porter would be finally taking responsibility for killing Brian.

Having shot two people, Porter now began shooting the messenger. When Porter's court-appointed attorney in New Hanover County, a capital case litigator with over 25 years' experience, suggested that he take the state's offer, Porter fired her. When a second skilled attorney was appointed, Porter fired her as well, and then he filed a restraining order against her, contending that she was harassing him by coming to the jail to speak with him about his case. A third attorney from the Duplin County case was appointed to work on both cases, but Porter had him removed from the New Hanover case when he acknowledged to Porter that, while the evidence in Brian's killing was weak, Porter could not escape justice in Obediah's homicide.

Judge Charles Henry then gave Porter a stern warning: fire the next attorney and he would not provide Porter with another. Defendants are entitled to an attorney, but that right is not unlimited. Through conduct similar to that which Porter was exhibiting, defendants can forfeit the right to a court-appointed attorney and be required to hire one or represent themselves. When the fourth attorney, equally experienced, was appointed, Porter again asked for the attorney to be removed. Porter wanted to represent himself. Judge Henry granted that request but appointed standby counsel to answer legal and procedural questions at any time that Porter requested it. This attorney, however, could not question witnesses or make objections during trial. Judge Henry drafted a 25-page order detailing all of Porter's legal maneuvers to support the reasoning for forfeiture of the right to counsel.

Porter was also evaluated by a psychiatrist who determined that he was capable of proceeding to trial; Porter was neither "insane" (which refers to not being in one's right mind at the time of the crime) nor "incompetent" (which refers to not being in one's right mind at the time of trial and therefore not being able to assist in his or her own defense).

Porter, now representing himself, rejected the plea offer that DA Ernie Lee and I had offered. It was time to try him for his crimes. I decided that Brian's case would be tried first. Not only was it two years older than Obediah's murder, but, if he was convicted, this prior conviction for murder would be yet another aggravating factor that a future jury in Duplin County could consider in voting for the death penalty.

The Trial of Nashid Porter

It must have galled Porter, a man so obsessed with weakening the state's case by killing the only witness to the crime, to realize that he had actually made it even stronger with his subsequent actions. The first break came when the "Ain't No Snitch" code was violated. While it has always been the case that silence on the street meant that Porter had little to fear from potential witnesses, that code might be overridden by another one: blood is thicker than water. Patrick Bragg observed Brian's murder and did not want to cooperate. Now that Porter had killed Obediah, Patrick's nephew, he was willing to testify despite his subsequent arrest for selling heroin. He was serving a decade in the federal penitentiary and snitching is not popular in prison. However, Patrick declared, "what is right is right and what is wrong is wrong." He expressed great regret that his earlier silence had contributed to his nephew's death.

Our second big break came when another neighbor, Mikeya Love, also agreed to testify. She had seen everything. Later, she would be threatened in her neighborhood for helping the police, but she stood firm even in the face of adversity. Brian was a good man and so was Obediah. She had grown up with both Ebony and Obediah and knew Porter by name.

But the biggest break came in a pretrial ruling by the Court. "Forfeiture by wrongdoing" holds that a defendant should not benefit from his wrongful conduct by making a witness absent.[6] Obediah had provided two videotaped statements to police about the limited details of what he knew. (Judge Henry relied on the precedent of *State v. Hewson* where Gail Tice's 911 call was admitted into evidence as discussed in chapter 3.)

Judge Henry ruled that Rule 404(b) allowed the state to share with the jury the fact that Porter murdered Obediah to keep him from testifying about Brian's homicide. This rule of evidence applies not only to prior bad acts but also to subsequent bad acts, which become admissible using the same test and for the same purposes highlighted throughout this book. Porter became unglued, and over the course of the evidentiary hearing he was held in contempt of court six different times.

The "Maybe You Did It" Pig

Nashid Porter is a sovereign citizen, a person who puts the very process on trial by testing the jurisdiction of the court at every turn. Armed with his own warped view of right and wrong, the sovereign citizen believes that the rule of law does not apply to him. He then either delves into the finer points of the procedural process, raising every objection possible, or refuses to participate at all.

Oddly, Porter did both, first raising every conceivable right during pretrial hearings and jury selection, and then refusing to leave his holding cell to hear any of the evidence against him when the trial took place. His standby counsel was present during the entire trial and was made available to Porter for consultation at any time. He availed himself of this assistance on a handful of occasions and mostly instructed the attorney to stop bothering him.

As for the Bill of Rights, Porter invoked eight of the 10 amendments. He likely would have raised all ten but the Third (quartering soldiers) and Seventh (right to counsel in a civil trial) clearly did not apply. Here were some of his arguments:

> **First Amendment freedom of religion and the press:** Porter is a Muslim and insisted, under the guise of religious freedom, on wearing special garb that he had never requested for any of his court proceedings over the previous years. He also liberally quoted the Quran, invoking Sharia law, and chanted prayers over the court's admonition. Next, the two witnesses to Brian's killing, Mikeya Love and Patrick Bragg, were concerned about their identities being made public. Judge Henry ruled that Porter could wear his holy garb and further allowed the press to cover the testimony of Mikeya and Patrick provided that their faces were concealed during the broadcast.

> **Second Amendment right to bear arms:** Because Porter was a convicted felon, he forfeited the right to bear arms. He did not deny his former felonies (in fact he had pled guilty to them in the past) but denied that he could be convicted because he denied being the killer.

> **Fourth Amendment freedom from unreasonable searches and seizure:** US Marshals followed Porter's movements using sophisticated tracking devices that located his phone. The Marshals obtained search warrants from a federal judge before using this technology and before barging into the homes of his family members and friends in an effort to locate him. Porter also raised the right of privacy. These arguments failed for two reasons: he could not raise the rights of a third party (the other homeowners as they

were not before the court), and he had lost his right to privacy when the federal judge found probable cause to believe that he had committed the charged crimes.

Fifth Amendment right to remain silent and due process: Porter made no statements when questioned by police and invoked his right to remain silent at the time of his arrest. Jail calls he made to his girlfriend, concerning the identities of witnesses who may have given up his location or might testify against him, were played before the jury. Defendants are notified before a call is connected while in custody that the call is being recorded and may be monitored. Additionally, the presumption of innocence and due process enabled Porter to claim a weak case and be released during the course of his pretrial confinement.

Sixth Amendment right to an attorney: Porter was appointed four different attorneys. When he forfeited this right through his outrageous conduct, Judge Henry appointed the fourth attorney to serve as standby counsel and to sit in the front row during the trial and assist whenever called upon by Porter at the breaks. The Sixth Amendment also gives a defendant the right to confront accusers. Porter refused to be present to hear the evidence against him. Extraordinary accommodations were made: video cameras were set up in the courtroom showing all the proceedings and were broadcast to Porter's holding cell behind the judge's chambers. At every break, Porter was given the opportunity to confer with the standby counsel and change his mind about being present in court for the next witness. Although he consulted with the attorney outside of the courtroom on a handful of occasions, he consistently refused to return to the courtroom for the trial.

Eighth Amendment prohibition against cruel and unusual punishment: This right prevents the court from setting excessive bail and cruel and unusual punishment, not an issue in this case. Porter's first attorney raised this point when the evidence weakened in Brian's case and his subsequent release led to the murder of Obediah. The prohibition against double jeopardy prevents the state from trying the defendant twice for the same crime. It does not, however, prevent the state from presenting evidence of one murder victim (Obediah) in the trial of a different murder victim (Brian) or vice versa, under Rule 404(b). Finally, the death penalty, which Porter faces in Duplin County, has been upheld by the Supreme Court of the United States. The case in Duplin County is expected to be tried in 2020.[7]

Ninth Amendment right of privacy: Porter claimed that his rights were violated when authorities "tapped" his phone, both in the apprehension and during his time in confinement. The state established that the Marshals did not exceed their authority in using the technology in locating Porter's cell phone. Also, for reasons raised in the Fourth Amendment, there is no expectation of privacy in jail—such calls can and should be monitored for the safety of everyone at the detention facility.

Tenth Amendment state's rights: WPD officers were the lead law enforcement officials in Brian's homicide. Duplin County Sheriff's detectives were the lead law enforcement officials in Obediah's homicide. Both agencies worked with the US Marshal Service in apprehending Porter. Law enforcement agencies must respect territorial boundaries, even though criminals do not. There is nothing improper about various police groups working together. Federal resources helped in the capture, but all of the heavy lifting of prosecuting the case would be handled at the state level.

Day of Reckoning

Jury selection proved to be difficult. In all cases, the goal of jury selection is to find a representative panel of citizens that can be fair to both sides. Due to pretrial publicity, the trial was moved from New Hanover to Pender County. Jury selection is really a process of jury "deselection" in which each side gets to remove up to six jurors for any reason. The judge can remove an unlimited number of jurors for cause (for example, knowledge of the case, inability to serve, or bias illustrated by the juror during the selection process).

The use of these peremptory challenges is limited to an important exception: no one can be removed on account of race under precedent from a Supreme Court of the United States case called *Batson v. Kentucky*.[8] If either side intended to remove an African-American juror, we would have to give a reason. I removed only one: the mother of the head bailiff in the courtroom.

Porter was very active in jury selection and ended up using all six of his peremptory challenges. He was then left to accept the remaining jurors, with the only option for the court to remove anyone on a challenge for cause if they said they could not be fair. All 12 jurors plus three alternates said they knew nothing of the case, did not know the witnesses, and could base their verdict on the facts and the law. After jury selection Porter refused to exit his cell to participate in the proceedings.

We summarized the state's case against Porter during the opening statement. The jury would hear from three witnesses who would testify about what happened: Mikeya, Patrick, and Obediah. They would also hear from law enforcement officers concerning their efforts to locate Porter and the lengths he went to in order to evade arrest. We also informed the jury that they would watch video testimony of one of Porter's friends, Obediah, but at this point the jury did not know that he was dead or that Porter was charged with his murder. They would hear Obediah speak from beyond the grave. Sometimes it is best not to rob the jury of the power of discovery.

The state's direct examination of all witnesses was followed by no cross-examination as the jury was left to watch an empty table where a defendant and defense attorney would normally sit. Judge Henry repeatedly instructed the jury to draw no inference from Porter's absence or refusal to participate and also told them not to watch the local news that was filming, tweeting, and streaming most of the proceedings in real time, then recapping the events of the day each night during the regular newscasts.

Testimony from the lead detective explained that Porter was released on an unsecured bond after no physical evidence or witnesses linked him to Brian's death. Then Porter's other crime was admitted under 404(b). The testimony of Obediah's friends who witnessed Porter executing him; the testimony from the pretrial release coordinator showing Porter's movement the night he allegedly killed Obediah; and the testimony of Duplin detectives who laid out a brutal crime scene and his second capture.

After all of the evidence was presented, here is part of what I said during closing arguments:

> You have now heard from 16 witnesses and considered 81 exhibits. And while the transcript will capture everything that was said by these witnesses, the evidence actually fits into a book. A book that is, unfortunately, nonfiction. It's a horror story. It is a horror story that has been authored by this defendant. And the book is not over yet. The last page is going to be a verdict sheet. Verdict means to speak the truth. And if we're going

to have a true story it should end with your verdict. You hold the power of the pen. You get to decide how the story ends.

Let's make it very clear at the outset. The defendant tried to control how this book would be written and you've now heard about him tampering with the process to include taking the life of a witness and of depriving us of the ability to call Obediah Hester. And, in doing that, he actually created another witness, Hester's uncle, Patrick Bragg. You will hear that that evidence can also be considered to show a similar modus operandi and the identity of who it is that fired the bullet that killed Brian Grant.

And, just as a book has a cover and a back cover, so too, sadly, do we have that in this case. Exhibits 1 and 81, the front cover and back cover, were very intentionally picked by the prosecution. If you've forgotten what exhibit number 1 is, let me remind you. This is exhibit number 1, Brian Grant, and it's his day in court. This is about getting justice for him.

And the very back cover, exhibit 81, how this trial ended, is Obediah Hester, a man who said he was going to bear witness, a man who said he was going to do the right thing if called upon to do so.

Speaking for the dead is an awesome responsibility. Remembering the absent is too. And that's what we do in a murder case. Let's not forget these two gentlemen as we consider this book. …

We're lucky to live in the first world, to live in a place where there's not a lot of disease or catastrophe or even death that we see every day. Many of you, maybe you've never seen death before looking at the picture of Brian Grant. If you've never seen death before, take a good look. This is it. Death in a bag. (Showing them the bag containing a bullet, the fatal shot). This was pulled from the severed spinal cord of Brian Grant as it lodged into his back top vertebrae, dropping him and killing him instantly.

The only issue before you is who fired this shot? Because whoever did is certainly guilty of first-degree murder (felony murder for firing into an occupied dwelling and premeditated murder for shooting Brian in the face). It's just not even a close call. And so, sandwiched right in the middle of our book, with the front cover belonging to Brian Grant and the back belonging to Obie Hester, state's 30A, removed by Dr. William Kelly from the body of Brian Grant, screaming from the grave, screaming the truth, he did this.

In closing, I covered all of the facts and fit them into the law. The jury already heard the evidence so I spent little time summarizing it for them. Instead, I gave them the legal definitions of first-degree murder, the elements of the crimes charged, and emphasized that the facts and law established Porter's guilt beyond a reasonable doubt.

Because there was only an empty chair on the other side of the courtroom, I raised the five defenses that any seasoned defense attorney might raise if they had been sitting at the table and I explained why none applied. The real defense that had been on display was the fifth defense, putting the process on trial. Porter had apparently remained confident that the jury would latch onto one or more of the conspiracy theories that he had suggested during the lengthy jury selection process.

Ninety minutes later the jury returned a verdict of guilty on all charges. In a continued show of disrespect for the process and Brian's family, Porter, whose presence was required for sentencing, chanted and yelled throughout the reading of the Grant family's victim impact statement. Porter was sentenced to life without parole for Brian's killing. His conviction was unanimously upheld on appeal.[9] He will never be released.

State v. Carter[10]

On a beautiful February afternoon in 1997, the first warm and sunny day in months, D'April Greene turned off the stove where she had been cooking a pot of corn and turned to her two boys, Demetrius, who had just brought home a great second-grade report card and his younger brother, Demarius, age four. "Who wants to go to Toys 'R Us?!" she asked more as an invitation than as a question.

The boys had been so good and had been pent up inside for so long, especially since the arrival of their baby sister. The boys answered by running for the door. As they approached their mom's car, parked on the street next to Johnson's Grocery Store, Demetrius yelled "shotgun!" and dove into the front passenger seat.

Around the corner, on the other side of the grocery store, a different scene was playing out. Ty Baker had finally found the men whom he had been looking for. Ty was a drug dealer from New York who recently arrived in Wilmington to sell heroin. He had been doing very well; so well, in fact, that the street was saying that he had sold his last bindle, thereby "turning product into paper" (meaning money). He was a prime target.

Shan Carter and Kwada Temoney were partners in crime. Temoney was from "The Bottom," a name commonly associated with the south side of Wilmington around the corner from the Jervay Housing Community. Carter grew up in a loving family. His father worked at the post office, and his mother had done well raising Carter and his sister.[11]

The Carter family resided in several cities before settling in Wilmington during his formative years. Carter and Temoney became fast friends and eventually set upon a familiar business strategy, robbing drug dealers who had plenty of cash and were reluctant to report their victimization to law enforcement.

Over the course of a few months, the two committed some of the most vicious crimes locals had ever seen, though few reported what happened and were uncooperative when neighbors called the police. The modus operandi they employed rarely varied: armed with guns, the two would don ski masks, force entry, and cut the phone lines. They also picked victims whom they knew would not be calling 911 for help.

During the attack, occupants inside, frequently including young children, would be rounded up, then bound and gagged. "Show us where you are hiding the stuff or we will start cutting off one finger at a time," they said to one dealer, holding a knife up to his baby's hand. In another horrific case, they beat a drug dealer in front of his family with an iron. When the blows knocked his teeth loose, the two defendants ordered their victim to "swallow your teeth, M.F."

The crime involving Ty was different. Temoney and Carter, employing the help of a junkie named Damont "Eli" White, who knew where Ty lived and where he hid his stash, broke into Ty's empty apartment and made off with over $30,000. Splitting up the proceeds, Carter referred to the haul as "blood money," aware that a guy like Ty would not report the crime but would instead become a bounty hunter in search of justice.

Over the next few days and weeks, however, Eli got careless. Following the theft, he was found at many different street corners, buying another fix. Ty eventually guessed the source of Eli's newfound wealth and kidnapped him for further interrogation and torture. After several hours, Eli gave the name and location of his accomplices: Carter and Temoney frequently hung out in front of Johnson's Grocery Store.

Ty walked up to Temoney and coldcocked him without introduction, dropping Temoney to the ground. What Ty did not expect is what happened next. Carter pulled out his revolver and started shooting at Ty from point-blank range. Ty rounded the corner of the store and started running. Carter followed, continuing to shoot Ty in the back. His aim was excellent: Ty dropped dead in the middle of Dawson Street.

Far from rendering aid, onlookers went to Ty's body and rifled through his pockets, stealing money and drugs from the dead man before first responders arrived. Carter and Temoney quickly drove away, confident that no one would come forward to report what they had seen.

One hundred feet up the street from where Ty was dying, there was a scream. D'April Greene was shaking her oldest child, trying to wake him. A bullet that Carter had fired had traveled down the street, through the windshield of D'April's parked car and, after ricocheting off the steering wheel, took a hard left toward the front passenger seat.

The projectile went straight into the left side of Demetrius' head. After several agonizing minutes, and despite heroic efforts to save him, the young boy known to his family as "Little Papa" for the love he showed his siblings took his last breath. He was eight years old.

Carter's distinctive car was seen leaving the scene and warrants were issued for his arrest. Temoney and Carter were found hiding in a Market Street motel the next day. They had just tied up and shot a drug dealer in his home in order to raise enough money to leave town and go on the run. They were both charged, with not only Ty's and Demetrius' murders but the several uncharged crimes that were now coming to light.

The Trial

The killing of Little Papa started a larger conversation about the need to report all types of crime before innocent people get caught in the crossfire. Despite the initial outpouring of support, few people wanted to help. The other drug dealers who had been terrorized by Carter and Temoney agreed to testify at trial, but only because they had been subsequently charged for unrelated crimes and wanted a plea deal for their cooperation. The same held for bystanders at Jervay who merely witnessed what had occurred. Eli wrote a letter from jail and later testified explaining the plot to break in. (Sadly, he committed suicide shortly after the trial.) Ty's family never even came to Wilmington to participate in the proceeding.

At trial, Judge Jay Hockenbury ruled that several of the prior armed home invasions were admissible under Rule 404(b) to show a similar modus operandi of robbing drug dealers, to more fully explain the circumstances for why Ty approached Carter and Temoney, and to illustrate why Carter was motivated to kill him. Dealer after dealer, victim after victim took the stand to recount the horrors that Carter and Temoney had inflicted. What became clear is that they were not fighting their own war on drugs. They were soldiers of fortune putting their own love of money over human life.

The most compelling 404(b) evidence came not from the testimony of a drug dealer but from his family who had witnessed his torture. Donald Brunson was literally pulled kicking and screaming from his home, his bloody fingerprints tracing down the walls, before he was put in the trunk of his own car, naked. After driving to a remote location, the masked men shot Donald in the back, killing him when he tried to escape, running for his life.

Donald's family, who witnessed the kidnapping from the home but not the execution in the woods, also testified that they initially called friends, not 911, fearing both reprisal from the attackers and the legal repercussions of alerting the authorities to Donald's drug activity. This case remained unsolved for the next two months until Carter and Temoney were apprehended after Baker and Demetrius were killed. Ski masks left in the woods and Donald's stolen burned vehicle were tested and forensically linked to Temoney. He ultimately pled and received a 115-year sentence. Temoney refused to testify against Carter for that crime or any other.

Despite no help from Temoney, the state was able to convict Carter of Donald's murder, which the state tried before a different jury immediately before the trial for Ty and Demetrius' murders. As with Temoney, we had offered for Carter to plead guilty to all three murders and a host of other offenses to give him a life sentence. He refused our offer and risked death penalty trials instead. Carter was convicted of first-degree murder in Donald's case. Despite finding multiple aggravating factors, the jury recommended that Carter receive life without parole.

Confronting the Defenses

By the time the state rested its case in the trial for Ty and Demetrius' murders, the jury had already heard tale after tale of a two-man crime wave. In addition to the incident in front of Johnson's Grocery Store, the jury heard from several other dealers and Donald's family about their encounter. Up to this point in the trial, Carter had invoked the SODDI defense, claiming that he was not at the scene during the deadly shooting of Ty and Demetrius.

Carter further claimed that Temoney must have acted with another partner when robbing and terrorizing the other witnesses who testified. He continued to maintain his innocence for Donald's killing even in the face of having just been convicted of the murder in a separate six-week-long trial.

Now Carter changed course midstream. In a move that surprised even his own family, Carter waived his right to remain silent and took the stand. For the first time, he admitted to firing multiple times at Ty but said "Of Course I Did It." Carter contended that Ty was armed and dangerous and deadly force was a last resort to defend himself and his friend from imminent death. No weapon was found on Ty's body, and there were no bullets at the scene to suggest any other shots were fired. Carter's attorney suggested that Ty's gun may have been stolen when onlookers were rifling through his pockets, but there was no physical evidence or testimonial evidence to back up the claim that Ty ever possessed a weapon on the day he was killed.

As for shooting Demetrius, Carter had to admit that the boy's death was a tragedy. Ballistic evidence concluded that the same weapon that killed Ty Baker had also killed Little Papa. Even if the jury believed the conspiracy theory that Ty fired a weapon, the bullet that was removed from the head of an eight-year-old child came from Carter's gun. To all of this, Carter's defense was "I Did Not Do It," arguing that he was not guilty of first-degree murder.

The state first argued that Carter was guilty of first-degree murder under the felony murder rule. Since Demetrius was killed when Carter was in the act of shooting and killing Ty Baker, and because the bullet went into an occupied vehicle, itself a serious felony, Carter was guilty of felony murder, irrespective of whether or not he had the specific intent to kill Demetrius.

We also argued that Carter was guilty of premeditated and deliberate murder of both Ty and Demetrius. Firing multiple shots means that he formed the intent to kill during the course of the crime. That is the definition of premeditation and deliberation. Under the "transferred intent doctrine," if Carter intended to kill Ty, he was equally responsible for killing Demetrius. This theory holds that the law does not reward a defendant for being a bad shot, as "hate follows the bullet."[12]

The New Hanover County jury agreed. They returned verdicts convicting Carter of first-degree murder, under both theories, for the murder of Ty Baker and for the murder of Demetrius Greene. The trial proceeded to the sentencing phase. The jury found that Carter had killed before, having been convicted of the first-degree murder of Donald Brunson; that he had engaged in a violent course of conduct over the preceding several months as he terrorized numerous other victims and their families; and that he was motivated by pecuniary gain in committing the crimes. The jury unanimously recommended that Carter should receive not one but two death sentences. He remains on death row to this day.

Caught in the Crossfire

Defendants like Porter and Carter are frequently not even required to stand trial because their crimes never get solved. Building and maintaining trust with neighborhoods like those where Brian and Little Papa were killed is the biggest obstacle in getting the case into the courthouse.

In a vicious cycle that pervades our inner cities, today's victim becomes tomorrow's defendant as he seeks vigilante justice in retribution for his earlier victimization, thus perpetuating a cycle of violence (Ty Baker's killing is an example of the Equivalent Group Hypothesis).[13] The victim's silence at the hospital speaks loudly about the mistrust he has in the justice system, a system with which he has likely had personal experience and a system that has likely incarcerated members of his family. For this victim-turned-bounty hunter, his view is simple: if he cannot find justice at the courthouse, he will look for it on the street.

How do we prevent tragedies involving innocent victims caught in the cross fire from occurring? Maybe we can't. Sometimes children die. But lifting up kids like Little Papa, my first victim in a murder case, has been an obsession of mine since I first met his family. This has caused me to expand the Equivalent Group Hypothesis to the Mirror Image Rule in an effort to give voice to the surrounding community that no one can blame for their victimization. If even one of Carter's many other victims had come forward to report their terror, he would not have been out of custody to kill an eight-year-old boy. If other witnesses had joined Obediah in talking to the police about Porter, he would never have been released from jail prior to Brian's trial. Building trust to encourage people to come forward not only slays the fifth pig, it might just save lives.

With good schools and job prospects, maybe D'April would not have been living in a place called "poverty." In chapter 7, we look at initiatives to prevent youth violence and programs to provide economic opportunity to people who are raising kids in that dangerous place. These efforts need to grow and spread across all levels of society. If the whole community saw Little Papa as their child too, I believe there would be far fewer murders.

In Porter's trial we saw a double killer who ended up representing himself and was completely unwilling to adhere to the procedural laws that are put in place to conduct a fair hearing. In essence, his defense was that the whole system is corrupt. Meanwhile, Carter and Temoney were so sure of the mistrust that others had in the system that they knew they could commit violent crimes with impunity, secure in the knowledge that witnesses would not come forward.

FIGURES 4.11 AND 4.12   Dedication of Demetrius Greene Park, April 2005. *Source*: WECT.

The "Maybe You Did It" defense is strengthened by individual cases of police misconduct. This defense also takes root on the street where systemic problems in the justice system are believed to exist, such as police brutality, mass incarceration, and disproportionate minority contact. We will look at these issues in chapter 6. Underlying whether this defense will be effective is whether "we the people" trust the police, prosecutor, and judge who are tasked with upholding the Constitution and ensuring equal protection.

Dr. Martin Luther King Jr. once said that "our lives begin to end when we remain silent about things that matter."[14] Good people die when crime goes unreported. The ultimate silent witness to the mistrust that needs repairing between the community most in need of protection and the justice system is evident in the shrines to the children like Little Papa who are caught in the crossfire of issues not of their own making.

With the heart of the community ripped out, the Jervay Housing Community was razed soon after the young boy's death. The Wilmington Housing Authority has since rebuilt the federally-subsidized neighborhood into a modern housing complex. In the new public square there is a park that bears the name of Demetrius Greene. And across the street, in the place where

Little Papa took his last breath, sits a makeshift memorial of flowers and balloons, and they are always fresh. In more than 20 years since the murder occurred, the family has not missed a week.

Notes

1 *State v. Delgado*, 364 N.C. 602 (2010). Co-counsel was Jon David.

2 *Washington Post*, as reported by San Diego News 7, December 10, 2018. (In-depth analysis of a decade of killing of women in 47 major US cities revealed that almost half were murdered by an intimate partner. Moreover, 36 percent of the men were publicly known to be a potential threat prior to the attack because of a prior restraining order or a prior conviction for a violent crime.)

3 The Delgado case has been featured on *Dateline NBC*, Mystery on Reminisce Road, aired July 12, 2010, http://www.nbcnews.com/id/38158659/ns/dateline_nbc-crime_reports/t/mystery-reminisce-road/#.XpfJXOpJHIU); *Unusual Suspects*, "Hiding in Plain Sight," aired September 11, 2011, https://www.investigationdiscovery.com/tv-shows/unusual-suspects, and Southern Fried Homicide (Terror in the Tar Heel State, aired January 10, 2013; https://www.investigationdiscovery.com/tv-shows/southern-fried-homicide/.

4 Sometimes victims break the mold and find the strength to help others. Ana Cruz now delivers "Baskets of Hope" to women trying to restart their lives after escaping their abusers. https://dfw.cbslocal.com/2016/07/22/domestic-violence-survivor-gives-hope-one-basket-at-a-time/

5 *State v. Porter*, 787 S.E.2d 16 (N.C. 2016). Co-counsel was Connie Jordan.

6 This is also known as the Doctrine of Unclean Hands. See generally, James Markham, The Forfeiture by Wrongdoing Exception to the Confrontation Rule, July 2006, https://www.sog.unc.edu/sites/www.sog.unc.edu/files/course_materials/200610SmithForf.pdf

7 Given the existence of these final two aggravating factors, Porter was clearly eligible for the death penalty for the killing of Obediah in Duplin County. Not only was Obediah a witness and the murder was carried out to prevent him from testifying—the circumstances of the death indicate that it was especially torturous.

8 *Batson v. Kentucky*, 476 U.S. 79, 86 (Apr. 30, 1986).

9 N.C. Court of Appeals, COA 17-738 (unpublished opinion decided July 3, 2018). In upholding Judge Henry's ruling that Porter had a fair trial, the court of appeals rejected Porter's arguments that his public defender "was a puppet of the prosecution" or that I had "exhibited a pattern of governmental

misconduct and prosecutorial misconduct so outrageous that it violates fundamental fairness and is shocking to the universal sense of justice." See pages 9 and 12, respectively.

10 *State v. Carter*, 156 N.C. App 446 (2003) (murder of Donald Brunson); *State v. Carter*, 357 N.C. 345 (2003) (Murders of Demetrius Greene and Ty Baker). Co-counsel was John Sherrill.

11 His upbringing would later be offered by the defense at sentencing as mitigating evidence to show a large network of family support. We argued the reverse—Carter had every opportunity to be a productive member of society, like his sister, and chose a life of crime instead.

12 *State v. Wynn*, 278 N.C. 513, 519 (1971). "The malice or intent follows the bullet."

13 Anderson, James F. *Criminological Theories*. (Jones & Bartlett Learning,) (2015), 50

14 Dr. Martin Luther King Jr., Selma, Alabama (Feb. 12, 1965).

Figure Credits

Fig. 4.2: Leesville Police Department, Louisiana, "Lorraine Frew in Hospital Profile," Leesville Police Department, 1996.

Fig. 4.3: Leesville Police Department, Louisiana, "Lorraine Frew in Hospital," Leesville Police Department, 1996.

Fig. 4.4: Dr. Bill Oliver, "Oliver Imaging for Mooney and Cruz Noses," 2008.

Fig. 4.5: New Hanover County Sheriff's Office CSI, "Relation Between Mooney and Delgado Houses," New Hanover County Sheriff's Office, 1999.

Fig. 4.6: New Hanover County Sheriff's Office CSI, "Bootprint on Door," New Hanover County Sheriff's Office, 1999.

Fig. 4.8: Ben David, "Delgado Victim Chart," 2008.

Fig. 4.9: Copyright © 2010 by NBCUniversal Media, LLC.

Fig. 4.10: Federal Bureau of Investigation, "FBI Director Award Presentation," Federal Bureau of Investigation, 2009.

Fig. 4.11: Copyright © 2005 by Gray Television, Inc. Reprinted with permission.

Fig. 4.12: Copyright © 2005 by Gray Television, Inc. Reprinted with permission.

Chapter 5

The Body of the Crime

In this section, we look at the challenges confronting police and prosecutors when handling a classic murder mystery where there is no confession, no murder weapon, no crime scene, and no body. We examine the different types of evidence: circumstantial and direct, testimonial and physical. We also look at the factors that go into trying a defendant for the death penalty. Finally, we meet a remarkable group of people who make up the Homicide Family Support Group.

State v. Bradley[1]

Roberta grew tired of waiting for her daughter to open the door. If her daughter, Shannon, was sleeping, she would have woken up by now. Roberta and her sister, Beverly, took the balloons they bought for Shannon's 54th birthday and tied them to a nearby post and left the carefully wrapped presents on the porch. Apparently, this year's birthday would not include a brunch at their favorite restaurant. The three women had planned the meal for weeks, and Roberta left the porch with a feeling that mothers sometimes have, a sinking feeling that something was terribly wrong.

Fear turned to dread in the hours that followed. Shannon was not answering her phone, which was very unlike her. Roberta and her daughter spoke every day, sometimes several times per day. None of her friends had heard from her since the day before either. Shannon had battled with alcoholism for many years; she also suffered from low blood sugar. Was she passed out in the apartment in some kind of medical distress?

Later that same afternoon, April 6, 2014, several friends and family formed an impromptu search party and fanned out around the historic district of downtown Wilmington where Shannon lived, as well as the central business district that she frequented. After more than 24 hours with no contact, Roberta went to WPD to report her daughter missing.

When officers forced entry into Shannon's apartment they found an empty home. Nothing looked out of place and there were no signs of forced entry. Income taxes she had been working on were spread out on the kitchen counter. The bed was made and did not appear to have been slept in. A half bottle of wine sat on the kitchen counter as if waiting to be returned to the refrigerator. Nothing appeared to be missing except Shannon's phone, keys, and purse, which she routinely carried with her wherever she went.

Her trusted scooter was parked and locked outside. Because of a prior DWI, Shannon did not have a driver's license. Since she lived downtown, she frequently walked to bustling restaurants and small stores. Shannon relied upon her scooter, which did not require a license to operate, when longer commutes were necessary and a friend was not available to give her a lift. Shannon Rippy Van Newkirk's name was entered into the National Crime Information Center (NCIC) database, and she was treated as a missing person on Monday, April 7.

The Boss

When a person goes missing, investigators routinely work their way back from the last place they were seen in order to establish a time line. Detectives began by interviewing friends and asking a superior court judge to issue an emergency order to obtain Shannon's phone records to locate her phone. T-Mobile reported that the phone had been turned off, making it impossible to trace by pinging its location. However, the incoming and outgoing calls before it was shut off gave detectives a good place to start.

To no one's surprise, there were many calls to and from Steve Mott in the days and hours leading up to Shannon's disappearance. For the last decade, Shannon worked as a bookkeeper at Mott Landscaping, Steve's business, which provided lawn care and high-end landscaping in the counties around the Cape Fear River. During that time, Shannon and Steve also had an open dating relationship and intermittently spent the night at each other's homes. Everyone knew that Shannon loved Steve; everyone also knew that it was a largely unrequited sentiment, borne more of convenience than mutual affection. Steve quickly became a suspect.

The afternoon before she went missing, Shannon had enjoyed drinks with her best friend, Dawn Hubbard, at The Husk, a downtown bar three blocks from Shannon's apartment. Shannon was sporting a new haircut and fresh spray tan, a birthday gift from Dawn. According to Dawn,

Shannon was all dressed up with nowhere to go. Both women watched as the Mott Landscaping truck, with Steve behind the wheel, passed the bar at 4:00 p.m. Shannon kept calling him, but he didn't answer. Dawn did not think Steve was good for Shannon, and while Shannon disagreed, she also realized that she would not be ringing in her birthday with Steve.

Steve, as his phone records and Shannon's would later corroborate, did finally call Shannon from his friend's house downtown at approximately 6:30 p.m. The two spoke for a few minutes. According to Steve, he invited Shannon over to

FIGURE 5.1   Shannon entering The Husk.

his place. She declined and told Steve she was going out to brunch with her mom the next morning and did not want to have a late night. Steve did not hear any background noise and assumed that Shannon was back at her apartment alone. This turned out to be an incorrect assumption.

Steve cooperated with detectives, giving them full access to his phone and helping them interpret Shannon's phone records. One number popped up numerous times. There were 14 calls between Shannon and this person in the four days leading up to her disappearance. The calls came from a co-worker, James Bradley. He abruptly stopped calling Shannon at the same time she disappeared.

The Co-Worker

James Bradley was hired by Steve as a landscaper and worked alongside Steve's three other employees, including Shannon. He was a reliable worker, was entrusted with a work truck, and had unfettered access to large tracts of Steve's private property. Steve stored equipment and grew starter plants on this land. In addition to keeping the books, Shannon worked in the field. When paired up with Bradley, she often rode with him to clients' homes or to the remote staging area for Mott Landscaping, a 15-acre tract of land off Hoover Road in Pender County. Detectives later learned that Shannon also rode in Bradley's personal vehicle, a red two-door Chevy Tahoe SUV, when the two spent time together socially, which, to everyone's surprise, happened occasionally.

Steve believed in second chances and was not bothered by the fact that Bradley recently had been released from prison. He also did not run his new employee's criminal history, which is available online in North Carolina, because Bradley was open about it at their very first meeting. He told Steve he had spent 25 years behind bars for killing his ex-wife's paramour. This was the story he served up to any and everybody he encountered in his new community. In reality, Bradley had strangled his eight-year-old stepdaughter.

Bradley was convicted of killing Ivy Gipson in Fayetteville, North Carolina, in 1988. He was married to Ivy's mom and they had a young daughter together. On the day he killed his stepdaughter, Bradley was home from work, apparently too sick to leave the house. Ivy's mom left Bradley in charge of the girls, Ivy and 18-month-old Rita, while she went to work. Ivy rode the bus to and from school. Later in the afternoon, Bradley called 911 to report that his daughter did not return from the bus stop, and he feared that she had been kidnapped. The Cumberland County Sheriff's Office responded in a hurry and found the child's lunchbox scattered on the ground and immediately started searching.

Bradley's story had holes in it from the very start. Ivy never made it to school. On top of that, Bradley's time line kept changing and he appeared nervous. For the next 48 hours, Bradley dodged the Cumberland County detectives' requests to take a polygraph examination, while comforting his inconsolable wife. He finally relented and took the polygraph, believing that taking a bottle of pills might throw off the machine. He failed it miserably. After hearing the test results, which he likely did not know were inadmissible in a court of law (and still are), Bradley confessed.

The details of the killing and concealment of Ivy's murder were laid out in a chilling eight-page confession that detectives typed as Bradley spoke (he later signed the beginning and end of every page to endorse his words—a way for police to be thorough in an age before recorded interviews were the standard). Bradley claimed that he had pushed Ivy into the TV when he told her to turn it down. She hit her head and started to scream. To make her stop, he began to choke her, first with his hands and later with a sock that he used as a ligature around her neck.

Bradley confessed to flushing the sock down a toilet and staging a crime scene. He went to the bus stop where Ivy was supposed to hop off and walk home and placed an open lunch box on the ground to suggest a stranger abduction scenario. Bradley also admitted to putting Ivy's body in two trash bags, tying them up, and placing her in a dumpster. She was found in a landfill 72 hours later. The dumpster where Bradley threw her had been emptied, and Ivy had been crushed among the debris in the back of a dump truck.

On January 22, 1990, after having been in jail for a year-and-a-half awaiting trial, Bradley pled guilty to first-degree premeditated murder in exchange for removing the death penalty as a possible punishment in his case. He was sentenced to life with parole. The laws at the time allowed well-behaving defendants to be eligible for release after serving 25 years of a life sentence. That law changed in 1994, and today, parole has been abolished in North Carolina: now life means life.

While in prison, Bradley apparently regretted the decision to confess and to plead guilty to first-degree murder. On April 6, 1994, acting as his own lawyer, he filed a Motion for Appropriate Relief (MAR) seeking to withdraw his guilty plea.[2] In the filing, Bradley contended, "I simply lost control of my emotions and reacted to the situation violently." Bradley sought to "enter a plea to a lesser charge of second-degree murder, although I disavow guilt of this charge ..." He claimed that he never used a murder weapon, the sock, which suggested he acted with malice, and that he was only responsible for voluntary manslaughter because he killed the girl while he was blacked out. Bradley also expressed great regret for leading authorities to Ivy's body since this evidence enabled authorities to obtain the highest murder charge against him.

> I believe that the detectives added the statement to my confession; about using socks to commit the act of strangulation in order to obtain an arrest warrant; without having a body to justify the warrant. When I told them what I had done with the body, they were faced with having to search for it. They needed to have me in official custody, but they didn't have the evidence to show that I had committed a 1st degree murder. So the sock inclusion came as the result of the detectives needing to secure a warrant for first-degree murder; without having a body to justify it. (Page 7 of MAR)

The trial court did not reopen his conviction and Bradley remained in prison to serve out the quarter-century that the plea had imposed. He was released on parole on February 11, 2013. He was to reside in Wilmington.

Talking in Circles

Although Steve did not know the truth about Bradley's past, it did not take long for the WPD investigators to learn about Ivy's murder. Bradley became a prime suspect in Shannon's disappearance. He was interviewed by the police on three separate dates and was inconsistent on major details each time. Detectives first questioned Bradley at his home on April 9. He expressed shock when learning that Shannon was missing and denied having any contact with her on April 5, the last day she had been seen alive. Instead, he claimed that he and Shannon had a landscaping job at a client's house on April 3 and he had not seen her since. He also claimed that they had no relationship outside of work and was perplexed as to what may have happened to her.

Bradley repeated the same version of this story on April 11, when the police again interviewed him, this time on videotape at the station. The only significant new detail he added in this second interview was that he had spoken to Shannon on the phone the day she went missing—a fact that investigators already knew since, by that time, they had her phone records. When detectives asked Bradley if they could look at his call history, Bradley said that he had erased all of his calls because he did not want to have backlog on his phone. Detectives later got a court order and obtained a copy of his records, which are still logged with the carrier even when deleted from the phone.

Phone records not only keep track of incoming and outgoing calls, they can also tell investigators where a mobile phone is located because the cellular devices communicate with nearby cell towers.

FIGURE 5.2   Bradley's vehicle at the Exxon station.

At around 5:30 p.m. on April 5, Shannon had called Bradley. Cell towers and surveillance video indicated that she was at The Husk and he was in, or near, his apartment. Bradley's phone then began moving through town, consistent with a route to pick Shannon up. The two phones then traveled through the city together, eventually arriving back at Bradley's apartment by 6:05 p.m. The phones also stopped at the intersection of Third and Dawson Streets for several minutes, suggesting that they may have stopped at the gas station on that corner.

Detectives were able to pull images from cameras that monitor traffic throughout the city and located Bradley's distinct older model, two-door Chevy Tahoe driving along the route consistent with the times and locations provided by the phone records. The detectives also pulled videos from the Exxon station and Bradley was there, purchasing alcohol. The video of his vehicle at the gas pumps appears to show a passenger wearing a white V-neck shirt, just like the one Shannon was wearing when last seen at The Husk.

For a third time, Bradley was interviewed by WPD detectives, and for a third time he lied. This time, on April 15, Bradley was fully aware that he had been spotted on videotape with Shannon. The explanation for his discrepancy: he had been nervous in the earlier interviews and acknowledged that his background made him a prime suspect. As Bradley put it, "if a piece of cake is missing, you are going to blame the fat kid." He admitted to picking Shannon up downtown, but here Bradley served up his third lie by telling detectives that after driving around for a brief time, he dropped her off at a convenience store called The Village Market. Bradley didn't know that investigators had already reviewed footage from this store, a place Shannon frequented near her home, and knew that she was not on video there at any time on April 5.

When confronted, Bradley began to shake and sweat profusely and changed his story yet again. He admitted he had a strong attraction to Shannon and expressed anger at her relationship with Steve. Bradley claimed that instead of letting her off at The Village Market, he let Shannon out of his vehicle around Greenfield Lake during a heated argument. The area around Greenfield Lake is considered an unsafe place at night; like most parks in America, even men are advised against running there alone after dark.

This intrigued the detectives, and they asked Bradley to join them on a drive around the lake and show them the location where he let Shannon out of his SUV. When he showed them the place where she supposedly exited the vehicle, investigators pulled surveillance videos from a nearby clinic that offered an angle that would have captured her image. For the second time on the same day, Shannon was nowhere to be found on a videotape that would have corroborated Bradley's story.

Detectives drove Bradley back to the station and continued the interrogation. Bradley continued to stick to the story that he had let Shannon out at Greenfield Lake. He did say, "I was the last one to see her alive," and, "It's my fault she's missing." Bradley never apologized for misleading the police for 10 whole days, when he could have helped them find Shannon, a person who was his friend, colleague, and love interest, by telling them the truth from the start. And, during the three long questioning sessions, he never once expressed concern for Shannon and her well-being. Instead he said: "I want my life back." Unfortunately, despite a strong circumstantial case, investigators did not have enough to hold Bradley. He walked out of the police station on April 15, still a free man. But only for the moment.

Searching for Shannon

Over the next two weeks everyone desperately searched for Shannon. Family, friends, and multiple police agencies combed nearly every wooded area in New Hanover County. In addition to physical searches at all locations where Shannon was known to frequent, authorities scanned missing persons' databases, banking transactions, and cell phone activity. Detectives also spent a great deal of time searching the remote areas in a tri-county region where they believed Bradley might have disposed of Shannon's body. Places of particular interest were the vicinity of Greenfield Lake in New Hanover County and the storage areas for Mott Landscaping, one near The USS *North Carolina* battleship, the other off Hoover Road in Pender County.

Finding a Needle in a Haystack

On April 29, WPD detectives drove to the Hoover Road property where Bradley and Shannon frequently went as part of their job with Mott Landscaping. A 15-acre parcel on a dead-end road next to 68,000 acres of state game lands, the property was used by Mott Landscaping as a staging area for growing trees and shrubs that would later be brought to clients' homes and yards. According to Steve, Bradley had recently cleared a section in the northwestern corner of the property with a bush hog, a machine that cuts thick brush and shrubbery. The northwestern corner could only be reached by a dirt road, which was secured by a cable wire that had a combination lock. According to Steve, only he and Bradley had the combination, making this section of the property accessible by vehicle only to them.

During a walkaround search, one of the detectives identified a stump that looked out of place and when the team approached it, they saw a patch of disturbed earth. When they stepped onto the ground, still wet from the April rains, a foul smell came bubbling up from the swampy ground. The unmistakable smell of human remains was overpowering. Shovels in hand, the detectives set to work, soon pulling from the shallow grave trash bags containing the decomposing body of a white female.

Detectives immediately contacted the patrol division, who still kept Bradley under surveillance. He was arrested while in his daughter's car (Rita, who had been a baby when Ivy was killed) at a drive-thru restaurant and charged with first-degree premeditated murder. At Bradley's first court appearance the following morning, I showed the presiding judge that he had a prior record for murdering a child and suggested that the capital defender's office be appointed to represent him. Bradley was given no bond. At long last, this case appeared solved and the trial looked to be a slam-dunk.

The Unexpected

In cases where a body is partially or badly decomposed, we request the help of the Office of the Chief Medical Examiner, which has the very best resources. On May 1, detectives went to Greenville, North Carolina, where an autopsy would be performed.

For the first time, investigators removed a set of three trash bags that contained the crime victim's body to render a better view of the corpse. What they saw was a cruel and lonely way to die. The woman was naked and bound in the fetal position with duct tape wrapped around her ankles and around her legs and midsection, as if to keep her in that position. Multiple broken ribs and chipped teeth suggested that she had been badly beaten. The massive blunt force trauma to her head caused the skin to split in multiple locations. Bruising on her neck indicated she had been grabbed with great force, maybe even strangled.

I got a call from WPD Chief Ralph Evangelous.

"Are you sitting down?" he asked.

"Yes," I replied.

"It's not Shannon," the chief said. "We have another victim."

FIGURE 5.3 *Star News* headline, May 1, 2014. Bradley was given no bond at his first appearance in light of the fact that his first-degree murder charge in Shannon's homicide made him death-penalty eligible.

The detectives had called him, shocked, at the discovery of two tattoos on the body, one on the neck and one on the back. Shannon had tattoos, but they didn't match the ones on the body. Things just got complicated. I now faced a whole new scenario. Did I have a serial killer in my district?

Types of Evidence

Prosecutors rely on different types of evidence to prove every criminal case. Evidence falls into two large categories: direct and circumstantial. Within these categories, there is testimonial evidence and physical evidence.

Direct evidence is something that can actually be seen. The most common example is an eyewitness who comes into court and testifies about what they have observed. For instance, if I had to prove to the jury that it was raining at the moment and we were sitting in a windowless room, a witness could take the stand and testify that they were just outside and it was raining. The witness would be under oath and subject to cross-examination. The jury could assess the credibility of the witness and believe all, part, or none of the testimony.

Circumstantial evidence, on the other hand, is not something that is directly observed but a group of circumstances that, when taken together, suggest that an event took place. To prove it is raining, I could call a witness from inside the same windowless room who reports that she just saw someone on the elevator who was dripping wet and shaking off an umbrella. Juries are frequently asked to examine physical evidence: things that they can see, hear, and even touch, like a weapon, gunshot residue, fingerprints, and DNA. Pieces of physical evidence at a crime scene are called "silent witnesses," though sometimes they speak volumes. To help further explain this physical evidence, I might also call an expert witness, such as a meteorologist, to testify about the forecast.

The law makes no distinction between the two types of evidence, and a case can be proven by either direct or circumstantial evidence or a combination of both. The burden of proof in all criminal cases is proof beyond a reasonable doubt. Because a jury cannot directly see whether it is raining or not, they may have doubts. Therefore, when possible, prosecutors try to use a mix of direct and circumstantial evidence in order to verify and corroborate their case. They couple this evidence with arguments to the jury, urging the use of reason and common sense to make logical inferences in order to come to conclusions about things that cannot always be seen.

Corpus Delicti

For someone to be guilty of a crime, prosecutors must establish the "body of the crime," or *corpus delicti*.[3] This is almost always a given, especially when someone dies. In Shannon's case, however, the body of the crime became a real question. The state had to prove not only that Shannon was missing but that she was murdered, despite having no confession, no crime scene, no murder weapon, and no body.

The first rule of any murder case is that dead people do not speak. A related concept is that murder is rarely committed in the presence of witnesses. In nearly every homicide, however, the state at least has proof that a crime occurred. Blood and other DNA present at a crime scene might say a lot about the nature of the assault and perhaps establish the identity of the killer. The presence of a weapon can establish the existence of malice, the crucial element necessary for second-degree murder. The number and nature of wounds on a victim's body can speak volumes about premeditation and deliberation to convict for first-degree murder.

The old adage "no body, no crime" is actually not the law. As one court said, in upholding a conviction where the victim was never located, "The fact that a murderer may successfully dispose of the body of a victim should not entitle him to an acquittal. That is one form of success for which society should have no reward."[4] This same court gave this rationale years earlier in a similar case: "It is not necessary in order to support the conviction that the body actually be found. To require direct and positive proof of *corpus delicti* would be most unreasonable ... the worst crimes are naturally committed at chosen times, in darkness and secrecy."[5]

In Shannon's case, we had no body, no weapon, and no crime scene. Obviously, the burden of proving the guilty act (*actus reus*) in a "no-body homicide" is very hard, but it can be proved with two logical steps: first, that the missing person is dead and, second, that the person on trial did it.[6] If Shannon had committed suicide or died of natural causes, her body would most likely have been located through our extensive searches. Several factors could be considered to show that Shannon was dead and not just hiding: her good health, close family relationships, future plans, dependability at work, limited financial means, and that she was not known to travel and had no such plans. As one court said, given all of these factors, "the unlikelihood of such a voluntary disappearance is circumstantial evidence entitled to weight equal to that of blood stains and the concealment of evidence."[7]

Circumstantial Evidence of Bradley's Guilt

To prove that Bradley caused Shannon's death, and that he did it with the requisite mind-set (*mens rea*) to make him guilty of murder, the state had to rely on circumstantial evidence. We had no witnesses to the actual disappearance or killing. To prove that Bradley killed Shannon and that he murdered her with malice and with premeditation and deliberation, we focused on three things: Bradley's words, Bradley's actions, and Bradley's other crimes.

1. Bradley's Words: Spoken and Written

In addition to the constant lies that Bradley told investigators over multiple days, he also provided details that proved to be very significant. From the very beginning, Bradley suggested that Shannon was financially destitute and may have needed to sleep with men for money. There was absolutely nothing in Shannon's background or anything that was discovered in the lengthy investigation to suggest that she was ever a prostitute. On the other hand, Bradley admitted to having sex with prostitutes since the time of his release. Even more telling were the chilling stories he penned years earlier that were found in his apartment, which provided us with a motive for what he may have done to Shannon and the woman we found while searching for her.

While he was in prison from 1988 to 2013, Bradley authored two short stories that seemingly foretold what he would do upon his release. "The Beast Within" and "Serial Killer" are stories that he wrote in 1993 and 1994 that revolve around the killings of young women and prostitutes by a serial killer. In "The Beast Within," the killer is described as a man who, while in the act of having sex with a prostitute, transforms into a savage jaguar to eat all but the heads of his female victims. In the story, Bradley also marvels at how quickly one can dispose of a body. Many of the female characters die when their throats are eaten. In "Serial Killer," an English professor abducts young women and strangles them by tying a scarf around their necks.

The woman, whom investigators found at the remote property off Hoover Road, as dental records would confirm, was Elisha Tucker, age 34. Elisha had an extensive drug history and convictions for prostitution. Like Ivy, Bradley's stepdaughter and first victim, she had great trauma to her neck and was dumped in trash bags. During their investigation, detectives also located two other prostitutes that Bradley had been courting. Among other similarities with the women he wrote about in his fictionalized accounts, they were poor and struggled with addiction.

Let's back up a little. Bradley was arrested for Shannon's death on April 29, 2014, the day the body was discovered on Hoover Road, and he was once again interrogated. Still denying any involvement in her disappearance, he was shown a picture of the full trash bag that had been unearthed at the Hoover Road property. When he saw the photo, Bradley smiled and remained silent. That smirk proved to be telling. At that moment, he knew something that would take investigators another 24 hours to learn—they had the wrong body. The only way Bradley could have known that was if he had killed both Shannon and the second victim.

After his arrest, Bradley wrote letters to friends and family from jail. In some of the letters, he acknowledged that detectives might read his letters. He was right. Bradley took great pains to put forth yet another version of the night Shannon disappeared. It was also in these letters that Bradley, for the first time, admitted that Shannon had actually been in his apartment on April 5 and that she drank a bottle of wine. This was most likely an attempt to explain the presence of her DNA, hair, or fingerprints that the CSI investigators might find during their extensive searches. While investigators ended up finding no trace of Shannon in Bradley's apartment—most likely because of his meticulous cleaning—they now knew she had been there at the time her phone was turned off.

2. Bradley's Actions

Cell phone records and video cameras around town conclusively established that Bradley was with Shannon at the time she went missing. This gave him the means and opportunity to commit the crime. When analyzing a case, prosecutors look for MOM: motive, opportunity, and means. Motive is not part of the burden of proof in any crime, except hate crimes. Prosecutors must prove who, what, where, and when but not *why* a crime happened. Nonetheless, it is helpful to know the motive. Looking at Bradley's actions, not just from the night Shannon went missing but also at the almost 14 months since his release from prison, gave strong indications that he was a sexual predator. He clearly had the means and opportunity to act out the sick fantasies he had written about when he took Shannon back to his apartment.

During the three weeks in which Bradley was investigated by the police, he cleaned the exterior of his vehicle on at least three occasions, including washing the undercarriage of the red Chevy Tahoe. Investigators also learned that Bradley asked his landlord for a carpet-cleaning device despite the fact that his apartment had new carpets that were only three months old. A search of

Bradley's residence and vehicle, and testing of several seized items, revealed no forensic evidence indicating that Shannon was ever present in either place, despite cell phone evidence that proved the opposite: she had been in both on April 5.

Shannon's cell phone was turned off in the area of Bradley's apartment and was off the network when investigators tried to ping it in the days after her disappearance. Bradley also turned his cell phone off for 13 hours around the time of Shannon's disappearance. If he was worried about her walking around alone in an unsafe area, a dark and wooded park surrounding a lake with snakes and alligators, why would he turn off his phone? Bradley could provide no explanation for why he would do that, especially since he cared for Shannon and he acknowledged that he had left her in an unsafe place before immediately regretting the decision and searching for her.

It certainly didn't make Bradley less of a suspect when investigators discovered that he had searched the internet for ways to defeat cell phone tracking. FBI agents determined that Bradley had conducted this computer search and had downloaded an article about cell phone tracking on April 20, five days after he'd been pushed on the cell phone issue by detectives in an interrogation room.

Finally, Bradley's failure to act was very telling to family, friends, and investigators. Despite being a co-worker and friend, and Bradley's expressing to detectives he wanted to be more than that, he never helped search for Shannon. He was the only person in Shannon's phone records who had called her numerous times leading up to April 5, but not a single time after her disappearance. At this point, we were sure he didn't call because he was the only person on the planet who already knew that she would not be answering the phone. And now we had to prove it.

3. Bradley's Other Crimes

Typically, the fact that a defendant has engaged in other bad conduct in their life, like premeditated murder of an eight-year-old girl in Bradley's case, is not admissible evidence in a trial. People cannot be punished merely for having bad character. If they have already been convicted of a crime, it would violate the principle of double jeopardy to allow them to be punished again by putting the same evidence before another jury in a different case.

As we saw in chapter 3, however, evidence of other crimes may be admissible under Rule 404(b) in certain circumstances. This includes showing that a defendant used a certain modus operandi in carrying out a crime, that he was driven by a certain motive to commit a crime, or that he carried out that crime with planning, preparation, premeditation, and deliberation. Prior bad acts and crimes can also be used to show the identity of a perpetrator.

It was easy to prove that Bradley killed Ivy Gipson: he confessed to her murder, pled guilty as charged, and spent 25 years in prison. While the killing happened more than a quarter-century before Shannon's disappearance, Bradley was incarcerated nearly all of that time. The period spent in confinement stops the clock when considering temporal proximity, that is, the time between the 404(b) offense and the currently charged offense.[8] Ivy was killed in 1988 and Bradley was immediately jailed and not released until February 2013. Accordingly, the length of time between Ivy's murder and Shannon's murder was actually only 15 months in calculating time for the purpose of 404(b).

It was much harder to produce sufficient evidence to prove that Bradley had killed Elisha. In fact, it would take investigators another two years before they could charge Bradley with her murder. Elisha was reported missing by her mother on October 21, 2013, six months before her body was discovered. Her mother had expressed concern that she may already have been missing for a couple of months. At the time of the missing persons report, detectives didn't even know who Bradley was and everyone assumed that the rumor on the street was true: that Elisha went to Florida and was now prostituting to support her heroin addiction.

To establish that Bradley had killed Elisha, and make her murder admissible in Shannon's trial, the state relied on a combination of circumstantial and direct evidence.

First, the circumstances of her disappearance put her in Bradley's orbit. Elisha would frequently work as a prostitute out of the Market Street motels but was also known as a streetwalker along Dawson Street. At the time Elisha went missing, Bradley lived at 711 Dawson Street.

Second, Elisha was found in a remote area, down a long road that had a chain with a lock blocking off vehicle traffic. Only Steve and Bradley had access to this path, and Bradley had been in the area clearing the land in the time between Elisha's disappearance and when she was found. This was not a crime scene in Times Square, New York, where millions of people might visit; the pool of potential suspects who had access to this property was very small.

Third, the judge considered Elisha's manner of death and disposal. The medical examiner who performed her autopsy concluded that Elisha died from blunt force trauma to the head. She had suffered terribly. The same doctor also noted bruising to the right side of the neck, consistent with manual pressure. Ivy died from strangulation. Both victims had been killed in a highly premeditated manner.

Fourth, Elisha had been disposed of in multiple trash bags. In his 1988 confession, Bradley admitted to double-wrapping Ivy in two trash bags. The medical examiner who performed Elisha's autopsy testified that in the nearly 5,000 autopsies she had performed, she had seen victims disposed of in trash bags in only six other cases. Unusual, even bizarre methods of carrying out a crime such as this rise to the level of being a signature—an insight into Bradley's modus operandi.

Fifth, detectives were able to develop that Elisha, like Shannon, fit into a class of women who Bradley desired and pursued. In the 14 months between the time Bradley was released from prison for Ivy's murder and Shannon's disappearance, Bradley had or attempted to have sexual relations with at least four different women: Shannon, Elisha, Crystal Sitosky, and Schnique Miller.

All four women were single with limited financial means. Bradley provided financial support to these women through various means: Shannon (co-worker/driver), Crystal (money/handyman), Schnique (paid for sex), Elisha (dating relationship). All had a history of substance abuse: Shannon (alcohol), Crystal (pills), Schnique (crack cocaine), and Elisha (heroin). Bradley believed that all four women would prostitute themselves for money and gained their trust and confidence through sustained relationships.

Crystal testified that she saw Bradley with Elisha on at least four different occasions. She also saw photos of them together on a phone that Bradley lent her. Bradley was with Elisha on numerous occasions and referred to her as his girlfriend to Crystal. He later said Elisha left to work in Florida. Crystal remained in constant contact with Bradley at the time Elisha went missing and was also introduced to Shannon by Bradley. Crystal went to prison on probation violations surrounding prescription drug fraud in January 2014. She would later testify that getting locked up saved her not just from the streets but also from Bradley.

Schnique testified to having sexual relations with Bradley for money. While being questioned by police, Bradley volunteered that he was paying Schnique for sex. Schnique, who had convictions on her record for prostitution and drug offenses, described being tied up by Bradley during sex and treated violently.

Murder is rarely carried out in plain sight, and Bradley would bring these women to isolated places. Elisha was found in a remote location and Shannon was never found. Schnique had sex with Bradley at Steve's other remote property off Battleship Road on the other side of the Cape Fear River. Crystal testified that Bradley invited her to the Hoover Road property twice around the time that Elisha went missing. She went there to have intimate relations with Bradley for money in his red SUV. Despite his invitation, she refused to get out of the car and go into the woods because of the rain. It may have saved her life. Part of Bradley's modus operandi was to physically isolate his victims to stifle their cries for help.

Bradley told detectives that he fancied himself as a "knight in shining armor" when explaining why he was providing financial help and free labor to Shannon. His text messages to Crystal also showed a willingness to provide financial support to a woman he knew was a substance abuser. Investigators concluded that Bradley looked for "damsels in distress" and fed them, or gave them money for drugs, in order to keep them under his control. Another part of Bradley's MO was to find women who were socially isolated and on the fringes of society—if they screamed, no one would listen.

As for physical evidence in Elisha's murder, there were two big breaks that took investigators almost two years to develop. Eighteen months into the investigation, the defendant's former landlord came forward with a roll of duct tape. She found it behind a dryer in Bradley's apartment while cleaning it for new tenants. While not as precise as a fingerprint, the duct tape had the same class characteristics (color, weave patterns, materials, style of manufacture, etc.) as the tape found wrapped around Elisha's body.

But the biggest break came several months later when the physical evidence that police seized from Bradley's SUV, while looking for Shannon, was retested. He was the only one with access to his SUV, and with Elisha's DNA now in hand, scientists at the state crime lab compared her DNA to a stain on a floor mat of the Chevy Tahoe seized by the CSI unit of the WPD in April 2014. At the original testing, the stain appeared to be animal blood. Upon closer examination of the padding under the mat, it was determined that the substance was indeed human blood. It had given false results in a previous test because it had been chemically altered due to the presence of cleaning agents. When retested, a spot on the floorboard had been missed during Bradley's cleaning. The DNA found matched that of Elisha Tucker.

Pretrial Hearing

In April 2016, Judge Paul Jones conducted a lengthy 404(b) hearing, essentially a mini-trial of all three murder cases, to hear the facts and determine the relevancy of the prior bad acts evidence as it related to the prosecution of a no-body homicide case. He ruled that the murders of Ivy and Elisha would be admitted in Shannon's murder trial, as well as the short stories "Serial Killer" and "The Beast Within."

Ivy's murder was relevant under 404(b) because it showed a common plan or scheme and similar modus operandi: the means by which Bradley attempted to carry out and get away with murders through acts of deceit, concealment, and disposal. Ivy's murder was also relevant to the issue of the killer's identity, as well as malice and premeditation and deliberation.

Elisha's murder was also deemed relevant under 404(b) to show motive, malice, and common plan or scheme: to kill vulnerable women who were addicted to substances in varying degrees, and believed by Bradley (correctly or incorrectly) to be prostitutes, whom he befriended and took to remote locations owned by his boss. Elisha's murder was admissible to show intent, motive, malice and premeditation and deliberation.

In both Ivy and Elisha's murders, Bradley abused a position of trust and confidence. He lied to authorities, destroyed potentially incriminating evidence, and, in Ivy's case, he even staged a crime scene to mislead investigators. Bradley's bizarre disposal of Ivy and Elisha, now a signature, was crucial in showing why Shannon could not be located after exhaustive searches.

Judge Jones found that Bradley's short stories illustrated his criminal mind-set and manner of disposing of victims' bodies.[9] Bradley's Motion for Appropriate Relief, where he expressed remorse at leading detectives to Ivy's remains, was admissible to show why he continued to lie to authorities regarding Shannon's disappearance. As Bradley said to detectives during intense questioning on April 15, "I am not going to help you put a noose around my neck." In his mind, he'd been punished for his honesty in Ivy's case and would not make the same mistake twice.

The Death Penalty

Only first-degree murders are death-penalty eligible and not every first-degree murder qualifies for capital punishment. Instead, one or more statutorily defined aggravating factors must be present to seek the maximum punishment.[10] Among the 11 aggravating factors set forth in the law include the record of the defendant (where he has either killed before or been previously convicted of some other violent felony, or engaged in a course of uncharged conduct that came to light upon his arrest when the crime spree ended). James Bradley clearly qualified for the death penalty in that he had already been convicted of first-degree murder (Ivy) and had allegedly killed someone else (Elisha) before being arrested for killing Shannon.

Other aggravating factors for seeking the death penalty include killing a member of a protected class (like a police officer or judge), killing a witness, killing for pecuniary gain (i.e., money), or causing risk of death to multiple victims during the murder (like using a weapon of mass destruction, such as a bomb). None of these factors appeared to apply to Bradley's crimes.

Yet another category of aggravating factors looks at the circumstances of the killing. When a murder involves torture (where the victim is conscious of impending death and powerless to prevent it), or where a premeditated murder is coupled with other violent felonies (such as armed robbery, kidnapping, or rape), the defendant is death-penalty eligible. Because we did not know the circumstances of Shannon's death, we could not know whether her murder was "especially heinous, atrocious, or cruel" or whether Bradley had committed other felonies. As for Elisha's death, we had a body and there was evidence that she suffered mightily. Elisha had numerous skull fractures and broken ribs that bled internally and externally. Bruising around her neck further indicated that the trauma and choking she experienced occurred prior to her death. According to the medical examiner, Elisha was likely still alive when she was bound with duct tape, and may have been alive even when she was placed into trash bags and into a shallow grave.

Since the year 2000, prosecutors have been given discretion to seek the death penalty.[11] (Prior to that time prosecutors were required to seek the death penalty if one or more aggravating factors existed.) This is perhaps the biggest decision that a prosecutor will make and it should not be done lightly, arbitrarily, or alone.

All homicide cases in the Sixth District are subjected to a critical case review where a team of prosecutors evaluates the strengths and weaknesses of the case, suggests investigative strategies, and discusses potential plea offers.[12] For first-degree murder cases, I take the additional step of convening a committee comprised of three to five senior prosecutors to review the facts and consider the law before voting whether or not to proceed capitally. If the committee concludes by a majority vote to seek the death penalty, the lead prosecutor is instructed to seek it. If, in the course of plea negotiations, the defense offers to plead the defendant to life without parole, then the same prosecutors who comprised the original review committee must reconvene to determine whether to accept the plea.

FIGURE 5.4   DA's office critical case review.

In exercising our discretion regarding the death penalty, the review committee goes through a checklist of factors. We obviously do not consider things like race, religion, socioeconomic status, or national origin of the defendant or the victim. We do, however, consider such factors as: the danger posed by the defendant (including his record and any uncharged conduct); the presence of co-defendants and their relative role in the case and whether the evidence is based upon their testimony; the mental health of the defendant; the defendant's relationship to victim; whether the victim was engaged in any illegal or immoral conduct at the time; and the likelihood of a jury recommending the death penalty (i.e., past jury action in similar cases).

For the prosecutors on the review committee, the decision to put someone on trial for their life is not a theoretical exercise. When the review committee convened to consider Shannon's murder, we voted against seeking the death penalty. There were simply too many legal hurdles in convicting

Bradley of first-degree murder, and it seemed unlikely that, given the absence of a body, he would ever be put to death. We were also mindful of the fact that while there are approximately 150 inmates on North Carolina's death row, not one has been executed since 2006.[13]

Justice for Shannon: Bradley's First Trial

More than three years after Roberta and Aunt Beverly first knocked on Shannon's apartment door, the trial of her killer began on June 12, 2017. Jury selection was moved to Pender County due to pretrial publicity.

The jury listened to 27 witnesses and reviewed 150 exhibits. In addition to testimony from Shannon's family and friends, they also heard from FBI agents who tracked Shannon's and Bradley's cell phones and searched his computers. The jury listened to and watched many hours of Bradley changing his story during interrogation by detectives at his home, around Greenfield Lake, and at the police station.

We also called on the lead detective from Ivy's murder case from 1988 who read Bradley's confession aloud in the courtroom. The detectives who found Elisha while looking for Shannon took the stand and shared details of their investigation. The jury also listened to Elisha's mother and the doctor who performed her autopsy. They met Crystal and heard her story. Jurors also read "The Beast Within" and "Serial Killer" with rapt attention.

The defense did not call any witnesses and Bradley did not testify. His attorneys, both seasoned capital defenders, vigorously defended the case through cross-examination of the State's witnesses, relying on a mixture of two defenses. First, they argued the "I Did Not Do It" defense, contending there was not enough evidence to suggest that Shannon was even dead. They were adamant that a crime had not even occurred. The second defense they advanced was "Some Other Dude Did It." With no witnesses to the crime and no physical evidence, there was nothing directly linking Bradley to Shannon's murder. With no murder weapon, no crime scene, and no body, the case was without precedent. No one had ever been convicted in North Carolina where all of these things were lacking.

When it was time for the closing argument, I acknowledged the tough task before the jury. There were complex evidentiary issues, logical inferences to be made, and lots of dots to connect. While Shannon's murder was a no-body homicide, there were two other bodies that Bradley had thrown away like trash. Experience is the best teacher and murder is a learned behavior. Through trial and error, Bradley was refining his craft.

Despite his efforts to conceal evidence and extensive lies, Bradley could not outrun his past. The man the jury saw, dressed in his suit and appearing professional, was far different than the murderous man whom Ivy, Elisha, and Shannon saw in their last moments. Appearances can be deceiving. Bradley seemed innocent. He was not. To sum up our confidence in his guilt, I took the jury on a hypothetical boat ride, incorporating all the circumstantial evidence we had against Bradley.

Imagine that two people, James and Shannon, go out to sea in a boat. Only James returns. What happened to Shannon? Is she still on a vacation? Did she accidentally slip and fall over the side of the boat? Or, was she killed and thrown overboard?

We knock on James' door and ask him a simple question: "Where is Shannon?" At first he says that she never got on his boat. But then we show him a picture of both of them leaving the harbor together and going out to sea. "That's right," he says. "Now I remember. I dropped her off on a remote desert island." So we go out and look for her in a place where we know his boat has traveled, and while we are looking for Shannon we find Elisha floating in the water. She went out to sea with James but she did not slip off the side of the boat. Elisha was murdered and thrown overboard.

We look into James' past and learn that years earlier he took a little girl out to sea in a boat. He killed her too and threw her overboard. He pretended that she never got on the boat as well, but after a while he told the U.S. Coast Guard what he had done and where to find her. He spent the next 25 years in the brig regretting that he ever helped find the girl's body. Every day he vowed that he would not make that mistake again.

We also checked what he wrote in the captain's log. There were other women James planned on taking out to sea and he felt the same about them as he did about Shannon. In that same captain's log, James also wrote about killing women and pushing them off the boat to make it look like an accident.

The reason we cannot find Shannon is that when she went out to sea, she entered the Bermuda Triangle. She went missing and has never been heard from again. But we don't have to guess why she is missing. We know without doubt.

We frequently speak of triangles in court. We speak of lovers' triangles and the things that motivate people to kill. We speak of triangulating information, like when we are tracking phones:

taking two fixed points and moving toward the unknown. What we have here is a Bermuda Triangle of death. We know what happened to Ivy. We know what happened to Elisha. Bradley killed both of them with malice and with premeditation and deliberation. They are now shouting from the depths: "Don't let this man get away with killing Shannon too."

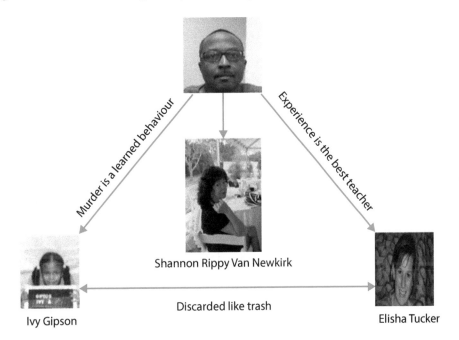

FIGURE 5.5   Bermuda Triangle of death.

The Verdict

The jury took two days to deliberate. They asked to review some of the exhibits that had been introduced at trial and for clarification on some of the legal definitions of murder they had been given in jury instructions. At one point, they were polled by the court and indicated that they were not in unanimous agreement. (Afterward, we learned that 10 jurors wanted to convict Bradley of first-degree murder, one juror wanted to convict for second-degree murder, and one juror was leaning toward not guilty.)

A knock finally came on the door from the jury room. They had reached a decision. Bradley sat stone-faced, while Shannon's supporters were so numbered that some had to stand in the packed courtroom. The clerk read the verdict: guilty of second-degree murder. The jury found that Bradley acted with malice in killing Shannon, but not with premeditation and deliberation. Judge Jones sentenced him to over 30 years in prison.[14]

Because Bradley was still on parole for Ivy's murder, the conviction also meant that he had violated the terms of his release. He was brought before the parole board within a week of the verdict. The parole board immediately reinstated the life sentence for Ivy's case. He was never getting out, even if he lived to be 100 years old.

Justice for Elisha: Bradley's Second Trial

Nearly two years after realizing that the body at the autopsy belonged to Elisha and not Shannon, Bradley was charged with Elisha's murder. The cumulative evidence we had collected in searching for Shannon, especially finding Elisha's blood in Bradley's SUV and duct tape in his home that was consistent with bindings around Elisha's body, gave us enough confidence to charge Bradley with first-degree murder.

A group of senior prosecutors once again convened a meeting to determine whether to proceed capitally. The committee voted to seek the death penalty and try Bradley for his life for Elisha's murder. The committee also made the recommendation that Bradley could receive life without parole (in addition to the sentence he was already serving on Ivy's parole revocation plus Shannon's 30 years) instead of the death penalty on Elisha's case if he would do one simple thing: take investigators to Shannon's body. Bradley promptly rejected this offer and demanded a trial.

Capital Jury Selection

On January 22, 2019, a special session of court was declared for the first death penalty trial to take place in the Sixth District in nearly 15 years.[15] An out-of-town judge with extensive capital litigation experience, Douglas Sasser, presided over the case. Ultimately, more than 1,000 citizens from Pender County were summoned as potential jurors. When they arrived at the courthouse, jurors were required to complete a 15-page questionnaire that covered everything from their family histories, to prior knowledge of the case, to their views on the death penalty.

The death penalty is the only instance where a jury, not the judge, decides the sentence. The prospective jurors were told that in the event that they convicted Bradley of first-degree murder, the trial would proceed to a second phase, known as the sentencing phase, where the only two possible sentencing options are life without the possibility of parole or death. Prospective jurors were further told that if they found Bradley guilty of second-degree murder, the judge would be in charge of sentencing and death would not be an option. Obviously, if Bradley was found not guilty of Elisha's murder, there would be no sentencing hearing.

Many people have strong views regarding capital punishment. Some are strongly for it and some are strongly opposed to it. No one is required to violate their beliefs (moral, religious, or political) to be on a jury. Jurors must be able to fairly consider both life and death as sentencing options. People who could never consider the death penalty under any circumstances, or those who believe it is the only proper punishment for someone who has been found guilty of first-degree murder, are not eligible to sit on a capital case. Only people who are able to base their verdict on facts and law and not on personal beliefs, emotion, or sympathy can ultimately sit as jurors.

Jurors were instructed by the judge and then rigorously examined by both sides about the four-step, tightly structured process they would be required to follow in arriving at a sentencing recommendation.[16] In step one, the jurors would be asked to consider if aggravating factors (the 11 statutory factors calling for death) have been proven beyond a reasonable doubt. If the answer is yes, they must proceed to step two. If the answer is no, they are duty bound to return a sentence of life without parole.

In step two, the jury is asked to consider whether mitigating factors exist. These are factors which do not excuse a killing but make the murderer less deserving of the maximum punishment. In this stage the burden is on the defense to prove the existence of one or more mitigating factors, which include things like mental illness, gross impairment, and having a diminished role in the commission of the crime like involving one or more co-defendants, to name just a few. Unlike aggravating factors, which are limited to 11 and defined by statute, there is no limit to the number of mitigating factors that a defense team may put forth and argue. In this stage, the burden shifts to the defense to prove, by a preponderance of the evidence, the existence of one or more mitigating circumstances.

FIGURE 5.6 Scales of justice.

Once the jury has found aggravating and mitigating factors, all of the factors are then put on the proverbial scales of justice in order to conduct a balancing test. In this third step of the process, the jury is asked to decide which way the scales tip. If the mitigating factors outweigh the aggravating factors, the jury must recommend life without parole. During the weighing process, it is not a numbers game: one aggravating factor may outweigh multiple mitigating factors, or vice versa. If, however, the aggravating factors outweigh the mitigating factors, the jury is instructed to move on to the fourth step.

In the fourth and final stage of the sentencing hearing, for the jury to recommend death, they must find, unanimously and beyond a reasonable doubt, that the aggravating factors outweigh the mitigating factors and are "sufficiently substantial" to call for the imposition of the death penalty. If even one juror fails to agree that death is the appropriate punishment, the judge declares a hung jury and the sentence imposed is life without the possibility of parole.

Judge Sasser ordered that every juror had to be individually questioned to avoid the danger of someone with pretrial knowledge of the defendant's former convictions contaminating the rest of the jury pool. If they already knew about the defendant's prior convictions or could not follow the law regarding the four-step process, the judge excluded them from serving. To learn about each individual's views and educate them about what would be required to sit on the case, both sides were also allowed to meticulously question every prospective member of the jury. The selection process took over seven weeks and over 250 people were individually questioned, sometimes over several hours each, before the 12 jurors and three alternates were ultimately impaneled.

The Trial

The trial was relatively straightforward. Elisha's family testified that she had endured trauma throughout her short life, including multiple sexual assaults, and had turned to heroin and then to streetwalking. She had gone missing for over two months, not seeing any of her five children who all lived apart from their mother, before they had reported her missing. This had been the third documented time in a decade that Elisha's mother had gone to authorities to file a missing person's report.

Detectives testified that they looked for Elisha off of Dawson Street where she was known to walk the streets and in the Market Street motels (the same group of motels that were the focus of our enforcement efforts, discussed in chapter 2) where she frequently slept. Detectives also put out a press release asking the public for help but gave up the search after a couple of weeks, believing the rumors on the street that she had gone to Florida with a pimp or a john.

The other challenge with the law enforcement search for Elisha was that they couldn't use the traditional means for searching for a missing person. Elisha did not have a cell phone, so there was no pinging or tracking to pursue. Elisha did not have a set schedule of traditional work or life commitments that would have caused concern if she was late or didn't show up for a period of time. She did not have a bank or a credit card to query for activity in Wilmington or in another state. Elisha had few friends who could account for her movements or articulate where they had last seen her or who they had seen her with. Elisha's transient existence meant that the leads went cold quickly and it seemed plausible that she had left the area. But there was no way to verify that.

Detectives were also permitted to testify that months later, when Shannon went missing, they made a grisly discovery of Elisha's remains far outside the city limits of Wilmington. Judge Sasser ruled prior to trial that detectives could testify that Bradley was a suspect in Shannon's disappearance but would not allow the jury to know that he had been convicted in a prior trial of her murder. (This ruling was based on Rule 403, which says that the judge may exclude evidence where its relevance is substantially outweighed by the danger of unfair prejudice to the defendant. For the same reason, we did not present any evidence of Ivy's murder during the case in chief.)

Crystal, the young drug-addicted woman with whom Bradley had met on multiple occasions, including at the remote Hoover Road property, testified that Bradley frequently gave her money for drugs. Crystal further testified that she knew Elisha and saw Bradley with her on multiple occasions.

Crime scene investigators with the WPD testified about sending evidence to the crime lab in Raleigh to test for everything from fingerprints to DNA. Once those results came up empty, they thought all was lost until Bradley's landlord, Alice, delivered a roll of duct tape to detectives two years after they had searched the home and missed this evidence hiding behind a dryer. Agents from the crime lab later testified that the tape bindings from Elisha's body was highly consistent with the tape found in Bradley's apartment, matching on 28 points of similarity through visual inspection and chemical testing.

Crime scene investigators also testified about combing through Bradley's apartment and car looking for any signs of Shannon or Elisha. What was evident to investigators is that Bradley had thoroughly scrubbed both places to the point that cleaning agents made lifting any forensic evidence nearly impossible. Despite initial testing from Bradley's SUV giving inconclusive results (most likely caused by severe chemical contamination from bleach or some other chemical), retesting of the floor padding found under the carpet, on the driver's side, left no doubt that Elisha's blood had soaked through to the floor board.

Elisha proved to be the ultimate silent witness. Not only did her blood catch Bradley but her body left no doubt about the suffering he had inflicted upon her. As I reminded the jury in closing arguments, the extensive injuries made clear that whoever had assaulted Elisha meant to kill her. The defense could not simultaneously argue that an innocent man was on trial and that "Some Other Dude Did It" while also contending that Bradley was guilty of second-degree murder or something less ("I Did Not Do It").

The jury took only four hours to find James Bradley guilty of first-degree premeditated murder. He would now face a sentencing hearing where the only two options would be life without parole and death. Still desperate to find Shannon, the detectives and I agreed to renew our offer to Bradley to plead to life without parole if he would help us find Shannon. He once again refused to help. The only power Bradley still had to inflict suffering on people outside of prison was to continue to hold on to that information. That was apparently enough for him to risk a sentencing hearing.

The Sentencing Hearing

The jury had already convicted Bradley of a brutal murder. That alone would be enough for the death penalty under North Carolina law. What they heard next was something far worse. He had killed twice before.

The lead detective from Ivy's case took the witness stand. No one moved as photos of a 30-year-old crime scene were shown and Bradley's confession was read aloud just as it was in Shannon's trial. They also heard, for the first time, that Bradley had been in prison for most of his adult life and had only been out six months when he killed Elisha. Shannon's mother also testified. The jury now heard that not only was Shannon still missing, five years later, but that another jury had convicted Bradley of her second-degree murder 18 months earlier.

It was now the defense's turn to present evidence. There were no mitigating factors set forth in statute (like drug use, mental incapacity, domination by other co-defendants, etc.) that applied to any of his crimes. Instead, the defense called two witnesses, a prison expert and a psychologist, to discuss a host of nonstatutory mitigating factors that fell into three broad categories: Bradley's difficult childhood; his exemplary military service; and time served as a model inmate without any infractions during his 25-year sentence.

Through cross-examination of defense witnesses, we established that while Bradley had been abused as a child, his older sister grew up in the same environment and went on to receive a PhD and write a book. We further had defense witnesses agree that whatever good Bradley had done in military or in prison did not excuse the behavior that would follow when he was discharged from the Army and released from prison.

The jury was now sent back to deliberate on the sentence and follow the tightly structured process that they first learned about during jury selection. They found all three aggravating circumstances: that Elisha's murder was "especially heinous, atrocious, and cruel"; that he had been previously convicted of another capital offense (Ivy); and that he had engaged in a violent course of conduct by killing another person (Shannon) before he was arrested and charged with Elisha's murder.

The jury also found, by a preponderance of the evidence, that there were many mitigating factors relating to Bradley's military service and his difficult childhood, including that he had an ACE score of 6 (we will discuss ACE scores in greater detail in chapter 8). All further agreed, however, that the aggravating factors outweighed the mitigating factors. In other words, the jury moved on to the fourth and final question: In view of all the evidence, were these aggravating factors "sufficiently substantial" to call for the death penalty?

After two days of deliberations, the jury announced that they were hopelessly deadlocked: 11 jurors were voting for death and one was voting for life. No amount of evidence or further discussion was going to change the outcome. Judge Sasser brought the jurors back into the courtroom and did the only thing he could under the law: he declared a hung jury for the sentencing phase because there was not a unanimous verdict as to the recommendation. Since a death penalty verdict must be based on a unanimous verdict of all 12 jurors, the only sentence Judge Sasser could impose was the one Bradley was already serving for his other crimes: life without parole.

The Death Penalty and Second Chances

Serial killers are driven by an obsession. So am I. After seeing so much victimization over the last couple of decades, I stay up nights wondering how we can prevent the tragedies that wash onto our shores at the courthouse. Much of what occurs is preventable.

First-degree murder, perpetrated by an individual who enjoys killing, is the least preventable crime that I have ever encountered. While there are no throwaway people and everyone deserves equality, there are some defendants who truly deserve to spend the rest of their lives in prison or to be sentenced to death for their crimes.

Many critics of the death penalty contend that the punishment is unfair because it is arbitrary. The argument goes that some defendants who are less deserving than others are on death row, usually for insidious factors like the race of the defendant and/or the race of the victim, rather than for the gravity of their offenses. While there are safeguards in place to protect against a "runaway jury," it is also true that verdicts, including the ultimate sentence of death, can change from one jury to the next.[17]

In chapter 2, you were introduced to Terrance Campbell, who brutally murdered Buddy Hall during a "gay panic" attack, and Paul Cummings, who tortured Jane Head to gain access to her bank account. In chapter 4, you met Shan Carter, who killed Ty Baker and Demetrius Greene during a string of violent crimes. All three men currently sit on North Carolina's death row. Do you think any of them are more deserving of death than James Bradley?

I am an advocate for rehabilitation and second chances. I applaud employers who give ex-offenders a job upon their release, provided there is a full background check and full transparency about the offender's past. Steve Mott took an ex-offender at his word. The disruption to his work caused by the investigation ultimately led Steve to lose his business. His girlfriend lost her life. Prison has its place. Violent and career criminals need to be locked up to protect society.

Let us also not forget about the victims. Incarceration is costly, but life is precious. How much is Shannon's life worth? Or Elisha's? We failed Elisha and Shannon the day Bradley walked out of prison on parole. Bradley should never have been released after he killed Ivy.

The two other women whom Bradley was grooming for the short time he roamed free, Schnique and Crystal, both struggled with drug addiction. Schnique was in a Florida prison serving out a three-year sentence for robbery by the time of Shannon's trial. Crystal testified that prison saved her life as it abruptly halted her relationship with Bradley. It is likely to have saved Schnique as well.

And what about healing? For all families who have a loved one taken from them by a murder, there is no such thing as closure. Their absence has left a wound that cannot heal. Elisha's five children will grow up without their mother. For Shannon's family, there will always be a missing chair around her family's table at brunch each year on April 6, her birthday.

I first met Shannon's brother, Shawn, as I walked the 15 acres of Hoover Road to visualize Elisha's crime scene. Shawn was there with a metal rod in his hands, plunging it into the ground to look for his sister's grave. To this day, he continues to drive around the region in his free time, getting out of his car with that rod when he sees an open field or dense stand of trees.

The Homicide Family Support Group

Nothing could be harder than losing a child. For relatives who have lost a loved one to crime, an added layer of anger, fear, and uncertainty is mixed into the equation as they wonder who will be held responsible, what will happen in court, and if their wishes will be considered. The members of my office have come to know the family members of murder victims through interactions that go well beyond a park dedication. To foster these relationships and support families, my predecessor, John Carriker, established the Homicide Family Support Group (HFSG). This group is made up entirely of victims' relatives who have experienced tragedy through acts of violence, ranging from DWI offenses to capital murder cases. Family members counsel each other through their grief and, in the process, learn about the road ahead as the case winds its way through the unfamiliar territory of the criminal justice system.

When a murder occurs, members of my office and members of the HFSG are aware that a family in shock will soon be coming to the courthouse. At the first meeting with the district attorney's office, we tell them about the HFSG. We ask them if it is okay for a current member, typically from a family that has experienced loss in a similar crime, to call them. A call from a family who has been there too, who can tell the new family that the prosecutors who handled their case are trustworthy and professional people, goes a long way.

Imagine when the mother of a child murdered last week gets a call from a mother who lost a child eight years ago and is told that it took her four years to smile and really laugh again. That is hope given by someone who has been there. HFSG members get incredibly close with each other and frequently check in with one another. Veterans educate new members about the grief they experienced along the way and help demystify the process by talking firsthand about their journey through the system.

The group meets one night every month. Food is served and childcare is provided. In lengthy cases, or when a family is coming in from out of town for a loved one's trial, HFSG members provide homecooked meals to the family. Members become like family to each other and attend big life events, whether it is the birth of a child, a wedding, or a funeral.

There is a confidentiality pledge that every participant must take to enter the room. Media is strictly forbidden. Members agree not to discuss the facts of pending matters, other than to give a brief description of the date of loss and manner of death. Some seasoned members have also shared their experience of discussing the case with "an investigator from the county" only to be cross-examined later about the statement they actually gave to an investigator from the public defender's office.

No professional counselors are present during these monthly meetings, and participants are cautioned that the HFSG is not intended to replace the counseling they may require from psychologists, psychiatrists, pastors, or other forms of support. The only professionals in the room are senior prosecutors and victim witness legal assistants. If the members have specific questions or want to provide new information about their case, they are told to schedule a time during the business day to meet with the detective and prosecutor who are assigned to handle it.

Family members typically have lots of questions: What are the steps in the process (first appearance through trial)? Why do some cases plead and others go to trial? Is the death penalty an option? Is probation even possible? For many of these questions, the moderating prosecutor may be able to provide an answer. Other times, this same prosecutor will report the family members' concerns to the prosecutor handling the case the next day.

In North Carolina, like many states, homicide victims' families have a constitutional right to meet with the prosecutors handling the case, to be present at critical stages of the proceeding, and to speak to the judge at the time of sentencing or plea.[18] The HFSG gives members a meaningful and continuous connection to the district attorney's office for the time the case is pending—which, in many cases, can seem excruciatingly long. Frustration with the system can be addressed and sometimes allayed by those who have been there before. By the time a new family member comes to court, they know about the process and a detailed letter or impact statement has frequently been written.

The HFSG not only supports the relatives of victims, but it also helps members of the DA's office. As the fog lifts in the days after a funeral, some relatives of the victims have meaningful information to provide that may aid in the investigation, help the prosecutor, or provide more insight into the life and personality of a victim whom we will never meet. It may be information or observations that lead us to important follow-up interviews, details informing our trial strategy, or new leads. The support that members give each other frees up very busy prosecutors and victim witness legal assistants to focus on the hearing or trial.

Members of the HFSG often attend court proceedings, lending each other support. Imagine the impact the presence of this group has on a judge and jury. Without uttering a word, a sea of people, diverse in many respects but united by grief, conveys the magnitude of crime and sense of loss to everyone in the courtroom. Some defense attorneys have tried to bar the HFSG from the trial. Their motions have never been granted.

Every year around the holidays, the families get together to remember their loved ones in a ceremony that is partly a celebration of life and partly a call to end violence. A slideshow displays images of the victims during happy times. People sing and play music, and flowers are brought forward as the name of each victim is called out. Members of my office, law enforcement officers, and community leaders come to what can only be described as a second funeral for these victims. No one can show the senseless loss through violence or impaired driving better than the Homicide Family Support Group.

The message is clear: people must learn from these senseless tragedies if these crimes are to stop. As a constant reminder of the lives that have been taken, these same pictures of the victims are on permanent display in the lobby of the district attorney's office (see appendix A). To the members of my office, these images provide perhaps the most persistent reminder of why we do what we do: giving a voice to victims.

Notes

1 *State v. Bradley*, 14CRS053046. Co-counsel was Barrett Temple. The Bradley case was featured on *On the Case with Paula Zahn*, "No Body, Two Crimes," aired January 26, 2020, https://www.investigationdiscovery.com/tv-shows/on-the-case-with-paula-zahn/full-episodes/no-body-two-crimes.

2 *State v. Bradley*, 88CRS20519 in Cumberland County. The Motion for Appropriate Relief was filed on April 6, 1994.

3　The corpus delicti rule provides that there must be corroborative evidence, independent of a defendant's confession or admission, that tends to prove the commission of the crime. *State v. Parker*, 315 N.C. 222 (1985).

4　*People v. Charles Manson*, 71 Cal.App.3d. 1, 42 (1975).

5　*People v. Cullen*, 37 Cal.2d 614, 624 (1951).

6　In *State v. Head*, 79 N.C. App. 1 (1985), a real estate agent went missing on a call and was never heard from again. Despite a massive search, her body was never recovered. Initially, suspicion turned toward the husband, but then the investigation turned toward a man who had called into the real estate office as a potential customer and had given a fake name. Id. at 11. Eventually, the victim's clothes were found near a creek, along with circular pieces of duct tape to suggest that she had been bound. Id. at 11-12. Trash bags found at the scene were later determined to be consistent with trash bags from the defendant's home; torn clothing matching the victim's was determined to be consistent with fibers from the clothes found at defendant's home. Id. at 12-13. There was also evidence that the defendant had lured two other female real estate agents to meet him at a listing where witnesses would not be present but fortunately those encounters ended without incident. Id. at 15.

7　*Epperly v. Commonwealth*, 224 Va. 214, 228-229 (1982). "[In the 1700s] a person might disappear beyond all possibility of communication by going overseas or by embarking on a ship. It would have been most dangerous to infer death merely from his disappearance. Worldwide communication and travel today are so facile that a jury may properly take into account the unlikelihood that an absent person, in view of his health, habits, disposition, and personal relationships would voluntarily flee, 'go underground' and remain out of touch with family and friends. The unlikelihood of such a voluntary disappearance is circumstantial evidence entitled to weight equal to that of blood stains and the concealment of evidence."

8　*State v. Castor*, 150 N.C. App. 17 2002 (murder committed 27 years before second murder being tried admissible under 404(b) to show defendant's intent and identity and the 18-year incarceration between crimes were excluded in determining remoteness issue).

9　See, *State v. Hayes*, 768 S.E.2d 636 (2015). (Rap lyrics to a song entitled "Man Killer" were found in the defendant's apartment containing references to strangling a female and taking her car keys. The court rules that the lyrics were sufficiently similar to the evidence of the victim's murder by stabbing and strangulation and moving her car. The song was admitted under 404(b) to show the defendant's identity, motive, and intent in committing the crime.) See also, *State v. Allen*, No. COA05-1480, 2006 N.C. LEXIS 1880 (N.C. Ct. App. September 5, 2006) (unpublished). (Rap lyrics written by the defendant while incarcerated prior to the trial were sufficiently similar to the facts surrounding the murder to be relevant to show motive and intent.)

10 N.C.G.S. § 15A-2000. Sentence of death or life imprisonment for capital felonies; further proceedings to determine sentence.

11 N.C. Gen Stat. § 15A-2004.

12 First Assistant District Attorney Lillian Salcines Bright runs the critical case reviews and is also a member of every death penalty review panel.

13 *Death Row Roster*, NC Public Safety, North Carolina Department of Public Safety, (Aug. 11, 2017), https://www.ncdps.gov/Adult-Corrections/Prisons/Death-Penalty/Death-Row-Roster.; "Ten Years after NC's Last Execution, AG Candidates Concur Death Penalty Should Stay Law," WRAL.Com, (Aug. 13, 2016), http://www.wral.com/ten-years-after-nc-s-last-execution-ag-candidates-concur-death-penalty-should-stay-law/15912008/.

14 *State v. Bradley*, No. COA17-1391, 2018 N.C. App. LEXIS 1054 (N.C.Ct.App. Nov. 6, 2018).

15 *State v. Bradley*, 16CRS007232. Co-counsel was Barrett Temple.

16 N.C.G.S. 15A-2000(b).

17 The North Carolina Supreme Court has a procedure in place to guard against the death penalty being arbitrarily handed down. The Court undertakes a "proportionality review" anytime a jury sentences an individual to death. In this review, the case is compared to every other case on death row. If the sentence is considered disproportionate when compared to the other cases, the Court is empowered to commute the sentence to life without parole. N.C.G.S. 15A-2000(d)(1).

18 N.C. Const. art I § 37 (h).

Figure Credits

Fig. 5.3: Copyright © 2014 by Star News. Reprinted with permission.

Fig. 5.3a: Copyright © 2014 by Star News. Reprinted with permission.

Fig. 5.5: Ben David, "Bermuda Triangle of Death," 2017.

II Community

Chapter 6

The First Two Arms of the Starfish

In this section, we look at the role that government and faith, the first two arms of the Starfish model, play in giving structure to community. America's town square has long been built around the duality of these two institutions, even as the Constitution provides that the church and state shall remain separate. We look at police use-of-force and misconduct cases and mass incarceration as we take on the thorny issue of race and justice and see how peace and calm, restoration and reconciliation can come through acts of forgiveness and through honestly confronting our past.

Protests in the Port City

Tear gas hung heavy in the air over the streets of downtown Wilmington on May 31, 2020.

George Floyd, a black man from North Carolina, had died begging for his life while a white police officer in Minneapolis, Minnesota, put a knee on George's throat for 8 minutes and 46 seconds. The officer and three of his colleagues, who stood by but did not act to save a helpless citizen they took an oath to protect, had been charged with murder. Now protests erupted around the country, including in my hometown.

Mayor Bill Saffo and I walked through the crowd of protestors, a bubble of SWAT

FIGURE 6.1   The view from the district attorney's office as police in Wilmington prepared for protests on May 31, 2020, in the wake of the George Floyd murder. Protests the day before were peaceful, but indications that this protest would turn violent led police to prepare for unrest.

team members surrounding us, to join NHSO Sheriff Ed McMahon and WPD Interim Chief Donny Williams, to announce a citywide curfew and call for calm. To the crowd, at least four with guns, and the thousands at home watching live on TV and social media, I asked the same question that Dr. Martin Luther King Jr. made the title of his last book, "Where do we go from here: chaos or community?"

In re McIver[1]

On April 5, 2007, Phillipe McIver, a 23-year-old African-American man, lay dead in the center of the road. The cause of death was a gunshot wound to the head. The young man was wearing only a white t-shirt. Two armed, white police officers with the WPD stood over him. To most of the crowd that gathered outside Creekwood's Section 8 Housing Community, it appeared that a "cover-up" was in the works. While the officers awaited the arrival of SBI agents from outside the city to handle the investigation, some members of the crowd fired shots into the air. A police tactical team was called in to disperse the crowd.

The city's collective fear was that Wilmington might soon descend into looting and violence. Rumors were flying around that there might be citywide riots; marches took place. Some walked with signs that read "Just Us," referring to the prospect of getting "justice" against the police. At the height of it, a group of concerned citizens pled with me to prosecute the officers. These leaders were men and women whom I admired: heads of the NAACP, and pastors and bishops who presided over large congregations of law-abiding citizens. Felicia McIver, Phillipe's mother, was prominent in the group. I asked her to join me in calling for calm.

If there was ever a time for using a case as an opportunity to build trust with a disenfranchised segment of the community, this was it. Here was a chance not only to get justice for McIver, but also for all other similarly-situated victims who did not have a well-publicized case attached to their names. The community was watching. The group of leaders who came to my office wanted me to send a message, one they had heard me declare before: "no one is above the law, and no one is beneath its protection."

There was one big problem with prosecuting the officers who fired the lethal shots: they were innocent of any crime. An independent investigation later showed that the shooting was entirely justified, and in-car cameras captured the entire event on film. Toxicology tests confirmed that

McIver was high on "love boat," a combination of marijuana and formaldehyde, which was likely the reason that he was wearing just a shirt and sitting in the street blocking traffic at the time the officers approached him. As they attempted to remove him from the road, McIver wrestled one of the officers to the ground, removed the officer's service revolver, and began shooting at him at point-blank range. The other officer, seeing that deadly force was being used against his partner, shot and mortally wounded McIver. Both officers then secured the scene, removing the weapon from McIver's hands, before the crowd came.

Confronted with these facts, the legal conclusion was clear: McIver's death, while clearly tragic, was precipitated by his illegal and violent conduct and not due to any racism on the part of the officers. The officers' actions were consistent with their training and any other response would have been unreasonable and potentially fatal for them or for others. I made the decision not to release the videotape, which showed a close-range shooting of a young man to his head. I also did not show the tape to Ms. McIver, knowing it would be too painful for her to watch. Instead, I showed the tape to the African-American leaders who came to my office and I released a detailed synopsis of the case to dozens of pastors to help spread the word about the true facts.

It turned out to be the correct course of action. There were no fires or looting in the days following the press conference. And yet, when the case was over, the conversation about race and justice in our community had ignited a movement. While the leaders who met with me admitted that the McIver case was not an example of profiling or racism, there had been other examples, too numerous to be coincidence, that needed to be addressed. Real peace and lasting calm could only come through confronting these much larger concerns.

Race and Police Shootings: Lighting the Long-Simmering Fuse

Deadly encounters between the police and minority motorists and pedestrians are now filmed on squad car dash cameras, officer-worn body cameras, and bystanders' cell phones. Many of these videos have gone viral and play continuously on 24-hour news channels hungry for ratings. Riots and marches, and sometimes violence and looting, have followed in cities as diverse as Ferguson, Baltimore, Cleveland, Oakland, and Charlotte. Officers have been specifically targeted for murder following these use-of-force cases in New York, Dallas, and Baton Rouge.

The lack of trust between police and minority communities has been present for years, fueled in part by disproportionately high minority contact involving the war on drugs and mass incarceration. Code enforcement, heavy fines, and court costs have also become a de facto "poor tax" that fuels the hatred that explodes when use-of-force cases occur.[2]

The familiar blue line bumper sticker is heavy with symbolism: a solid black line on top and bottom with a blue line in the center. The top black line represents law-abiding citizens in the community. The bottom black line represents the criminal element that would do them harm. In the middle, separating them, is the Thin Blue Line, the men and women of law enforcement who are there to serve and protect us.

Many are now asking the question openly: if this is "Us" against "Them," who is the "Us" and who is the "Them"? It should be obvious that all peaceful members of the community should support the police in fighting crime, even as they simultaneously call for transparency in the investigations of police misconduct and criminal prosecution when warranted. But when the community turns against the officers, we observe that officers begin to retreat from the very neighborhoods that need them most, fearful that aggressive stop-and-frisk policies will be

FIGURE 6.2 Thin Blue Line.

viewed as racial profiling and heavy-handedness. In instances where this has been the case, community-based policing was replaced with the "Blue Flu"[3] or "The Ferguson Effect."[4] The response has been disastrous. With the Thin Blue Line erased, "black-on-black crime" has run rampant,[5] the disastrous display of the Mirror Image Rule discussed in chapter 1.

How did this happen? Historically, when officers were involved in use-of-force cases, other officers who witnessed the encounter would either turn a blind eye to the abuse or fabricate details to back up a false account of what occurred. This "Blue Wall of Silence"[6] led to deep mistrust about whether truthful internal investigations into police misconduct were even possible. It also led to the opinion that the authorities were modeling the very worst kind of behavior—expecting cooperation on the street from reluctant witnesses—when these same officers were unwilling to speak up themselves.

The response in my district has not been to retreat and thereby fuel the victimization that runs rampant in high poverty, largely minority communities. Instead, I have advised law enforcement to step up patrols in these areas and have applauded them when they have relocated sub-stations and training centers in high crime areas. The important shift is for officers and community members to reimagine the role of police in these areas from warriors to guardians, where police are not seen as an occupying force, but rather allies who earn respect through sincere outreach.

Prosecuting the Police

There is a profound question that has been asked for over two millennia, "quis costodiet ipsos custodies?" which translates to "who guards the guardians?"[7] The answer to that question is the district attorney. When a use-of-force case happens, we must decide whether a crime has or has not been committed. Doing that involves employing a process that I call "the Integrity Diamond."

The hard call cases are not when officers commit crimes, but when they use force and there is a question as to whether the force was justified. When a suspect is killed by the police or dies in custody, there will be many questions asked by many people. Public scrutiny can be especially intense in cases involving police shootings, inmates hanging themselves in jail cells, or high-speed pursuits. A triangle is formed between the three Ps: prosecutor, police officers, and the public. Perceptions are formed about whether justice can truly be done. Some may scream for leniency, while others demand maximum punishment. These reactions, however, are typically based more on relationships and agendas than on the facts of the case.

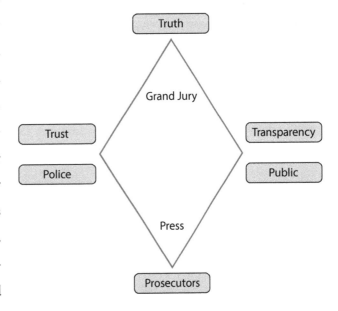

FIGURE 6.3   Integrity Diamond.

In these situations, the key for building and promoting trust among all parties is for the DA to remain independent and transparent while maintaining a commitment to doing the right thing.

The protocol never changes for these cases and the goal throughout is to adhere to the three Ts: truth, transparency, and trust. When an officer is a defendant or a victim of a serious felony, I call for an outside investigation by the SBI. I also give the head law enforcement officer of the involved agency a chance to make a joint request for an external investigation so that it is clear to everyone that we both welcome outside scrutiny.

If felony charges are filed against an officer, they come from the grand jury, not from the prosecutors. While these cases often cause division in the community, it is the community that ultimately decides the outcome through its charges and verdicts.

In cases where there are no charges and no grand jury is impaneled, I release a detailed synopsis of the investigation to the press and invite a member of the deceased's family and his or her attorney to review the complete file and interview the lead SBI agent. I also hold a press conference and answer questions when possible. While it would be easier to duck from the responsibility of handling these controversial cases, I choose to involve myself in their prosecution and only refer the case to an outside prosecutorial authority in extraordinary circumstances.[8]

Media and Police-Involved Uses of Force

When a use-of-force case occurs in my district, I am frequently in front of the cameras within the first few hours. My goal is to keep the calm by focusing on the process rather than the facts. I promise a complete and thorough outside investigation. I tell the community that my office will go wherever the truth leads. Most importantly, I promise full transparency. Essentially, I try to project calm by focusing on the three Ts and the three Ps which make up the Integrity Diamond.

The press is responsible for reporting the pertinent facts so that the public can keep a check on those in power. Tension arises when a use-of-force case occurs because the media moves fast while the wheels of justice grind slowly. Prosecutors and police will not talk about a pending investigation for fear of getting the facts wrong and potentially causing prejudice to future court proceedings. There are also ethical rules prohibiting pretrial publicity by police and prosecutors.[9]

When a high-profile use-of-force case occurs, I know that if I say nothing, there will be others, from the decedent's family members, witnesses, or policemen's leagues, who will rush into the vacuum, potentially setting the tone and often spreading misinformation. Saying nothing can feed the fear and conspiracies that may be swirling out on the street and through social media.[10]

Optics are important during these press conferences. I frequently stand with the head of the law enforcement agency in calling for this outside investigation.[11] I try to simultaneously convey that everyone in the justice system is committed to the truth, and that I will remain independent when making the call on whether a crime has occurred. I am the district attorney, not the police attorney.[12]

FIGURE 6.4   I joined Chicago Police Superintendent Garry F. McCarthy and Judy Woodruff on the set of *PBS News Hour*. During this appearance, Woodruff asked McCarthy about rumors regarding a video of a police shooting in his city. Within two weeks McCarthy was fired, the video was released, and the officer was indicted for first-degree murder.

When a racially charged use-of-force incident occurs or a contentious trial is about to take place, a group of African-American pastors remain on call to meet with me and the head of the affected law enforcement agency. When there is a damning video that is about to go public, we show it to them first. When I have decided that a case may be perceived as controversial, I do not try to explain my reasoning to the media in sound bites. Instead, I send out a detailed summary of the facts, together with my legal analysis of the decision. Approximately 100 of these faith leaders receive this packet of information so that they can talk to community members with the benefit of all the pertinent facts.

In the time since the McIver shooting, the use of the Integrity Diamond has been tested many times, and it has withstood the test. For example, during a four-month period, from October 2013 to January 2014, four people were killed in three different police-involved shootings in Wilmington.[13] A few months earlier, George Zimmerman was acquitted in the shooting death of Trayvon Martin in Florida in July 2013.[14] This incident gave birth to a national movement known as "Black Lives Matter."[15] The riots in Ferguson, Missouri, began in August 2014.[16] The Wilmington shootings fell squarely within the time frame when Americans were having a big debate about race, justice, and officer involved use-of-deadly-force incidents.

The Revolutionary Black Panthers

One feature of the protests that occurred throughout the country is that an outside group typically arrives in the affected community to lead the protest. Such was the case in my district. The Revolutionary Black Panthers employed antipolice protests in several such instances and marched with weapons to underscore their militant opposition to a system that, they believed, oppressed people of color.

FIGURE 6.5   Members of the Revolutionary Black Panthers on the New Hanover County Courthouse steps, January 30, 2017. *Source: Star News.*

The group hailed from Milwaukee and knew little about our community. In requesting a parade permit to gain attention for their cause, they requested to carry loaded firearms during the march. In response, I, along with the city attorney, issued a public statement notifying the Panthers of a state statute prohibiting marches with weapons. The First Amendment guarantees peaceful assembly but does not allow for an armed gathering that can potentially turn violent.

The permit was denied, but that did not deter the group from coming to town. They announced plans to gather in Creekwood to recruit participants for the parade. Almost no one showed up. The Panthers, failing to see why no one would engage with their effort, accused law enforcement of creating an atmosphere of fear where people would be afraid to join in the protests.

Next, with guns in hand, they marched on the sidewalk, instead of the street, claiming that this would not constitute a parade subject to state laws. Soon after, they assembled on the steps of the courthouse to hold a press conference. Having loaded weapons on county property, including the courthouse, violated a county ordinance, punishable as a class 3 misdemeanor.

Instead of making an arrest on this technical violation, the chief of police, sheriff, and I made a joint call from our command center and gave the group a verbal warning: the group was ordered to either put down their weapons or be arrested. Numerous deputies, who were also armed, approached the group and asked them to lay down their guns. The Panthers complied and the weapons were seized.

The Panthers disbanded after this encounter only to regroup later in the day at a private residence in downtown Wilmington. Taking up new weapons, the Panthers stood on the front porch and conducted a "tribunal." They had a list of grievances about the chief, the sheriff, and me, ultimately accusing us of genocide and other war crimes. Their call and response to the crowd included other grievances, specifically 1898, the closure of Williston High School, and The Wilmington 10, discussed below. They stomped on an American flag, all the while remaining on private property.

I was with law enforcement officers throughout the day, monitoring the events through several hidden cameras used by undercover officers in the crowd. As much as we disagreed with what was being said and done, we respected the First Amendment and the Panthers' right to free speech. We also could in no way countenance an illegal arrest—one that would have given them a larger platform and prove their assertion that the law and courts overreach and deprive people of their rights. Bored by our show of restraint and by speaking for several hours to a crowd that was not growing, the Panthers quietly returned to their hotels and ended their protest.

We agreed to return the Panthers' weapons the next day, provided they could prove ownership and lawful possession. Two of the guns were determined to be stolen from Wisconsin and one of the individuals attempting to retrieve a weapon had an active domestic violence protective order issued against him from the same state. With those exceptions, the guns were returned within 48 hours of their seizure. The group left Wilmington without incident.

Legitimate Grievances

Protesters take to the street with legitimate grievances, and it would be wrong for anyone in the criminal justice system to say otherwise or ignore their pleas for reform. The mistrust that bubbles to the surface following a racially charged police shooting is boiled in a cauldron that is heated by the slow burn of a painful history. Confronting that past is important and speaking honestly about the court's role in perpetuating racism through the years is necessary.

Our laws, starting with the Constitution itself, have given lip service to equal protection while that ideal has frequently been lost in the interpretation or implementation of the law. Profiling does occur and mass incarceration has disproportionately impacted communities of color.

As justice officials, we can do better and we must do better. Especially after the murder of George Floyd, there will be sweeping criminal justice reform around racial equity during arrest, conviction, and sentencing. This will include bail reform and the establishment of citizen review boards in communities where they did not previously exist. Every district attorney should welcome those conversations and want to be a part of those efforts. It will be our handling of cases, especially in violent crimes where overwhelmingly the victims are minorities and below the poverty line, where our actions will demonstrate that black lives matter.

And of course, people in power, including elected officials and the police, do commit crimes and must be held fully accountable. The impact goes far beyond the individual officer and official and can impact the entire system as cases are affected and trust is further eroded. And where an official or officer relies on his status to either perpetuate a crime or attempt to escape punishment, he should be punished more severely as a result.

In the sections to follow, we will look at how the government arm of the starfish is most responsible for spearheading reform. This includes holding police officers and public officials accountable, as well as a policy to ensure that damage is limited to the extent possible. We will look at how education, through officer and community training, can reduce harm and build trust. We will also explore efforts to reduce crime and mass incarceration at the same time. Finally, we will see how confronting the past, rather than denying it, can bring about a better community for everyone.

State v. Sloan[17]

The car looked a little too nice to be prowling around Houston Moore, a Section 8 housing community. The new model Buick was furtively starting and stopping, coming to a crawl by alleys and staying too long at stop signs. Was this a stolen vehicle? Was it a drug deal in the works? WPD Officer Stephen Griffith ran the license plate and the registration was valid. With no basis to stop the car, Officer Griffith let it go.

An hour later, he saw the same car again. This time there was a passenger in the front seat. Officer Griffith fell in behind it and followed at a distance. When the vehicle failed to use a turn signal and cut off a taxi, he initiated a pretext stop, using a minor traffic offense to conduct a more thorough investigation.

The car was driven by Mark Sloan, age 46, who spent his entire adult life working in Pender County law enforcement. Sloan's home was located only 30 miles up the road on US-17, but a world away from Houston Moore. Over more than two decades, he rose to the rank of captain with the Pender Country Sheriff's Office. His primary duty was operational authority over the entire patrol division.

Sloan was a deacon and active member at his Baptist church. He was also an elected official, serving as a town council member in Topsail Island. When visiting his office, it was not uncommon for visitors to hear the voice of Rush Limbaugh on the radio. A picture of Ronald Reagan hung prominently behind Sloan's desk. If a casting agency called looking for a white, law and order, God-fearing, conservative law officer, they could have asked directly for Sloan.

"What brings you to this part of town?" Officer Griffith asked, while also requesting license and registration. Sloan produced his license, showing himself fully dressed in his captain's uniform. "I just dropped off my nephew at his apartment around the corner and now I am completely lost," he replied.

It seemed unlikely that the passenger was Sloan's relative: Alton Ross was a 25-year-old African-American man who, at first glance, appeared to be a woman. Sloan added, "after leaving my nephew's house, I became hopelessly lost in this neighborhood. This nice young man has offered to show me back to civilization if I drop him off at a Burger King."

Officer Griffith was skeptical, and asked Sloan if he had dropped off his nephew in the last few minutes. Sloan said yes. But Officer Griffith knew he was lying, as he had seen him an hour earlier. "What is the name of his apartment complex?" Officer Griffith asked. "I don't know," Sloan replied, and pointed in a direction where there were no apartment complexes. "And what is your nephew's name?" asked the officer. "Cody Suggs," Sloan said. "We will be checking into that one, Captain," Officer Griffith said, and radioed for backup.

When the backup officer arrived, Sloan and Ross were separated. Officer Griffith again interviewed Sloan, this time in front of his squad car to capture the questioning on film. The lies continued. Sloan reiterated that he had dropped off his nephew and was lost. He had passed Ross on the road and said that Ross had flagged him down and he was giving Ross a ride to Burger King.

Meanwhile, Ross was giving a different story to the assisting officer. He was a male prostitute from Durham (a background check confirmed his address there as well as a recent conviction for solicitation). He had come to the Port City to stay with relatives and hustle on the street when Sloan flashed his lights at Ross, a signal that the driver was soliciting prostitution.

Ross further told the officer that he got into Sloan's car and they negotiated the terms of their arrangement, though Ross tried to put him off initially, telling Sloan, "you're not my kind of guy." Sloan offered Ross $60, which he put in the center console of the vehicle.

As he pulled across the street from some apartments on Wellington Avenue, Sloan asked Ross to expose himself to ensure that Ross was not an undercover police officer. Ross complied. Sloan then started to search for a more discreet location, but cut off the taxi without signaling, leading Officer Griffith to initiate a traffic stop. Ross never asked Sloan to drive him to Burger King. "I know what I am," Ross told the assisting officer. "Apparently you don't know who he is."

The name of the "nephew" came back as an unrelated white male who lived in rural western Pender County and wasn't related to Sloan at all. In an interview later that same day, Cody Suggs confirmed that he barely knew Sloan. Suggs stated he did not have an apartment in Wilmington, and he had not been in a car with Sloan the night before or ever, for that matter.

"He kept coming by my house to talk to me after the call," Suggs said, referring to a noise complaint that Sloan had responded to six weeks earlier. After that incident, Sloan returned several times for no obvious reason, leaving Suggs uncomfortable. "… I did not report it. Who was I going to tell?" Suggs' name was simply part of the cover story, the first thing Sloan came up with when being questioned.

Sloan relied on the fact that, between his word and the word of a common criminal, his version would go unquestioned. He was wrong. Officer Griffith arrested Sloan on three charges: soliciting prostitution, soliciting crimes against nature, and directional signal equipment violation. To the friends who knew him, or thought they did, Sloan's arrest was baffling.

Pender County Sheriff Carson Smith called me before the sun was up. "There has been a mistake," Sheriff Smith said. "Mark was giving a young man a ride to safety when he was pulled over by WPD officers who do not know him." Sloan had obviously called his sheriff, who now repeated the same version that Sloan had given to Griffith hours earlier. "Why don't you come to my office, Sheriff," I said. I had already received the call from WPD and had anticipated Sheriff Smith's involvement.

Sheriff Smith came to my office later that morning and we watched the videotaped interrogation together. The facts spoke for themselves. Whatever the outcome of any future trial, Sloan was caught lying to fellow officers. Putting aside his personal friendship with Sloan, Sheriff Smith took immediate action and fired Sloan within 24 hours of the incident.

Sloan was unrepentant and continued to profess his innocence, presumably confident that Ross would not return for the trial. He was wrong again. Months later, at trial, DA Investigator J.W. "Skip" Hedge located Ross in Durham, and the young man agreed to cooperate. Sloan was convicted of soliciting crimes against nature.

While the misdemeanor charge did not carry active jail time, District Court Judge Shelly Holt stripped Sloan of his badge and sent the judgment to Law Enforcement Training and Standards, effectively banishing Sloan from law enforcement for life. Limiting the damage that an officer, like Sloan, causes to the larger system is not only achieved in individual cases but through a policy known as *Giglio*.

Giglio and the Police Integrity Policy

People are presumed innocent until proven guilty. This right frequently makes it difficult for employers to act while charges are pending. "Let's wait and see and let the process run its course before taking any action," is the common refrain. But what happens when a police officer is charged? There are a whole host of concerns other than the crime itself. In Sloan's case, for example, we can no longer rely on his word as a witness in other pending cases when he lied to fellow officers. If his veracity is called into question, it calls all his arrests into question.

Following Sloan's November 3, 2011, conviction, I formalized a district-wide policy to handle these situations. The policy is based upon two United States Supreme Court cases, *Brady* and *Giglio*, which frame a prosecutor's obligations to be transparent with the court and with defendants' attorneys.[18] In introducing the policy to every officer, I emphasized that the credibility of the judicial system rests on the foundation that public servants are truthful and have integrity that is beyond reproach.

Brady material includes "exculpatory evidence," either testimonial or physical evidence, which might be favorable to the defense. *Giglio* material requires disclosure of "impeachment evidence" of any witness who is called to testify at trial. That includes not only criminal convictions, but anything that bears on the veracity of the witness (such as a prior statement by a witness that is inconsistent with the witness's testimony, false reports, etc.), as well as evidence of prejudice or bias (racial, religious, or personal bias against the defendant individually or as a member of a group). This evidence is important for jurors who will weigh the credibility of the witness testifying in court.

The *Giglio* policy puts the burden on the internal affairs (IA) division of each police agency to review the file of every sworn officer, reaching back a period of 10 years, and disclose to the DA's office the information mandated by *Giglio*. Next, three senior prosecutors in my office examine the file. If disclosure is required, prosecutors meet with the "*Giglio* impaired" officer to inform them that the information will be disclosed to the defense attorney and the trial judge and will be the subject of examination in open court whenever the officer testifies in the future.

In egregious cases, like Sloan's, where the conduct is such that a witness's credibility cannot be rehabilitated, we send a letter notifying the officer and their supervisor that we will not call them as a witness in the upcoming trial or in any future case. We call this the "death letter" because it may cause the officer to lose his or her job.

A brief example will illustrate the policy. Suppose that Officer Green routinely drives his patrol vehicle to and from work and typically leaves it at his residence when off duty. Department policy requires that the vehicle be used for work purposes only. On one occasion, Officer Green drives his patrol vehicle to the supermarket to go shopping on the way home from work. A concerned citizen takes a picture of his license plate and sends an email to the chief, upset that the officer is wasting taxpayer money. Confronted by IA about the incident, Officer Green lies and denies that he ever took the car to the store. The IA investigator then shows Officer Green the picture of his license plate and Officer Green is reprimanded.

In this example, had Officer Green been truthful when first questioned, there would be no *Giglio* violation. Misusing a company vehicle may or may not constitute an internal departmental policy violation, but it does not affect Officer Green's credibility as a witness. But his lie during an internal affairs investigation calls his veracity into question. He would then become "*Giglio* impaired" for 10 years and would be questioned about this incident each time he testifies in the future in any proceeding where he is an officer.

Of course, when an officer commits a crime, a conviction would automatically call his or her credibility into question. When that crime involves moral turpitude, it may result in the officer losing his or her badge. In extreme cases, where that officer is the only witness, it may require the DA's office to dismiss all pending cases of that officer: better to set several guilty people free than risk sending an innocent person to prison on the word of a disgraced officer.

Ending Mass Incarceration

Many see mass incarceration as disproportionately affecting people of color. Some claim that prison growth has exploded over the last few decades as a way of separating and segregating minority communities from privileged society.[19] The argument continues that after the 13th Amendment outlawed slavery, a racist criminal justice system has reinstitutionalized the economic engine of the South as prisons house mostly men of color. Chain gangs have become free "slave labor."

Today there are about 2.5 million people in jail or prison in America: 1.5 million in state prisons, 300,000 in federal prisons, and approximately 700,000 in local jails.[20] In a country with five percent of the Earth's population, we account for over a quarter of the Earth's incarcerated. The prison industrial complex has exploded in growth over the last few decades. And, while crime rates have generally decreased, big concerns about prison practices remain.

In 2015, police, sheriffs, and prosecutors from all 50 states traveled to Washington, DC, to call our nation to a higher purpose. The mission of the Law Enforcement Leaders to Reduce Crime and Incarceration was to simultaneously lower crime rates and the prison population. Major metro chiefs, rural sheriffs, and DAs from big cities and

FIGURE 6.6   Law Enforcement Leaders to Reduce Crime and Incarceration event at the National Press Club, October 2015.

FIGURE 6.7   President Obama met with members of the Law Enforcement Leaders to Reduce Crime and Incarceration in October 2015 at the White House.

small towns stood united in their purpose: by locking up only the right offenders, we can make our communities safer.

Of course, this group was not advocating for going light on crime. The founding members had made a career of being tough on criminals and rose through the ranks of their respective professions by being good at what they do. Many of the members are conservative politically, and few likely voted for President Barack Obama, with whom we met after announcing our group's mission to the National Press Club.

After the leaders assembled, five of us were asked to speak—to give our perspective on the importance of the issue. The police chiefs for Los Angeles, Chicago, New Orleans, and Houston all spoke passionately on topics ranging from community policing to outreach efforts to use-of-force protocols, as well as the need for more drug and mental health treatment. I was honored to be the only prosecutor or official from a small community to make remarks.[21]

Freed from the political pressure that many lawmakers face, these law enforcement leaders were telling the country that there can be a different path forward, one that works more intelligently and dispels several myths that have become part of the national discourse. Here are some myths and the reforms that we sought:

Myth 1 of Mass Incarceration: The government is making money by reinstitutionalizing slavery. *Fact*: Prison is expensive, averaging $30,000 per year per inmate, and nearly all prisons are run by governments, not private individuals or business, and are funded by state and federal taxes. While politicians who maintain tough positions on crime across the country agree that locking up offenders scores high on approval ratings, reality set in during recessionary times that government cannot continue the pace. Far from building more prisons, states, including North Carolina, are starting to close them.

Reform: Widely viewed as a nonpartisan issue, efforts to confront mass incarceration have been undertaken by all areas of government. The legislative branch has written new laws; the executive branch (police and prosecutors) has come together to advocate for a shift in resources and priorities; the judicial branch has followed suit with a change to the sentencing structure and even a deep examination of the goals of punishment. In 2012, the North Carolina Legislature, working closely with law enforcement and judicial officials, passed the Justice Reinvestment Act (JRA).[22] The goal was to reduce the number of people serving time in prison for drug and property offenses in order to make room for more violent offenders. With savings realized from fewer inmates, the money was "reinvested" into probationary community-based punishment that was able to focus on treatment. Seven years after the law was passed, the prison population in North Carolina fell by over 10 percent, or more than 3,000 people. Eleven prisons have been closed (even as the state population continues to grow) and there are 14 percent fewer people returning to prison now than in years past.[23]

Myth 2 of Mass Incarceration: Prisons are filled with nonviolent drug addicts and young men of color who have been caught with marijuana cigarettes. The war on drugs is really a war on people in poverty. We should follow the European model and save scarce bed space for violent offenders.

Fact: If we let everyone out of prison today, except for murders and rapists, the United States would still maintain a higher rate of incarceration than most industrialized countries.[24] Over 53 percent of state prisoners are incarcerated for violent crimes—murder, manslaughter, rape, robbery, and assault.[25] Violent criminals receive lengthy sentences, not property offenders or drug addicts. The content of the crime and the magnitude of a defendant's criminal record, not the color of a defendant's skin or whether their attorney is retained or court-appointed, are the driving factors at the time of sentencing.

Moreover, less than 1 percent of federal prisoners are incarcerated on drug possession convictions. In the state system, only 14 percent of the prison population is there on any type of drug offense; of those, nearly all are incarcerated for trafficking and selling.[26] Still more of these drug-dealing inmates are serving time for cases where prosecutors have pursued violent criminals by using the drug laws, which are easier cases to prove than violent crimes.

Reform 1: An important reform at the federal level corrected a racial injustice. Crack cocaine, long viewed as a drug of impoverished users, was sentenced much more harshly than powder cocaine, a drug preferred by wealthier, more privileged users. These differential punishments had a disproportionate impact on the minority community. Federal courts found the sentences violated equal protection. In 2010, the Fair Sentencing Act was passed that drastically reduced, and in some cases commuted, sentences to rectify the injustice.[27] Additionally, the Law Enforcement Leaders to End Mass Incarceration advocated eliminating or greatly reducing mandatory minimum sentences for drug cases, getting judges and prosecutors back into the job of sentences and plea bargains, rather than having their discretion handcuffed through legislative decrees.

Reform 2: The JRA required that defendants receive deferred prosecutions for first-time drug offenses, meaning that while probation is mandatory, offenders have a chance to keep the conviction off their records. The law further allowed for expunction—permitting one nonviolent felony or misdemeanor to be removed from a record after a certain period of time.[28] Additionally, the JRA reduced the time that habitual felons serve in prison for nonviolent underlying felonies.

Myth 3 of Mass Incarceration: The greatest abuses are done at the local level in jails where nonviolent offenders, who are presumed innocent and frequently destitute, languish in custody awaiting trial.

Fact: Local officials, like DAs, sheriffs, and county commissioners, must bear the cost of incarceration at the local level, about $80 per day per inmate in my district, and are accountable to the voters. Many defendants in jail have been convicted and are serving out sentences of six months or less (longer sentences get shipped to prison).

Reform: My office teamed with the NHSO to hire a full-time deputy to work daily alongside my prosecutors to monitor the jail population. Nonviolent persons who cannot afford small cash bail (for example, a homeless person panhandling or a teenager shoplifting) are released from custody even before the defense attorney meets their client. In just the first two years of operation, this program saved more than $2 million in the cost of incarceration and resulted in dozens of low-risk defendants being released from custody prior to trial.[29]

Respecting Authority, Not Fearing Power

While deadly police encounters are extremely rare, what is very common is the everyday heroism of the men and women who serve and protect our communities. Most officers do their jobs with honor and distinction, with little pay or recognition. To help create a better awareness or their roles and a respect for their positions, we have created two programs in my district.

The first program is called "Know Your Rights," where members of my office join with police officers to conduct a series of summits with community members. The meetings are held at nonprofit centers and houses of faith, frequently in high-crime areas. Participants learn that if they are stopped by the police on the street, in a car, or at their front door, they have basic protections guaranteed by the Bill of Rights.[30] We give real-life examples of how these rights may be involved in everyday circumstances.

Searches require probable cause or an admission of guilt for a specific crime. For encounters on the street, participants learn they have the right to calmly leave if they are not under arrest, or they may invoke their right to remain silent. If they get stopped in a car, they have the right to pull over in a safe and well-lit area or to put on their hazard lights and call 911 to explain that they are looking for such an area. Drivers should keep their hands on the wheel. They have a right to know the reason for the stop, to record the incident, and to get the officer's name. If there is an arrest roadside, the participant is told they have a right to leave their car in a secure place so it will not be towed.

If police stop by someone's home, participants are told they have a right to know that the person knocking is an actual law enforcement official by asking for credentials or calling 911 to see if officers have been dispatched to the property. Participants also learn that they have a right to ask why officers are at their home and to view a search warrant before allowing anyone to enter.

In all these instances, the basic message is reinforced: officers are there to do their job, which is to serve and protect. Law enforcement officers will have an open dialogue with the subject of their investigation, and, if the situation allows, they will listen to concerns raised at the time and explain their actions during a stop, search, or arrest. For their part, citizens are expected to comply with the officers' commands, even if they object to the law enforcement action at that moment. Citizens at the summits are given contact information for the internal affairs division of the police agency as well as my office, in case they ever want to file a formal complaint to have the matter reviewed.

These summits start the conversation and set the tone that law enforcement officers uphold rights that are the same for everyone under the Constitution. As part of these outreach efforts, the heads of area law enforcement agencies joined forces to illustrate the best way for citizens to interact with their officers to prevent misunderstanding and escalation. The campaign is called "Listen, Explain, Comply, Complain." With the motto "We are all in this together," their goal is simply to "make sure everyone gets home safe, and to encourage positive relationships and mutual respect." The compact is simple: officers will listen and explain; citizens should comply then complain.[31]

The second program in my district to build better relations that officers have with the community is the "Service Above Self Awards," named for the motto of the host organization, the Wilmington Downtown Rotary Club. When out of uniform, only a few people in law enforcement are recognizable to the community at large. Most officers work in obscurity and become famous only when they are injured or killed in the line of duty, criminally charged, or when a use-of-force incident gets media attention. In this respect, heads of agencies are like the quarterback of a football team, receiving the praise, and occasionally the blame, for the whole team's work. Most officers, by contrast, are like the offensive linemen who do the hard, punishing work and only get singled out for recognition when they jump offsides. Rank and file officers need to be made famous in their hometowns for their everyday acts of heroism.

FIGURE 6.8   From left: UNCW Police Chief David Donaldson, Wrightsville Beach Police Chief Dan House, Kure Beach Police Chief Dennis Cooper, New Hanover County Sheriff Ed McMahon, Wilmington Police Chief Ralph Evangelous, and Carolina Beach Police Chief Chris Spivey. *Source*: Positiveleoencounters.com.

At the "Service Above Self Awards" ceremony, officers from several different police agencies are recognized for valor in the line of duty. Friends and family are invited to hear the stories of these men and women, sometimes for the first time in public. Life-saving decisions, major arrests, courage in high-stress situations, and simple acts of kindness are all recognized as honorees hear their stories and biographies retold by the peers who nominated them. Alex Haley, the author of *Roots* and *The Diary of Malcolm X*, held as his personal motto, "Find the good and praise it." On this day, with this ceremony, we do.

History: Sometimes the Truth Hurts

Our country's founders ignored the reality that slavery remained even as they "secured the blessings of liberty" by guaranteeing "equal protection" and "justice for all" in the Preamble of the Constitution Our courts were complicit in the sin of this contradiction. The *Dred Scott* decision declared that the Constitution does not apply to slaves.[32] Then, in the wake of the 13th Amendment abolishing slavery,[33] a series of US Supreme Court decisions, *Plessy v. Ferguson*[34] prominent among them, created the absurd fiction that people could peacefully coexist in a "separate but equal" world.

Jim Crow laws kept blacks and whites separated at restaurants, hotels, athletic fields, and schools. In the years that followed, local police and prosecutors were cast into the role of upholding these evolving laws as lunch counters in Greensboro and buses in Birmingham became battlegrounds. Many faith leaders, including Dr. Martin Luther King called the contradiction out, noting that politicians in every branch of government were feeding their constituents "the stale bread of hatred and the rancid meat of racism."[35] Nonviolent protests were often met with police brutality.

The History of Wilmington in Black and White

In the weeks surrounding McIver's death, I watched the Duke Lacrosse scandal play out in Durham (discussed in chapter 2). At the height of the controversy, Duke embarked on a quest to hold a citywide discussion around the thorny issue of race and justice and it enlisted the assistance of Dr. Tim Tyson. Dr. Tyson, who is white, majored in African-American studies as an undergraduate. He gained a national reputation for his writing about the civil rights struggle both in formal studies and in novel form.[36] The son of a preacher, Dr. Tyson approached the issue of race relations with a fervor that was just short of religious zealotry, and he considered equality for all people to be a moral imperative.[37]

Dr. Tyson, who grew up in Wilmington, witnessed its racial history firsthand, and became a celebrated author for chronicling it.[38] His approach was original and bold in its execution. Instead of having an academic lecture on Duke's campus (that few would likely attend), he instead opted to teach a class to 300 students, diverse in many respects, at the Hayti Heritage Center, a historic African-American church.[39]

One hundred community members (including my mother, who had attended Duke as a young woman and lived five houses from the Duke Lacrosse house at the time of the incident) were invited to audit an eight-week course that would explore the history of race and justice in Durham. The lectures might address the Greensboro sit-ins one evening, while another night might have involved race relations in Durham during World War II. Toward the end of Dr. Tyson's talk he would moderate a panel of local leaders who would provide their own firsthand accounts. Time was devoted to either an open microphone discussion or breakout sessions in small work groups for community-based action on current issues.

To underscore that the purpose of the gathering was not merely an academic exercise, Dr. Tyson elevated the conversation by inviting a gospel singer to teach the class with him. Mary Williams, with a powerful singing voice reminiscent of Aretha Franklin, could take over the room at any moment. Williams drew everyone into singing well-known songs from the civil rights struggle and hymns from the slave era. When the songs were finished, Williams would explain the oral history that was transmitted through the music. As she did, she peeled back the secret codes and buried lessons that inspired the crowd in a way that Dr. Tyson could not do alone.

I audited one of the classes and explained to Tim and Mary that while I was a DA, I had a much different approach to handling cases than did my counterpart in their community. Within minutes of observing the class, I knew that I had found a great vehicle to engage community outreach in Wilmington. Over the next several days, I met with the same leaders who had come to my office after the McIver shooting. I encouraged them to come to see firsthand what I had witnessed and brought 16 of them to the next class. All were similarly impressed and agreed to approach Tim and Mary about replicating this class in our community. Both were excited by the opportunity and said yes.

The group was called the "Big Picture Talkers."[40] Our goal was to bring together unofficial leaders of the community: public educators, pastors, and heads of nonprofit agencies. We were not aiming for one event, but for the beginning of a process, one that would reflect the words of the class mission statement: "We are committed to bringing together a new multicultural community in order to create a space and time to dissect, discuss, and confront Wilmington's racial history. Furthermore, we wanted to attempt to understand history's persistence in the present and its possible effects in the face of the future." Our purpose was not to wallow in our city's painful history but to celebrate its many triumphs and highlight the achievements of our residents.[41]

The class we created, "The History of Wilmington in Black and White," was held in the old Williston High School building, to underscore its historical significance. (In the 1970s the facility was reopened as Williston Middle School, and it remains open to this day.) First-year attendance numbered over 300 participants. The class was held for four consecutive years and came close to reaching 1,000 graduates. It was funded through grants from the Z. Smith Reynolds Foundation and was run, in its first year, through UNCW's Osher Lifelong Learning Institute. In subsequent years, the class was run through the YWCA.[42] The friendships that were formed out of this shared experience survived the end of the semester and led to community action.

Three historical events covered in "The History of Wilmington in Black and White" deserve special mention: The coup d'état of 1898, the assassination of Dr. Martin Luther King Jr., and the Wilmington 10.

1. Coup d'état of 1898

Going back over 100 years, a great divide had been created in our community along racial fault lines. Once a shining example of racial equality in the Jim Crow South, Wilmington's black middle class was run out of town in 1898, and black elected leaders were forced to resign at gunpoint in the only coup d'état in American history. The Cape Fear River was said to be "choked with black bodies" after the massacre.[43]

This defining event in the life of our region is highlighted in the National Constitutional Center Museum in Philadelphia as a watershed event in our country. Unfortunately, it is all but forgotten in textbooks and class studies in our area schools. The diaspora of the black middle class that followed forever altered the neighborhood structure and economic vitality of the minority community in our region that remains to this day.

Obviously, no one is alive today who directly witnessed the events of 1898. But the "massacre," "riots," and "coup d'état," as it is alternatively known, is still with us in quiet whispers and in public discourse. Some call it "The Ghost of 1898."

2. Wilmington's Tie to Dr. Marin Luther King Jr.

When the US Supreme Court finally ordered the desegregation of public schools through *Brown v. Board of Education*, they added an important qualifier that it should be done "with all deliberate speed."[44] With no real timetable established to implement the law, needed integration was delayed, in some cases for years. In Wilmington, that delay lasted 14 years.

Williston High School was long considered a model for education and boasted many elite graduates who went on to prominent colleges and universities, making the school the pride of the African-American community. When the New Hanover County School Board ordered its closure and required black students to attend the formerly all-white New Hanover High School, the black community was outraged. This plan would surely relegate their children to second-class status and a loss of community identity. Dr. Martin Luther King Jr. agreed to visit and to speak at a rally in April 1968, less than two months before the school doors would be shuttered.

Dr. King was in Memphis, Tennessee, lending support to sanitation workers who were demanding higher wages and better conditions in the days before his scheduled appearance in Wilmington. He was to arrive in Wilmington on April 4 to deliver a speech encouraging voter registration at Williston. But the sanitation strike gained momentum and he decided to remain in Memphis to support the effort. The *Wilmington Morning Star* newspaper made a passing reference to the cancellation, noting in the Tuesday, April 2 edition that "King Cancels Stop in Wilmington Thursday." His decision to stay in Memphis proved deadly. King was shot by James Earl Ray as he exited room 306 of the Lorraine Motel at 6:01 p.m. CST at the very moment he was to speak at Williston.

The April 5, 1968, edition the *Wilmington Morning Star* led with the headline, "Dr. King had been slated to speak here." The next day, the same newspaper wrote: "200 students and adults from Williston High School paraded to downtown Wilmington for a short prayer service at the New Hanover County Courthouse. WPD Chief H.E. Williamson lauded the citizens' restraint and noted that 'no parade permit was needed for the march since the group stayed on the sidewalk.'"[45]

On the 50th anniversary of his assassination, I called upon Bertha Todd, a career educator who was born two months before Dr. King and who taught at Williston High School on the day he was murdered. Even at 89, Ms. Todd proved to be a tireless strategist and agreed to be my co-chair of the MLK50 Commemoration Commission.

The initial idea to hold one event quickly evolved into two: a daytime assembly for students and an evening event for members of the community. On April 4, 2018, hundreds of students from several area schools assembled at Williston during the school day to honor King's legacy by calling out school violence and bullying. Later that night, nearly 2,000 community members filled every available seat and stood in overflow spaces to hear the Williston choir, elected leaders, and other community members laud Dr. King (an open letter I penned to Dr. King was read aloud: see appendix B). At both events student essay writers were honored for standout passages they prepared about Dr. King's mountaintop speech.[46] They wrote about how the world looked from the mountaintop today and how it might have been different had King come to our city.

At the appointed hour, 7:01 p.m. EST, Major General Joseph McNeil, a graduate of Williston Senior High School and one of the four young men who refused to stand up from a white's only lunch counter at Woolworth's in Greensboro, rang a bell to remember the precise moment King was shot. The bell was rung an additional 38 times at Williston and in churches throughout the city to honor the 39 years that Dr. King walked the earth. (In 2020, Major General McNeil returned to his hometown for a ceremony finally recognizing his contribution to the Civil Rights Movement. The street in front of the courthouse was renamed Major General Joseph McNeil Commemorative Way through a vote by Wilmington City Council.[47])

A plaque was hung at the entrance of Williston that, like a plaque outside the Lorraine Motel in Memphis, bore an inscription from the Book of Genesis 37:19: "Behold, here cometh the dreamer. Let us slay him. And we shall see what will become of his dreams." We also engaged members of the nonprofit and faith-based communities to hold joint services and stand against racism throughout the year in regional public and private events.

3. The Wilmington 10[48]

The race riots that followed the painful closing of Williston High School spawned the celebrated trial of The Wilmington 10, at which nine African-American men and one white woman were convicted of firebombing a white-owned grocery store and sentenced to prison for a collective 280 years. Much of this history was never documented in school textbooks, but it has been handed down through oral tradition. This was especially true in Wilmington's African-American community, leaving an entrenched mistrust of established power for decades. Dr. Tyson invited some of the members of The Wilmington 10 in for a panel discussion, and the heavy-handed tactics of the lead prosecutor, Jay Stroud, became evident to me and others watching.

When the Wilmington 10 were convicted in 1971, many questioned their guilt. Their case made international news and Amnesty International declared them to be political prisoners. In 1978, their sentences were commuted by Governor Jim Hunt. In 1980, the Fourth Circuit Court of Appeals reversed their convictions.

The case file, made up of press clippings and the trial notebook of Assistant District Attorney Stroud, sat in a closet in the district attorney's office, gathering dust, for the next several years. I gave Dr. Tyson the case file, thinking it belonged more to history than to my office. What Dr. Tyson discovered during his in-depth review of the file was jaw-dropping.

Notes taken during jury selection by Stroud made clear the worst kind of tampering and racial discrimination. Stroud's own words left no doubt that he tried to select jurors who were known members of the Ku Klux Klan (KKK). He also selected token African-Americans who were likely to go along with a guilty verdict. When 10 African-Americans and two whites were selected to hear the case, Stroud knew that a guilty verdict would be less likely than if more white members were on the jury. His notes document a deliberate plan to fake an illness (before the jury was empanelled and double jeopardy would attach to the proceedings) so that a mistrial would be declared.

Stroud got his wish. A mistrial was declared, and the retrial of the case was moved to Pender County, a far more favorable venue for the prosecutor. Ultimately 10 whites and two African-Americans were selected onto the jury, a complete reversal in the racial composition of the first jury. The Pender County jury convicted The Wilmington 10 of all counts.

When the details of this injustice came to my attention, I knew that action was required, even four decades later. Stroud's behavior was not merely unprofessional, it was unconstitutional. While all 10 defendants had been let out of prison many years earlier, the criminal stain remained. All faced the same challenges that every convicted felon faces, and nearly half of the defendants had died without ever getting closure.

The only person who could pardon them (a move long-sought by the surviving members of The Wilmington 10 and their family members) was the governor. Dr. Tyson and I reached out to Governor Beverly Perdue and her legal team with this newly discovered evidence. On her last day of office, Governor Perdue pardoned The Wilmington 10.[49]

The Town Square: The Power of Symbols

America's earliest settlements reflected the significance that church and state played in moderating human conduct. Even before building their own homes, the first two structures erected in many of the colonial-era town squares were a church on one side of the town square and a jail on the other. Together, the pulpit and the prison acted as a hammer and anvil to shape the behavior of the townspeople. The same organization of buildings exists in towns across America. Religion inspires while the law requires.

Law sets the ground floor, the minimum standard for a decent society. These codes were enacted in view of what the "bad man" might do. The church was more aspirational, promoting ideal behavior that people might attain, even unwitnessed, because God would be watching. Both sides of the town square support each other. As President John Adams wrote, "Our Constitution was made ONLY for a moral and religious people. It is wholly inadequate to govern any other."[50]

Thomas Jefferson, who authored the Declaration of Independence and the Virginia Statute of Religious Freedom, later recognized that core rights are fundamental and that keeping the church and state separate was essential. That did not mean that citizens should abandon faith. As Jefferson wrote, "God, who gave us life, gave us liberty. Can the liberties of a nation endure when we remove a conviction that they are a gift of God?"[51]

In our nation's capital, the balance of power and the larger goals of our government are reflected in the city's design, where symbolism is heavy. The three branches of government and monuments to three great founders of our democracy are aligned in a cross. At one end of the cross is the US Capitol. Immediately behind the Capitol, keeping a check on the laws that are created there, stands the US Supreme Court (iconic turtles appear throughout the architecture, representing the slow and deliberate pace of justice).

In the center of the cross stands the Washington Monument. On the side opposite of the Capitol and Court is the Lincoln Memorial, which honors the president who oversaw the creation of the 13th Amendment abolishing slavery. On the other side of the cross is the Jefferson Memorial. Jefferson faces the White House on the far side of the cross and, not by coincidence, looks toward the Oval Office and over the shoulder of every president who would follow him.

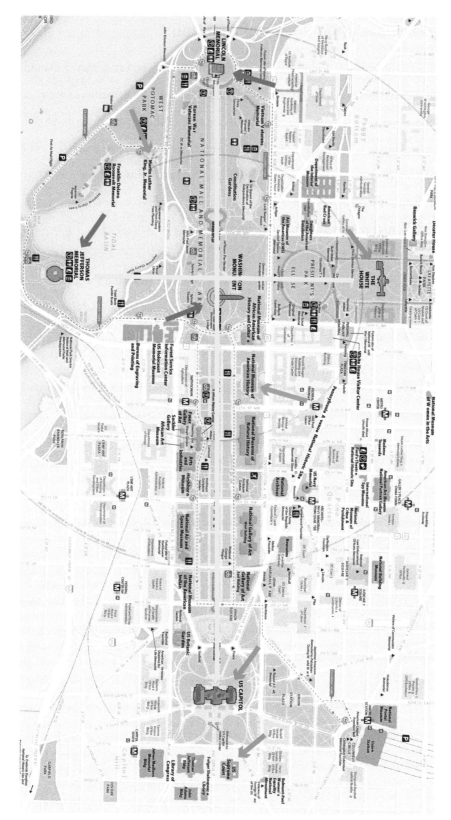

FIGURE 6.9 An aerial view of the National Mall in Washington, D.C.

Two new monuments have recently been added, giving recognition to the struggle that has been ongoing for over 200 years in our country. Next to the Washington Monument, an important addition has been added: The National Museum of African American History and Culture. Sandwiched between the Jefferson Memorial (honoring the president who owned over 600 slaves yet wrote that "all men are created equal") and the Lincoln Memorial stands an exhibit honoring the legacy of Dr. King. Appropriately, the monument is called "A Stone of Hope."

History does not change but the lens through which we view it can evolve. And what we choose to emphasize will guide us, now and in the future. In my district, statues of Confederate heroes guard both courthouses. Many question why this history is celebrated next to the halls of justice, rather than at the Fort Fisher Battlefield, one of the defining battles of the Civil War. There is a difference between remembering this history and venerating it. Conversations about the continued prominence of these memorials throughout cities in the south are challenging how history is portrayed in public spaces.

In addition to the memorial to the Coup d'état of 1898, we should erect a monument to the greatness of 1897. Freed slaves and poor whites formed a Fusion Party to create an inclusive

FIGURE 6.10 Wilmington Police Department Interim Chief Donny Williams addresses a crowd at the 1898 Memorial Park, the terminus of a peace march in the days following the murder of George Floyd. *Source: Port City Daily.*

community that was so politically powerful and so ahead of its time that it was perceived as a threat by some whites in the Jim Crow South. By recasting the pain of 1898 into the glory of the years that proceeded, we can remind everyone that it is possible to recapture the greatness that is in the DNA of the Port City.

The Faith Arm of the Starfish

Many people violate the Ten Commandments in search of the happiness that Jefferson included in the Declaration of Independence. Some seek pills or alcohol; some look for affection outside their marriages. They face consequences for these actions when they come to the side of the town square that dispenses justice.

Others pursue happiness by engaging in conduct that takes them to the other side of the town square. For them, true happiness comes from JOY: Jesus first, Others second, Yourself third. That sense of belonging comes more readily when there is a belief in something larger than oneself. For people who live by the Golden Rule, it is easier to obey the law. On this side of the town square, the truth can set them free.

When we talk about peace, we recognize that the word connotes something more than the absence of conflict. If malice is defined as having a depraved heart, peace speaks to having an untroubled one. And when we speak of doing justice, we are talking about more than punishing the wicked—it equally means uplifting the poor.

Ours is a nation that was founded on the belief that everyone is free to choose which god to worship, or even whether to worship at all. Yet we also recognize that we are one nation, under God, indivisible with liberty and justice for all. We are rooted in ancient traditions with profound implications: "And what does the Lord require but to do justice, love mercy and walk humbly."[52]

In chapter 1, I shared the case of a baby who was accidentally left in a hot car to illustrate the four reasons that we punish: general deterrence, specific deterrence, retribution, and rehabilitation. There is a fifth reason we punish that is gaining ground in modern day thought: restorative justice.[53] In this process, victims who have been harmed are given the opportunity to have the defendant make amends by coming face to face with them. For many, real healing involves confession and forgiveness. These concepts, of course, are at the core of the Christian faith, and they have sustained some families in heart-wrenching moments. Consider this next case as an example.

State v. Deans[54]

On Saturday, May 23, 2015, around lunchtime, Matthew Deans was traveling south on US-17 near the intersection of Sloop Point Loop Road in Hampstead. He drove a red 2012 Freightliner commercial box truck, carrying a full load of seafood.

Up the road were three cars, occupied by three generations of the same family, parked in a single file line at a traffic light. In the first vehicle, a 2008 Ford Edge, sat Gentry Dobbs Eddings and Patricia Eddings, a retired couple who just watched their daughter get married. In the second vehicle, a 2012 Kia Sedona, was their daughter-in-law, Hadley Eddings and her two-year-old son, Gentry Dobbs Eddings III ("Dobbs"). The third vehicle was a 2015 Kia Soul, occupied by Gentry Dobbs Eddings II, Hadley's husband and a pastor, who had just officiated his own sister's wedding.

When questioned later, Deans admitted that he was looking down to eat a sandwich and returned his eyes to the road just in time to see the back of the Kia Soul. He locked the brakes, but there was not enough time. After jerking the wheel to the left, Deans' vehicle struck the Kia Soul in the rear, sending the car, driven by Gentry, flying into the median of US-17 where it came to rest on its roof. After impact with the Kia Soul, Deans' truck next collided with the Kia Sedona, thrusting it forward and striking the rear of the Ford Edge, driven by the senior Eddings couple. Deans' truck rolled over onto its right side and crushed the back roof of the Kia Sedona in the process. Gentry, in the Soul, and his parents, in the Edge, were uninjured. Things were far different in the Kia Sedona, the car Hadley was driving.

At the time of the collision, Hadley was eight months pregnant. Her two-year-old son, Dobbs, was secured in a car seat in the back, the area that had been crushed under the weight of Deans' truck. Rescue personnel focused their efforts on removing Dobbs from the vehicle. Tragically, he had been killed on impact. Hadley was transported to NHRMC, where an emergency cesarean section was performed to save Reed, the unborn baby. The great joy that everyone experienced when he was born alive gave way to unspeakable grief when he succumbed to his injuries and died two days later.

Back at the scene, over a dozen law enforcement officers from three different police agencies, along with personnel from Pender Fire and EMS, began their investigation into the cause of the collision, starting with Deans. Several officers who were trained to investigate impaired driving cases spoke with him and knew to look for specific signs of impairment: slurred speech, problems with coordination and balance, and lack of mental focus. While they observed that Deans was visibly shaken, no officer observed anything to suggest that he was impaired.

Trooper Hendrickson, the lead investigator with the North Carolina Highway Patrol, escorted Deans to NHRMC to draw his blood as required by state law.[55] When questioning Deans as to what he thought he would test positive for, Deans replied marijuana. When pressed further, Deans stated he smoked marijuana a few days prior. The blood draw was conducted at approximately 6:30 p.m., more than six hours after the collision.

Deans was charged with one count of misdemeanor death by motor vehicle in the death of Dobbs Eddings and taken to the Pender County Jail. After Reed died, Deans was subsequently charged with a second count of misdemeanor death by motor vehicle on May 26, 2015. Both charges, while involving death, do not typically result in incarceration upon conviction.

Around 8:30 p.m., while at Pender County Jail, Deputy Patience Shepard was conducting a frisk search of Deans when he suddenly bent over in pain. Deans admitted to Deputy Shepard that he was withdrawing from heroin, a drug he now claimed he had used approximately two days earlier.

In the days and weeks after the collision, Trooper Hendrickson and the State Highway Patrol established a time line of Deans' movements in the 24 hours leading up to the collision. They determined that Deans began his workday at around 7:30 a.m. by picking up a spare refrigerator truck from his employer, Blackburn Brothers Seafood in Carolina Beach. He was asked to make a seafood run to Beaufort and Sneads Ferry, North Carolina, and was returning to Wilmington when he caused the fatal collision on US-17. None of the co-workers and customers who had encountered Deans in the hours leading up to the collision believed he was impaired.

Trooper Hendrickson executed a search warrant on Deans' phone. Deans' text messages revealed that he was a daily heroin and marijuana user. These text messages further revealed that he purchased heroin from the same dealer every day in Wilmington and that he smoked it to get high. At approximately 2:45 a.m. on May 23, 2015, less than 10 hours before the fatal collision, Deans purchased and used what he believed to be heroin from an unknown drug dealer near the area where he usually purchased his drugs. He sent a text to his regular dealer, who had made the referral to the other dealer, at 10:34 a.m., complaining that the substance he had purchased "tasted like sh … but got me high tho …" Deans' phone records also revealed that he texted and made phone calls throughout the lengthy drive before the crash.

On July 6, 2015, investigators received a toxicology report detailing the findings from Deans' blood sample. It was found that Deans had trace amounts of: (1) THC (the derivative from marijuana), (2) fentanyl, and (3) acetyl fentanyl. The report also concluded that the trace amounts of THC and fentanyl were not psychoactive, meaning they were not likely impairing at the time the substances were drawn from his blood, six hours after the collision. Heroin is undetectable in blood after a delay of this long.[56]

At the time of the incident, fentanyl was available on the illicit market in powder or tablet form[57] and had no accepted medical use in the United States.[58] Drug addicts, like Deans, were beginning to seek it as an alternative to heroin or were unknowingly ingesting it when the highly potent substance was mixed with heroin. At the time, acetyl fentanyl had been responsible for numerous deaths across the United States.[59] Before May 23, 2015, the federal government and the North Carolina General Assembly began the process of including this deadly substance on the controlled substances list, but at the time of the collision it was still not listed as an illegal drug.[60]

On July 17, 2015, Session Law 2015-162 was signed to include acetyl fentanyl as a Schedule I controlled substance under the North Carolina Controlled Substances Act[61] and came into effect December 1, 2015. (This law change would mean that driving with any amount of fentanyl would constitute driving while impaired, subjecting a defendant to far harsher punishment when causing a fatality. We will see this in chapter 8 in the case of *State v. Hayes*). This law was not retroactive to the collision and the deaths of the Eddings children.

The driver of a commercial vehicle, such as a Freightliner box truck, has a special duty to operate his vehicle with heightened caution and care. The state contended that Deans violated this duty in three ways when he (1) ate a sandwich while driving; (2) continuously texted and talked on the phone, including making a call at 12:18 p.m., which was determined to be the exact moment that the collision occurred; and (3) operated the vehicle with no more than 4 hours and 45 minutes of sleep and after ingesting a deadly substance (even if the state could not prove that he was impaired at the time).

Involuntary manslaughter is the unlawful killing of a human being, unintentionally and without malice, that results from either the commission of an unlawful act, not amounting to a felony (like careless and reckless driving or texting and driving) or when a person acts in an unlawful or culpably negligent manner, where fatal consequences are foreseeable.

Culpable negligence in the criminal law requires more than mere "negligence" as that term is used in the civil law. Rather, culpable negligence is reckless or careless behavior that demonstrates a thoughtless disregard of the consequences or shows a heedless indifference to the rights and safety of others, such as gross and flagrant conduct, evincing reckless disregard of human life. (Like the definition of "implied malice" discussed in chapter 3 in *State v. Grooms*, the degree of recklessness is proven through a combination of circumstances.) On a continuum of guilt, culpable negligence for involuntary manslaughter is less in degree than implied malice necessary for second-degree murder.

Deans' actions, taken as a whole, prevented him from stopping his truck before slamming into three stopped vehicles, thereby causing the deaths of a young boy and an unborn baby. His actions constituted reckless behavior that showed a heedless indifference to the safety of others. These facts supported two counts of involuntary manslaughter, charges we indicted him on when the circumstances of the collision came to light.

Even two counts of involuntary manslaughter seemed to be an inadequate label for the crimes that Deans had committed. Had we been able to prove impaired driving, Deans would have faced at least a decade in prison, for two counts of felony death by motor vehicle, with the possibility of more than twice that amount of time if his recklessness rose to the level of malice for second-degree murder. (Refer to the sentencing chart in chapter 1: Involuntary manslaughter is a class F felony; felony death by motor vehicle is a class D felony; second-degree murder, under an implied malice theory, is a B2 felony).

Far from wanting the maximum sentence, however, the Eddings family did not wish to see Deans spend a day a jail. Their focus was on healing and forgiveness, not punishment. Their statements to him, as well as what Deans, the judge, and I said during the sentencing hearing, will take you inside the courtroom when Deans threw himself on the mercy of the court.

Matthew Deans

I'm sorry. There's not enough words to explain to you guys how sorry I am. And if there was anything I could do to trade places, it wouldn't take me a second to think about it. There's not enough words to tell you how sorry I really am and how my irresponsibility ruined you-all's lives. And you seem to be some of the nicest people I've ever seen.

I'm going to live a better life, living it for you and your kids, you-all, and your whole family. That's just something I'm going to work on. And after everything is said and done, I'm going to work on it. And I will make a better--I will improve my life and make it better and live a life for both Reed and Dobbs.

Hadley Eddings

From the day this happened, I've been very concerned about you … while losing my children has been the most devastating thing of my entire life, I know, without a doubt, that they are in heaven and that they are whole and that they are perfect. So I look at you and I say, I want you to have that too. I know that you did not intend for this to happen. I know you didn't do it on purpose. I know that mistakes happen and accidents happen and we make poor choices. I just want you to know that. I'm not mad at you. I forgive you. I want you to be rehabilitated. I want you to have a good life. I don't want this to be the end for you. I want you to have, I want you to make something of yourself.

Gentry Eddings

Dobbs' and Reed's life obviously was so significant to us. Words cannot describe how important they are to us. I firmly have hope—our resurrection hope to see them again. And that gives us hope. So we understand the magnitude of what's happened.

We know that it was not your intention for them to die. And that is significant and meaningful for me and for Hadley, and it's important for you to remember as well. And I know that that impacts the way we look at everything that's happened.

Still, mistakes were made that led us to this place. But I want you to know that I sincerely forgive you completely for everything that's happened. I have no grudge or ill will for you. I forgive you completely, because I've been forgiven much as well. I was a sinner in need of a Savior. I hope that you know that resurrection hope. That there's life after death for our sons, for us, and that God, Jesus Christ, loves you. He's a merciful and gracious God. It would bring us joy to hear that you are doing well in the future. We want to know a Matthew Deans that is free from addiction and that's doing well with his life.

Dobbs and Reed would want you to one day experience a life of peace and joy. I just have an image of them wanting to give you a hug. They are gracious boys. I believe they want to give you a hug and want what's best for you as well. We will continue to pray that that would be true for you. Ultimately, we pray that you would see--that we will see you in heaven with us in the end. We want you there. Our sons want you there too. I hope to one day join hands with you to worship the God who is our redeemer that's gracious to all of us. So we will be praying for you. And we love you. God bless you.

Ben David

Speaking for the dead and remembering the absent is the highest duty of a prosecutor. The obligation to see that justice is done is even more pronounced when, as here, two innocent children have been killed. The deaths of Dobbs and Reed Eddings ripped out the heart of our community. The sympathy that all of us feel for the Eddings family has been exceeded only by the compassion that they have displayed for the man responsible for causing their unfathomable loss. ...

The Eddings have forgiven Deans because they know that they have been forgiven. Their faith has not been shaken, it has been deepened. They have about them a peace that passes all understanding, and, in that peace, they have expressed great compassion. All of us are in awe of their example. While compassion plays a vital role in this case, my duty is to focus on consequences.

Today Deans is pleading guilty to the highest charges possible under North Caro-lina Law. He has come into court, without a negotiated plea, and thrown himself on its mercy. ...

The Eddings have asked for some good to come out of this tragedy. There has been. The North Carolina legislature has moved very quickly. On July 17th, after this incident and before this plea, Governor Pat McCrory signed into law that acetyl fentanyl will become a Schedule I controlled substance effective December 1st of this year. What that means and the message that will hopefully resonate from this courthouse all through North Carolina today is that ... driving with any amount of acetyl fentanyl is now impaired driving ... And so that is a good thing today. ...

While the family talked about compassion, I must speak of consequences. Some amount of incarceration is absolutely warranted and necessary here. And that's not coming from this family. That is coming from this District Attorney. I have a community to represent and a message to send. And that message is: Accidents happen when you engage in conduct like this—and this is in fact no accident at all … and should be punished that way.

I would like to end by saying something to Mr. Deans. … There's a reason why you lived. You need to find what that is. You need to do something with your life that goes beyond just living for yourself now. … If you ever put a pill in your mouth or a joint to your lips or any illicit drug in your body, you're dishonoring these children. But if you lead a good life, do everything that Hadley and Gentry said far better than I can, that will be a life well lived. You can be defined by this tragedy or your response to it. And we're all hoping that your response is a good one. Be somebody.

We have a job here on earth to assign labels to certain conduct. That's what our justice system does. … It gives you, your Honor, some discretion in terms of what to do next. And I think anything you could hand out would pale in comparison to the prison that this young man's conscience can become if we don't handle this correctly.

So, compassion does play a role, forgiveness plays a role, and it's a beautiful thing to see. But we also must send a message. The reasons we punish are not only to look at a specific individual, but to look at society in a larger sense and say some conduct is not okay. The reason that we elevated this charge is that what we had at the time of this incident was more than a mere accident caused by a distracted driver. It was a collision really of two worlds.

Having met the Eddings family, it's impossible not to feel the magnitude of the loss and the deep regret that the world will be deprived of getting to know the men that their children would have become. This is a day for Matthew Deans to stand before you in judgment. But make no mistake, this is also a day that Dobbs and Reed have their day in court. We're here for justice for them."

Judge Gorham

First, I want to say to the Eddings, I am so sorry for your loss. I cannot fathom the loss that you have and what you've been through. But it is clear that you have a hope. And I am thankful for the hope that you have; thankful for the compassion even that you have for the defendant in this case. It is a very difficult case. It is a very difficult time for you. I do wish you well.

Mr. Deans, if you will stand up, sir. And even as for you, I can't even imagine what you are suffering through because of what happened. I can tell that you are sincere and that you are very remorseful.

Madam Clerk, there will be two judgments. The Court orders that the defendant be imprisoned for a minimum term of 15 months and a maximum term of 27 months in the custody of the North Carolina Department of Correction.

The next judgment. 15 CRS 1117, count one, the defendant has pled guilty to involuntary manslaughter, Class F felony. In this case, the Court does find mitigating factors, numbers 11A, 17, 18, and 19. The Court finds that the mitigating factors outweigh the aggravating ones. The Court finds that the defendant shall be sentenced in the mitigated range of punishment. The Court orders that the defendant be imprisoned for a minimum term of 12 months and a maximum term of 24 months in the custody of the North Carolina Department of Correction. This sentence shall run at the expiration of the (prior) sentence imposed.

Subject to the following conditions, the execution of this sentence is suspended, and the defendant is placed on supervised probation for a period of 36 months. The Court imposes special condition of probation that the defendant is to report for initial evaluation by Treatment Accountability for Safer Communities (TASC) and follow all of the recommended treatment. The Court orders special condition of probation that the defendant is to serve an active term of five months in the custody of the North Carolina Department of Correction. This shall run at the expiration of the (the prior) sentence imposed."

Effectively, Judge Gorham sentenced Deans to approximately 3.5 years in prison. This was followed by three years of supervised probation for drug evaluation and treatment. If Deans violated either the terms of his probation or committed a new offense, he would face one to two years of confinement.

New Life

In the immediate aftermath of their loss, the Eddings, together with members of their church, opened a child center in Haiti after raising $2 million on a GoFundMe page. They named the center after Reed and Dobbs. In the following year, the couple continued to inspire many with their message of faith and forgiveness. On July 10, 2017, Hadley gave birth to identical twin boys: Isaiah Dobbs and Amos Reed. Their birth made international news and confirmed for many the existence of a good and benevolent God.[62]

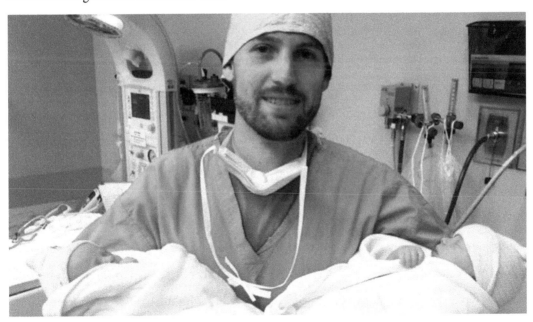

FIGURE 6.11   Gentry, Amos, and Isaiah Eddings.

Charleston

Less than a month later, three hours down the same highway where the Eddings lost both of their children, another agonizing story of loss and the power of forgiveness happened in the city of Charleston, South Carolina. On June 17, 2015, Dylann Roof, a troubled young man who had white supremacist leanings, went into Mother Emanuel AME Church, the oldest African Methodist Episcopal church south of Baltimore. After quietly praying with the group for nearly an hour, he opened fire on the dozen African-American congregants who had welcomed him into their prayer circle. Nine were killed. Roof ran away but was soon apprehended in North Carolina. He was returned to Charleston for his first court appearance.

Roof confessed to investigators that he carried out the massacre in the hopes that it would trigger a larger race war, both in Charleston and around the country. National news networks had been covering stories frequently throughout the preceding year, sometimes on a weekly basis, of cities on fire across America. A similar pattern had emerged from these many flashpoints, showing an African-American suspect killed by a white police officer and the entire incident caught on film. Thereafter, the local authorities quickly cleared the officer of any wrongdoing. Furthermore, the justice system was slow to act in pronouncing guilt. Riots and rallies by groups like Black Lives Matter followed as protestors demanded justice.

Weeks before the Mother Emanuel Church massacre, Charleston had the classic case of excessive use-of-force by a white police officer on an African-American suspect. On April 4, 2015, Walter Scott was gunned down while running away from Officer Michael Slager. The officer, seemingly under no continuing threat to his safety, shot Scott five times in the back. The entire incident was captured on a bystander's cell phone. Even to dispassionate observers, the video was shocking. It looked like murder, caught on film.[63]

The state was unable to secure a conviction in Officer Slager's 2016 trial, which resulted in a hung jury. Instead, he negotiated a plea with federal authorities to a charge of deprivation of rights under color of law. As part of the plea agreement, Officer Slager had to admit that he used excessive force, that he was not acting in self-defense, and that his use of force was unreasonable. In exchange, the state dismissed its second-degree murder charge.[64]

While there were initial attempts by outside groups to duplicate the riots in Charleston that had only recently quieted down in places like Ferguson and Baltimore following interracial officer use-of-force incidents, the Charleston residents seemed willing to be patient. They trusted in the system and would await a decision in a courtroom, not the court of public opinion. Outside groups soon left. Roof, however, thought that one more high-profile interracial killing and the entire country might descend into chaos.

Despite his planning, something unexpected happened to foil Roof's desire to incite a riot. At his first court appearance, the families of the several victims were permitted to speak. They stunned the judge and the world by forgiving the defendant. They forgave him for the same reason that the Eddings family forgave Matthew Deans.

The victims' families of the Mother Emanuel AME Church massacre forgave Roof because they too had been forgiven. As followers of the faith, they were now compelled to do the same. Justice, of course, would still be handled by the system. But these families refused to let anger rule. In the book they believe in, you pray for your enemies.[65]

After seeing this example, several leaders in Wilmington were moved to reach out to the leaders of Charleston, long considered a sister city and linked by a common history. When their Mayor, Joe Riley, announced his retirement a few months after what he called "the city's finest moment," a group of us drove to Charleston to see up close the people who kept the peace. We wanted to meet the people of Mother Emanuel AME Church. We wanted to meet the police officers who had operational control of the command station shortly after the church shooting. We wanted to know how it was done.

A few large points emerged from our discussions. First, as it related to the officer-involved shooting, focusing on the process and swiftly condemning the act proved to be crucial. Everyone knew that the criminal process would take months, but the officials, for example, the chief of police, the DA (called the solicitor in South Carolina), and the mayor, moved to assure all that justice would be served. The tone they set muted the outside protesters' intent to burn the American flag in the city center. We are a nation of laws, and no one is above them.

Second, as it relates to the church massacre, in the immediate aftermath officials requisitioned a hotel across the street and gathered together numerous family members. There were many, of course, with very raw emotions. Roof was still on the run. Some family members spoke in private, just as they later would in public, about immediate forgiveness. Not all family members were of the same mind, but all agreed that a unified call for peace would be essential.

Third, without compromising the case, officials were transparent about the status of the investigation and the resources employed to find the shooter. They also called out the motive for the killing and offered no excuses that it was anything else. Together with the victims' families, they organized a march involving thousands of people, walking across the Cooper River Bridge as a demonstration of solidarity.

Finally, the events of that terrible summer tested the years of intentional work to create a city that lived up to the ideals of equal protection. Early in the 1970s, at the start of his term, a young Mayor Riley was repeatedly tested. Despite being raised in a white aristocratic Charleston family and attending the nearly all-white Citadel, Riley was ahead of his time in his inclusive approach. For example, he embraced the arts community, establishing the Spoleto Festival as a major annual arts event, despite anxiety by some that the city would be overrun with gay and lesbian visitors.

Riley was also intentional about improving race relations. He gained the nickname "LBJ" or "Little Black Joe" as he went to AME churches, after the election, not just before, and worked with informal leaders to improve conditions for everyone. After Riley conducted a national search, he found a well-qualified African-American police officer from Florida, who was also Jewish, to serve as chief of police. When the KKK sought a permit to hold a march through downtown, Riley obliged, fully aware of the First Amendment. He asked Chief Reuben Greenberg to lead the parade. "All the Klansmen could see was a black guy in power watching over them and keeping them safe, and the ass end of his horse," Riley told us. The KKK seemed ridiculous and they have yet to hold another public rally in the city.

What our delegation brought back to the Port City was this: justice is not an event, but a process. What the world witnessed in a racially charged police shooting and a mass murder in a church could have happened anywhere. The peace that prevailed in the aftermath was years in the making. Different voices joined together in a call for peace, rooted in the shared traditions that had unified many of the formal and informal leaders for years. Through consistent inclusion, transparency, and a show of grace, Charleston did what a SWAT team in Ferguson and indictments in Baltimore failed to do: it kept the peace.

Healing the Divide

Many people of deep faith look at the root causes of crime—poverty, racial and income inequality, and the breakdown of the family—as moral issues, not political ones. Yet, political leaders are the ones who must give structure to communities in order to deal with these pressing moral issues. While the church and state must remain separate under the Constitution, the faith and government arms of the starfish are vital to our outreach efforts when confronting the touchy subject of race and justice.

Reconciliation can come through shared understanding and suffering. For many people, that shared understanding of belonging comes from faith. As my friend Pastor Rob Campbell of New Beginnings Church in Wilmington said, "These are not black children or white children dying in the streets of Wilmington—they are God's children."

He and many of the other faith leaders I have befriended are committed to having the different congregations come together. As Dr. King once observed, 11:00 a.m. on Sunday is the most segregated hour in America. They are helping to heal the divide in our community by hosting each other's congregations in their respective churches. The results were encouraging. Eight pastors from some of the most established churches, four white and four African-American, formed a joint Bible study to increase the bonds between the members of their congregations. They met weekly at rotating congregations. In time, they joined Habitat for Humanity to construct a house for a family in need.

A person's zip code defines his or her destiny far more accurately than race, religion, or creed. At the core of crime and victimization is poverty. The fact that an overwhelmingly high number of people of color live below the poverty line can lead many to mistake causation with correlation. People who fight crime, and study it, acknowledge that preventing victimization and lowering the rate of incarceration starts with improving the economic conditions of the poor. We are better served when we strive for equality throughout an area code rather than a zip code.

Unquestionably, racism has existed and continues to exist in all segments of society. No group is immune, and no sector should be ignored in this analysis, especially the justice system. A strong police presence in a high crime area will lead officers to stop more cars carrying guns and drugs. However, a collateral consequence of these pretext stops will be innocent people who are profiled based upon the color of their skin or the neighborhood in which they live. Trust is lost when law-abiding citizens question if the law really is being applied equally.

It is not enough to talk about black-on-black crime to excuse the disproportionate effect that over-policing and aggressive prosecution has on the minority community. There are deep wounds.

It is not inconsistent to both support law enforcement while also listening to and supporting groups who are raising legitimate concerns about officer use-of-force incidents, disproportionate minority contact, or mass incarceration.

As Wilmington native Michael Jordan, a basketball star at the University of North Carolina at Chapel Hill and the National Basketball Association, said when donating one million dollars each to the NAACP and the Policeman's Benevolent Association: "As a proud American, a father who lost his own dad in a senseless act of violence, and a black man, I have been deeply troubled by the deaths of African-Americans at the hands of law enforcement and angered by the cowardly and hateful targeting and killing of police officers."[66] Promoting the general welfare of every citizen makes us all safer.

My last two decades as a prosecutor have given me more hope than concern when reflecting on the difficult challenges we face. The reality of the role of race and how people are treated from arrest to sentencing is far different than the viral videos and sensational cases that crowd the national scene. To be sure, there are segments of the community who do not like or support the police. But people from high-victim areas hunger for justice in a way that people in gated golf course communities can only partially understand. For this group, crime is not a theoretical threat, it is an ever-present reality. They respect the rule of law, support the police, and want crimes reported and solved.

We must also confront the reality that, while it is exceedingly rare, there are some people working in the justice system who are racist. But these actors are not merely outliers; they are outcasts who tarnish the badge and undermine the oath of office that all of us take. Most public servants choose the profession to help people, knowing that those most in need would be coming from challenging circumstances. Any dialogue to the contrary comes from people with agendas who have not looked through the eyes of people handling and experiencing the toughest cases in their community.

Police officers and prosecutors are not perfect; like all humans, we make mistakes. These issues are complicated and cannot be classified as black or white or blue; they are gray and must be considered in an appropriate context. True reconciliation, whether bringing a city together in the aftermath of police use-of-force cases, in heart-wrenching moments involving restorative justice, or throughout a community and even a whole nation in search of healing, requires forgiveness.

Respect for authority begins with confronting the truth, even when it is painful. Just as we have seen that unearthing the past gives insight to a defendant's crimes, confronting our nation's history gives insight to the depth of America's "original sin," the legalization of human slavery and the painfully slow abolition of it and its aftermath. The truth does hurt, but it also sets us free.

Notes

1 There are many press accounts of the McIver Shooting. Co-counsel was Jon David.

2 In Riot-Hit Ferguson, Traffic Fines Boost Tension and Budget, Reuters, (August 19, 2014).

3 Marty Roney and Alvin Benn, Alabama Officers Call in Sick in 'Blue Flu' Protest, *Police-One.Com* (Copyright 2017) (August 12, 2016), https://www.policeone.com/Officer-Safety/articles/209489006-Ala-officers-call-in-sick-in-Blue-Flu-protest/.

4 Shaila Dewan, "Deconstructing the 'Ferguson Effect,'" *The New York Times*, March 29, 2017, https://www.nytimes.com/interactive/2017/us/politics/ferguson-effect.html.

5 *See* Richard Rosenfeld, "Documenting and Explaining the 2015 Homicide Rise: Research Directions," US Department of Justice Office of Justice Programs, June 2016. Criminologist Richard Rosenfeld analyzed FBI crime figures and found that the murder rate in 56 major US cities went up a stunning 17 percent in 2015 after years of steady decline. The problem was even more pronounced in cities with increased tension. As Heather Mac Donald observed: "… it was in cities with large black populations where the violence increased the most. Baltimore's per capita homicide rate last year was the highest in its history. Milwaukee had its deadliest year in a decade, with a 72 percent increase in homicides. Homicides in Cleveland increased 90 percent over the previous year. Murders rose 83 percent in Nashville, 54 percent in Washington, D.C., and 61 percent in Minneapolis. In Chicago, where pedestrian stops are down by 90 percent, shootings were up 80 percent through March 2016."

6 Bill Berkowitz, The Blue Walls of Silence among Police Enables Cop Brutality, *BuzzFlash.Com*, (March 5, 2015), http://www.truth-out.org/buzzflash/commentary/the-blue-wall-of-silence-among-police-enables-cop-brutality/19187-the-blue-wall-of-silence-among-police-enables-cop-brutality.

7 Juvenal, *Satire VI*, lines 347-348 (first century Rome).

8 In rare circumstances, an actual or apparent conflict requires the district attorney to refer the case to either the Attorney General's office or a neighboring prosecutorial authority. N.C. Gen. Stat. § 7A-64 (2004); N.C. Gen. Stat. § 114-11.6 (2010). I took this action after a NHSO deputy shot and killed

an unarmed college student through the front door of the student's home on December 1, 2006. My office originally presented an indictment charging the officer with second-degree murder. When the grand jury did not return a true bill, I referred the case to the attorney general's office. They sent the case back before the grand jury on a charge of voluntary manslaughter. The grand jury again did not return a true bill, effectively ending criminal prosecution. Ken Little, "Long Cleared in Death," *Star News Online* (July 12, 2007).

9 See Model Rules of Professional Conduct: 3.6, Trial Publicity and 3.8, Special Responsibilities of a Prosecutor.

10 Jim Salter and Eric Tucker, "Federal Report Faults Police Actions during Ferguson Unrest," *NewsOK. Com*, (June 30, 2015), http://newsok.com/federal-report-faults-police-actions-during-ferguson-unrest/article/feed/858010. Consider what was said by the Department of Justice following the DA clearing the officer in the shooting death of Michael Brown in Ferguson: "Had law enforcement released information on the officer-involved shooting in a timely manner and continued the information flow as it became available, community distrust and media skepticism would most likely have been lessened."

11 Rad Berky, "SBI Launching Investigation into Keith Scott Shooting, McCrory Says," WCNC.com, (September 22, 2016), http://www.wcnc.com/news/local/keith-scott-shooting/sbi-launching-investigation-into-keith-scott-shooting-mccrory-says/324039249. In the Scott case, many of the factors that typically produce protests and riots were not present: the suspect was armed with a loaded firearm found at the scene; the officer who used deadly force was African-American, as was Scott; and the Charlotte Police Department, led by Chief Kerr Putney, who also happens to be African American, had a long history of great outreach efforts. The *Charlotte Observer* identified what many believed to be the problem:

> The Charlotte-Mecklenburg Police Department is the only one in North Carolina that generally investigates its own officers' shootings, absent a request from victims' relatives for an outside probe. Real change, and real trust, will require a recognition by CMPD's leaders and officers that they must open themselves to new perspectives and potential changes. ... Showing openness to the outside investigations idea would be one way to help boost trust right now.

Charlotte DA Andrew Murray had immediately called for an outside investigation by the SBI and his senior prosecutor, Bill Stetzer, was at the scene to monitor the investigation. When DA Murray was ultimately able to speak weeks later, the outside investigation left no doubt that the shooting was entirely justified. By then however, riots had already occurred and the city had been damaged. The current DA, Spencer Merriweather, has recently changed the policy to require investigations by the SBI when police use-of-force cases occur.

12   While DAs in my state advise officers in terms of enforcing the law, they cannot defend officers when they break the law, write policies for them, or give advice in civil proceedings.

13   There are many press accounts, including the detailed synopsis of each shooting and my legal reasoning for not charging the officers, available for all three cases by searching for the names of the deceased: Brandon Smith, killed by NHSO and ATF officers, October 13, 2013; Teven Robinson and Ronald Roland, killed by WPD officers, October 25, 2013; and Grace Denk, killed by a WPD officer, January 28, 2014.

14   Lizette Alvarez and Cara Buckley, "Zimmerman IS Acquitted in Trayvon Martin Killing," *The New York Times*, July 13, 2013, http://www.nytimes.com/2013/07/14/us/george-zimmerman-verdict-trayvon-martin.html.

15   *About the Black Lives Matter Network*, Black Lives Matter, (August 8, 2017), http://blacklivesmatter.com/about/.

16   "What Happened in Ferguson?," *The New York Times*, August 10, 2015, https://www.nytimes.com/interactive/2014/08/13/us/ferguson-missouri-town-under-siege-after-police-shooting.html.

17   *State v. Sloan*, 11CR055727. Counsel was Kristen Robinson.

18   *Brady v. Maryland*, 373 U.S. 83 (1963); *Giglio v. United States*, 405 U.S. 150 (1972).

19   See for example Michelle Alexander, *The New Jim Crow: Mass Incarceration in the Age of Color Blindness* (2013).

20   Bureau of Justice Statistics—Total Correctional Population (Last revised October 15, 2016).

21   http://lawenforcementleaders.org/law-enforcement-leaders-launch-event/

22   N.C. Gen. Stat. § 90-96, 15A-145.2 (2012).

23   *Figure 21: NC Prison Population*, Justice Reinvestment Act Implementation Evaluation Report 2018, North Carolina Sentencing and Policy Advisory Commission, North Carolina Department of Public Safety, Division of Adult Correction and Juvenile Justice, Daily Unit Population Reports and Inmates on Backlog Reports (July 17, 2019).

24   "American Prisons—The Right Choices." *The Economist* (June 20, 2015).

25 US Department of Justice Statistics, 2013

26 Id.

27 See generally, www.sentencingproject.org, October 20, 2012, discussing the Fair Sentencing Act and the attempts to rectify disparities in sentencing between crack and powder cocaine.

28 *Summary of NC Expunctions 2017*, The North Carolina Justice Center, August 9, 2017, http://www.ncjustice.org/?q=second-chance-alliance/summary-nc-expunctions-2017.

29 Ray Jazayeri, the NHSO deputy who monitors the jail population every day joined me in meeting with a group that organized a "black mothers' bailout" for Mother's Day. We explained to the group that we shared their goal of making sure impoverished non-violent offenders should not languish in jail pretrial because of inability to pay a case bond. See *Star News Online* "Activists Give Jailed Moms a Mother's Day Gift: Bail" May 11, 2019. However, we disagreed with their fundraising efforts to bail out four women who had a combined 100 convictions on their records. Three of these women reoffended within weeks of their release.

30 US Const. amends. I-X

31 *Listen, Explain. Comply, Complain*, Wilmington Police Department, (August 9, 2017), http://www.positiveleoencounters.com/.

32 *Dred Scott v. Sanford*, 60 U.S. 393 (1857).

33 US Const. Amend. XIII.

34 *Plessy v. Ferguson*, 163 U.S. 537 (1896).

35 Dr. Martin Luther King, Jr. "Eulogy for the Martyred Children," September 18, 1963. https://kinginstitute.stanford.edu/king-papers/documents/eulogy-martyred-children

36 Tyson's best-selling book, *Blood Done Sign My Name*, recounts the story of an interracial murder in Oxford, North Carolina, and the race riots that followed in that community and later in Wilmington, in the early 1970s. *See generally* Timothy Tyson, *Blood Done Sign My Name* (2004).

37 Dr. Tyson's father and five uncles all attended Duke Divinity School to become Methodist ministers.

38 See generally Timothy B. Tyson, *Wars for Democracy: African American Militancy and Interracial Violence in North Carolina during World War II*.

39 One hundred students came from Duke, 100 from North Carolina Central, and 100 from University of North Carolina at Chapel Hill.

40 The "Big Picture Talkers" reference is from the book *Their Eyes Were Watching God*. *See* Zora Neale Hurston, *Their Eyes Were Watching God* (HarperCollins Publishers, Inc., 2006) (original 1937), 1–2. "The sun was gone, but he had left his footprints in the sky. It was the time for sitting on porches beside the road. It was the time to hear things and talk. These sitters had been tongueless, earless, eyeless conveniences all day long. Mules and other brutes had occupied their skins. But now, the sun and the bossman were gone, so the skins felt powerful and human. They became lords of sounds and lesser things. They passed nations through their mouths. They sat in judgment."

41 Great athletes who grew up in Wilmington include basketball superstar Michael Jordan; boxer Sugar Ray Leonard; tennis great Althea Gibson, the first African-American to win Wimbledon; and NFL hall of fame quarterbacks Roman Gabriel and Sonny Jurgenson. Great artists include painters Minnie Evans, Ivey Hayes, George Pocheptsov, and jazz musician Percy Heath.

42 To see a syllabus, please visit "The History of Wilmington in Black and White," http://www.wilmingtoninblackandwhite.org.

43 Zucchino, David. *Wilmington's Lie: the Murderous Coup of 1898 and the Rise of White Supremacy.* New York, NY: Atlantic Monthly Press, 2020.

44 *Brown v. Board of Education*, 347 U.S. 483 (1954).

45 *Wilmington Morning Star*, April 6, 1968.

46 Often referred to as *I've Been to the Mountaintop*, this was King's final speech, delivered in Memphis the night before his assassination.

47 "Maj. Gen. Joseph McNeil Commemorative Way Signs Now Up on 3rd Street." WECT, January 3, 2020. https://www.wect.com/2020/01/03/maj-gen-joseph-mcneil-commemorative-way-signs-now-up-rd-st/

48 The Wilmington 10 were widely covered locally, nationally and internationally. The 10 defendants were charged in New Hanover County and tried in Pender County. Counsel was Jay Stroud.

49 "Gov. Perdue Issues Pardon of Innocence for Wilmington 10." WECT.com. December 2012.

50 "From John Adams to Massachusetts Militia," October 11, 1978. Founders online: https://founders.archive.gov/documents/adams99-02-02-3102.

51 Quotations of The Jefferson Memorial, Thomas Jefferson Foundation, Inc. http://www.monticello.org/site/jefferson/quotations-jefferson memorial.

52 Micah 6:8.

53 See generally, restorativejustice.org. Frequently the defendant, victim and the community at large gather for a meeting to focus on the harm caused.

54 *State v. Deans*, 15CRS00114. Co-Counsel was Jason Smith.

55 N.C. Gen. Stat. §139.1(b5).

56 Lautieri, Amanda, "How Long Does Heroin Stay in Your System?" November 12, 2019. https://americanaddictioncenters.org/heroin-treatment/how-long-in-system

57 See Bahar Ghoulipour, "The New Street Drug to Watch: Acetyl Fentanyl," *Live Science*, PURCH (August 20, 2014), https://www.livescience.com/47451-emerging-drug-acetyl-fentanyl.html.

58 Drug Enforcement Administration—Office of Diversion Control (Drug & Chemical Evaluation Section). *Acetyl fentanyl (N-(1-phenethylpiperidin-4-yl)-N-phenylacetamide)*. July 2015.

59 *Acetyl Fentanyl*, Office of Diversion Control, Drug and Chemical Evaluation Section Drug Enforcement Administration, US Department of Justice, (July 2015), https://www.deadiversion.usdoj.gov/drug_chem_info/acetylfentanyl.pdf.

60 *Rules-2015*, Diversion Control Division, Drug Enforcement Administration, US Department of Justice, (May 21, 2015), https://www.deadiversion.usdoj.gov/fed_regs/rules/2015/fr0521_7.htm ("The Administrator of the Drug Enforcement Administration is issuing this notice of intent to temporarily schedule the synthetic opioid, N-(1-phenethylpiperidin-4-yl)-N-phenylacetamide (acetyl fentanyl), into schedule I pursuant to the temporary scheduling provisions of the Controlled Substances Act.").

61 H.B. 341/S.L. 2015-162, 2015-16 General Assembly, (N.C. 2015).

62 Jamie Gwaltney, "2 Years Ago a Tragic Wreck Killed Their Sons. Now They Have Twin Reasons for Joy," *The Charlotte Observer*, July 10, 2017, http://www.charlotteobserver.com/news/local/article160639684.html.

63 "A Closer Look at the Walter Scott Shooting." nbcnews.com, April 8, 2015.

64 "Michael Slager, Officer in Walter Scott Shooting, Gets 20 Year Sentence." nytimes.com, December 7, 2017.

65 "'I Forgive You.' Relatives of Charleston Church Shooting Victims Address Dylann Roof." washingtonpost.com, June 19, 2015.

66 Megan French, "Michael Jordan 'Can No Longer Stay Silent,' Donates $2 M to Police, NAACP, after Police Shootings." *US Weekly* (July 25, 2016).

Figure Credits

Chapter 7

The Other Three Arms of the Starfish

Young people hunger for structure. When they do not find it at home, they find it in each other. In this section, we look at three arms of the Starfish model (schools, businesses, and nonprofits) and see how these arms of outreach can come together to combat gang violence. Just as people can act in concert to commit crimes, members of the community can join forces to reduce it.

State v. Haugabook[1]

They hung out on the basketball court at Williston Middle School during a hot summer day in June 2012. Five teenagers, mostly 15- and 16-year-olds who were longtime friends, were just passing time. The man they met for the first time that day was a stranger, but he had their instant respect. Cornell Haugabook was 23 years old, recently released from prison, and a validated gang member (VGM) with the tattoos to prove it; a series of them covered the entirety of his chest.

The stranger had two guns and a plan, but he needed some help. Would anyone be interested in ordering up an armed robbery? The scheme seemed plausible: call a restaurant with a delivery service and lure the driver to an abandoned house where there would be no witnesses and no cameras. Bait money would be needed. When the man arrived to deliver the food, hand him the money, take the bag of food, and wait for his wallet to come out with change. It would be easy to take the food plus the driver's hard-earned money.

The man they lured into the spider web was Zhen Bo Liu, a father of two and a grandfather of one who had left China in search of a better way to support his family. He went to work at China King, a Cantonese takeout service in "The Bottom," a name commonly associated with the south side of Wilmington. Liu spoke almost no English; his boss taught him how to put his hands up in the air if he was ever robbed. "Just give it up if you are ever held up," he was instructed.

Haugabook had two revolvers. He kept the .38 special for himself and gave the "double deuce" (a long-barrel .22) to a 15-year-old named Mustafaa Friend. Two other teens joined in the conspiracy; Rasheed Thompson supplied the bait money, a $100 bill, and Manije Johnson-Martin used his cell phone to call China King and order about $40 worth of food.

Two more teens, Marvin White and Nathaniel Lawrence, came upon the scene while the robbery was in progress. They hid in the bushes while Haugabook and Friend waited on the porch of an abandoned house.

Night fell as Liu drove up to the shotgun house on 10th and Queen Streets. He had to use a flashlight to see the house numbers in the neighborhood but found the location where the food was to be delivered. Haugabook and Friend advanced on the car.

Things were going according to plan. Liu, who remained in the front seat, handed the food through the driver's window and had his wallet out to make change. The young men became agitated as Liu fumbled around for the correct change. They drew their weapons and began shouting, "Give us all the money!" Liu became terrified and confused as he struggled to understand the commands.

There was more shouting and then a gunshot, straight down through the open window, as Friend shot Liu in the foot. He immediately began to scream in pain. "Now we have to kill him," said Haugabook. Without saying another word, he shot Liu in the face at point-blank range. Friend and Haugabook, along with the four others who had watched from the sidelines, ran around the corner to Johnson-Martin's mother's house.

Safely inside the home, all six men ate every bit of the food that they had ordered. Some of the teens later claimed that they lost their appetite after Haugabook informed the group that if anyone snitched, they would be killed.

White and Lawrence, who at this point would not have been charged with a crime since they did not conspire to commit the armed robbery, returned to Liu's car. It had been 20 minutes, but still no police had arrived; despite the sound of two gunshots, no one in the neighborhood had called 911.

White and Lawrence took the car keys and cell phone from Liu's dead body. A few blocks down the road, they threw both down a drain: they would never drive the car and the phone was password-protected and formatted in Chinese.

After a time, Liu's manager became worried when his employee did not return to work and did not return multiple phone calls. He went to the address where Liu was last dispatched, and there he found his body. Police were finally notified of this senseless killing, in which a man was lured to his death while just trying to do his job.

It did not take police long to learn the identities of the defendants. The incoming call to China King for the fatal order was easily traced to Johnson-Martin's phone. He quickly confessed, likely unaware that the law made him just as responsible for Liu's death as the men who had fired the weapons.

Defendants who join forces to commit a specific act are responsible for that crime and any other crimes that are related to it under the theory of "acting in concert." Each is held responsible for the actions of the other if those actions are foreseeable and done in the furtherance of a shared purpose.[2] When two defendants join forces to commit an armed robbery and a murder occurs, both may be charged for the killing.[3]

White and Lawrence were arrested next. They had not participated in the plan to commit the robbery, meaning that they were also not responsible for the foreseeable murder that occurred during its commission; but they were charged with the robbery of Liu's keys and cell phone. They took detectives to the storm drain where they had thrown the items away and agreed to testify against the others.

Detectives found Thompson, the young man who provided the bait money and was present for the robbery and murder and charged him with everything: conspiracy to commit robbery with a dangerous weapon, robbery with a dangerous weapon, and first-degree murder. With these charges hanging over him, Thompson would likely plead.

At the time, the age of majority in North Carolina to be tried as an adult was 16 years old. Friend was the only defendant under that age. A special provision allows juveniles to be tried as adults, and juveniles charged with serious crimes can face a hearing in juvenile court to have their case moved to Superior Court. Friend was treated as an adult after this hearing due to the severity of the crime.

The defendants were not deemed eligible for capital punishment. No one under the age of 18 can face the death penalty; Haugabook was old enough to face capital punishment but was spared the prospect after a battery of tests established that he was "mentally retarded," which the statute defines as having an IQ below 70.[4] Even where aggravating circumstances are present, however, the state has the right to seek a life sentence in lieu of the death penalty.

Additionally, a defendant under the age of 18 cannot receive more than 25 years in prison for first-degree murder under the felony murder rule (in this case, murder during the commission of an armed robbery). An exception is made if the jury finds that the killing was premeditated and deliberate. Such defendants, regardless of age, can face a life sentence.

The state tried Haugabook for his various crimes. During the investigation, police found one of the two murder weapons at his home. By monitoring jail calls, they learned the location of the other one and were able to find it. Every co-defendant, except Friend, testified against Haugabook. The jury convicted him of first-degree murder under the premeditated and felony murder theories. He was sentenced to life in prison without parole.

The other five co-defendants pled guilty as part of plea agreements. For all except Friend, this required that they testify truthfully against Haugabook. Three of them had conspired together and all pled to second-degree murder. White and Lawrence pled guilty to common law robbery for their role in taking property after the murder.

Why was Friend unwilling to testify against a man he had only known for two hours? While only Haugabook was a VGM, Friend represented the "Ain't No Snitch" agenda that is so prevalent in gang culture. Gangs, like criminal conspiracies, cannot survive without loyalty to the common purpose. But perhaps the biggest motivator is the fear of being known as a snitch, and the reprisal on the street or in a jail cell that often accompanies such a label.

Even after the others had testified against Haugabook, Friend held out. The other co-defendants didn't have a hard time testifying against a stranger, but they struggled with testifying against Friend, whom they had known their whole lives. We gave Friend another week to come around. After showing him that we had his fingerprints on one of the guns and that the bullet from it matched the slug in Liu's foot, he finally pled to second-degree murder and robbery with a dangerous weapon.

While equal protection ensures that all people must be treated equally for the same offense, clearly there is a difference in the ultimate degree of responsibility between the one who pulled the trigger and those who were along for the ride. Prosecutors, through their plea offers, and judges, through their sentencing decisions, apportion fault based upon the level of conduct. In this case, the sentences were as follows: Haugabook (life without parole); Friend (23–31 years); Johnson-Martin (12–15 years); Thompson (10–13.5 years); Lawrence (1.5 to 3 years); White (1–2 years).

The teenagers who joined forces with Haugabook thought they were ordering up a robbery. Unfortunately, they joined forces with someone who was far more brazen, and they got more than they bargained for. None of the recruits likely realized that they had just signed on for a murder. As we saw in chapter 3, however, these teenagers were held responsible for the foreseeable consequences of their actions.

Gangs

Organized crime has been around for decades, especially in the larger cities. These groups include not only organized crime families like the Mafia, but also street gangs like the Crips, Bloods, and MS-13, to name just a few. Gangs have come to small cities and rural areas. I first saw them come to my district in the early 2000s. Many at the time dismissed it as young kids playing a game. Today that has changed.

There are hundreds of VGMs in Wilmington and many others who have evaded detection but associate with these groups. Being a gang member is not itself a crime. However, defendants attaining VGM status can receive enhanced punishment for the crimes they commit.[5]

In Wilmington, as is true everywhere else, there used to be established "gang leaders," but as these leaders have been incarcerated or killed, the streets have run wild. Of the 15 homicides in Wilmington in 2015, 10 involved guns and eight were gang-related. The lifestyle the gang members lead is extremely violent: it has been suggested that if you are a gang member you are 60 times more likely to be a victim of homicide.[6]

State v. Johnson[7]

When family members are in gangs, it is not uncommon for their relatives to be pulled into the vortex of violence. Al'quon Flowers, age 18, went missing in July 2011. Hours turned into days and then weeks. Investigators had few leads but a lot of suspicions. It had been a turbulent summer and the local gang problem was impossible to ignore.

Al'quon's three older brothers were all high-ranking gang members of a local Bloods set. Investigators believed he was killed in retaliation for another senseless murder—a deadly shooting outside a nightclub, Club 609, of a rival gang member by Al'quon's older brother. Rumors swirled that he had been first kidnapped in Wilmington, later killed, and finally dumped in a remote area across the Cape Fear River. Nobody wanted to talk, and investigators were stymied. Nearly four years went by, and nobody would share details.

When a man arrested for a string of armed robberies in Wilmington abruptly found himself serving 50 years in federal prison, it didn't take long for him to talk. In exchange for time reduction—which is possible only in the federal justice system—Alan Johnson, a person rumored to have been peripherally involved in Al'quon's disappearance, agreed to cooperate. What ultimately forced Johnson to help was not doing the right thing, but a desire to help himself.

FIGURE 7.1   Family of Al'quon Flowers holds a vigil one year after his disappearance.
Source: WECT.

With the information in hand, I reached out to DA Jon David. We had a defendant willing to talk, and my brother had the crime scene and body of the missing teenager somewhere in the vast reaches of his prosecutorial district. Jon met with the Flowers family, and they agreed that if Johnson could lead authorities to Al'quon's body, he would be allowed to plead to second-degree murder.

A cross-sworn federal prosecutor in my office, who had tried Johnson for the armed robberies, also agreed that his federal sentence would be reduced for giving substantial assistance. Johnson led WPD officers deep into the swamps of Brunswick County where Al'quon's remains were located, and the Flowers family was finally able to bury their son.

Getting justice for young men like Al'quon must be one of the highest priorities in the criminal justice system. Preventing these murders in the first place involves out-of-the-box thinking, building alliances with people who, historically, have not been at the table, and engaging the community most affected by gang violence.

As we will see, in the cases and initiatives that follow, we started to reduce gang violence and not just react when we turned to the often-overlooked power of the civil nuisance abatement laws. (These laws are like the ones used to reduce the nuisances at the motels on Market Street, discussed in chapter 2.) We also adopted some best practices from High Point, North Carolina, and Harlem, New York, and came up with some homegrown programs in the process to really begin to change the seemingly never-ending cycle of gang violence.

State v. Farrow[8]

The Rhino Club was located on 125 Market Street, a prime location for a restaurant, and was once a favored spot for young professionals to have a drink after work. Located in the heart of downtown on the corner of 2nd and Market Streets, it was, for a time, the very epicenter of the action. Eventually, sales lagged as many new clubs and bars in the Central Business District opened, vying for the same customers. As competition increased, there was a race to the bottom as standards were relaxed to increase the pool of eligible customers, including those under 21 and those already impaired.

The Rhino Club went even further: it became a known gang hangout for the local United Blood Nation. The walls were painted red, the color of the gang. Mayhem and fights ensued; the owner reportedly had a bullwhip to keep the peace. Nightly calls to the police documented the rapid descent of a once reputable establishment. The most common anonymous calls were about bar fights inside and drug activity in the parking lot. Girls as young as 15 were served liquor. Something had to be done.

As part of "Operation Last Call," I sent out a letter to dozens of bars requesting that the owners attend a summit at the police station to discuss the problems we were seeing downtown. We were especially concerned with the Rhino Club. Along with ALE officers, I explained that we were going to ramp up enforcement, using the same nuisance abatement laws to seize property.

In the meeting with the bar owners, I explained that the unruly crowds spilling onto the street at closing time were more of a disorder issue than a crime problem. Responsible adults needed to get back in control. Equally important, disorder and crime were bad for business. Word was out that downtown Wilmington was not safe after 10:00 p.m. Most bouncers and bar owners enthusiastically agreed to support the initiative to curb loitering.

No one from the Rhino Club showed up for the meeting. In the nine months following the written warning, WPD and the 911 center received over 200 calls for service to the Rhino Club and the connecting parking lot. Documenting the constant chaos proved important in establishing the record for the eventual nuisance claim.

FIGURE 7.2 AND 7.3   The Rhino Club was shut down following a homicide there in 2011. Slice of Life Pizzeria renovated the historic building and moved into the space in 2014. *Source*: Wilmingtondowntown.com.

On Sunday, January 24, 2011, what we had all worried about finally happened. Just before midnight, a melee broke out in the Rhino Club and spilled into the street. Taaron Jones, a local rapper and United Blood Nation gang member, was stabbed to death on the sidewalk in front of the club's entrance. Ronald Farrow was soon arrested and charged with Taaron's murder. We immediately filed a petition to suspend the Rhino Club's alcohol license, and it was granted in less than 48 hours.

When the Rhino Club could no longer serve alcohol, it quickly went bust, and the owners filed for bankruptcy.[9] Slice of Life Pizzeria, which occupied a small space across the street from the Rhino Club (and caught some of the murder on film with its security cameras), purchased the old club. Significant remodeling took place and now the building at 125 Market Street is once again a crown jewel of downtown and is a favorite restaurant for businesspeople, tourists, and families.

However, our work was not over when the Rhino Club closed. It took nearly four years to get justice for Taaron. Many who witnessed his murder would not testify. A co-defendant who had been arrested was released when we realized he was innocent. Farrow fired multiple attorneys, unwilling to listen to any plea offer they brought up. Finally, in December 2014, Farrow was convicted by a New Hanover County jury of second-degree murder.

One problem remained even after closing the Rhino's doors: merely shutting down an establishment does not automatically stop the violence. Displacing crime is like squeezing water: it just squirts out somewhere else.

The patrons of the Rhino Club moved two miles away to Club 609, at the midtown corner of Kerr Avenue and Market Street. Three months later, another young man was murdered, in front of the same gallery of characters that had been present at Taaron's killing. A fight erupted in the club when one of Taaron's songs played and soon some patrons started flashing gang signs. Gunshots followed and Cornelius Blanks was killed. Garry Orlando Hines was ultimately charged with his death. Two months later, Hines' brother, Al'quon Flowers, was kidnapped and killed.

The ABC quickly revoked the liquor license. Promoters then moved the party to a farm in rural Columbus County, where yet another murder was committed by the same gang. A young man was fatally wounded in the crossfire and two young girls, ages 14 and 15, were wounded as well. DA Jon David met with the farm owners and threatened civil action against the property if the same tenants continued hosting large parties at the location. The tenants were evicted, and the gang lost another place to congregate.

Intervention: The High Point Model

At the end of 2012, law enforcement and justice officials invited several VGMs to City Hall to have a talk. The process we were using came from elsewhere in the state and had swept across the country with great results. The High Point Model, named for the North Carolina town where it was piloted, employs a focused deterrence approach with the involvement of several community actors to promote the success of the program.[10] In this model, created by David Kennedy, members of local street gangs who are on probation and facing real prospects for rehabilitation are called to a meeting. This group comprises carefully screened young offenders who are heading down a path that, if left unchecked, will lead to a prison cell or the morgue. Examples are given of other people they know who have already received heavy sentences or who have died as a result of criminal conduct.

State and federal law enforcement officers, probation officials, and members of my office deliver a consistent message: life, as they know it, is now over. The group is shown actual videos, captured by city cameras, of themselves engaging in criminal activity, including hand-to-hand drug deals with undercover agents and fights with each other. Instead of being arrested, the authorities "bank the case" and commit to not prosecuting the violation if the activity ceases immediately. From here forward, their actions, and those of their known associates, will be heavily monitored by a combination of a gang task force and probation officers. If the young offenders are arrested again, prosecutors will advocate for a high bond, charge the "banked case" in addition to proceeding on

FIGURES 7.4, 7.5, 7.6, AND 7.7   On December 6, 2012, law enforcement leaders organized a gang call-in, which was designed to put gang members and their families on notice that their criminal behavior must cease. Clockwise from top left: Chief Ralph Evangelous, DA Ben David, call-in participants, Chaplain James Jamison.

the new charges, and change the venue to federal court to maximize the time of active incarceration.

The effectiveness of the High Point Model hinges not only on severe consequences but also on second chances. To lend support to their success, participants are given a way to save face and to escape a life of crime through bimonthly call-in meetings. Present at the meeting are members of the young offender's family, as well as pastors, educators, and other community leaders. A member of our Homicide Family Support Group is also present to share a testimonial about the effects that criminal activity has had on his or her family.

The young offenders are given the opportunity to continue their education by enrolling at CFCC either to earn their GEDs or to earn college credit. Members of two other organizations are also on-hand to offer employment opportunities: the Wilmington Housing Authority Youth Build U.S.A. Program[11] (a program, much like Habitat For Humanity, where youth are paid through a grant to build a home together) and Leading Into New Communities (a group of ex-offenders who will be reintegrated into society through work, with grant money used to pay for the first four months of employment).[12] The message coming from the meetings is simple: everyone, from police to the offenders' families, wants them to succeed and to avoid further contact with the criminal justice system. It is the young person listening who chooses which path to travel.

Disappointingly, our crime numbers were not dropping in the months following the meeting as we had expected, when compared to the data from other communities. In the process, we learned several valuable lessons.

First, unlike places like High Point, where there is a strong line of succession of gang leadership, gangs in Wilmington are more fragmented and less structured. We could not target the Bloods, for example, and assume that all members of the Bloods report up the same chain. The gang had several factions that are sometimes in competition with one another. As a result, the midlevel individuals who we brought in as the call-in group did not have allegiance to the same "big fish" up the chain.

Second, we learned the importance of communication. The call-in allowed us to create a dialogue with some VGMs that did not previously exist. Ties between agencies that were supposed to be working with these young people were also strengthened. The mere act of getting everyone into the room together led to greater collaboration on gang prevention and intervention efforts.

FIGURE 7.8   Koredreese Tyson, one of the Gangster Disciple leaders, was served with the injunction shortly before his release from federal prison. He was rearrested within months of his release, charged with violent felonies perpetrated against another Gangster Disciple and his family member. Tyson also worked at Tru Colors.

Third, at the time we did our call-in, we did not have the right people and programs in place to provide viable alternatives to the street. While some existing programs were successful for other populations, young gang members needed more support to engage with these programs than we had estimated. Instead of serving as an opportunity for VGMs to get out of a dangerous lifestyle, our offer seemed to them an empty promise that authorities could not ultimately fulfill.

Finally, we saw that in taking a tough love approach, we had to ensure that we were backing up what we promised regarding severe consequences for those who would disregard our advice and return to the same lifestyle. We had to pull out all the tools from the tool belt, even some that had never been used before, if we were going to save lives.

The Gang Injunction

The right to peaceful assembly is protected under the First Amendment. But if the purpose of two or more people coming together is to commit crimes, that is a different matter. Violent assembly has never been protected under our Constitution, and there are civil laws to prevent gang members from being in one another's presence.

Taking a page from the work we had done to shut down the Rhino Club and later working to clean up the motels on Market Street, in December 2015 we turned to the civil laws to help combat the gang violence in our city. Our quest to prevent violent gang members from assembling with each other in public came soon after when 15-year-old Shane Simpson was murdered in broad daylight while he stood on a downtown Wilmington street corner with several other teenagers. In total, five teenagers were shot, all from the same gang. Several other teenagers from a rival group, the Gangster Disciples, were eventually arrested. Not surprisingly, none of the wounded members wanted to help the police.[13]

In light of the case, the mayor, the chief of police, the sheriff, and I convened a press conference at the Martin Luther King Jr. Center to talk about preventing similar gang violence.[14] We announced the formation of a task force (made up of officers from the vice and narcotics unit and gang detectives from the WPD, members of the DA's office, and attorneys from the Wilmington City Attorney's Office) to enforce the civil laws which might lessen the impact of area organized crime. Specifically, we highlighted the North Carolina Street Gang Suppression Act, N.C.G.S. §14-50.16, which allows officers to serve injunctions upon VGMs prohibiting them from congregating with each other.

Daniel Thurston, a city attorney who formerly served as a prosecutor, worked with members of my office to put this law into practice as a way of preventing future tragedies. The numbers, through crime mapping (discussed below), would dictate who would be the focus of our attention. For the next year, a criminal analyst, working with gang detectives, looked at the activity of the Gangster Disciples and identified their members and their leadership.

This focused effort took us nearly two years. In November of 2017, a 100-page civil complaint was filed, listing me as the plaintiff and the 24 most influential members of the Gangster Disciples as defendants.[15] The complaint documented multiple crimes that each had committed and established (through tattoos, social media posts, and jail interviews) that each of these leaders belonged to the gang that had been wreaking havoc on the north side of Wilmington. All defendants, whether on the street or in jail or prison, were individually served and given an opportunity to come to court two weeks later to either contest the allegations or deem them admitted through their silence.

Approximately half of these named defendants appeared in court, some with attorneys, to claim either that they were not members of the gang or that the allegations of their criminal conduct were untrue. All of them wanted to know how gang officers had developed this information, but it wasn't hard to do since there were numerous posts to social media demonstrating their affiliation. The city attorney, working on my behalf, convinced Superior Court Judge Imelda Pate that, by a preponderance of the evidence, the named defendants were in fact gang members and should be subject to the injunction.

The injunction prohibited the named defendants from associating with one another within the city limits of Wilmington, committing any crime, or doing drugs for three years. If they did any of those things, they could be placed in custody for up to six months and fined up to $1,000. They were allowed, however, to be together for legitimate purposes such as work or school, or to meet with an attorney. They were also allowed to petition to be removed from the list after two years.

Almost immediately, several members were found to be in violation of the law and the injunction. Judge Pate imposed civil sanctions, including fines and imprisonment, to send the message that being in contempt of the terms of the injunction would have very real consequences. With their strength in numbers gone, their power to control neighborhoods vanished. Data in the areas where the Gangster Disciples once held the most sway (which included Creekwood and the surrounding neighborhood) revealed that violent crime was up 25 percent in 2016, the year before the injunction was filed. For the same area in the two years following the injunction, violent crime (murder, rape, robbery, and aggravated assault) fell by 46 percent and part one crimes (violent crimes plus burglary, larceny, motor vehicle theft, and arson) fell by 50 percent.[16]

A Sense of Belonging

In *Community: The Structure of Belonging*, Peter Block compares communities that work to those that are completely broken.[17] Where would you rather live, San Diego, California, or Detroit, Michigan? How about Austin, Texas, or Gary, Indiana? Without knowing much about the local elected leaders, crime rates, educational opportunities, or the main industry in the city, I'd bet you would say San Diego and Austin. Why is that and how does your community rate?

According to Block, there is a structure to community. Communities that work are intentional about giving structure to connections, to giving their citizens a place where they "belong." When children of a certain age do not have structure in the home, they find it in each other. The place where they end up belonging may be in a street gang.

The word "belong" has three meanings: the first is "ownership," as in "this property belongs to me." When citizens feel ownership in a community, they are stakeholders. Do you take better care of a place when you rent it or when you own it? The same is true for community: high poverty areas are frequently ravaged by high crime, where Section 8 housing and slumlords are far more common than neighborhood crime watch groups.

The second meaning of the word "belong" is "membership," such as belonging to a club. Most of us want to believe in something greater than ourselves and contribute to the whole. For many people, that is family. As we shall soon see, many gang members come from areas of the community where the concept of a nuclear family is almost nonexistent. Most of us would rather be members of something other than a gang, but some have few options.

The third thing that gives people a sense of "belonging" comes from scrambling the word order: "longing to be." Do members of the community have true opportunities for advancement, or do they think that the game is rigged? Stated another way: does everyone really matter?

In his book *The Fractured Republic*, conservative writer Yuval Levin says much the same thing as Peter Block, but from the opposite side of the political spectrum.[18] He believes that for community to really thrive it should resemble desirable fruits and vegetables—organic and local. Community must be established between neighbors, not through federal government programs or mandates. Government must support the "middle layers" separating the state from the individual, institutions like the ones I have identified in the Starfish model.

Joining Forces for Good

What do we do when the population most affected by crime does not want to participate in the criminal justice process? To break the cycle of violence where street-level crimes are going unreported, engagement with the community is essential. Part of the solution involves making it easier to report crime and to protect informants once information is given.[19] As we highlighted in chapter 4, for real reporting to take place, victims and witnesses must believe in the justice system and trust in its ability to protect them.

There are no quick-fix solutions; just as the problems have been decades in the making, meaningful solutions take years of work, years that outlive election cycles or grant funding. But children have only one childhood, and crime and safety require an emergency response. The balance is to engage in long-term strategic planning while simultaneously being possessed by what Dr. King called "the fierce urgency of now."

Breaking the cycle of violence also involves a change in mind-set and language. Just as labeling crime sets expectations regarding punishment, the labels we put on our children shape their expectations and those of our larger society. Kids do not know they are "at risk" unless we tell them they are.

Several years ago, leaders in the criminal justice system reached out to other area leaders who had a stake in helping to confront youth violence: business leaders, religious leaders, school officials, and nonprofit organizations. Membership reflected the components of the Starfish model, though I did not yet have a name for that structure when we formed the group in 2008. The result was the Blue Ribbon Commission on the Prevention of Youth Violence (BRC).[20]

The business leaders understood that crime greatly influences quality of life and that the reality (or even the perception) of crime in the downtown business district greatly affects our ability to attract investment. They also knew that displacing crime to another area of the community would not solve this issue for the entire area. The executive director of the Greater Wilmington Chamber of Commerce was made a part of the BRC and has worked to engage this vital part of the team by hosting power breakfasts, applying for grants, and encouraging corporate investment in our prevention efforts.

Religious leaders, who came together around a movement to start a unity and reconciliation effort, were also made part of the endeavor. Two pastors, one from an established African-American church and the other from one of the oldest and largest white congregations downtown, were each given a place on the commission.

The school superintendent was also invited to join the team. He faced the same racial divide with greater suspensions, dropouts, and a minority achievement gap. If there was a part of our community where fence-mending was needed to confront our present by looking at our history, school officials knew they had a role to play.

More than 40 nonprofit groups worked directly with the young people we were seeing at the courthouse. Many of them had been doing great work in diverse areas such as Boys and Girls Clubs, after-school arts programs, and apprentice programs. While they all had the same desire to help, many of the groups were in direct competition for scarce grant dollars. To bring the groups together behind a common cause, we gave them all a seat at the table by forming a distinct arm of the BRC, known as the Tactical Advisory Committee, and invited the director of the local United Way chapter to join the BRC board.

With the BRC established, we next hired a strategic director from the community to work full time on the effort and created three sub-teams to focus on specific areas. The Youth Violence Action Team's goal involved reducing crime by 25 percent over the next three years. The Education Action Team was tasked with reducing out-of-school suspensions and the dropout rate by 25 percent over the same time period.

The Community Engagement team had the goal of enlisting a volunteer army of 4,000 members and promoting our efforts to the larger community. The BRC created a Youth Enrichment Zone (YEZ) patterned after the Harlem Children's Zone.[21] The idea behind the YEZ was to engage in crime mapping by analyzing crime statistics, ShotSpotter data (that uses sound waves to identify locations of gunfire and is automatically communicated to law enforcement to dispatch), and hospital reports (which might identify crimes of violence that were going unreported) to see where in our community kids faced the most danger. In other words, we did not pick where to focus our efforts, the numbers picked the location for us.

YOUTH ENRICHMENT ZONE

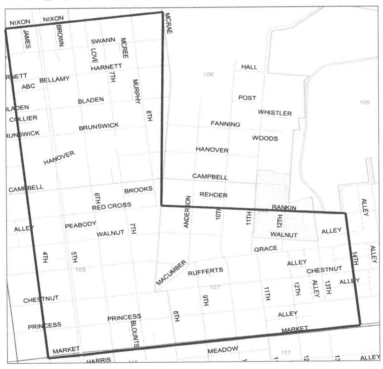

FIGURE 7.9   The Youth Enrichment Zone in downtown Wilmington.
Source: Star News.

After an exhaustive analysis of this data, we identified a 15-block area on the north side of Wilmington, a place where poverty runs rampant and single-parent homes are the norm. The concept behind the YEZ was to start with a small geographic area and focus resources on the schools, houses of worship, businesses, and nonprofits that work directly with the young people living there. Young children, especially in the critical zero- to five-year-old population, are assessed to determine the resources necessary for their long-term success. Additional areas may be annexed in the future as success is demonstrated.

Many of the problems that we jointly confronted could better be addressed at the child's house rather than at the schoolhouse or at the courthouse. We hired a caseworker to go door-to-door to assess residents' needs and to perform a de facto census of who was living at each residence. What he found was alarming, but not altogether surprising. He visited 84 homes and found that of school-aged children living there, 90 percent were at or near the poverty line, 98 percent were African-American, and just four fathers lived under the same roof as their children.[22]

We adopted the philosophy that, while resources would come from the outside, ultimately this needed to be an organic process wherein residents were part of the solution. We held town hall meetings to hear from residents about existing problems and current services to identify both gaps and redundancies and to encourage the community to buy into the concept of the YEZ. We created a youth ambassador group, made up of young men and women in the YEZ, who went door-to-door with caseworkers. Instead of these young people joining gangs and becoming part of the problem, they were now setting a positive example.

We also made it a goal to clean up the blighted areas in the YEZ. Under the broken windows theory of law enforcement, first implemented in New York City, one way to drive away violent crime is to invest in areas of disrepair.[23] When buildings are abandoned or have broken windows, they are far more likely to be vandalized and become dens of criminal activity. In contrast, when areas are cleaned up and when there is pride of ownership, crime watch neighborhoods are formed, cooperation with police and crime reporting goes up, and crime rates go down. Physically changing the surroundings changes the mind-set of the larger community and that of criminals who would otherwise come into the area to deal drugs. It is like turning on the lights in a dark place. What worked for the motels on Market Street could also work for the parks in the YEZ.

Four separate murders occurred in and around a park located on 10th and Rankin Streets in a short amount of time. Drug deals and gang activity were commonplace. Members of the BRC teamed with employees from Corning, Inc., to take back the park. Today, Portia Hines Park is the heart of the YEZ and hosts many area events. It boasts a community garden, hosts a youth sports league, and even welcomes families to movie nights, something once unthinkable for the location.

FIGURES 7.10 AND 7.11   Portia Hines Park, before and after.

Another facet of the broken windows theory is a relentless focus on minor crime: the idea being to nip it in the bud before it grows into more serious crime. Evidence suggests that code enforcement for things like jaywalking, graffiti, and abandoned vehicles cleans up an area. While these "stop and frisk" encounters are constitutional, so-called "Terry frisks" are also perceived by some as profiling.[24] A balance must be struck so proactive programs that retake the public square and proactive policing that seizes drugs and guns do not override the trust of those within the area most affected by crime. Impunity, the phenomenon that occurs when victims and witnesses fail to report crime, resulting in offenders being exempt from punishment, can be an unwelcome backlash when people do not trust that the law is being fairly applied or enforced.

When a prosecutor at the end of a 30-year career told me that preventing one person from going to prison would be more meaningful than putting 100 more in, I knew what he was talking about. Getting people out of the cycle of poverty and crime, and getting them through school and into solid careers, will do as much for public safety in any community as building more jails or prisons. It is a credit to the schools, business communities, and nonprofits to see how we have worked to reduce youth crime in my hometown.

The School Arm of the Starfish

Young people who succeed in school rarely appear at the courthouse, and our crime prevention efforts are ultimately tied to keeping them in school. It is estimated that two out of three inmates in prison today were high school dropouts.[25] Statistically, a person is on a better path if he or she stays in school through the 12th grade.

After the Columbine tragedy in April 1999, there was a dramatic increase in the number of school resource officers (SROs) in high schools and even middle schools. After the mass killing of elementary students in Newtown, Connecticut, in December 2012, more SROs were put into schools, even at the elementary level. Issues that previously went to the principal's office were now being handled by SROs and court officials. Administrative sanctions like time out and lunch duty were replaced with juvenile petitions and even detention. Threats and fighting, both in person and online, were treated as criminal justice issues and were addressed in the courthouse instead of the schoolhouse. The unfortunate side effect was that more young people were being placed into a courtroom environment, giving them a greater likelihood to reoffend.

Over the long term, we saw an increased frequency of kids coming to court for things that were once considered minor. In North Carolina, 42 percent of the overall charges filed against young people under the age of 16 are from violations occurring at school; most are very minor offenses.[26] As for the overall filing of juvenile petitions, only three percent involve violent felonies.[27]

Young people are impressionable and how SROs use their power greatly affects their view of all law enforcement. With the increased police presence at schools, it may be that many young people grow up to distrust officers, rather than to see them as guardians.

If young people are long-term suspended or expelled, they are now on the street, possibly committing crimes. What was once a mark in a confidential student record has now become a criminal record. Delinquents were starting to lose the healthy fear of court as it became routine, and the law was nearly powerless to impose any remedial punishment for these crimes. Something had to be done.

Chief District Court Judge J. Corpening brought school officials together with law enforcement officials to institute a protocol to limit the impact that arrests and suspensions were having on increasing dropout rates and later arrests, or what some have called "the school-to-prison pipeline."[28] Court officials and school officials entered into an understanding to provide students with administrative sanctions at school, rather than criminal penalties for many nonviolent offenses.

Most of the offenses that come from schools should be addressed in that setting. The priority is still maintaining a safe environment for students and staff, so violent offenses continue to come to the courthouse, while bullying, sexting, and outbursts in class are handled in-house by school administrators. The program resulted in a 47 percent reduction in the number of juvenile petitions being filed at the courthouse. Meanwhile, schools remained safe and SROs remained on campus to focus on crimes of violence.

Another juvenile program that worked to give teachable moments rather than criminal records to kids was Teen Court, a program I was first introduced to in Winston-Salem in 1996.[29] Since 2000 our district has run the court in both counties and the numbers show that Teen Court has reduced the number of repeat offenders and has allowed many young people to learn about the justice system through a positive experience.[30]

For first-time offenders of nonviolent misdemeanors, cases are diverted from the juvenile justice system and put in the Teen Court where nearly every participant, including the prosecutor, defense attorney, and members of the jury, are also teenagers. The sole adult in the process is an attorney serving as the judge. To qualify for Teen Court, the defendant must admit liability so that the "trial" is really a protracted sentencing proceeding where the jury is given a range of options for a community-based punishment. This program was recently expanded. Now all 16- and 17-year-old nonviolent offenders are automatically given deferred prosecutions rather than getting marked with a criminal record.

FIGURE 7.12   DA Ben David, Governor Roy Cooper, and Chief District Court Judge J. Corpening during the Raise the Age proclamation signing, July 28, 2017.

Judge Corpening and I went further. North Carolina was the last of the 50 states that still treated 16- and 17-year-olds as adults. (Think back to the case in chapter 3 involving Gail Plourdes and Josh Mortimer in the days after Columbine—Judge Corpening and I handled their first appearance together in district court). When the North Carolina Legislature was debating whether to change the age of adulthood from 16 to 18, we were the only two elected officials from the justice system to testify before the representatives in support of raising the juvenile age.

Ninety-seven percent of the arrests of kids who are 16 and 17 were for nonviolent misdemeanors and felonies.[31] The unintended consequences of over-policing in schools created permanent marks on their record, forever branding them as criminals.[32] For example, colleges will not admit them, and the military is no longer an option.[33] Felonies also bar applicants from receiving student loans or federally assisted housing.[34] Job prospects are greatly diminished.[35]

When defendants can reasonably foresee the danger that their actions can create, they are held accountable. It should be no different for the leaders passing and enforcing the laws. Standing by and watching our children drown in an ocean of unintended consequences was not an option: we had a duty to act. The North Carolina Legislature agreed and voted overwhelmingly to raise the juvenile age to 18. The law went into effect December 1, 2019.[36]

Creating Successful Schools

Strategies in the YEZ have specifically focused on successful educational models that do not operate like business as usual. In 2011, a middle school in the heart of the YEZ closed amid much controversy. The school, D.C. Virgo, was historically underperforming, causing parents to pull their children out and reducing the number of students to only half the capacity.[37] The school board made the financial decision to close the school and bus the remaining students elsewhere. To the children and parents in the neighborhood, the school was a treasure, reminding many of the closing of Williston High School in 1968. Many worried that history was repeating itself.[38]

It was imperative that something be done. With District Court Judge James Faison, who runs the drug treatment court (discussed in chapter 8) and has long been regarded as a leader in the African-American community, we co-authored a resolution on behalf of the BRC requesting that the school board reopen D.C. Virgo within one year. The school board adopted the resolution.[39]

D.C. Virgo appointed an advisory board made up of community members, equally appointed by the BRC and the school board, to help decide its future direction. It is worth noting that the two major goals of the BRC, to reduce youth crime and increase graduation rates by 25 percent within the first three years in the YEZ, were achieved largely through this exemplary collaboration.

Today, D.C. Virgo has one of the highest school attendance rates of schools in New Hanover County. Every student has a laptop computer and school uniform and most stay after school for several enrichment activities. The BRC remains vitally involved in the day-to-day operations. UNCW has since teamed with New Hanover County to run D.C. Virgo as a year-round public charter school.[40]

Another school based on a national best practice is the Girls Leadership Academy of Wilmington (G.L.O.W.). G.L.O.W. is the region's first all-female charter school, which was modeled after Young Women's Leadership Network (YWLN) in New York City. The founder, Judy Girard, invited me, Mayor Bill Saffo, school board leaders, and Live Oak Bank CEO Chip Mahan to Harlem to see this single-sex education program firsthand.

FIGURE 7.13   G.L.O.W. principal Laura Hunter (center, in black) and founder Judy Girard (center, in white) are joined by elected officials and celebrity chefs during the school's new facility opening in 2019. G.L.O.W. is the first single-gender public charter school in North Carolina. *Source*: Ken Oots, *Star News*.

When I met her, Judy was new to Wilmington, having recently retired as the CEO of the Food Network. She was intrigued by our adoption of the Harlem Children's Zone and wanted

BRC leaders to see the success of the YWLN model, which Anne and Andrew Tisch founded in 1996. Judy saw an opportunity for the model to work in her new town as it has already been successfully replicated in Philadelphia, Baltimore, and parts of Texas. The community responded overwhelmingly to G.L.O.W. and Judy and her team were able to raise millions of dollars and plant a beautiful campus in the high-poverty area of the north side of Wilmington that borders the YEZ.

Launched in the fall of 2016, the inaugural class consisted of 116 sixth-grade girls. Like D.C. Virgo, the plan is for the school to grow incrementally by one grade every year so that by 2023 G.L.O.W. will have over 600 students in sixth through 12th grade classes. On the first day of school, sixth graders are told they will go to college, and over the next seven years that seemingly distant hope becomes a reality.

The 20-year track record of the YWLN leaves little question about the long-term impact that this model will have on these women and their futures. With all the challenging demographics of poverty and first-generation college-bound students, we can expect to see only 60 of 100 of these women graduate from high school utilizing traditional models. That number rises to 93 high school graduates out of 100 under the YWLN model.

Preventing young women from dropping out of high school is only the start. In the traditional model, of those 100 girls, only eight will one day go to college. In the YWLN model, all 93 who graduate high school will go on to college. Think of the ripple effect for each young woman and the family she has and will have when this school is successful.[41] Child literacy correlates with mothers who can read, so educating a young girl also helps the next generation. Making these young women career-ready also gives them a more meaningful way out of poverty.

Two other programs that we introduced into the schools have paid huge dividends. We saw that many students with behavior issues were acting out on Monday mornings. With over 50 percent of the public-school children on free and reduced lunch in my two-county district, sometimes the meals these children receive at school are the only meals they get all

FIGURE 7.14   Nourish NC's "Backpack Program" sends food home with kids in need. My son Fitz and daughters Maddie and Sophie, walking to their school, Forest Hills Global Elementary.

day. A significant amount of the students come from "food deserts," where access to fresh food is limited. The result is that their diets consist primarily of inexpensive, high-calorie, fast food that does little for them nutritionally. A local nonprofit, Nourish NC, discreetly sends home food in backpacks on Fridays with kids who might not otherwise have it over the weekend.

The other program was Watch DOGS (Dads of Great Students). This program, which has proven to be effective in thousands of schools in big cities and small rural areas, aims to improve involvement in schools by fathers and other adult males.[42] For too long, dads only showed up when their children were in trouble. Watch DOGS is designed to bring fathers into schools on a more routine basis, serving as hall monitors, readers, and test proctors. At a minimum, fathers are asked to serve just one day a year (ideally near their kid's birthday) in a school activity assigned by an administrator. We have experienced much greater participation in the 18 elementary and middle schools in my district where these programs are established, and we are trying to recruit more schools every year.

Having an Adult Conversation

A young man had just been killed in an impaired driving crash, mere blocks from where he grew up. His best friend was driving. Two police officers were sent to notify the victim's family. The worst job for any law enforcement officer is delivering the news of death, especially that of a young person. As the officers walked up the path to a beautiful home to deliver the news that would be any parent's worst nightmare, they saw the mom and dad through a bay window, enjoying break-fast, unaware that their son was no longer alive. As the sergeant was about to knock on the door, the younger officer stopped him.

"Wait, wait, I want to give this family something," he said.

"What on earth could you give this family right now?" his supervisor asked.

"Five more minutes," the officer replied.

That's all they could give them. Five more minutes before the new normal would set in forever.

I experienced this same scenario two months after being elected DA. The defendant was from a great family and lived on my street. The victim's family lived in the same neighborhood, and they were also amazing people. The victim's mother was the first to speak. "I just wish he had called," she said with a shocked gaze. "We would have come and picked him up, no questions asked." As I came to know them better over the next few weeks, the dad offered this suggestion: "Maybe when you go out and talk to young people, you can remind them that we were once young too. We get it."

Since 2004 it has become my practice every year to visit each public middle and high school in New Hanover and Pender Counties, as well as many of the private and charter schools, to talk about choices and consequences. While I talk to them about being leaders and doing the right thing, I also remind them that all of us are imperfect and that we need to own our mistakes, learn from them, and forgive ourselves when they occur.

What I share with students will vary with the age of my audience, but I am not trying to teach them right from wrong—a concept they have been learning since kindergarten. Rather than teach them how to act, I want to remind them that their actions have consequences.

High school seniors receive a real-world perspective regarding the laws surrounding driving, drug use, and relationship violence. I also devote several nights each year to welcome incoming freshman at UNCW and to introduce them to the expectations we have for them as adults in their new hometown. I tell them about the five minutes the officers gave the family whose son was killed in a DWI crash, and that it was the victim's good friend who was driving the car. Then I remind them to call a friend, a taxi or Uber, rather than making my phone ring.

For students in eighth grade, I remind them that they will soon be treated like adults, so they need to start acting like it. My theme of being a leader is unwavering, and I try to give concrete examples that they are likely to encounter and to encourage them to report crimes. I talk to them about peer pressure and the concept of acting in concert and remind them to choose their friends wisely because they can be held accountable for each other's actions. "The Chinese delivery" case, the now common moniker for Liu's murder, provides a concrete example of this principle.

Eighth graders also hear about bullying, dangers on the internet, and the dangers of drug use. If students are being harmed or if they are being touched inappropriately at home or at school, they must report it. If they have stumbled across an online predator, they should not just ignore it; they must tell a parent or teacher.[43] Over the years, many students have responded by reporting their victimization to appropriate adults (including SROs, teachers, or guidance counselors) following these talks.

I also talk about the three Rs: responsibility, respect, and rationalization. Everyone can pick their response to a given set of pressures, whether that is to take a puff or a pill, to hit the button to send out a statement or picture on the internet that could destroy their reputation, or to take the car keys when a friend has been drinking. Role-playing extends the line between the moment when pressure is applied, usually by friends, and how they react. Lengthening this line makes them more "response-able."[44]

I also tell students about the gift of fear.[45] Our instinct warns us of potential danger—the people and situations that make us uncomfortable. That instinctive feeling telling you to fight or flee is often that voice inside saying that danger is foreseeable. We must listen to it.

My purpose in sharing real-life cases is to get the assembled students to appreciate the foreseeable consequences that come out of situations we all faced when we were younger. Knowledge is power. If adults are not having conversations with young people about the dangers they face, someone else is, and they are probably not telling them the truth.

The Business Arm of the Starfish

In December 2013, a year after the call-in of the VGMs to City Hall, and still seeing too much gang violence in inner city Wilmington, I was asked to address approximately 500 civic and business leaders to propose a plan of remediation.[46] I challenged them to create Hometown Hires, a program that addresses employment through an alliance among existing private, public, and nonprofit agencies. It goes without saying that having a good, secure job is an effective crime prevention measure: on the street they say that nothing stops a bullet faster than a job. My goal was to combat crime and poverty through stability and opportunity.

Every good business needs a strategic plan and the right partners. I approached Chip Mahan, CEO of Live Oak Bank, a man who rose to success with the mantra that hope is not a strategy. We hosted a series of CEO-only gatherings to lay out the vision and asked them to hire just one Hometown Hires candidate. No press was invited. We didn't ask for money. Chip and I acknowledged to the CEOs that they do not run a charity and that we aren't asking them to hire anyone other than the best employees. We were surprised by the eagerness with which these leaders met potential employees and placed them within their organizations.

We started with an ambitious goal of placing 300 individuals who were firmly rooted in our community. Participants had lived in New Hanover, Pender, or Brunswick Counties for at least one year and came from deep poverty. The ripple effect created by individuals and families pulling themselves and their families out of intergenerational poverty and into jobs with opportunities for growth cannot be overstated. The force multiplier of so many individuals participating in this initiative means we can make the entire area safer with fewer defendants and fewer victims.

An existing relationship with Chris Nelson, the executive director of the United Way of the Lower Cape Fear, made that agency a natural choice to administer the program. They designated staff to screen the applicants and collect job vacancies. To be eligible, a prospective Hometown Hire must be nominated by a nonprofit partner, participate in a screening interview, and enroll in supplementary training or education as needed. CFCC created a certificate program for employers with specific training needs, all at no cost.

Mentors support the candidates by providing encouragement and professional guidance outside the workplace. Businesses that could not initially place candidates in jobs would often invite their employees to serve as Hometown Hires mentors to assist the effort.

Those who are not punctual or cannot demonstrate a commitment to continuing education are asked to leave the program. People who test positive for illegal drugs or those with a violent criminal history are ineligible. Criminal records are verified through a background check performed by Castle Branch, a national corporation headquartered in Wilmington.

Many candidates do not have a record at all. For those who do, my office works quickly with mentors and pro se defendants to resolve outstanding warrants or missed court dates. For those with nonviolent felonies and misdemeanors, which frequently become scarlet letters on a résumé, we look to see if the conviction can be removed.

There is a class of offenders who commit lower-level offenses, typically property crimes like car theft, breaking and entering, or drug possession. They cripple our community. Structured sentencing, discussed in chapter 1, and the Justice Reinvestment Act, discussed in chapter 6, virtually guarantee that these defendants will receive probation and return to the streets. It is only when these offenders "graduate" to crimes of violence or achieve habitual felon status that prison becomes a long-term solution (500 murders were committed over the last decade in North Carolina by people who were on probation at the time).[47]

Ninety-eight percent of the people we send to prison will eventually be set free.[48] Unfortunately, of these, two-thirds will be back in a prison cell within two years of release.[49] To keep the community truly safe in a state where we are not building more prisons but are shutting them down, our attitude and level of engagement must grow beyond a system of inputs ("lock them up and throw away the key") to a system of outputs: making sure that the defendants who are on probation or who return to the street following incarceration are succeeding and not committing new offenses.

FIGURE 7.15   From left: Chip Mahan (CEO, Live Oak Bank); Will Rikard (executive director, Step Up Ministries); Dr. Vito Sartarelli (chancellor, UNCW); Kevin Keats (former men's basketball coach, UNCW); John Monteith (CEO, Monteith Construction); Ben David (district attorney, New Hanover and Pender Counties); George Taylor (CEO, Tru Colors Brewery); Michael McWhorter (CEO, Mojotone).

One law that prosecutors fought for and the most conservative legislature in our state's history passed should not be overlooked when talking about jobs and reentry. Under North Carolina law, people who have one nonviolent felony or misdemeanor and no other intervening convictions are eligible to have the conviction removed after living clean for 15 years (five years if under 18 at the time of the original conviction).[50] My office partnered with Legal Aid of North Carolina and UNC Law School to hold a free expunction clinic in June 2014. Individuals whom I had met through the years as defendants in a courtroom were now filing into the public library, worn down by years of carrying the "mark" of a conviction and hoping for a second chance. Approximately 500 people showed up that day, and many were deemed eligible.

Expunction goes far beyond making a job applicant more competitive—with a felony removed, a candidate is also eligible for public housing, federal student loans, obtaining an occupational license, and military service. Some applicants literally cried, and few could believe that my office, the same that once prosecuted them, was leading the charge to enforce the expunction law. In the time since this clinic, the community's level of cooperation with my office and law enforcement has improved dramatically—many times as victims and witnesses in criminal cases. By enforcing the laws that are available to them, we are making these individuals stakeholders in the justice system rather than adversaries to it. We are also working to pass one of the most expansive expunction laws in the country.[51]

Another benefit of the Hometown Hires program was the impact of having a role model in the home who is gainfully employed, creating a greater sense of dignity and purpose. Whether that person is a parent, grandparent, aunt, or big brother, watching an adult go to a job on a regular basis is a great example to set for the young people in the home.

After participants are placed into jobs, they meet weekly for 13 weeks as a group in a life skills class where they learn about budgeting, fiscal literacy, and creating saving accounts. Job training for teenagers from the YEZ also happens through the VOYAGE program where dozens of young adults ages 16–18 are placed into boardrooms, courtrooms, clinics, and other professional settings. Several VOYAGERS have turned their internship experience into permanent jobs.

In the first year of its existence, 97 people were put to work through Hometown Hires.[52] One was a single mom of three who was able to move her family out of public housing once she completed training as a Certified Nursing Assistant (CNA) and earned a job at NHRMC. Another was hired by a local construction company and now serves as the foreman of his own team, making over $50,000 a year. Prior to Hometown Hires, his job prospects were limited to waiting tables. The felony he acquired as a teenager was removed at the expunction clinic.

In order to take Hometown Hires to the next level, we merged with another nonprofit, Phoenix Employment Ministry, in 2015.[53] Founded by a Presbyterian minister, Phoenix was already doing some of the work that Hometown Hires formalized. The synergy that resulted from the merger cannot be celebrated enough. In addition to nearly doubling the placement capacity, 164 people gained jobs in 2016–2017.[54] The following year, the group changed its name to Step Up Ministries and has as its goal to place people into 200 jobs, each year over the next five years.

Finally, another entrepreneur, George Taylor, building off the friendships forged through the Hometown Hires effort, developed a business plan to open Tru Colors Brewery, which employs VGMs. This model requires members to exercise their influence over the gang to keep the streets quiet while showing them that there is another way to earn a living. Tru Colors was specifically excluded from the injunction as a place where gang members could congregate. Ten of the subject Gangster Disciples found stable employment at Tru Colors Brewery for the two years that the injunction stayed in place.

The Nonprofit Arm of the Starfish

In 2004, the New Hanover County Jail was bursting at the seams. Four hundred prisoners were crammed into cells that had a maximum capacity of 350 inmates. Drastic measures were taken. Bed mats were placed in the hallways for some of the more trusted inmates. Others were rotated out through bond reduction hearings that would not have been granted if there was space. A prisoner's rights group threatened a lawsuit alleging that the existing conditions constituted cruel and unusual punishment.

The population in our city was growing and we needed a bigger jail. But, as we saw in chapter 6, confining people convicted of crimes is not just about the size of penitentiaries, it's also about which people belong in them. All around our country, those with mental illness and drug addiction are serving out life sentences a few days at a time at the local jail, as their underlying conditions remain untreated. A different approach was needed.

New Hanover County Commissioners moved quickly and built a new detention facility eight miles from downtown with a capacity of 600 inmates. Meanwhile, the old detention facility, located across the street from the courthouse and connected to it by a series of underground tunnels, sat empty.

Next door to the empty jail stood First Baptist Church of Wilmington, founded in 1808. Many of our community leaders, including then NHSO Sheriff Sid Causey and several of the county commissioners, were members of the congregation when the jail moved locations. The church's pastor, Mike Queen, a founding member of the BRC, saw an opportunity. He knew that the unmistakable power of the geography, a complex that stands between the church and the courthouse, would make the building a great place to house outreach ministries that could play an active role in crime prevention and rehabilitation. Through generous contributions from the church and the Harrelson Family, the Harrelson Center was born.[55]

Over the years, the Harrelson Center has come into its own as a family justice center—treating the whole individual and the whole family unit. A spirit of collaboration has taken hold of the nearly 20 nonprofit groups now working alongside one another. Silos have been replaced with synergy and conflict has given way to collaboration. Drug treatment is available through a variety of nonprofit providers. Mental health counseling for veterans in the grips of post-traumatic stress is found in the Family Recovery Center. Victims of human trafficking find refuge in A Safe Place. Habitat for Humanity provides long-term housing, and Communities in Schools focuses on making students successful in the classroom.

John Monteith, a prominent local builder who was one of the first business leaders to embrace the Hometown Hires model, built the headquarters for the new organization on the fourth floor of the Harrelson Center. The foreman who led the project was one of our first graduates of the program. Job applicants coming through the program get new suits for interviews from Philippians Ministries, a longtime tenant on the first floor of the complex.

Area houses of faith have pooled their resources to create the Help Hub on the ground floor where a magistrate's office once stood. When a destitute person knocks on the door of a downtown church or synagogue looking for assistance, they are directed to the Help Hub. There, they are not only given emergency relief (such as money for gas or an overdue light bill), they are assessed by an intake coordinator who can direct them to many partner agencies that work on long-term recovery and sustainability.

In February 2020, The Harrelson Center began an "unlock hope" campaign to accommodate the explosive growth it was enjoying. By knocking down more walls of the old jail in order to convert additional office space for area nonprofits, barriers are being removed both figuratively and literally. Both defendants and victims at the courthouse get the help and treatment they require, beyond what the justice system was designed to provide.

It is a powerful message that a former place of incarceration is now a place of transformation. In the town square in my hometown, between the courthouse and the oldest church, a new space and way of thinking has emerged as the best way to reduce crime—building community instead of more prisons.

Storms and COVID-19

It seems like every year, just as the summer ends and students are going back to school, a monster comes to town, bringing death and destruction and leaving misery and pain in its wake. Over time, these home wreckers have become legend, going by names like Hazel, Bertha, Fran, Floyd, and Florence. They are hurricanes and they rip through the Cape Fear region with such frequency that our area has become known nationally as "hurricane alley." Weather forecasts and advanced technology now enable us to predict when and where these storms will make landfall. Inevitably, most people flee inland for safety.

Two groups remain behind to ride out the storm. The first are law enforcement officers who are required to shelter in place at their station houses to deal with the inevitable search and rescue efforts that follow. They also must maintain order as empty homes, many without power for days after, become easy targets. I stay behind to ensure that court operations can carry on, even in the wake of a storm.

FIGURE 7.16   Looters stormed a Wilmington Family Dollar store in the days following the storm. *Source*: WECT.

The second group that does not evacuate are individuals with very limited financial resources. Many do not have transportation and few have the money to stay in hotels in distant places. They either hunker down in their homes or find a hurricane shelter. People in this category are the same ones falling through the cracks of our criminal justice system—many residing in the "high victim" areas like the YEZ, where crime runs rampant even on sunny days.

Warren Buffet, one of the richest men in America, famously said that "you only find out who is swimming naked when the tide goes out."[56] He was referring to people living with financial risk who were suddenly exposed and left vulnerable by the 2008 economic crisis. The same is true for these storms: they reveal who in our community is living in desperate poverty. The storms also reveal who will be jumping in to help those who are struggling when the need arises.

Times of crisis bring out the best and worst in people. Neighbors coming together to help neighbors, and individual acts of heroism are juxtaposed against con artists who emerge to swindle or price gouge and looters who break out store windows to go on a shopping spree. It is in these darkest times that the needs of the most vulnerable become magnified and the necessity of everyone working together to help each other becomes the most pronounced.

You most likely experienced a similar phenomenon in your hometown during the COVID-19 pandemic. The most vulnerable members of your community (because of advanced age and medical conditions) relied on everyone else to do the right thing (social distancing and sheltering in place) to limit the damage. Executive orders, not unlike the gang injunctions, were enacted and enforced to limit the movement of people, the places they could attend, and the size of the group that could congregate.

FIGURE 7.17   During the COVID-19 pandemic, law enforcement leaders kept their social distance while remaining united in fighting crime in the "together we can, together we will" campaign, March 30, 2020.

The virus also magnified the disparities that existed in communities, disproportionately impacting communities of color.[57] If the pandemic were the police, it would have been accused of profiling.

But what the statistics from the hospitals, unemployment centers, and morgues really magnified is not unlike what the crime statistics reveal from our jails, prisons, and YEZ; they highlight the structural racism that exists on so many levels of society. The virus is color blind. It hit hardest those living in poverty, who carry in their bodies years of unequal access to health care.

Do we blame the frontline workers, the medical professionals dispensing treatment, and the police attempting to keep order, during these times of crisis? Of course not. They go about their work even as their own homes are flooding and even as they are being exposed to the very virus that is lurking in the people they are encountering and treating. In the process, they disproportionately experience more harm than the average citizen.[58] The work of ending the conditions leading to unequal impact is not the responsibility of first responders alone; the entire Starfish model must be involved and it must be an ongoing effort, not just during a state of emergency.

One final lesson from hurricanes and pandemics: because we can see them coming, we can minimize the damage. While both are forces of nature, far bigger than any one of us, it is the communities who look at the data, whose leaders work together and act when they reasonably foresee the danger before the threat arrives, who will save the most lives. In my hometown, we call it "hurricane preparedness." You know it now as "flattening the curve."

As we will see in chapter 8, we find our focus when we remember the center of the starfish: health. To magnify this point, we will confront the opioid epidemic, a public safety emergency in need of a public health solution. And it turns out that just as we can predict the weather or see a major pandemic on the horizon, we can foresee who we will most need to help, even before trouble reaches our shores.

Notes

1   *State v. Haugabook*, 798 S.E.2d 436 (N.C. Ct. App. 2016). Co-counsel was Dru Lewis.

2   N.C. Pattern Jury Instructions-Crim. 202.10; *State v. Barnes*, 345 N.C. 184 (1997).

3   *State v. Bellamy*, 172 N.C. App. 649, 669 (2005)(Discussed in chapter 3. The North Court Supreme Court indicated that murder committed during the course of an armed robbery is normally a natural and probably consequence of the robbery but that a sexual assault may or may not be. The determination must be on a case-by-case basis).

4   N.C. Gen. Stat. §15A-2005.

5 See, generally North Carolina General Statute 14-50.22 (enhancing punishment for persons 15 years and older who are convicted of offenses committed for the benefit of, at the direction of, or in association with any criminal street gang).

6 Hannah DeLaCourt, Police Chief: Yesterday Was Not a Good Day in Our City. A 16-Year-Old Was Killed and Four Other Men Were Wounded in a Drive-By Shooting, *StarNews Online*. Dec. 21, 2015, http://www.starnewsonline.com/news/20151221/police-looking-for-gang-related-suspects-in-fatal-shooting-video (last visited Aug. 16, 2017).

7 *State v. Johnson*, 16CRS000002 in Brunswick County. Counsel was Jon David. Counsel for the federal case against Johnson was Charity Wilson.

8 *State v. Farrow*, 368 N.C. 679 (2016). Counsel was Janet Coleman.

9 The bar was shut down, and the owners have since filed for bankruptcy protection. See, Wayne Faulkner, "Major Downtown Wilmington Landowner Files for Bankruptcy," *StarNews Online*, Apr. 12, 2011, http://www.starnewsonline.com/article/20110412/ARTICLES/110419909.

10 *See* David Kennedy, *Don't Shoot: One Man, A Street Fellowship and the End of Violence in Inner City America* (2011).

11 Youth Build U.S.A., Wilmington Housing Authority, http://www.wha.net/Housing_Programs/Resident_Services/YouthBuild.htm (last visited Mar. 23, 2012).

12 About LINC, Leading Into New Communities, http://www.lincnc.org/AboutLINC/tabid/57/Default.aspx (last visited Mar. 23, 2012).

13 Murder of Shane Simpson, Dec. 20, 2015. Four teenagers indicted for first-degree murder. See generally, *State v. Shequan Palmer, et al.* 15 CRS 60567.

14 This press conference can be found at https://www.youtube.com/watch?v=QPwjRnva2X8.

15 New Hanover County docket number 17CVS4184.

16 Email from Daniel Thurston, October 2, 2019. On files with author.

17 Peter Block, *Community: The Structure of Belonging* (2009).

18 Yuval Levin. *The Fractured Republic: Renewing America's Social Contract in the Age of Individualism* (2017).

19 The WPD created a "Text a Tip" program for people to anonymously report crime. "Wilmington Police Introduce 'Text a Tip' Program," WWAY TV, (Sept. 23, 2008, 4:42 PM), http://www.wwaytv3.com/wilmington_police_text_a_tip_program/09/2008. I then appeared before the NC Legislature

to have the discovery law changed to protect the identity of confidential informants. *See* NC Gen. Stat. § 15A-904.

20 See, *Blue Ribbon Commission on the Prevention of Youth Violence*, http://www.brczone.org. The BRC was rebranded Voyage in 2020.

21 The Harlem Children's Zone was created by Geoffrey Canada. See generally Geoffrey Canada, *Reaching Up for Manhood: Transforming the Lives of Boys in America* (1998) (discussing the effects of growing up in the inner city).

22 Email from Tufanna Thomas, strategic director, New Hanover Cnty. Blue Ribbon Commission on the Prevention of Youth Violence, to author (Apr. 3, 2012, 16:11 EST) (on file with author).

23 See generally, George K. Kelling and James Q. Wilson, "Broken Windows: The Police and Neighborhood Safety," *The Atlantic* (March 1982).

24 *Terry v. Ohio*, 392 U.S. 1 (1968).

25 US Highschool Dropout Rate [2020] Statistics and Trends. Educationdata.org

26 Email from Judge Corpening to author. On file with author.

27 Jenna Kurzyna, "Governor Cooper Signs 'Raise the Age Proclamation,'" WWAY TV LLC, (July 28, 2017), https://www.wwaytv3.com/2017/07/28/gov-roy-cooper-signs-raising-the-age-proclamation/ ("District Attorney Ben David said only around 3% of crimes committed by juveniles are violent.").

28 Judge Corpening was inspired by Steven Teske, a district court judge from Clayton County, Georgia. Teske, who is credited with being an early innovator of the school justice partnership model, came to Wilmington to work with the leadership team in our district.

29 The ADR Center, *Teen Court: Building a Better Community One Agreement at a Time* (Copyright 2017), http://www.theadrcenter.org/our-services/teen-court/.

30 Benjamin David, "The Benefits of Teen Court," *Business Life* (Nov. 1997): 30, 63.

31 Jenna Kurzyna, "Governor Cooper Signs 'Raise the Age Proclamation,'" WWAY TV LLC, July 28, 2017, https://www.wwaytv3.com/2017/07/28/gov-roy-cooper-signs-raising-the-age-proclamation/.

32 *Id.*

33 Lauren Horsch, "Raise the Age Bill Gains Steam in One of the Last States to Prosecute 16-Year-Olds as Adults," *The News & Observer*, March 8, 2017, http://www.newsobserver.com/news/politics-government/state-politics/article137281928.html (" [Representative Duane] Hall said that as a lawyer

he's had teens in his office crying after finding out a nonviolent felony conviction would preclude them from joining the military or getting financial aid for college.").

34 Wiley Nichol, "Top Ten Reasons for Getting Your North Carolina Conviction Expunged," Expunge My NC Record.Com, (July 25, 2014), http://expungemyncrecord.com/uncategorized/top-ten-reasons-getting-north-carolina-criminal-conviction-expunged.

35 Jenna Kurzyna, Governor Cooper Signs "Raise the Age Proclamation," WWAY TV LLC, (July 28, 2017), https://www.wwaytv3.com/2017/07/28/gov-roy-cooper-signs-raising-the-age-proclamation/.

36 North Carolina General Statute §7B-1501 (7).

37 *See* Amanda Greene, "Superintendent Recommends Virgo Middle School Be Shuttered," *StarNews Online*, Feb. 16, 2011, http://www.starnewsonline.com/article/20110216/ARTICLES/110219727; Amanda Greene, "Virgo Middle to Close, Reopen as Charter or Magnet School," *StarNews Online*, May 17, 2011, http://www.starnewsonline.com/article/20110517/ARTICLES/110519640.

38 Greene, "Virgo Middle to Close, Reopen as Charter or Magnet School," *supra* note 92. The school was named for the first African-American principal in the area. Michael Jordan is counted among the alumni. *Id.*

39 Pressley Baird, "New Hanover Submits Charter-School Application for Virgo Middle," *StarNews Online*, Nov. 30, 2011, http://www.starnewsonline.com/article/20111130/ARTICLES/111139991 (stating that New Hanover County Schools submitted a fast-track application to charter D.C. Virgo and that a successful application would allow the school to open in the fall of 2012). *But see* Editorial, "Virgo's Success Will Require Strong, Competent Leadership and Public Support," *StarNews Online*, Jan. 5, 2012, http://www.starnewsonline.com/article/20120105/ARTICLES/120109875 (stating the application for charter school was denied).

40 https://uncw.edu/virgo/

41 Statistics provided by Judy Girard and Todd Godby of G.L.O.W. Academy (May 2017).

42 To learn more about Watch DOGS visit fathers.com.

43 FBI statistics show that "one in seven youngsters has experienced unwanted sexual solicitations online" and "[o]ne in three has been exposed to unwanted sexual material online." *Keeping Kids Safe Online—FBI Program Offered in Schools*, Fed. Bureau of Investigation, (Jan. 11, 2011), http://www.fbi.gov/news/stories/2011/january/online_011111/online_011111. To encourage dialogue between children and parents about internet habits, I leave internet safety contracts with school faculty to

distribute to parents. The contract, on my letterhead, lays out 10 points of agreement between child and parent, ranging from not talking to strangers or giving out personal identifying information, to reporting immediately to the parents if the child is approached.

44 Dr. Stephen R. Covey, *The Seven Habits of Highly Effective People* (1990).

45 Gavin de Becker, *The Gift of Fear: And Other Survival Signals That Protect Us from Violence* (1997).

46 The Power Breakfast can be viewed at https://www.youtube.com/watch?v=Yli0dJwPE0I.

47 Ben David, United Way of the Cape Fear Area, "Prevent Violence NC" (2015), http://www.prevent-violencenc.org/new-hanover-county-community-story.

48 National Institute of Violence, "Recidivism" (June 17, 2014), https://www.nij.gov/topics/corrections/recidivism/Pages/welcome.aspx.

49 *Id.*

50 N.C. Gen. Stat. § 15A-145 and 15A-146.

51 The Second Chances Act expanded eligibility but more important, accessibility, to expunction relief. The new provision automatically expunges the record of arrest if a case is dismissed or a defendant is found not guilty. N.C. Gen. Stat. § 15A-146.

52 Phoenix Hometown Hires. "Phoenix Hometown Hires History and Timeline," (August 8, 2017), http://phoenixhometownhires.org/about-us/history/.

53 *Id.*

54 Phoenix Hometown Hires, "Job Placements in Fiscal Year 2016–2017," August 8, 2017, http://phoenixhometownhires.org/.

55 Visit Harrelsoncenter.org for a full list of the nonprofit work occurring at the Harrelson Center.

56 Berkshire Hathaway Inc. letter to shareholders by Warren E. Buffett, February 28, 2002, https://www.berkshirehathaway.com/2001ar/2001letter.html

57 "Why Black Americans Are at a Higher Risk for Coronavirus," CNN, April 7, 2020. (While making up roughly 30 percent of the population in places like Chicago and Louisiana, African-Americans accounted for 70 percent of the deaths; "Black Americans have more existing medical issues, less access to health care, and are like to work in unstable jobs—all factors that have made the coronavirus pandemic disproportionately hurt blacks more.")

58 It was widely reported that police officers in hotspots experienced far greater rates of COVID-19 exposure than the overall population. See for example, "The Military, Policing and Covid 19," www.

brookings.edu, April 1, 2020 (15 percent of the New York Police Department recently reporting sick

Figure Credits

Fig. 7.1: Copyright © 2015 by Gray Television, Inc. Reprinted with permission.

Fig. 7.2: Copyright © by Gannett Company, Inc. Reprinted with permission.

Fig. 7.3: Copyright © 2014 by Wilmington Downtown Inc. Reprinted with permission.

Fig. 7.8: Daniel Thurston, "Kordresse Tyson," 2017.

Fig. 7.9: Copyright © 2010 by Gannett Company, Inc. Reprinted with permission.

Fig. 7.13: Copyright © 2016 by Ken Oots. Reprinted with permission.

Fig. 7.16: Copyright © 2018 by Gray Television, Inc. Reprinted with permission.

Fig. 7.17: New Hanover County Sheriff's Office, "Together We Can ," https://www.youtube.com/watch?v=gN0-BOu6-g8. Copyright © 2020 by New Hanover County Sheriff's Office.

Chapter 8

The Center of the Starfish

I n this section, we look at health, particularly the well-being of our children. Keeping them safe is not only the desire of every parent, it is the highest duty of professionals in every arm of the starfish. We confront the opioid epidemic and see that the real gateway drug to heroin is not other substances, but trauma. By understanding the impact of adverse childhood experiences and how to make children resilient, we can help young people have a much brighter future. This should give us all hope, especially in the darkest of times.

State v. Edwards[1]

There is beauty in the world. We see it in the kindness of strangers and in the bravery of first responders. We find it in the midst of terrible days, like when a rainbow emerges after a storm. But mostly we know that there is beauty in the world because children exist. Childhood is a magical time. A time for dressing up and playing outside until dark. A time of potential and possibilities. A time of innocence.

There is also evil in the world. Coming face-to-face with it is very rare, even for a prosecutor, but when evil is in the room there is no mistaking it. Thieves take things; child predators steal a childhood. When innocence and evil collide, horror results. Our children need special protection and the law recognizes that those who would do them harm are the most deserving of severe punishment. When heinous crimes are perpetrated on children, I am especially reminded of why we build courthouses and prisons.

Eva and Raul Hernandez came to the United States in search of a better way of life.[2] They left Honduras and traveled many miles, crossing over our border illegally, fueled by the belief that America held the most hope for their future. Hard work had paid off. A decade later they were proud parents of three young children, Pablo, age 9, Maria, age 6, and Graciella, age 4. The children were born on American soil making them citizens of our country. They spoke English at school and Spanish at home.

The Hernandez family lived in the Royal Palms Mobile Home Park, home to over 200 illegal immigrants, who mostly worked as maids, lawn maintenance workers, and dishwashers. Nearly everyone in Royal Palms, including the Hernandez family, attended the Basilica Shrine of St. Mary Church every Wednesday night and Sunday morning for Mass. Extended families lived together under one roof, and everyone in the neighborhood had a hand in raising the children. Crime in Royal Palms, despite the bleak economic conditions, was almost nonexistent.

On September 14, 2016, Eva sat on the front steps of her modest home and watched Maria and Graciella playing in the front yard. Pablo was doing homework in the dining room. "Ayúdame, Mamá," her son yelled through the screen door, calling out to his mother for help with his math assignment. She left the girls to play for only an instant.

No more than 45 seconds later, Graciella came bursting through the front door screaming to her mom that a bad man on a moped had just driven off with Maria. At first Eva thought it must

FIGURE 8.1   Maria's photo was circulated as part of the Amber Alert. *Source*: WECT.

be a joke. She circled the outside of their home, peering into bushes and looking underneath the small crawl space, hoping that the girls were playing a game of hide-and-seek.

A neighbor, Rodrigo, arrived as Eva was frantically circling her home for a second time. Rodrigo confirmed her worst fears. He had just returned from chasing a man on a moped who had driven off with Maria as she flailed about between his legs. Rodrigo had lost the man on the moped in heavy traffic. Eva began to scream. Then she called 911. The time was 4:50 p.m.

The 911 operator did her best to translate the broken English of a hysterical mother. An Amber Alert was issued and the media was notified. The community would soon learn that a man with a long ponytail on a moped had kidnapped a little girl who he did not know.

Members of the Royal Palms community formed an impromptu search party. They went across the street to Walmart and bought supplies to mass-produce posters. A recent picture of Maria was distributed in rush hour traffic and broadcast by local news channels.

Sergeant Larry Ward with the Carolina Beach Police Department had received the Amber Alert. He drove his vehicle to the entrance of the Snow's Cut Bridge, the only access point to Carolina Beach. Royal Palms was five miles to his north. If the suspect travelled south to Carolina Beach, this is the bridge he would cross.

At 5:45 p.m., 55 minutes after the abduction, Sergeant Ward saw a man with a ponytail riding a moped and coming into view. Even though the man was alone, Ward stopped him anyway. Douglas Edwards had recently been released from prison after serving nearly 20 years for raping a six-year-old girl. Now, as a registered sex offender, Edwards was being monitored by law enforcement, along with the other 600 registered offenders who had returned from prison to the region.[3] Sergeant Ward knew Edwards by name: since his release from prison, unsubstantiated reports of a man with a ponytail trying to lure children away from their homes had circulated on the island. Edwards was a prime suspect.

Where Is Maria?

Sergeant Ward asked Edwards if he knew anything about a missing girl. No, he did not. Edwards claimed that he had just finished painting a home and was now going to his aunt's house to take a shower. Ward took a picture of Edwards with his cellphone and sent it to the command center. "Don't let him leave," came the immediate reply. Edwards matched the eyewitness identifications that were beginning to emerge.

FIGURE 8.2 Carolina Beach Police stop Edwards within 55 minutes of the issuance of the Amber Alert. Note the two helmets.

Lisa Hudson, a detective with the NHSO, materialized at the foot of the Snow's Cut Bridge within minutes. "Where is Maria?" she asked Edwards almost immediately. "I have no idea what you are talking about," came the reply. "Do you have a cell phone?" Detective Hudson asked. "Yes," Edwards said. GPS tracking would later put Edwards at the abduction site at 4:50 p.m.

Meanwhile, crime scene investigators at the abduction site were looking for physical evidence. They found cigarette butts in a lot across the street from Maria's home. When a neighbor reported that a man with a ponytail had been standing in the lot around 4:45 p.m., smoking and watching the girls play, the cigarette butts took on greater importance as they became physical evidence with the suspect's DNA.

Edwards agreed to come to the detective's division for a videotaped interview. He had claimed that he had nothing to hide, and the pounding rain that now fell from the sky made talking on the roadside difficult. Detective Hudson played the part of the good cop on the ride to the interrogation. She purchased Edwards a Big Mac and a coffee after he announced that he was starving. He also smoked cigarettes when she offered them.

In the interrogation room, Edwards ate his dinner and politely answered every question while professing his innocence. Outside, the rain continued to fall. The mood at the station, and everywhere else, vacillated between panic and desperation. Detective Hudson knew she had her man and got right in his face. The good cop routine was over, but Edwards did not break.

The decision was made not to arrest Edwards. Instead, over a dozen officers would covertly keep him under surveillance. It was thought that he might return to wherever he had left Maria in the 55 minutes between the time of the abduction and his encounter with Sergeant Ward. An out-of-custody suspect could take us there, one in jail could not. Most likely he would be leading us to a murder scene. But what if she was still alive?

Upon his release, Edwards drove to his aunt's house, a beach house overlooking the Atlantic Ocean, and closed the door at 10:00 p.m. At about 3:00 a.m., the surveillance team reported that Edwards looked out the window to watch them. He was not going anywhere except back to sleep.

The Long Night

The rain continued to fall throughout the evening. Over 200 officers from multiple police agencies slogged through several square miles, some by car, others by foot. The most likely route of travel that

Edwards took was either down Carolina Beach Road, a heavily traveled artery lined with homes and businesses, or River Road, one of the few rural roads left in the county. River Road snaked through dense forest hugging the Cape Fear River before joining Carolina Beach Road at the Snow's Cut Bridge.

Some officers went door to door with Maria's picture. The Highway Patrol set up a checkpoint and distributed posters. Members of the K9 team chased through miles of woods with flashlights. The mosquitoes were unbearable. A dive team came from Brunswick County to help. A WPD helicopter with infrared technology hovered over patches of dense forest that broke up sprawling subdivisions. Like the officers in the woods, the helicopter pilot saw plenty of coyotes and black bears, but not Maria. Midnight signaled the shift change, but officers on the case refused to leave. They would not stand down until Maria was found.

Back at Royal Palms, over 50 neighbors had come to the Hernandez home. They brought food for the family and wanted to help take care of Pablo and Graciella. Eva was inconsolable. At one point, at about 7:00 p.m., everyone joined hands to pray. A detective stayed with the family to give them any updates, but there was nothing to say.

The NHSO requisitioned a Moose Lodge that was near the abduction site to set up a command center. As officers from the field radioed in their unsuccessful efforts to find Maria, other officers documented the area on a large map that hung on the wall. This grid search continued with meticulous precision. Other detectives drafted search warrants and court orders to search Edwards' home and examine his computer and cellphone.

FBI agents with the Child Abduction Rapid Deployment Team (CARD) flew in from different parts of the country to lend assistance. They, along with the Cellular Analysis Survey Team (CAST), had the technology to see Edwards' movements in real time. In addition to seeing whom he may have called, the agents were interested in tracking the movements of the phone, especially the time between 4:50 p.m. and 5:45 p.m. (Recall the technology from *State v. Bradley* in chapter 5.) It would take a while to download and interpret Edwards' phone records, but time was of the essence. Agents would be doing in hours what would usually take weeks.

Daybreak

Two key parts of the investigation were happening simultaneously, and both would lead to the same patch of dense forest off River Road. At 7:30 a.m., Crystal McGirt called into the command center. She had just turned on the local news and saw the report about a missing child. Crystal, a school bus driver, reported that she was driving down River Road at 5:00 p.m. the previous day to return her bus to the county lot. She saw a man on a moped struggling with a little girl as he pulled to the side of the road. Her bus had a video camera and GPS. Within minutes, detectives were watching the bus video, capturing the grainy image of a man on a moped. The coordinates from the bus GPS were matched up to the time of the video and were radioed in to the command center.

FIGURE 8.3   Bus driver Crystal McGirt's dash camera captured Edwards and Maria on his moped.

Almost at the same time, Edwards' phone records were successfully downloaded and were being interpreted by FBI agents. On a big screen in the command center, an electronic map of the city showed where Edwards, or at least his phone, had been in the hours and moments leading up to the abduction. Red dots formed a trail of his whereabouts. All of us watched transfixed. A blinking dot meant movement. When the dot filled in and stopped blinking the phone was stationary.

As he had told Sergeant Ward and later Detective Hudson, Edwards had been at work all day in the northern part of the county painting a home. But then the movement of the phone started to contradict his accounts. Instead of leaving the job site at 5:00 p.m., Edwards left at 4:30 p.m. and drove straight to Royal Palms, arriving at 4:40 p.m. For the next 10 minutes, he stayed in the front yard of the home across the street from the Hernandez home. Then the phone started to move, indicating when he was driving away with Maria.

The dots continued to blink as Edwards drove down looping roads that connected subdivisions before finding his way onto River Road. And then, at the location that Crystal was now telling detectives she saw the man pull off the road, the blinking stopped, and the dots filled in. Edwards had gone into the woods. All of us watched the screen with growing dread. The dots continued to fill in while the phone remained in the dense forest for an excruciating 20 minutes; an eternity for a child molester to live out his sick fantasies.

Statistically, we had fallen off a cliff. The odds of finding Maria alive were bleak from the start. Now, 15 hours later and with visual confirmation that Edwards had been in the woods for an extended time, there was little question that the mission was pivoting away from being a search and rescue effort toward the awful direction of recovery and family notification. Sheriff Ed McMahon and I huddled with interpreters at the command center. The Hernandez family was standing by at Saint Mary Church with Father Bob, their priest. We would deliver the news together once detectives found their daughter's body.

Into the Woods

A search team deployed into the woods, following the path of Edwards' phone. Detective Sean Dixon, a Marine sniper, was among them. Like Sergeant Ward, who had served onboard a Blackhawk helicopter in the US Army, and dozens of other officers in local law enforcement, Detective Dixon had come back from a warzone to protect and serve people at home. Detective Dixon was accompanied by Bane, his Hanoverian hound.

FIGURE 8.4 K9 Bane and handler Detective. Sean Dixon.

The Hernandez family had allowed Detective Dixon to take Maria's blanket from her room, and Detective Dixon now had her scent to conduct an "article search." Bane's hair bristled, his tail went up, and his nose began to twitch as he ran down a sandy trail that led into the woods. Maria had been here; Detective Dixon was sure of it. Bane soon located a bag from a hardware store with the empty packaging of a deadbolt lock inside.

Detective Dixon's partner during the search, Lieutenant Scott Croom, broke off down another trail. In the distance, Lieutenant Croom saw the body first. He began to run, sick with the feeling that he was about to approach the corpse of a girl who was the same age as his daughter. Bugs were crawling across the little girl's pink shirt as he came upon her from the back, calling her name.

As he kneeled to roll her over, the little girl's face suddenly turned, lifting out of the mud where she rested. "Are you here to take me to my mommy?" she asked. "Yes, I am honey," he replied. Lieutenant Croom and Detective Dixon, who arrived with Bane within seconds, began to cry.

The two deputies radioed into the command center together. None of us will ever forget the words that came over the speaker: "She is alive. We are with her right now." A cheer went up. Officers began hugging each other. The family notification that the sheriff and I were preparing for took a decided turn. Prayers had been answered.

Two Types of Trauma

I met Maria later that morning at the hospital. Extended family and friends poured into the small waiting room as Maria's parents hugged and reassured their daughter. It was a reunion none of us will ever forget.

Two things became immediately apparent to me upon meeting this little girl. First, she had survived a very traumatic event—one that included not only hours of exposure to cold rain, bugs and wild animals, but sexual violation. The second thing that was obvious to me was that not only was Maria a survivor, she had a deep support network around her that would remain committed to her healing and happiness for years to come. I knew within minutes, and have since confirmed through watching her grow over the last few years, that Maria was going to be O.K.

Every year, members of my office meet untold numbers of people just like Maria who have endured a nightmare and lived to testify in court about their victimization. They might have suffered a physical or sexual assault or extensive injuries from a deadly weapon or car crash. In these cases, the trauma is isolated to a one-time occurrence, a traumatic event, what Dora called the "one bad hour in my life."

But there is a second type of trauma. Instead of a broken arm or bloody lip, there are some people who live with trauma every day. For kids who grow up in an abusive household or a high poverty neighborhood where violence is ever present, trauma is not confined to an event but is a part of life. These children are living with toxic stress that over time quite literally changes their body chemistry and their brain functioning. These children are in a survival mode response to this stress that not only affects them physically (increasing their heart rate, blood pressure, breathing and muscle tension) but mentally (reducing the ability to respond, learn, and maintain relationships and increasing the likelihood of fighting or acting out).[4]

In the mid-1990s, two doctors, Dr. Robert Adna and Dr. Vincent Felitti, began taking a different kind of patient history that did not focus on traditional things like the prevalence of heart disease and cancer in a family. Instead, these doctors conducted a study of 17,000 participants, from 1995 through 1997, to investigate childhood abuse and neglect and its tie to later in life health conditions.[5] Through this work, they developed an assessment tool to measure adverse childhood experiences (ACE). They used this data to come up with an ACE score that can draw connections between adverse childhood experiences and medical, social, and economic adversity later in life.

The assessment tool asked ten yes/no questions and generates an ACE score based on questions answered in the affirmative. Study participants were asked:

1.   Are your parents divorced?
2.   Is either parent incarcerated?
3.   Have you witnessed domestic violence in your home?
4.   Is there drug use in your home?
5.   Do you suffer from food insecurity or a lack of basic needs?
6.   Do you lack emotional support from family at home?
7.   Is there someone with mental illness in your home?
8.   Have you been threatened or emotionally abused at home?
9.   Have you been physically abused?
10.   Have you been sexually abused?

A child who answers 4 or more of the 10 questions in the affirmative has a challenging future to confront. They are 70% more likely to be victims or defendants of a violent crime. They are much more likely to become pregnant as teenagers, drop out of high school, or commit suicide. 62% of intravenous drug users have an ACE score of four or higher. Living with this toxic stress has long-term implications on health that leaves a dark legacy with a much greater rate of diabetes and heart disease, to name just a couple of ailments. The life expectancy, of someone answering six or more in the affirmative, is 20 years less than the rest of the population.[6]

What does that look like over time? In my more than two decades as a prosecutor, I have seen young people living with toxic stress who become the adults living on a cul-de-sac of despair. They are in a vicious loop that puts them in the never-ending cycle of bad relationships and bad choices. You have read about them in this book. Some are victims. Many are defendants. As we have seen time and again, this point is reflected in the Mirror Image Rule. When people are in pain, they tend to look for medication. Many find opioids.

The Opioid Epidemic

According to a 2016 study, 12% of individuals in Wilmington who were prescribed opioids were abusing them, making the Port City the number one place in America for abuse rates.[7] Many have speculated that Wilmington became the epicenter for the opioid epidemic because of our geography, midway between Florida and New York, with a bustling port and interstate traffic. Others say it is the economics of the rich users (tourists, college kids, and beachgoers) mixing with the very poor, concentrated in public housing communities. Whatever the reason for our problem, the collateral consequences have been profound.

The unintended deaths both locally and around our country are alarming. In 2017, 64,000 people died of drug overdose in America, surpassing gunshot wounds and car accidents as the leading cause of death among Americans under 50 years of age.[8] If a foreign army parachuted in and inflicted this level of harm on American citizens, would we not be calling for an end to the war?

These statistics show up in terrible ways where I live. Nearly four people die every day of an opioid overdose in North Carolina, which equates to more than one a week in my district.[9] Perhaps the saddest ripple effect of drug use resides not at the courthouse but at the neonatal intensive care unit at the hospital. Babies are born trembling from opioid withdrawal and require specialized care in their first days and weeks of life. These babies suffer neonatal abstinence syndrome (NAS) and are feeling the effects of life without heroin and other drugs. In 2010, there were 34 NAS babies born at NHRMC. In 2017, the number had increased to 129.[10]

The courts are increasingly intervening to arrange care for these children through foster families. The New Hanover County DSS reported that in fiscal year 2015–2016, 137 children were accepted into foster care due to the drug addiction of a primary caregiver. The following year, that number more than doubled to 280 children.[11] What happens when these children are discharged from the hospital or when older children are found to have parents who can no longer care for them due to addiction? Consider the ACE scores for these children. Who is going to send them the lifeline to get the help they need today?

So, what can be done to keep those struggling with addictions from winding up in a motel on Market Street, in a jail cell, or in a grave dug by a serial killer? What works? Everything has been suggested from more drug treatment, to limited immunity, to outright legalization of all controlled substances. Let's look at our local experiences on these fronts:

Community Recovery Court

In 1999, long before other places had even heard of the concept, stakeholders in the Sixth District created a drug treatment court, now called the Community Recovery Court (CRC). The mission was to protect the community from the collateral effects of drug crimes while maintaining our focus on traffickers, violent criminals, and habitual felons.

The CRC operates on the premise that defendants with underlying substance abuse issues will never exit the revolving door of the criminal justice system if their addictions are not addressed. The goal is not incarceration but restoration. (And as we saw in the Eddings' case, discussed in chapter 6, there is plenty of forgiveness involved.) In this restorative justice model, criminal justice officials are committed to changing the nouns in the defendant's life: the company they keep (person), where they hang out (place), and what they crave (things). The result is a positive change in habits.

Change comes through rehabilitation, which, in theory, is one of the goals of punishment. The reality today is far different. Most experts agree that sending people to prison, especially the very young, has the opposite effect of healing. The root causes that lead to crime, such as addiction and mental health issues, are not effectively treated in prisons. Putting nonviolent offenders into an environment with violent offenders and career criminals can lead them in the wrong direction and increases the chances of recidivism.

Every two weeks, defendants stand before District Court Judge James Faison, a former prosecutor who has headed the CRC since 2002. These defendants and their probation officers update Judge Faison on their work progress, treatment sessions, and drug test results. This same team uses a similar approach for impaired driving offenses for habitual offenders. Defendants who are convicted of impaired driving offenses will only serve about 30 days of a two-year sentence under current Department of Adult Correction (DAC) policy.[12] Bimonthly monitoring by a team of professionals, along with encouraged family participation, maximizes the defendant's chances for recovery.

Participation in the CRC is voluntary and is only available for persons with a nonviolent criminal history. Offenders must be fully prepared for the rigors of the program. Those who are successful in the program receive reduced sentences, while judgment is imposed on those who drop out.

The CRC often shows great latitude when defendants initially fail drug screens or are delinquent in paying their financial obligations: getting out of the lifestyle does not happen overnight. To get the defendant's attention, Judge Faison may apply short jail sentences, called "quick dips," meaning sending an offender who fails a drug screen to jail for the weekend instead of revoking their probationary sentences (which may send them to prison for months or even years).

Sometimes prison is necessary for those who are unsuccessful. Recall from chapter 5 that Crystal and Schnique (two sex industry workers who were in the grips of drug addiction) credited their incarceration as the reason they did not share Elisha and Shannon's fate at the hands of James Bradley. If not for the probationary sentences of both women being revoked when they continued to commit other crimes, they would have remained out on the streets.

After one year of living drug- or alcohol-free and complying with the standard terms of probation, CRC participants graduate in an elaborate ceremony at which they are celebrated by all involved. We believe so strongly in this program that when state funding was cut in the 2011–2012 fiscal year, New Hanover County Commissioners, who also foot the bill to run our local jail, stepped up to continue the CRC's operation.

Treatment courts unquestionably reduce the number of defendants who are incarcerated long-term. They are also successful in getting some who are struggling with addiction to embrace sober living and change their lives. But even more common are young women like "Amber," whom I first met when I was a new prosecutor and while she was a teenager. At the time, she was shoplifting to support a crack habit. She graduated to prostitution, has had several children along the way, and has migrated to heroin, methamphetamines, and other drugs.

Amber has been in and out of our local jail and the DAC well over a dozen times. Whatever treatment has been ordered during her many years of incarceration has failed to treat her underlying issues. Amber has not succeeded despite the tireless efforts of committed professionals in the CRC, and those working next door at the Harrelson Center. It has been said that "a picture is worth a thousand words." Does it look like Amber has been benefiting from treatment?

Mug Shots of "Amber" in the time I have been a prosecutor

FIGURE 8.5   1999.

FIGURE 8.6   2001.

FIGURE 8.7   2010.

FIGURE 8.8   2016.

Legalize It?

Lurking in the background when discussing vice crimes is the question of whether we should end the "war on drugs" and wave a white flag of surrender by legalizing gambling and prostitution. Where products and enterprise can be regulated, the argument goes, safer business practices ensue by taking the black market and profit margin out of the equation.[13] Some people ask, "If Colorado has legalized marijuana, why not North Carolina?" or "If prostitution is legal in Nevada, why not here?" Others bemoan the hypocrisy of government-sanctioned gambling (state lotteries, for example, raise millions of dollars, usually given to school systems) and contend that private industry should be able to engage in the same conduct for profit. "Wouldn't it be more beneficial for society to regulate this activity and get out of the business of being the 'morality squad'?"

As a prosecutor, my response to these arguments is twofold. First, as an executive officer, I enforce the laws. It is the legislature's responsibility to look at the larger policy questions and decide whether to prohibit certain conduct. When DAs see gaps in the law (e.g., Raise the Age, adding emerging drugs to the schedule of controlled substances), we can work with legislators to improve these statutes, but ultimately the legislature gives us the framework. Second, my experience has led me to believe that trying to remove the stigma of drugs by making them legal would lead to greater use, thereby increasing the unintended collateral damage.

Look at alcohol, by far the most abused drug in America. The deadliest weapon in most communities is a car driven by an impaired driver, which can be just as deadly as guns or knives. It is very rare to handle a domestic violence case in which alcohol was not present at the time of the incident, let alone as an ever-present part of the abuser's daily habits.

Alcohol is also the number one date rape drug in our country. A 2015 study revealed that 15% of female college students reported that they were raped while under the influence.[14] That is one in six female college freshmen. Over 90% of the physical and sexual assaults on college campuses involve alcohol impairment by either the defendant or victim or both.[15] Normalizing underaged drinking has led to all sorts of unintended consequences.

Another legal drug that has caused great devastation are medications found at hospitals, clinics, and pharmacies. Prescription drugs are the poster child for a legalized, well-regulated substance that has turned into a national nightmare. Because they are prescribed by doctors, many assume that they are safe; nothing could be further from the truth. More doctors need to remember their Hippocratic Oath to "do no harm" and limit the use and availability of prescription pills.

Prescription drugs are a significant gateway to heroin. One national study reported that eight out of 10 heroin users first develop their habit after using prescription pills, either their own or stolen from others.[16] There are more prescription drug overdose deaths at our local hospital than those stemming from heroin and cocaine combined. Over the last decade there has been a four-fold increase in pain medicine prescriptions, and a four-fold increase in overdose deaths—a provocative correlation.[17]

High school students raid their parents' and grandparents' medicine cabinets to have "trail mix" and "pharm" parties, mixing pills of different colors into dangerous cocktails for fun or for bragging rights. They don't appreciate the importance of utilizing these drugs in a therapeutic manner and under the supervision of a doctor. The pattern rarely varies. Few people understand the dangers of taking prescription drugs that are intended for someone else. As occasional users become addicts, they run out of options for getting easy refills. They end up running to the street, where there are no license checks for filling prescriptions. The cheaper and more potent fix is heroin, now frequently mixed with the much cheaper and far more deadly drug, fentanyl. Now with a full-blown heroin addiction, all the misery and suffering for them, the family, and larger community is as inevitable as the sun rising in the morning.

Limited Liability?

Some suggest that a middle-ground approach, where drug use is still illegal, but people are not criminally charged for drug possession, if they reach out to authorities for help. Frequently when people die from drug overdoses, they are surrounded by friends, often others who are also struggling with addiction, at the time of their demise. North Carolina passed a law that gives immunity to those who call 911, as well as to the person in medical distress.[18] This was not an attempt to normalize drug use but a compromise to encourage life-saving: if someone is deciding between criminal sanctions and getting emergency medical assistance, most agree that we should remove the barriers to making that 911 call. To see why the law was necessary, consider this next case.

State v. Leutgens[19]

The 911 call came in at 1:15 p.m. on July 18, 2012. Jeremy Leutgens, a local boy who grew up selling ice cream on a beach in Surf City, was frantic. He had woken from a deep sleep to find his girlfriend, Stephanie Hobson, lying lifeless in the bed next to him. She was, in his words, cold to the touch and her lips were blue, as if she had been dead for hours. Ambulances and officers quickly arrived, and Stephanie was pronounced dead at the scene. She was 25 years old.

Leutgens told EMS workers that Stephanie had taken pills that she found on the internet. Officers noticed the distraught young man playing with his cellphone, as if trying to erase text messages and other contents on it. They seized it and later obtained a warrant. What they would find a few days later was horrifying.

Video on Leutgens' phone, recorded over a 12-hour period, showed Stephanie slowly dying. His original story about waking up to find her already dead was a lie. He had recorded everything, at first to amusingly document her gross impairment, and later as a crude way to seek medical advice from friends by texting them clips of Stephanie's deteriorating condition. The friends who watched these videos all said the same thing: "call 911 immediately!" Leutgens never called … until 10 minutes after she died.

An autopsy would later reveal the presence of lithium and an antidepressant known as Fluoxetine, both of which Stephanie took under a doctor's care. What was of special interest to the medical examiner, though, was the presence of a drug known as "25i"—a designer drug that was so new to authorities that the North Carolina Legislature had not yet made it illegal.[20] A toxicologist later established the cause of death, serotonin syndrome, which caused excessive stimulation of serotonin receptors in Stephanie's brain. There was an interaction between Stephanie's antidepressants and the 25i, also known as "N-bomb," which caused labored breathing and eventually led to cardiac arrest.[21] This was a condition entirely treatable with supportive care; she would have survived and fully recovered with immediate treatment.

Until her death, Stephanie was living with her parents in Kure Beach. She had graduated from Temple University in Philadelphia three years earlier with a degree in journalism. She had only known Leutgens for four months and, much to her parents' dismay, had been in an "on-again off-again" relationship with him. The week before, Stephanie had started a new job at a local car dealership and seemed to be doing well.

On July 17, Leutgens invited Stephanie on a date at an upscale restaurant in downtown Wilmington. While downtown, Leutgens met with two friends, Ben and Jessica, and shared two pills of 25i with them. He told them the pills were "pretty strong." At dinner, Leutgens tried to sell a pill of 25i for $20 to their server. The server declined.

Stephanie was intrigued. Could she try some? Leutgens promised to "take care of her." After having some drinks downtown and later at a friend's house, Leutgens made good on his promise. At approximately 1:30 a.m., back at Stephanie's apartment, Leutgens gave Stephanie a double dose and took one dose for himself. According to Leutgens' later statements, the drug kicked in around 3:00 a.m. Leutgens reported that he was having extremely strong hallucinations, and that during that time Stephanie appeared to be having a "bad trip." She was incoherent and not speaking.

At 3:20 a.m., Leutgens began recording a cell phone video that showed Stephanie spinning around the room, confused and mumbling and falling on the ground. Just 25 minutes later, at 3:45 a.m., the video showed Stephanie facedown on the floor and not speaking. On the video, Leutgens is heard narrating the apparent effects of the drug and apologizing to Stephanie for giving her too much.

Leutgens moved Stephanie to the bedroom around 8:00 a.m. He was no longer feeling the effects of the drug. He texted Ben and Jessica and sent them the video of Stephanie on the bed having what appears to be seizures. They told him to call 911. At 9:00 a.m., he texted his friend, Alec, that "Steph took way too much" and had not moved or spoken since she took it. Alec told him to call 911. For the next three hours, Stephanie's condition continued to deteriorate. At 12:15 p.m., Leutgens took yet another video of Stephanie on his bed. She was clearly having trouble breathing. She was moaning and her eyes were fixed in a steady stare. She was unresponsive to anything Leutgens was saying to her.

At 12:35 p.m., Leutgens took another video. In these images, Stephanie's breathing was very shallow, and she continued to moan and be unresponsive. It is believed that she died at 1:15 p.m. It was only after her death that Leutgens finally called 911.

The Duty to Act

Imagine that two people are sitting on a beach and see a small child, walking alone near the water's edge. Without warning, the toddler wades into the water and is quickly engulfed by the waves. One of the onlookers says to the other, "I bet that baby will not last a minute." Over the next several seconds, the toddler dips beneath the surface and drowns.

Horrified and outraged, every person would want the two strangers who refused to render aid charged with the highest crime possible. Can they be charged? The answer is probably not. The criminal law imposes no duty to rush to another's aid. There may be civil liability, but the criminal law is powerless to make people do the right thing. Those who step up to render aid to the helpless are called Good Samaritans. Those who fail to act or choose to look the other way are not called criminals. Except in very limited cases, the moral outrage that all of us feel does not find redress in the criminal courts. These onlookers might be social pariahs, but we may not be able to charge them with or convict them of a crime.[22]

As is often the case with the law, there are exceptions. If one or both onlookers were lifeguards, EMS workers, or police officers, the obligation would be imposed through their profession. Failing to act could expose them to liability under the concept of *"parens patriae,"* Latin for "parent of the nation." Additionally, if one of them were a relative, like a parent, or took on the responsibility of the parent, like a nanny, there would be a duty imposed by law or contract. (Note: In the case of the infant hot car death in chapter 1, there was no liability because the mother was unaware of her child's plight.) Finally, if one of the onlookers had created the peril, such as by pushing the toddler into the water, they would have a duty to jump in and try to save the child.

Using the drowning child hypothetical, there is clearly moral outrage in Leutgens watching Stephanie die, but is there a crime? There is nothing about their relationship that compelled him to act. (In conducting exhaustive nationwide research, we determined that only the state of Oregon imposed a duty to act upon non-married persons who were living together.) Similarly, Leutgens did not have a duty imposed by any job.

However, his behavior was egregious. Not only did he supply the drugs, effectively pushing Stephanie into the water, but he took steps to conceal their source by telling investigators that she purchased them off the internet. Leutgens attempted to destroy evidence (the numerous videos and text messages on his phone) that established that he had been sober enough to realize Stephanie's distress and recognize that she needed immediate help. Reaching out to friends only further established that the reason he did not call 911 was that he was afraid of the consequences of being revealed as a drug dealer, effectively putting his own legal concerns above those for his girlfriend's health. Because Leutgens created the peril, he had a duty to act.[23]

Failing to act in this situation was tantamount to the culpable negligence that underlies involuntary manslaughter. We charged Leutgens with this offense and braced for a trial. To our surprise, and to Stephanie's family's relief, Leutgens came into court and pled guilty as charged. He showed great remorse and threw himself on the mercy of the court. He was sentenced to 17–30 months in prison.

Everyone, especially Stephanie's parents, would have given anything for Leutgens to have called 911. This is the purpose behind the limited immunity law. I share Stephanie's story every time I speak with a group of high school seniors.

Our Best Intentions

The immunity laws went even further. Frontline officers who respond to the scene, frequently before EMS arrives, are cast into the role of bringing people back from the grave by administering a drug called Naloxone or Narcan. The law gave officers immunity if they acted negligently in attempting to deliver treatment. If they saw criminal activity (drugs laying around, paraphernalia such as syringes, etc.) during their lifesaving efforts, they were required to walk away after giving the medical intervention.[24]

Justice officials in my district worked closely with a nonprofit group that disperses Narcan to equip law enforcement agencies with this lifesaving drug. Statewide, 785 of the first 3,000 Narcan shots administered by law enforcement officers were in New Hanover County. Law officers were not able to arrest the people they were bringing back to life, but they were saving their lives, sometimes, the same person, multiple times. The motto to "serve and protect" took on a whole new meaning as even those who were committing crime were now being served and protected.

Who could question the success of these efforts? We soon learned the answer to that question, on the morning after Halloween in 2016. That is when we saw that sometimes the road to hell is paved with our best intentions.

State v. Hayes[25]

On the clear morning of November 1, 2016, Mason Richardson was in his car seat. His dad, a long-distance trucker, had the day off and he was running errands with his pregnant wife, their four-year-old son, Jordan, and youngest child, Mason, three days shy of his third birthday. The family car came to a stop at a traffic light near Independence Mall.

Twenty-four-year-old Jonathan Hayes grew up in this area of Wilmington and still lived with his parents. His downward spiral through drug addiction, mostly with opioids and heroin, is chronicled in a series of mugshots for various DWI arrests and property offenses. Though his physical appearance was not affected in the same way as Amber, his crimes began to escalate. The breaking and entering charges are a clear sign that his habit had become too expensive to maintain.

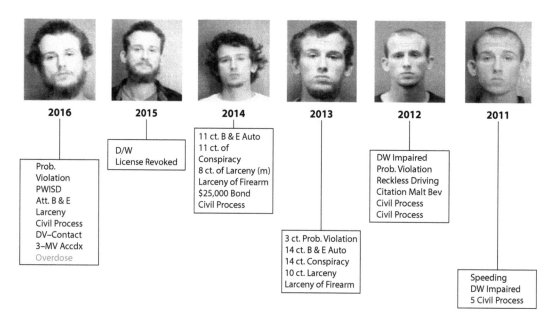

FIGURE 8.9   Summary of Jonathan Hayes arrests, 2011–2016.

Hayes was not only known to law enforcement as a defendant, he was also brought back to life with Narcan by police three different times in the calendar year for 2016. Each time he was revived he woke up a free man—the immunity laws meant that officers could not arrest him for the drugs that almost killed him.

Less than two months after Hayes' most recent overdose, he was once again on the streets of Wilmington. He now carried a personal Narcan kit in his car in the event he would need to be revived again. On this day, he was again heavily impaired, driving wildly through city streets in a pick-up truck that his family had provided to him.

A Good Samaritan called 911 as Hayes passed him at an intersection and swerved into the oncoming lane of traffic to pass slower vehicles. The caller reported that the truck he was now intently watching was being driven out of control and it was only a matter of time before there would be real trouble. Less than a minute later, the call proved to be prophetic. Hayes never stopped at the busy intersection of Independence Boulevard and Oleander Drive. He slammed full speed into the back of the Richardsons' stopped car. Mason was killed on impact.

As the EMS personnel revived and treated Hayes for his minor injuries, he asked the first responders if immunity laws would once again protect him from criminal prosecution, confident that this fourth time would be like his three prior events. The answer, of course, was a resounding no—immunity extends to drug possession, not the crimes one might do while impaired. Hayes was charged with second-degree murder and given a $59,000,000 bond—a million dollars for every mile per hour he was allegedly driving when he hit the Richardson family vehicle.

The investigation had some wrinkles that we didn't initially anticipate. When Hayes' lab report came back, there was no indication for the presence of heroin. Meanwhile, a needle found in the vehicle tested positive for fentanyl. At the time, the crime lab was not testing blood for fentanyl, and we learned that we would have to make a special request for this testing. Additionally, a judge ruled that although Hayes' prior DWI convictions were admissible at trial, under Rule 404(b), the previous times he was revived by law enforcement with Narcan were not.

Learning from past painful experiences and changing the law and practices to avoid repeating those mistakes must be the goal of everyone in the justice system. Recall from chapter 6 that when Matthew Deans killed Reed and Dobbs Eddings in a terrible traffic collision, the officers could not charge impaired driving because he was showing no signs of impairment and the heroin that Deans had taken had left his system by the time of the blood draw six hours later. Further, the fentanyl that was in Deans' system was not considered an impairing substance at the time. Changes to protocol (requiring blood draws within the first two hours of a fatality) and changes to the law (adding fentanyl to the Schedule I controlled substances list to make any amount of the drug DWI per se) that were born out of the Eddings' tragedy ensured that the outcome would be different for Mason's family.

Additionally, once we make precedent, we rely upon it. Doug Carriker, my co-counsel from *State v. Grooms* (the defendant who ran over and killed David and Trey Doolittle as they rode their bicycles, discussed in chapter 3) was now lead prosecutor in the Hayes case. He relied on the same theory of implied malice that became the standard in that case, to argue to the jury that Hayes should be guilty of second-degree murder and nothing less because of the many instances of impaired driving prior to killing Mason. The jury agreed. Hayes was convicted as charged on June 4, 2019. He was sentenced to 15–19 years in prison. Using heroin mixed with fentanyl is suicidal. Driving while on it is homicidal.

FIGURE 8.10   Memorial for Mason at the site of the traffic crash. *Source: Star News Online.*

While law enforcement, the courts, and medical professionals all acknowledge that addiction should be treated, some have begun to question whom we are serving and protecting when addicts like Hayes are revived multiple times, only to kill a completely innocent child and forever alter the lives of everyone in the Richardson family. For the officers at the scene, and the prosecutors who fought so hard to create a culture where users would be saved instead of punished, this case rocked us all. As WPD Chief Ralph Evangelous sadly said, "in many ways we were complicit in this toddler's death."

Finding Our Focus in the Drug Haze

Justice officials were devastated by Mason's death and were committed to changing the practice of walking away from overdose revival cases, even if the law still provided immunity for the drug possession offenses that were in plain view. We joined forces with medical professionals and others within the addiction community and created a Quick Response Team (QRT). We believed it was lunacy to allow people like Jonathan Hayes to leave without any consequences and with no follow-up support.

Today, when someone is brought back to life with Narcan, the QRT (made up of a peer-support specialist, a licensed therapist, and police officer) arrives at his doorstep within 48 hours of the overdose. We also advocate for short-term incarceration through the civil laws known as "involuntary commitment" when those we are trying to reach present a clear danger to themselves and others.[26] The QRT is there to build rapport, encourage safer practices, and facilitate access to treatment and recovery resources.[27] In just the first year, 122 of the first 148 people who were seen by the QRT, or 82%, went into treatment and remained there for at least one year.[28] Wilmington is now the pilot site for a state-funded effort.[29]

We did not stop there. We also focused on the supply side of the drug epidemic that was devasting our community and started with the legal pills that were feeding the problem. Administrators at the NHRMC initiated policies that prohibited the emergency department from dispensing pain medications, requiring patients to either be committed to the hospital or turned away without receiving medication. This simple change reduced the number of pills on the streets (and correspondingly the demand for heroin) to such an extent that we urged our local legislative delegation to put this policy into law.

The North Carolina Legislature, led by the Wilmington delegation, unanimously passed the STOP (Strengthen Opioid Misuse Prevention) Act in June of 2017.[30] The STOP Act limits the number of pills that doctors can prescribe: a patient is given a maximum of a five-day supply of opioid-based pills for acute pain and a seven-day supply or less after surgery. (This is in contrast to the dozens of pills that patients were historically being prescribed, leading to massive surpluses that were ending up in the wrong hands.) Additionally, under the STOP Act, state-run databases, which are monitored daily by drug agents with the SBI, report when a patient is doctor-shopping or seeking pills from various providers. People are also now required to show a valid picture ID when purchasing prescriptions and their personal information is entered into the NC Controlled Substances Reporting System to prevent multiple refills from taking place.[31]

We also recommitted to going after the traffickers and dealers who were peddling poison for profit. These ruthless businessmen drop prices to coincide with school breaks in order to attract new clients, lace less dangerous drugs like marijuana to hook people quickly, and use the latest technology to stay in touch with customers. Drug kingpins are often viewed as heroes on film, or even in real life, but ultimately, they destroy their own communities.

We understood that drug dealers do not respect jurisdictional boundaries, but law enforcement agencies have power only in the geographic area under their control. This complicates the effort to prevent and combat crimes that span various counties or states, and criminals often take this into consideration in order to slip through the cracks. My brother and I coordinated a regional approach to cut out the confusion and loss of information that comes from traffickers playing cat and mouse across the Cape Fear River, crossing from the Sixth District (New Hanover and Pender Counties) to the Fifteenth District (Bladen, Brunswick, and Columbus Counties) and back again.

On March 6, 2018, officials from our five-county region came together on the deck of the USS *North Carolina*, the celebrated warship that is docked on the Cape Fear River. We announced that, moving forward, anyone arrested for the sale or trafficking of heroin or fentanyl would be subject to a million-dollar bond—virtually ensuring their confinement pretrial. We would insist on long prison terms for anyone found guilty of selling these substances.

FIGURE 8.11   Press conference calling for million-dollar bonds for individuals charged with trafficking in heroin and fentanyl. *Source*: WWAYTV3.

We also announced work on an initiative that has since become law: "death by distribution" mandates that those who sell lethal drugs like heroin, fentanyl, and cocaine are responsible for their customer's death.[32] The law specifically applied only to the sale of drugs causing death and excluded other users from prosecution for death by distribution. This meant that someone like Leutgens can still be prosecuted only for the lesser crime of involuntary manslaughter if he fails to call 911 and faces no crime at all if he does, in order to continue to encourage users to reach out for help during a medical emergency. On that battleship, we conceded that the war on drugs has been lost; we are now fighting a war on drug dealers.

Lessons Learned

Let's return to the demand side of the drug epidemic. As we discussed earlier when looking at ACE scores, a great majority of drug users are self-medicating to deal with childhood trauma. In March of 2019, I was in the middle of the capital sentencing hearing of James Bradley. To humanize their client and to evoke sympathy, the defense team called a psychologist to testify that Bradley had been given an ACE assessment and scored a six, indicating a difficult childhood. Bradley, they argued, deserved mercy and to have his life spared because of his challenging upbringing.

I was livid that Bradley would hide behind great science to excuse his conduct. Many people overcome adverse experiences and go on to achieve great things. It misses the point to suggest that a high ACE score dooms someone to become a serial killer—this argument vilifies and stereotypes all the children struggling with tough conditions. But even more to the point, by getting the jury to focus on Bradley's tough childhood, they were forgetting about his victims.

Elisha Tucker, whom Bradley had just been convicted of murdering, had five children, all by different men (including her mother's husband). My informal assessment of her is that she had an ACE score of eight. The other women he was grooming at the time of his arrest undoubtedly had high ACE scores too. They, like so many other victims I encounter in the criminal justice system, make bad choices, form bad relationships, and struggle with bad addictions because of the violence and instability they experienced and witnessed when they were younger.

On the same day we were cross-examining the defense's doctor, I walked across the street from the courthouse to Thalian Hall (the historic theater that doubles as City Hall) to give a TEDx Talk.[33] The organizers of the event wanted to know what brought our crime rate to the lowest point in decades even as we were closing prisons and reducing our jail numbers.[34] In the TEDx Talk, I framed the narrative around the Starfish model and discussed the people who are still falling through the cracks. I focused on the center of the starfish, health, and my belief that ACE scores hold the key to our future efforts in making our community even safer.

Think of the advances in science over the last few decades and how that has changed the way that cases are prosecuted in a courtroom; frequently delivering us the silent witnesses that are crucial to conviction. Science, however, can do more than simply help us solve and prove crimes: it can also help us stop crimes from ever occurring. That is because the social determinants of health are the same as the root causes of crime. When we treat those in need, we make all of us safer.

Let's review some of the larger points we have covered.

In **chapter 1, Foundations,** you were introduced to the role of the DA—to be a voice for victims and the conscience for the community. Our job is not only to respond to crimes but to try to prevent them. ACE scores allow us to identify the children who are most vulnerable, the ones we are most likely to meet at the courthouse as a defendant or victim, or even whose funeral we might attend. Today's victim is tomorrow's defendant as the cycle of violence continues. Of all the reasons we punish, the one most needed when looking at bad behavior of children is rehabilitation. We can shape a better future for our children by treating the underlying conditions today.

In **chapter 2, The Blame Game,** we saw how defendants blamed everything and everyone except themselves to avoid accepting responsibility for their crimes. The larger community does the same thing when speaking of "societal ills." Frequently, the ones getting blamed are the victims. It was only when we changed the paradigm, and began to think about how we think, that we shifted our focus back to the defendants and away from victims. Whether looking at domestic violence, human trafficking, or hate crimes, we removed from our creek the pigs we call "Maybe You Did It," "The Devil Made Me Do It," and "Of Course I Did It."

Shifting the blame from victims to defendants is crucial. Instead of arresting "a drug addict prostitute," we should go after the drug dealing pimp who "is prostituting a young woman struggling with addiction." We can do the same thing as a community when we see "kids with problems" instead of "problem kids." We must label a defendant's conduct (crimes), but we must not label those whom they are harming (victims). For young people in the criminal justice system, we must change our thinking from "what is wrong with you?" to "what happened to you?"[35]

In **chapter 3, The Power of the Past,** and **chapter 5, The Body of the Crime,** we saw how prior bad acts gave context to a defendant's later crimes. Tragedies that first appeared to be "accidents"

(Grooms and Pierce) turned out to be predictable, even inevitable, given their histories. These defendants were held responsible even for unintended consequences because their past made the offenses "reasonably foreseeable." Someone's past (whether looking at Hewson, Bradley or Delgado) also frequently proved the motives for their crimes. Similarly, ACE scores can make a child's future contact with the court system "reasonably foreseeable" and their diagnosed trauma gives insight into what might be motivating their behavior.

While motive is not a part of the burden of proof, it is nonetheless essential in looking at a child's behavior. The key to 404(b) evidence is to remember that it is not admissible to show that someone acted in conformity with their past (the argument Bradley's attorneys were making in the sentencing hearing). Rather, past acts are admissible to prove what someone may be thinking or help to explain their actions. ACE assessments have that same power.

In **chapter 4, The Cost of Silence**, we saw the danger of turning our backs on voiceless members of the community (drug users, battered women, and drug dealers getting robbed in their own homes) who were the victims of violence. Many suffered in silence while others in the community became concerned only after great harm was visited upon other innocent people, like an FBI secretary, or a child killed by a stray bullet.

Many also continue to blame whole parts of the community. Typically, they speak of "personal responsibility" and decry "the breakdown of the nuclear family" for why crime occurs. We do not have to live with the reality that kids in the YEZ will go to prison. Nor should we accept that children living in mobile homes in rural areas were never meant to go to college.[36] We can choose to accept responsibility for them because these are "our children." We can also admit that we created the peril, even unwittingly, through the larger structural inequality that exists in our society. Either way, we have a duty to act now. The cost of doing nothing leads to further victimization today and more tomorrow.

In **chapter 6, Church and State**, and **chapter 7, Schools, Business, and Nonprofits**, we looked at the Starfish model that gives structure to community. The sense of belonging that ideally every child should have at home is frequently being supplied by these arms of outreach. Coming together can lead to meaningful reform and long-term reconciliation. Shared understandings and strong relationships are far more effective at promoting peace and safety in a community than blaming and line drawing. Part of this involves forgiving ourselves and each other. Justice must be an everyday process, not an event. To protect life and preserve liberty, we must never forget about the pursuit of happiness for everyone.

Resilience

Here's the good news. A child is not washed up at age seven or beyond repair at age 12. The clay that is their brain is still being shaped. Children are resilient, and we can change the arc of their future if we change their present circumstances.

This lesson is powerfully demonstrated by Drs. Anda and Felitti and many others in *Resilience: The Biology of Stress and the Science of Hope*. In the movie, which I frequently share with other leaders in my district, the creators of the ACE assessment discuss their lengthy history and the ongoing work that can lead to far better outcomes. With the right support structure in place (I call it the Starfish model, others may come up with a different structure), those with high ACE scores can not only succeed but can flourish because "adversity builds character."

A high ACE score is not a death sentence; it is a diagnosis that can lead to early intervention and effective treatment. Many of the heroic first responders, leaders on the BRC, and criminal justice professionals whom you have met through this book have high ACE scores. For them, early adversity was overcome by even better support. There is a scale to measure resilience, which includes having resilient parents, building social connections, meeting basic needs, and building social and emotional skills.[37]

Intervention, dealing with a person already in crisis, is rarely successful. Amber, like countless others, still struggles with addiction despite our best efforts, because her underlying trauma was not addressed when she was younger. Even if she detoxes, she will still seek out substances within hours of her release. The same holds true for the young men in the Gangster Disciples. We can prevent them from hanging out with each other, bank their cases, and confront them with police and pastors standing together, but many still end up in the system. These are noble efforts, but CRCs and call-ins frequently come too late or without the reinforcement to change.

Seeking to help those already doing damage to themselves and others also leaves the community vulnerable to more crime. By giving limited immunity to Hayes, he was left on the road to later kill a child. The same can be said for the gang violence that eats up some neighborhoods. At some point, the focus must shift from rehabilitation to incarceration.

There is no question that Thomas Grooms and Mathew Deans had long-standing, untreated addictions, but they were punished to the fullest extent allowed by law when they each killed two innocent people on the roads. They, like three of their four victims, were once children. It is impossible to know, but motivates me to believe, that if these men had received treatment years earlier, maybe David, Trey, Reed, and Dobbs would be alive today. What would that be worth?

The key to resilience is starting early. For the NAS babies at the hospital, we still are within the first 2,000 days of life when 90% of their brain is being developed.[38] For five-year-olds walking into kindergarten, already far behind academically, the achievement gap will grow unless immediate steps are taken.[39] It is when we see the critical need early that we must act.

Spending money on our children provides the greatest return on our investment. Doctors and lawyers should agree that "an ounce of prevention is worth a pound of cure." From a purely economic standpoint, we can spend $1 in treatment to save $8 on incarceration, and much more on the costs to victims.[40] The same principles of the Justice Reinvestment Act (where money saved on incarceration is reinvested into community-based treatment) magnify the necessity of building better schools and providing better medical care for our youngest citizens.

In my community, leaders from diverse backgrounds have rallied around medical professionals to form the Resiliency taskforce—the starfish has even become our brand. Of all the efforts I have seen in my 20 years as a prosecutor, I believe that understanding ACE scores and translating them into the larger work of the community holds the greatest promise for crime prevention. To be sure, there will always be crime. But we can help kids now and prevent them and others from becoming victims later.

FIGURE 8.12   Resiliency logo.

It is still too early in our journey to speak specifically about the success of the Resiliency Task Force. But what I can say is that it has mobilized people around a common language and core mission. Our early work includes having the ACE test given to those working with children in trauma: the same frontline medical professionals and police officers who respond to crisis situations. We believe that self-awareness is key, as is providing support for the people who are caring directly for our children.

I have also challenged my community to undertake universal screening of all children by the first grade. From surviving many hurricanes, we instinctively know in the Cape Fear area that planning can lead people to safety. Storms will always bring a new wave of "washed up" individuals who need to be saved. The science behind adverse childhood experiences can greatly assist us in our rescue efforts. It can tell us where on the beach we should look to find the next starfish. What we do does make a difference for many and especially for one child at a time.

Setting a Child Free and Locking up a Predator

Before Maria was reunited with her family, work had to be done to free her from the woods and bring Edwards into custody. Lieutenant Croom called into the command center to give the dozens of assembled officers an update of the little girl's condition. "Guys, we still have an issue," Lieutenant Croom said. Maria was chained to a tree. The chain was wrapped twice around her neck, and there were two padlocks securing it. She had slid the chain down to the base of the tree and lay facedown on the ground tightly secured against the base of the oak. She would not be going anywhere until they could be cut off.

Other officers quickly arrived. One hailed a utility vehicle to get cutting tools while others came in with a first aid blanket to wrap around Maria for warmth. Extreme exposure had set in. Maria had been bitten by every bug in the forest and, although it was September, the temperatures dropped during the relentless overnight rain. Soaked to the bone, Maria was showing signs of hypothermia. She was carried out of the woods in a tarp fashioned into a stretcher. To the world watching on live TV, everyone thought officers were carrying away the remains of a little girl.

FIGURE 8.13   Maria was carried out of the woods in a blanket and immediately taken to the hospital for medical attention. *Source: Star News.*

Amid the celebration, it was almost easy to forget about Edwards. The surveillance team was following Edwards as he was driving away from the direction of where we had just found Maria. He never intended to go back for her.

Edwards was pulled over to the side of the road. He was frisked before being led away in handcuffs. Keys were found in his pocket. Later we would try these keys in the padlocks that had been cut away from Maria's neck: they opened both locks. As if phone records and cigarette butts were not enough, we now held the key to Edwards' conviction—at least for the kidnapping charge.

When a Victim Speaks

To make sure that the punishment fits the crime, it is important to hold defendants responsible for their actions that can be established beyond a reasonable doubt. At this point in the investigation, Edwards had been arrested for first-degree kidnapping, a charge that would be easy to establish but one that would carry only a decade in prison. We suspected that other crimes had been committed, but we needed to be sure.

The miracle of Maria's survival afforded us the opportunity to have a firsthand account of the horror she experienced. The first person to interview Maria was Colleen Mistovitch, RN, who had completed extensive forensic training, including the proper techniques for collecting physical evidence and how to testify as an expert in court, to become S.A.N.E. (Sexual Assault Nurse Examiner) certified. According to Nurse Mistovitch, there were abrasions in and around Maria's vagina, suggestive of sexual assault, most likely digital penetration. However, at this point, Maria would disclose only that the "bad man," as she called him, had kissed her on the mouth.

Rain had washed away any DNA evidence that might have been present. Welts all over Maria's body came from multiple insect bites and stings. The abrasions that Nurse Mistovitch observed were strong circumstantial evidence of a sexual assault but were not conclusive.

Twenty-four hours later Maria was brought to the Carousel Center, a place that cares for children who are physically and sexually abused. Professionals at the Carousel Center do everything from critical evidence collection, to conducting videotaped interviews (in order to avoid the criticism later that young children were coached, led, or manipulated by a parent to report abuse during a nasty divorce), to providing long-term counseling. Maria disclosed additional details to a trained therapist on videotape, including that Edwards had performed a sex act on her and forced her to perform a sex act on him.

Sitting in his jail cell, Edwards knew that Maria was the only person on the planet who could send him away to prison for the rest of his life. He was able to slip a letter out of jail that was mailed to the Hernandez family in which he warned Maria not to testify.[41] "No policia, no testimonial" he wrote in a crude mix of English and Spanish.

The Hernandez family was terrified. Eva and Jose already distrusted the police. In their native country, corruption among authorities was rampant. In their adopted country, their illegal status made them vulnerable to deportation. They were reluctant to have their daughter go through the ordeal of a public trial but understood the necessity of having her testify.

Man's Best Friend

Within minutes of Maria's reunion with her family, Detective Dixon came into the hospital and gave her a stuffed animal, a dog that looked a lot his K9, Bane. Maria took great comfort in holding her new toy, and it became an inseparable companion over the next several weeks. Bane was a hero to Maria and the stuffed dog provided her comfort.

Watching Maria cradling her new stuffed animal reminded me of a great program I first saw at the elder abuse unit of the San Diego DA's Office and gave me an idea for how my office could help her and many other children. What if Maria could see a dog every time she came to my office and have that dog by her side when it was time to testify? It would make the courthouse and the officers, therapists, and prosecutors who now hovered around her wanting details of her assault much less intimidating.

I reached out to Paws4People, a nonprofit group based in Wilmington that has placed over 700 therapy dogs around the country with deserving clients, mostly veterans coping with post-traumatic stress and children with medical issues like epilepsy or diabetes.[42] Golden retrievers and yellow labs are bred specifically for the program and begin training immediately after being born. For the first four months they are vetted at a puppy development center. They spend the next six months in West Virginia prisons where they go through extensive training with inmates. It is only at this stage that prospective clients go to the prison to "bump" with the dogs, a process where the dog picks the owner. During my bump I met POTTER, a two-year-old yellow lab.

Despite learning that I was a prosecutor, the inmates were very glad to hear about POTTER's ultimate destination. "All the good that I have in me, I try to put into this dog," his inmate trainer said to me. They were especially willing to help in the case against Edwards. Those who perpetuate crimes against children are not eli-

FIGURE 8.14 Courthouse facility dog POTTER.

gible to be dog handlers, and child predators occupy the bottom rung of the ladder in prison. After a brief semester at UNCW to finish off his training, POTTER came to work at the courthouse as the state's first certified facility dog. Maria was his first client.

Maria first met POTTER on a playground at her church when my co-counsel, Lance Oehrlein, and I met with her to talk about the responsibilities of being a witness. Every time she would come to our office or go to Clinica Latina (a therapy center serving Hispanic clients within Coastal Horizons), POTTER would be there with her. By the time trial came around, we filed a motion to allow POTTER in the courtroom to be with Maria and her family, even when she testified. The motion was granted.[43]

No Mercy

Look back at the felony sentencing chart in chapter 1. Edwards was a prior record level IV. Aside from the former sex offense conviction, Edwards had been convicted of dealing drugs after his release from prison. Because Maria was especially young, and because the crime was especially heinous, we contended that aggravating factors (which must be found by a jury beyond a reasonable doubt in a separate hearing) would enable a judge to sentence him to far more time for each offense. The judge would also have the discretion to run the sentences consecutively to each other (one sentence served after the other) or consolidate them into a single sentence.

Edwards was charged with two different class B1 sex offenses, the class B2 felony of attempted murder, a class C felony of first-degree kidnapping, a class E felony of assault with deadly weapon inflicting serious injury (the chain was the alleged weapon and Maria's emotional distress was alleged to be the serious injury), and lesser offenses of intimidating a witness and obstruction of justice. If Edwards was convicted of everything Maria was now alleging, he faced over 100 years in prison.

Sensing impending doom, Edwards' attorneys offered to plead him guilty to various charges in exchange for making him parole eligible in 40 years when he would be well into his 80s. We rejected that offer. Edwards had already shown that rehabilitation was not effective after the first time he attacked a child. Additionally, by leaving Maria alone and chained to a tree, Edwards showed total indifference to her well-being, even as rain and darkness descended on the woods where he left her. We believed that Edwards should die in prison, and nothing less.

We also charged Edwards with attempted murder, which requires a showing of specific intent to kill. Attempted murder is one of the hardest charges to prove. Jurors surmise that, if a man wanted to kill a vulnerable child, there would be nothing preventing him from carrying out that intent. The reasoning goes that the fact that she was found alive is strong evidence that death was never intended. Defendants, however, are held accountable for even unintended consequences that are reasonably foreseeable. Moreover, Edwards had a duty to act because he created the peril.

Leaving a child chained to a tree in the woods raised the issue of what Edwards would have done to her if he ever returned. Even if he had initially planned to come back, those plans changed once he realized that police were watching him. He made the choice to value his freedom more than her life. Other cases in North Carolina supported the idea that Edwards could be convicted of attempted murder under these facts.[44]

With community outrage at a boiling point, jury selection was moved an hour up the road to Sampson County. Members of that rural community would decide the outcome.

The Trial

The state called many witnesses to the stand. We began by calling Eva, who recounted the nightmare of Maria's kidnapping, the excruciating 18 hours that followed, and the miraculous reunion at the hospital. She also talked about her daughter's struggles with trusting strangers and sleeping at night. Neighbors from Royal Palms came in to identify Edwards as the man who stalked and then drove off with Maria. They also spoke about the broken tranquility of their neighborhood.

Law enforcement officers from many different police agencies took the stand to describe the search. Todd Radabaugh, a captain with the NC Wildlife Commission, testified as an expert witness about the many large predators, other than Edwards, that inhabited the woods, as well as the snakes and insects that were all around Maria when we found her. Captain Radabaugh remarked that many hunters mimic the sound of a whimpering child to draw predators to an area. Maria, as it turned out, was stoic throughout the night, which may have saved her life.

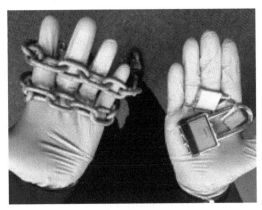

FIGURES 8.15 AND 8.16   Key in Edwards' pocket unlocked the lock around Maria's neck.

FBI Agent Mike Sutton testified about the cell phone location technology that pinpointed Edwards' location and explained his time in the woods. Scientists from the state crime lab confirmed that Edwards had smoked the cigarettes that crime scene investigators collected across the street from the Hernandez home. Sergeant Ward and Detective Hudson recounted Edwards' persistent denials, and the jury watched video of Edwards eating dinner, drinking coffee, and smoking cigarettes, requesting to go home after a long evening of questioning.

Detective Dixon and Lieutenant Croom each took the witness stand and brought the jury into the dense forest to where they found Maria chained to a tree, facedown in the dirt. Nurse Mistovitch described the little girl's injuries and her belief that they were consistent with sexual assault and not from environmental factors.[45] Therapists from the Carousel Center and Clinica Latina were also permitted to recount what Maria had shared with them.

Edwards winced when we called a 31-year-old woman named Michelle as a witness. Twenty-five years earlier, she had been a six-year-old little girl who had been sexually assaulted by Edwards, an apartment maintenance man who had befriended her single mother. She was the little girl who had bravely testified and previously put Edwards away for two decades. Now, as a grown woman and with POTTER at her side, Michelle relived the horror of her childhood experience like it had happened the night before. Her description of the sex acts that Edwards performed on her and that he made her perform on him were not only identical to what Maria had claimed, it begged the question: how could little girls even know how to describe this conduct unless they had experienced it firsthand?

This 404(b) evidence proved to be crucial. As we have seen throughout this book, while motive is not part of the burden of proof in nearly any criminal case, finding the why of a defendant's conduct frequently results in holding the right person accountable and appropriately labeling their conduct. Seeing this prior conduct made the jury fully appreciate that the darkest place that we took them was not into the deep woods where we found Maria, it was into the mind of a child predator.

Of all the witnesses who testified, however, none was more composed, or as riveting, as Maria. She showed great courage and was able to speak for herself as she testified by closed-circuit TV from the judge's chambers with POTTER by her side. While the Sixth Amendment gives defendants that right to confront their accusers, making in court testimony necessary in nearly every case, an exception has been created to allow child victims of sexual assault to testify by closed-circuit TV.[46] She recounted all the details of the assault, hitting all the elements necessary to sustain every charge. She also talked about the long night and how she prayed instead of cried to pass the time.

Faced with few options, Edwards surprised many of us by taking the witness stand. He threw the "I Didn't Do <u>It</u>" pig into the water. He admitted to kidnapping Maria but said that nothing else had occurred. Edwards had confessed to a crime carrying a 10-year sentence but denied any sexual activity or intent to kill that carried much more substantial time in prison. Edwards also said the "Devil Made Me Do It" by contending that he experienced an almost sleepwalking state where he did not remember any of his actions until he was in the woods trying to calm Maria.

Edwards claimed he only kissed Maria on the forehead to reassure her that he would be coming back. He explained that he chained her to the base of the tree so she would not fall and accidently hang herself or run away. He insisted that he was trying to find a break in the surveillance team's coverage to come back to free Maria and let her go. It was an incredible story and most of it was self-serving and untrue.

The jury needed only four hours to deliberate. They convicted Edwards of every charge except the witness intimidation charge since it was Eva, not Maria, who opened and read his letter. In a separate sentencing hearing, the jury found aggravating factors (that Maria was especially young, and that the crime was especially heinous, atrocious, and cruel) beyond a reasonable doubt. Judge Phyllis

FIGURE 8.17   River Road traversing the woods in which Maria was found. The X on this aerial photo indicates where she was located.

Gorham not only sentenced Edwards at the highest end of the aggravated sentence for each charge, she made sure that every one of the sentences ran consecutively to each other. Edwards was given a sentence of between 80 to 120 years.

Good in the World

Prosecutors are often asked how we stay upbeat and positive after witnessing the death and destruction that comes with being exposed to the worst cases imaginable. The answer to that question lies in part in finding a balance. We search for the opposite of what we see in our cases: where we see sickness (addiction, stress, anguish, and disease) the members of my office focus on health (diet, exercise, sleep, and vacations). Where there is doubt, we look for certainty. We battle falsehoods with the truth. There is evil in the world but there is also good. Surrounding yourself with great people is essential, and where I work, they are in rich supply.

Members of my office thrive because they remain focused on doing the right things for the right reasons. They build up rather than tear down. They do important work, but don't take themselves too seriously. They engage in physical activity. They appreciate what they have. They connect with family and friends. They show deep compassion and serve others.[47]

While we sometimes experience secondary trauma in witnessing horrific events, we see acts of bravery and kindness far more often than cowardice and cruelty. As a prosecutor, I have seen the heroism of first responders and the benevolence of strangers daily. But what has affirmed my belief about the goodness of people, more than anything else, is meeting the people whom I have written about in these pages. If they, and their families, can still see the good in the world after having suffered unspeakable loss, it makes the daily inconveniences the rest of us suffer seem trite in comparison.

The portraits of homicide victims hang at the entryway to the DA's office as a reminder that while people die in an instant, they live for a lifetime. These victims laughed and loved and pursued happiness just like the rest of us. And when their voices were silenced by crime, the awesome responsibility and privilege falls on prosecutors to speak for them. Their portraits serve to commemorate that the absent are not forgotten.

But there are no portraits of the thousands of victims, like Dora and Maria, who have lived through their ordeals. They have survived to tell their own stories, sharing their worst pain and their most private suffering in the presence of their attackers and the public. It is watching that courage that has inspired the rest of us to confront our own fears. It is their resiliency that has shown us that suffering can lead to a deeper sense of gratitude for the things you have.

Remember what Dora said after her assault? She did not bemoan her fate. She celebrated the fact that over almost 80 years she had experienced only one bad hour. She was grateful, not bitter.

FIGURE 8.18   A full rainbow was in the sky while Maria was chained to the tree. *Source*: Sean Ruttkay.

Maria was the same way. Her strength made the rest of us calm. She was not going to die in those woods, and she was not going to let Edwards steal her childhood. Both made sure that the abuse ended with them by having the courage to find their voice in a courtroom.

Two hours into the nightmare of Maria's disappearance, a beautiful rainbow appeared. Many remarked at the time, and later testified at trial, that it was one of the most beautiful skies that ever looked over Wilmington. During the frantic search to find a little girl, it seemed like cruel irony that something so wonderful should appear. Finding Maria alive seemed as elusive as finding a pot of gold beneath one of the colorful arches.

When the verdict was announced, I took Maria and her family into my office and gave them a large framed picture of that rainbow. Through time lines and witness interviews, we know that it appeared at almost the precise moment that Eva and Raul gathered with dozens of friends and neighbors to pray for their daughter's safe return. Unbeknownst to them, Maria was doing the very same thing, alone in the woods, chained to a tree, a few miles away.

In the conference room where the members of my office regularly meet, a picture of that same rainbow is the only image that breaks up the otherwise bare walls. It is there to remind all of us to keep the same kind of perspective that Dora kept after her attack and to hold onto the same hope that the Hernandez family and Maria clung to in their darkest hours. It is the same hope that we hold out for the future of the children we encounter in our jobs who have experienced trauma. The picture is there to remind us that even in the midst of storms, there is still beauty in the world.

Notes

1　*State v. Edwards*, 16CRS57399. Co-counsel was Lance Oehrlein.

2　The names of this family have been changed.

3　Sophie Whisnant, "Sex Offender Registry: Effective Deterrent or a Step Too Far?" *Star News Online*, July 20, 2017.

4　See http://acestoohigh.com/aces-101.

5　Drs. Robert Adna and Vincent Felitti created the ACE assessment tool. "About the CDC-Kaiser ACE Study," Centers for Disease Control and Prevention (June 11, 2018, 10:23 p.m.), https://www.cdc.gov/violenceprevention/acestudy/about.html.

6　See *Resilience: The Biology of Stress and the Science of Hope.* (KPGR Films, 2016).

7   Castlight Health, "The Opioid Crisis and America's Workforce." (June 11, 2018, 11:29 a.m.) https://www.scribd.com/document/363231012/Cast-Light-Report-Opioid-Crisis#from_embed

8   Josh Katz, "Drug Deaths in America Are Rising Faster Than Ever," *The New York Times*, June 5, 2017, https://www.nytimes.com/interactive/2017/06/05/upshot/opioid-epidemic-drug-overdose-deaths-are-rising-faster-than-ever.html ("Drug doses are now the leading cause of death among Americans under 50.").

9   "STOP Act Provision Takes Effect Jan. 1, Will Limit Opioid Prescriptions" (June 11, 2018, 11:43 a.m.), https://governor.nc.gov/news/stop-act-provision-takes-effect-jan-1-will-limit-opioid-prescriptions.

10 Email from Judge J. Corpening to the author. April 17, 2018. *NAS baby data and DSS Stats.*

11 Id.

12 Jamie Markham, "Sentence Reduction Credits and Parole for DWI Inmates," UNC School of Government blog. (Jan. 13, 2010, 9:09 AM), http://sogweb.sog.unc.edu/blogs/ncclaw/?p=988.

13 Johann Hari, *Chasing the Scream.* Bloomsbury Publishing, 2015.

14 Dennis Thompson, "One in Six Female College Freshmen Raped while Incapacitated: Study," *US News and World Report.* Nov. 18, 2015.

15 Ibid.

16 "Facts: Heroin." (June 11, 2018, 10:52 a.m.), https://www.drugabuse.gov/publications/drugfacts/heroin#ref

17 See, www.drugabuse.com, National Institute of Drug Abuse, revised April 2020.

18 S. 20, 2013 Gen. Assem. (N.C. 2013).

19 *State v. Leutgens*, 12CRS057871. Co-counsel was Barrett Temple.

20 "What Is N-Bomb?," Foundation for a Drug Free World, (Aug. 2, 2017), http://www.drugfreeworld.org/drugfacts/synthetic/what-is-n-bomb.html ("N-BOMe, commonly referred to as 'N-bomb' or 'Smiles,' is a powerful synthetic hallucinogen sold as an alternative to LSD or mescaline (a hallucinogenic drug made from a cactus plant). There are several variations of this drug, but 25I-NBOMe, often shortened to '25I,' is its most abused and potent form.").

21 Id.

22 The landmark case on failure to act involved the murder of Kitty Genovese, a young woman who was stabbed 14 times and bled to death during a brutal half-hour attack as dozens of neighbors in a crowded neighborhood in Queens, New York, turned their backs and shut their windows. The 1964

case drew widespread condemnation and is credited with bringing the term "the bystander affect" into the American vernacular and was also the driving force behind the creation of the 911 system. See generally, "How the Death of Kitty Genovese Birthed 911 and Neighborhood Watches," *Inside Edition*, March 21, 2020.

23 In re Z.A.K., 189 N.C. App. 354 (2000).

24 *Id.*

25 *State v. Hayes*, 16CRS058725. Counsel was Doug Carriker and Kristi Severo.

26 See, www.mentalillnesspolicy.org, surveying the laws of the 50 states regarding involuntary commitment for mentally ill persons who are a danger to themselves or others. These same civil laws, which send people to jail for short term evaluation and treatment, can and should be applied to drug overdose situations.

27 Ben Smart, "Quick Response Team Is Latest Effort to Reach Opioid Overdose Victims in Wilmington," WECT (March 21, 2018) https://www.wect.com/story/37778909/quick-response-team-is-latest-effort-to-reach-opioid-overdose-victims-in-wilmington/ (July 25, 2019).

28 Quick Response Team Summary, report compiled 10-1-2019. Funded by the North Carolina Department of Public Safety. Sponsored by the City of Wilmington. Email from Tony McEwen, October 2, 2019. On file with author.

29 House Bill 325. See, "Governor Cooper Signs the Opioid Response Act and Other Bills into Law," July 22, 2019, https://governor.nc.gov/news/governor-cooper-signs-opioid-response-act-and-other-bills-law (July 25, 2019).

30 See Strengthen Opioid Misuse Prevention Act, House Bill 243. www.ncleg.gov, STOP Act overview, CTCF 9-26-2017.

31 *Id.*

32 Death by Distribution Law HB 474/SB 735. See, www.ncmedsoc.org, July 9, 2019.

33 David, Ben. "Fixing the Bridge: Treating the Root Causes of Crime." TedxAirlie. Mar. 2019. Lecture. https://www.newhanoverda.com/community-engagement

34 See, "Chief Evangelous: Part I, Crime Rates in Wilmington Hit Record Low since 1993," PortCityDaily.com, February 6, 2019.

35 *Resilience: The Biology of Stress and the Science of Hope.* (KPGR Films, 2016).

36 For a great narrative on the despair that rural people living in extreme poverty face and the toxic stress that pervades their environment, read *Hillbilly Elegy*, by J.D. Vance. It is a mistake for anyone to confine crime prevention efforts to inner cities and drug addiction. I have worked with Pender County officials to form a Resiliency Task force to address the needs of children in this setting.

37 By pairing ACE scores with resiliency scores, one can assess the tools that an individual needs to respond to their ACEs. In other words, a high resiliency score can help to combat a high ACE score. See, "Got Your ACE Score? What's Your ACE Score? (and, at the End, What's Your Resilience Score?)" (June 11, 2018, 10:35 p.m.) https://acestoohigh.com/got-your-ace-score/

38 See First2000days.org. Great efforts have been made in my hometown around this movement, especially by faith- based leaders, including Rev. Clifford Barnett, who is also a member of Wilmington City Council.

39 Smart Start of Wilmington was one of the early adopters of the ACE score model and invited over 200 leaders from diverse fields to a screening of the movie *Resilience: The Biology of Stress and the Science of Hope*, to first jump-start our local efforts.

40 See, www.drugabuse.gov, "Is Providing Drug Abuse Treatment to Offenders Worth the Financial Investment?" In 2007 it was estimated that it cost $14.6 billion annually to treat drug abuse (including health costs, hospitalizations, and government specialty treatment. It cost $113 billion annually to combat drug-related crime (including criminal justice costs and costs borne by victims of crime).

41 Letters are screened at the detention facility looking for incriminating evidence or threats to potential witnesses, but this letter somehow managed to escape detection. Eva Hernandez called my victim witness legal assistant upon reading the letter and we immediately reached out to detectives.

42 See, Paws4People.org.

43 Increasingly, courts around the country are allowing dogs to be present in court when vulnerable victims testify, especially children during sexual assault cases. State v. Devon D., 321 Conn. 656 (2016) (child witness allowed to testify with the aid of a dog); State v. Reyes, 505 S.W.3d 890 (Tenn. 2016) (dog allowed to be present in courtroom where dog's handler testified in a hearing that she saw the child become less frightened and more able to focus and talk with the dog present); *People v. Chenault* 227 Cal. App.4th 1503 (2014) (Judge allowed a facility dog to accompany two girls, ages 11 and 13, while they testified against their uncle in a sexual abuse trial; any possible prejudice to the defendant was limited by positioning the dog carefully out of the presence of the jury.)

44 *State v. Pittman*, 174. N.C. App. 745 (2005) (Defendant convicted of first-degree kidnapping and attempted first-degree murder where he kidnapped a six-week-old infant and abandoned it in a collapsing shed; baby found two days later with severe hypothermia after temperatures dropped into the 30s.); *State v. Edwards*, 174 N.C. App. 490 (2005) (Defendant convicted of attempted first-degree murder where he carjacked and murdered a mother and left an 11-month-old baby for dead; baby discovered eight hours later in a field wearing only a diaper with second-degree burns from sun exposure and suffering from severe dehydration.)

45 The defense contended that the abrasions in and around Maria's private area came from sticks on the ground underneath where Maria was found and that she had rolled over them during the multiple hours at the tree, including when she had to pull down her own pants to use the bathroom.

46 See generally, N.C. Gen. Stat. 15A-1225.1.

47 *Happy*, directed by R. Belic. (2001), DVD. Documentary that analyzed the pursuit of happiness by traveling to five continents and interviewing hundreds of people, from rickshaw operators in Kolkata, India, to centenarians in Okinawa, Japan, to Cajuns in the swamps of Louisiana.

Figure Credits

Afterword

Monuments and Memory

We erect monuments in public places to remember our past. Some of our past is immediately venerated, while other memories take a while to surface. Ancient, and sometimes crumbling, structures give insight into the persistence of memory. On the banks of the Cape Fear, the hollowed-out foundation of the area's first courthouse stands next to the remains of a once-magnificent church. American society was founded on the duality of these two institutions.

The DA must walk both sides of the town square in order to assume the mantle of being the keeper of the public conscience. Our laws recognize the separation of the church and state, and yet we were never meant to live without a belief in something greater than ourselves when serving others. Being the DA is about showing tough love.

On the courthouse side of the square, we punish and demand accountability. Here we say the truth hurts. On the side of the town square reserved for faith, we speak of forgiveness and mercy. Here we say the truth will set you free. On both sides of the square, we simultaneously tend to those who have sinned and show compassion for those who have suffered.

The past does not stay buried for society or for individuals. We tend to run from our past and run toward the future. Sometimes, after a long journey, we arrive back at the same place from where we first began. The past shapes our thoughts and, in turn, our actions. Our habits become like currents, leading us on good and bad journeys. where individuals and whole communities arrive at predictable destinations.

Few things are permanent. Attitudes change and, with them, people's actions. Laws get overturned and are rewritten. Things once prohibited become possible. Priorities change. Prisoners become patients and warriors become guardians. We look to our past with the hope that good traditions may be repeated and bad ones avoided. A precedent is a guide, not a talisman. It is up to individuals to set the course.

There will come a time when this office that I occupy will be occupied by someone else. I hope that this living history helps to guide them in their journey, just as the stories of my predecessors have helped me in mine. The precedents and programs I have discussed, like the monuments in our town square, have meaning and provide memory. They are also ephemeral and fleeting. Whoever is at the helm would be wise to look to the past but must always keep their eye on the horizon.

The Light and the Water

Lighthouses, on the other hand, remain stationary and do not shift with the sands of time. In a dark place, they provide light and help others safely navigate through treacherous waters. Lighthouses appear on the horizon and draw people in from distant shores. The very freedoms set forth in our laws have become a beacon for the rest of the world.

Crime occurs in private and in the shadows. Trials are public affairs and justice is dispensed in well-lit courtrooms. We bring attention to the things that hurt us by taking them out of the darkness. We march in the street to end violence in the home. We shut doors to places that have become dens of inequity and erect playgrounds and parks to drive away drug dealers. When public officials are corrupt or peacekeepers act violently, we demand transparent processes, believing that sunlight is the best disinfectant.

There is an interplay between the light and water. If we stay on the shimmering surface, we see our own reflections. Other times we plunge the depths to see what stirs in an individual's heart or moves whole communities to action. We dredge these things up and expose them to the light of day to find what connects past principles to present situations and people to each other.

What we choose to drop into the water has meaning. Choices have consequences and even those on distant shores can feel the impact. We are held accountable for the things that we can foresee. Heedless indifference can be viewed as malicious, even intentional, when there is a demonstrated pattern of wanton disregard over time. Choosing to do nothing works only up to a point. Inaction is unacceptable when we have created the peril.

By throwing the starfish back into the water, we end up saving ourselves. The water offers forgiveness. Forgiveness for the sin of society's indifference to the plight of a child living in a dangerous place called poverty. Forgiveness for the sin of silence, where speaking could have prevented that child from getting caught in the crossfire of crime. Forgiveness for saving an addict only to have him drive down the road, paved with our good intentions, toward a car filled with a family on an errand. We need forgiveness for our indifference, for our good intentions, and for all of our imperfections.

The End of the Journey

At the end of a long journey, the Cape Fear River empties into the Atlantic Ocean. There, at the river's mouth, is Bald Head Island. Water simultaneously allows for disconnected places to open lines of communication and trade, yet also separates places from each other by drawing borders and creating islands. Such is the case with the Cape Fear River. Mapmakers have placed Bald Head Island into Brunswick County, in the Fifteenth District, just beyond the reaches of New Hanover County in the Sixth District.

To the inhabitants of this island, it must seem like a world away from places I have written about in these pages. Bald Head is the richest zip code in the entire state of North Carolina. Homes sell for millions of dollars and golf carts are the only permitted form of transportation. The residents of this exclusive enclave have always prided themselves on being far from the fray. Few probably give much thought to life upstream or the waves lapping onto the beaches.

FIGURE 9.1   Old Baldy Lighthouse on Bald Head Island, North Carolina. *Source*: Oldbaldy.org.

In the center of Bald Head Island stands Old Baldy, an iconic 200-year-old lighthouse that has guided people through treacherous waters through the ages. Next to the lighthouse there is a church, but no jail or courthouse. The side of the town square reserved for doing justice is not needed here, at least not in the view of its residents. The rare trouble that occurs on the island gets shipped back to the mainland to be handled out of view.

Recently, the pounding ocean surf and the pulsing tides have caused the sands around the island to shift. A channel that once separated Bald Head Island from the mainland has filled in, forming a land bridge connecting this remote neighbor to the rest of us. People in Fort Fisher in New Hanover County can now walk to Bald Head Island in Brunswick. Bald Head Island is an island no more.

At the base of Old Baldy, next to the church, is a rock. On it is inscribed these words: "No man is an island entire." I could not have brought justice to the victims in this book had it not been for the help and dedication of those around me. This includes individual victims and their families who have shown incredible bravery. It also includes my fellow prosecutors, past and present, the guardians in law enforcement, and members of the public.

In the district attorney's office we will continue to be guided by the light of the law as we watch the water. We will also continue to walk up and down the beach looking for the next starfish. I hope that wherever you are reading this book you are doing the same. For if there is one thing I have learned on this journey, it is this: community is the best way to combat crime.

Figure Credit

Appendix A

Honoring Victims of Violent Crime

Ty Baker

Cornelius Blanks

Joe Bradshaw

Donald Brunson

David Doolittle

Trey Doolittle

Dobbs and Reed Eddings

Ivy Gipson

Brian Grant

Demetrius Greene

Buddy Hall

Jane Head

Obediah Hester   Stephanie Hobson   Taaron Jones   Officer Rich Matthews

Melissa Mooney   Mason Richardson   Shane Simpson   FIGURE A.20   Gail Tice

Zhen Bo Liu   Elisha Tucker   Shannon Rippy Van Newkirk

Figure Credits

Fig. A.7: Copyright © 2015 by The Eddings Family. Reprinted with permission.

Fig. A.10: Copyright © by Gray Television, Inc. Reprinted with permission.

Fig. A.15: Copyright © 2011 by Gray Television, Inc. Reprinted with permission.

Appendix B

Dr. King frequently wrote letters, especially while incarcerated, to remind society about the injustices he experienced. On April 4, 2018, the Wilmington Star News *ran this open letter that I wrote to him:*

Dr. King, fifty years ago, in the midst of the civil rights storm, you planned to come to Wilmington and speak at Williston Senior High School, heralded by its alumni as the Greatest School under the Sun. Instead, events kept you in Memphis, Tenn., where you boldly proclaimed your mountaintop experience to the world and foretold your own death. Even in that darkest hour, you refused to despair.

From a jail cell, you wrote that "today's despair is a poor chisel to carve out tomorrow's justice." In your time you had every reason to complain; the world rejects its prophets, and so it was with you. Your home was bombed on three occasions. You were punched, kicked and stabbed by strangers. You braved attack dogs, billy clubs and water hoses, while holding true to the principles of nonviolence. You were jailed 14 times. Yet you marched on.

You stood up for Rosa Parks, who remained seated on a bus in Montgomery, Alabama. You fought to desegregate water fountains, lunch counters and hotels across the Jim Crow South. You fought for voting rights, equal rights and you peacefully protested the Vietnam War. When four young girls were killed in the bombing of their church in Birmingham, Ala., you preached from its pulpit the next day. On the morning after returning from Norway to accept the Nobel Peace Prize, you marched with workers in your hometown of Atlanta, demanding better wages.

You took on the suffering of others and called our nation to a higher purpose. On the 100th anniversary of Abraham Lincoln's Emancipation Proclamation, which granted freedom to 3 million enslaved Americans, you echoed the sentiments of conscientious humanity that while all men are created equal, we were not living as equals. You stood in Lincoln's shadow to remind us of the better angels of our nature and of the unfinished work remaining for our republic.

Even today we turn away because reality is sometimes too painful to confront. But you did not run from the truth—you embraced it. You knew that sometimes the truth hurts, but also that it sets us free. You looked beyond your present reality and told us of a dream. In that dream you said that from a mountain of despair we would hew out a stone of hope.

Your life, your words and your vision inspired others to march for freedom and commit to the greater good. Like the stone that David picked up to slay Goliath, you threw yourself against the injustice of the world and toppled giants of hate and intolerance. Chiseled by your experiences and your time, you emerged from a mountain of despair to sacrifice yourself for the cause, secure in the belief that your God was bigger than your enemies.

Fifty years ago today, your powerful voice was silenced on a hotel balcony in Memphis. But while a bullet killed the dreamer, it could not kill the dream. For you cast the stone of hope into the troubled waters of discrimination on both sides of our nation's shores. Ripples brought about tidal waves of change from sea to shining sea.

Justice, you said, would flow like a mighty river, but only once we recognized that injustice anywhere is a threat to justice everywhere. Water raced over the lowlands of the American South, across the heartland plains, through dry deserts and up mountainsides to the far North and West. And as it spread, the water showed us that we are all connected to each other, and reminded us of the power of forgiveness.

Today, in our nation's capital, your 30-foot statue emerges from a mountain in view of monuments dedicated to our founding fathers, symbolizing the enduring power of hope and reminding us all that one individual can truly change the world. From the mountaintop today we can look back and see the miles we have traveled since you were taken from us. We can also look forward and see the miles we must go before we can take our rest.

At times it feels like an uphill fight—poverty, hate, racism and sexism still exist, and the violence that you decried is being visited on our schoolchildren. But just as you ran the race with perseverance, we know that the torch has been passed to our generation. This is a relay race that can only be won together.

The title of your last book is a question, "Where Do We Go from Here: Chaos or Community?" We answer community. We will go forward together. We will remain committed to each other and to the things that bind us. We are one nation, under God, indivisible, with liberty and justice for all.

Tonight we despair because you are not here. But we also rejoice in knowing that, just as you are our stone of hope, you also spoke about the light of hope, a resurrection hope. The final chapter of that story says that love wins.

When you died, you were indeed free at last. And although we were deprived of your presence in Wilmington 50 years ago, your words and deeds have transcended time and boundaries. They constantly remind us to recommit ourselves to one another and to keep hope alive. A bullet took your life in Memphis, but your dream lives on in Wilmington, Washington and the world.

Acknowledgments

I have traveled to many countries and have had to learn how to navigate different cultures by learning a few words upon my arrival in every new land. The most important phrase in any place is "thank you." As I think about the birth and painful delivery of this book, there are not enough ways for me to express my gratitude to all the people who helped make it possible. There are many more who have contributed to my upbringing and education to individually recognize. To say thank you, in any language, seems inadequate.

I start with my family. You have loved and supported me at every turn. Thank you for the encouragement, inspiration, and quiet time to document the journey in the middle of a hectic life. Stephanie, Maddie, Sophie, and Fitz, this book is for you. In the midst of the darkness, you remind me of the light.

For the people in my office, past and present, you inspire me. I have learned from you and watched you do the hard work of getting justice in individual cases. You don't get paid enough or thanked enough by me or by others for what you do every day. This book is my effort to give your families, friends, and neighbors an insight into the world where you live and work.

Jon, I would not be a prosecutor, or even a lawyer, today without your influence. Thank you for talking me out of becoming a doctor and then talking me into a life of public service. In walking away from money, I have become rich beyond measure, and we have both found our calling.

For the men and women of law enforcement, you have the hardest job in the criminal justice system. You are in the heroes in your individual families for a reason. Thank you for allowing me to take your cases into a courtroom and for what you do while the rest of us are asleep.

I am fortunate to be surrounded by great professionals in the criminal justice system. The same is true for business leaders, educators, faith leaders, and those working in nonprofits. The Starfish model that I write about in these pages was inspired by you as we work together to build community.

I called upon several people for the editing of this book and any errors that remain are mine. Samantha Dooies kept me organized when I tried to put my thoughts on paper and has done the same as my assistant whenever I have walked into a courtroom or onto a stage. Majsan Boström, whom I first met as a crime reporter, tirelessly worked to make this book readable and relevant. Matthew Ledford, a brilliant law student, is representative of the many interns who have volunteered to work in my office and lent their time and talent to these pages. Caroline Scorza and Perry Fisher edited and formatted the final version of the book with poise and professionalism. Michael Chaney, an assistant DA, is representative of the dozens of prosecutors who toiled, as they often do, to correct my many mistakes contained in this book.

Six people with PhDs also provide invaluable assistance. Dr. Michael Maume of UNCW and Dr. Gary Smith of Grove City College helped shape early versions of this book. Dr. Robert David, Dr. Elizabeth Randall David, Dr. Sara Jarvis, and Dr. Judith McBride helped shape the final version of this book. These last four doctors have also helped shape me to be the man I am today.

Finally, I want to thank the people in my hometown. For the people touched by tragedy, either directly or indirectly, it has been the privilege of my professional life to be your voice in a courtroom. For those charged, I have tried to treat you with respect even though we have been on opposite sides. For those who live in the Sixth District, thank you for believing in a 34-year-old who first ran for office and for supporting me in the years since. It is my hope that in sharing your stories we might learn from our mistakes, prevent some of the sadness we too often see, and make some sense of it all.

FIGURE 10.1   The David family: Sophie, Stephanie, Ben, Fitz, Maddie, Finnegan, and Bogey.